COMPLETE BOOK OF
Rifles and Shotguns

COMPLETE BOOK OF
RIFLES and
SHOTGUNS

WITH A SEVEN-LESSON RIFLE SHOOTING COURSE

Jack O'Connor

Drawings • RAY PIOCH

Editorial Supervision • WILLIAM SILL

OUTDOOR LIFE • HARPER & ROW • NEW YORK

Contents

COMPLETE BOOK OF
Rifles and Shotguns

PART 1

CHAPTER ONE

The Origin of Shoulder Arms

THE EXCELLENT SPORTING RIFLES AND SHOTGUNS THAT ARE ENJOYED today are the outgrowth of the work of many people over a period of six centuries. The original incentive to develop firearms was a military one. There are many chapters in the story of how the first crude cannons, which tossed iron balls and sometimes only stones, evolved into the light shoulder arms that were reliable and accurate enough to be used for hunting.

BASIC SHOULDER ARMS COMPONENTS

The basic parts of any weapon fired from the shoulder are (1) the barrel, which confines the powder charge and directs the bullet or the shot, (2) the stock or wooden part of the weapon that the shooter holds to his shoulder, and (3) the lock, which today is part of the action.

The components of the charge are (1) the missile, which can consist of a single projectile (bullet), many small projectiles (shot), or a bullet and shot, a type of ammunition once used with United States Army muskets; (2) the powder charge, which creates gas as it burns and propels the missile; (3) a priming powder or cap, which ignites the powder charge. From the earliest days of shoulder arms in the Fourteenth Century until development of the self-contained cartridge in the Nineteenth Century, these components were carried separately—the bullets or shot in a pouch, the powder in a horn and the percussion caps in a little box.

THE HISTORY OF GUNPOWDER

The development of any sort of firearms had to wait, of course, for the invention of gunpowder. That event didn't take place until late in the Middle Ages. It is now generally agreed that gunpowder was

9

invented in the East, probably in China. It seems to have been used there, however, only for firecrackers. Some authorities believe that gunpowder is an outgrowth of Greek fire, an incendiary composition or "liquid" fire. Its chemical nature is not definitely known. The inventor of Greek fire, Callinicus of Heliopolis, is said to have used it at Constantinople to set fire to enemy ships. The German alchemist-monk, Berthold Schwartz, has been credited with inventing gunpowder, and the English philosopher, Roger Bacon, was also credited with the discovery because a formula for gunpowder is given in a work attributed to him.

COMPONENTS OF GUNPOWDER

Gunpowder is basically a mixture of saltpeter (potassium nitrate), charcoal (carbon) and sulphur. Mixed in certain proportions, these burn rapidly and generate a large amount of gas. When gunpowder is burned in a confined space, such as the bore of a gun, it explodes and the impact of this explosion is the force that propels the missile.

Often called black powder, early gunpowder was a finely ground mixture of these three basic ingredients. But as "powder" it had its faults. If it was packed too tightly, there was no air space between the particles to promote a flame. The powder would either smolder or not burn at all. If the powder was packed too loosely, the gas generated by its burning escaped past the projectile.

Powder makers eventually learned that by moistening the fine mixture of powder and making it into a cake, it could then be broken up into uniform "grains." This was done by passing the cake through fine screens. The powder makers also discovered that the burning rate of black powder could be controlled by the size of the grains.

THE FIRST PORTABLE ARMS MECHANISMS

The first portable arms were hand cannons which were used in the late Fourteenth Century. They had bores that ranged between $\frac{1}{2}$ and 1 inch in diameter and straight wooden stocks that were little more than handles. To fire one of these hand cannons, the gunner thrust a piece of heated wire into a touchhole in the breech. This meant that there had to be a fire or hot coals nearby. This clumsy and dangerous process continued until the development of the "match,"

Among the earliest shoulder arms was the roughly constructed "hand-culverin," an adaptation of the cannon with a crude wooden stock.

which was a long cord of hemp, flax or cotton saturated beforehand in saltpeter or the lees of wine. The match burned slowly without a flame, in much the same way as a piece of punk which children use to set off firecrackers. Both ends of the match were kept burning, so that if one went out, it could be relighted from the other.

In order to fire, the gunner had to hold the gun with one hand and with the other touch the lighted match to the priming powder in the touchhole. This method was improved upon when weapons makers moved the touchhole from the top of the breech to the side. A small metal pan was placed beside the touchhole to hold the priming powder. This "flashpan" was eventually outfitted with a cover that kept the powder dry. Aiming, of course, was only approximate, but all the essentials of the gun—lock, stock and barrel—were there, crude as they were.

THE MATCHLOCK

The first "action" used with shoulder arms was the *matchlock*, which employed a serpentine or an S-shaped piece of metal that held the smoldering match. When a shooter was ready to fire, he pressed one end of the serpentine. This pressure brought the opposite end, which held the glowing match, into contact with the priming powder in the pan. The powder went off, propelling the projectile. The end of the serpentine that the shooter pressed was actually the first trigger. This trigger allowed the matchlock to be held with two hands and thus enabled the shooter to aim more accurately. The next innovation was a match holder that could be locked under spring tension and released by a more fully developed trigger mechanism.

While the matchlock was being developed, the straight stock of the

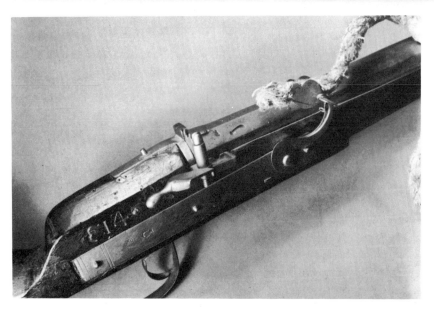

The first real firing "mechanism" was a snapping-type matchlock like this late Sixteenth-Century model.

hand cannon was given a bend, which made it somewhat resemble the form of the modern stock. A weapon of this type is called an *arquebus*. It was made famous in the Sixteenth Century by Spanish soldiers. Weighing between 40 and 50 pounds and requiring two men to operate it, the arquebus was rested on a forked stick and had a range of about 100 yards.

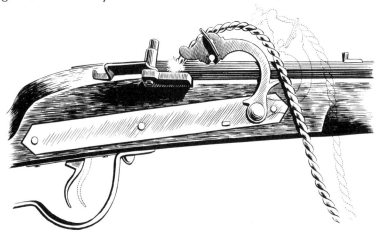

The matchlock firing mechanism holds a slow-burning fuse in a metal arm, which is pushed forward manually by the shooter into cocked position (dotted line). Pulling the trigger releases the arm, bringing the fuse into contact with the powder in the flashpan.

THE WHEELLOCK

Firing a portable weapon by means of a fuse had its disadvantages. If the fuse became damp, it was of no use. The necessity of having fire in close proximity to large quantities of black powder resulted in many accidents. The *wheellock* eliminated this hazard by doing away with the fuse. This new action worked by generating sparks from iron pyrites that were struck by the serrated edges of a revolving wheel. The mechanism was wound up against the tension of a strong spring, and when the gunner pressed the trigger the wheel revolved against the pyrites, causing the sparks to ignite the priming powder in the pan. This, in turn, ignited the powder in the chamber and sent the bullet on its way.

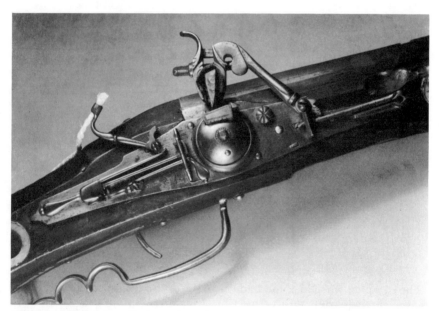

The complicated and expensive wheellock eliminated the burning match. The maker of this model, however, didn't quite trust his mechanism, and employed a match just to be sure.

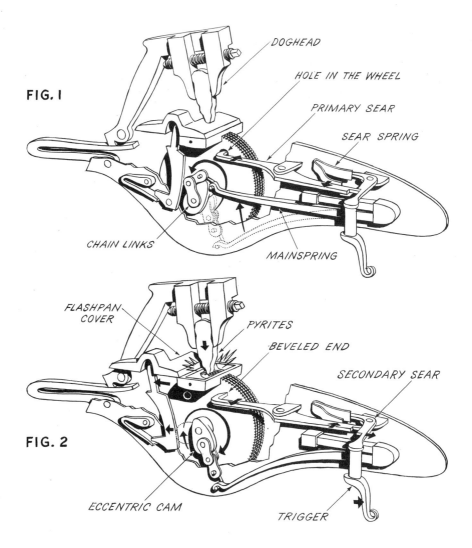

FIG. 1

DOGHEAD

HOLE IN THE WHEEL

PRIMARY SEAR

SEAR SPRING

CHAIN LINKS

MAINSPRING

FLASHPAN COVER

PYRITES

BEVELED END

SECONDARY SEAR

FIG. 2

ECCENTRIC CAM

TRIGGER

The complex wheellock mechanism requires the shooter first to wind the wheel three-quarters of a turn with a "spanner," or wrench. Chain links raise the mainspring to a position of tension (Fig. 1), cocking the trigger mechanism as beveled point of the primary sear slips into hole in the wheel under tension of the sear spring. Pulling the trigger (Fig. 2) releases the primary sear from notch in the secondary sear, and force of the mainspring spins the wheel, dislodging beveled point of the primary sear from the hole. The eccentric cam impels the flashpan cover back and the doghead down, causing the pyrites to touch the serrated edges of the wheel, sending sparks into powder in the flashpan.

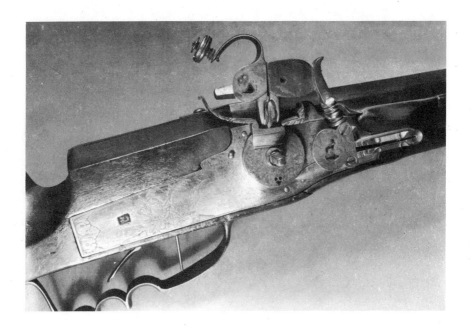

This .70-caliber wheellock boasted a rifled barrel and a trigger-safety device. It was designed in the sixteen hundreds to be fired from a Y rest or fortress wall.

FROM SNAPHANCE TO FLINTLOCK

But the wheellock was expensive, very complicated and had a fantastically slow lock time. It was superseded by the *snaphance,* which had a simple device consisting of a curved steel arm that held a piece of flint, a steel "battery" and a flashpan with a cover that was opened and closed manually by the shooter. When the trigger of the snaphance was pressed, the arm snapped forward, causing the flint· to strike the battery and create sparks to ignite the powder in the flashpan. Legend has it that the snaphance was invented by chicken thieves who operated at night and couldn't betray their presence by glowing matches, but who were too poor to afford expensive wheellocks.

The *flintlock* was a simplification of the snaphance mechanism. It also set flint against steel to ignite powder in the flashpan. The mechanisms differed, however, in that the flintlock's flashpan cover and steel battery were one piece. Consequently, when the flint struck

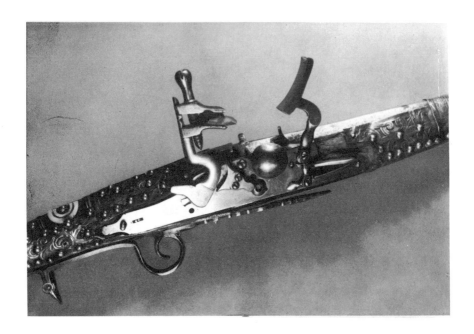

Enter the snaphance, forerunner of the flintlock. Instead of a wheel moving against flint, the flint moves, snapping down to scrape against a "battery" or "frizzen" (shown raised), showering sparks into the flashpan.

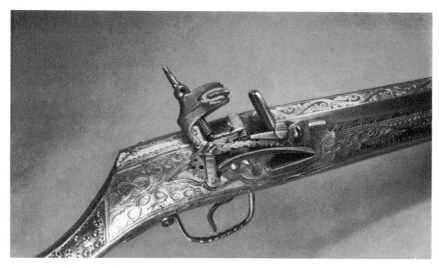

A Spanish version of the snaphance is the miquelet. This one is of Arabian make in .50 caliber.

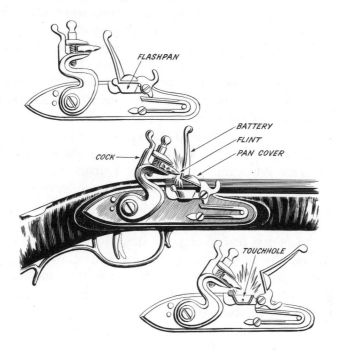

FLASHPAN

COCK →

BATTERY
FLINT
PAN COVER

TOUCHHOLE

Surpassing both wheellock and snaphance, the flintlock mechanism employs a one-piece battery and pan cover. Pulling the trigger releases the cock holding the flint, which snaps down and strikes the battery, forcing it back and sending sparks into the flashpan.

the battery, the battery and its extension, the pan cover, were automatically pushed up and out of the way so the sparks fell into the pan. This refinement made the flintlock's action a faster one, because the extra time it had previously taken to remove a separate flashpan cover was eliminated. The workability of the flintlock action is attested to by the fact that it was the universal means of ignition from late in the Seventeenth Century until the invention of the percussion cap in the early part of the Nineteenth Century.

PERCUSSION FIRING

The invention of the percussion cap was almost as important as the invention of gunpowder. Alexander Forsyth, a Scottish clergyman, invented an explosive that he called percussion powder and patented it in 1807. Composed largely of potassium chlorate and fulminate of mercury, this powder had the quality of igniting when violently compressed. Its invention was followed quickly by the development of the percussion cap by Joshua Shaw, an Englishman who had emigrated to America and settled in Philadelphia. This percussion cap was the ancestor of the modern centerfire primer. (The British still use the term *cap* for primer.) The cap, a small, deep copper cup, contained the percussion mixture, which was held in place with a bit of tinfoil. Shellac was used to waterproof the mixture. The cap was placed on a "nipple," the outside of which was shaped like the inside of the cap. When the trigger hammer struck the cap, the force of this strike compressed the cap against the nipple, detonating the percussion mixture and causing a jet of flame to be channeled into the powder charge, which, in turn, exploded.

By the end of the first quarter of the Nineteenth Century, caplocks were rapidly beginning to replace flintlocks; indeed, many flintlocks were converted to use caps. Although the Napoleonic Wars were fought with flintlocks, most American troops who fought in the Mexican War during the eighteen forties were armed with caplock muskets. However, flintlock muskets were used by some American troops as late as the siege of Vicksburg during the Civil War.

THE DEVELOPMENT OF RIFLING

All early firearms had smoothbore barrels (like modern day shotguns) as distinguished from "rifled" ones. As early as 1550, however, gun barrels were being rifled—a process whereby grooves are cut in the bore. Early rifling consisted of straight grooves that ran parallel to the line of the bore. Their purpose was probably not to stabilize the bullets, but to make loading easier, since the grooved barrel would have less friction when a bullet was thrust home. When some unknown genius, generally considered to be a German, cut *spiral* grooves in a barrel to give the bullets "spin" for greater stability and accuracy, the rifle was born.

The early rifle had the advantage of much greater accuracy than the smoothbore, but it also had very great disadvantages. It was slower to load, because the naked lead bullet, which was as large as the diameter of the grooves, had to be pounded down the barrel with a ramrod. The black powder used then was extremely dirty and left a heavy residue. As this residue built up within the bore, every bullet became harder and harder to seat, and the rate of fire became slower

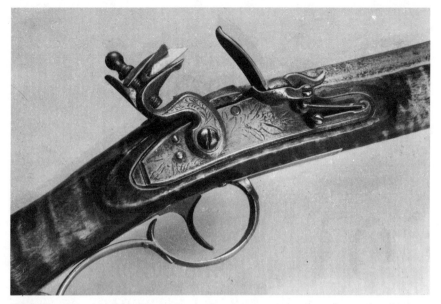

The simple, sure-fire flintlock mechanism was employed on the famous Kentucky rifle. The Kentucky was a light, "small" caliber (.40 to .50) flintlock with a rifled barrel.

and slower. It was this difficulty of loading and slowness of firing that prevented the rifle from becoming a widely used military weapon until the middle of the Nineteenth Century.

THE KENTUCKY RIFLE

The rifle played an important part in American history. With it the American frontiersman protected his goods and his family from Indians, and shot deer, wild turkey and black bear for food. Rifle-making was introduced into America by German immigrants who had learned the craft in the old country, and it was these Americans of German descent (Pennsylvania "Dutchmen") who evolved the famous Kentucky rifle, so called because in those days Kentucky was the frontier.

The Kentucky was a flintlock with a long, heavy barrel and a short, crooked stock. Its bore was comparatively small for those days, but pioneers wanted small-bore weapons because lead for ammunition was expensive. The practical frontiersmen had learned that small, light bullets carefully placed were sufficient in killing power for the game they encountered. The Kentucky's barrel was made of soft iron and when the barrel became worn, its owner took it back to the gunsmith, who "freshed it out" by recutting the rifling. Then the owner got a new bullet larger in diameter, to match the new bore size, and "old Betsy" shot as well as ever.

The Kentucky, like all the other guns discussed in this chapter, was loaded through the muzzle. First the shooter put the butt of the gun on the ground and poured the correct amount of powder from his powder flask down the muzzle. Then he took his bullet or shot from a pouch and rammed it down the barrel with a ramrod. He "primed" his piece by pouring priming powder from a second flask into the pan. In the days of the "percussion" shotgun and rifle, priming was accomplished by placing a cap on the nipple. Then the weapon was ready for firing.

An important American contribution to the history of the muzzle-loading rifle was the use of a greased patch of linen or buckskin. The greased patch enabled rifles to be loaded in a quarter of the time it had taken before. The patch was cut to correct size, seated over the muzzle with the bullet on top and then pushed home with the ramrod. A bullet of about bore diameter, which was easier to seat, could be used and yet the rifling would spin the bullet because the patch held it tight in the barrel. The greased patch also helped to keep the Kentucky's barrel clean as it drove the fouling or black powder residue in front of it as it was pushed by the ramrod.

Kentuckys were made in various bore sizes or *calibers,* ranging from .32 (32 hundredths of an inch) to .40 and larger, but the typical Kentucky was about .38 caliber. It used a ball weighing 78 grains with a velocity of about 2,000 feet per second and with about 690 foot pounds of energy. A skilled marksman using this rifle could break a buck's neck at 150 yards or more, or hit an upright man at 300. The Kentucky was the rifle that killed off the elk in the East, the buffalo that once ranged in Kentucky, and drove the Indians onto the plains.

THE PLAINS RIFLE

As the American frontier moved westward beyond Kentucky to the Great Plains and the Rocky Mountains, where tough buffalo and huge grizzly bear abounded, pioneers found that their small-bore rifles were not entirely satisfactory for use on this larger game. As a consequence the "plains rifle" was created in the early years of the Nineteenth Century. Typical of these was the Hawken, which was made in St. Louis, Missouri, at that time the jumping-off place for the West. The plains rifle was a saddle weapon of relatively short range but heavy shocking power; its barrel was only about 30 inches long. Ball caliber, which had been as small as .32 in the Kentucky, went up to .50 and larger in the plains. Because of its heavier recoil, the plains rifle was generally made with a wide, flat "shotgun" butt-plate, instead of the curved "rifle" buttplate used on the Kentucky.

Although the muzzle-loading plains rifle filled an important need for a few years, it was actually not an important step in the development of firearms. In fact, it was really a reversion to an older type of European rifle.

We still retain many sayings from the days of the muzzle loaders. People frequently incorrectly refer to cartridges as "bullets"; the bullet, as we have seen, is actually only a component of the cartridge. The saying "a flash in the pan," to mean *something that doesn't come off* derives from the fact that although the sparks from the flint would ignite the priming charge, the main powder charge sometimes failed

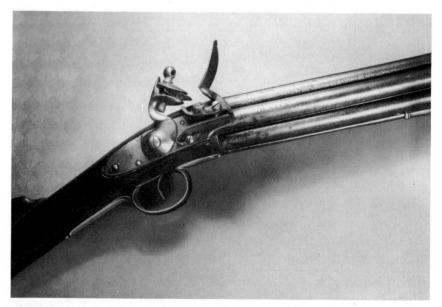

The flintlock mechanism was even adapted to the machine gun principle in 1790, though it wasn't very successful. At a single stroke of the flint, a train of powder was lighted at the base of each barrel firing all seven within a minute.

to burn. Use of the expression "lock, stock and barrel," as a term meaning *everything*, dates back to the era when guns and rifles were composed of only these parts, when there were no "actions" that ejected a fired cartridge or locked up a new one, in the case of a single-shot, or fed a new cartridge from the magazine, in the case of a repeater.

Today the old muzzle loaders, which played such an important part in the settling of the United States, are much sought after by collectors. And there are a few gunsmiths who still build them.

CHAPTER TWO

The Development of Breech Loading

THE DREAM OF PERFECTING A RIFLE THAT COULD BE LOADED IN THE breech, instead of through the muzzle, haunted gunmakers for a long time. Attempts to build such a weapon were recorded in England during the reign of Henry VIII, a forward-looking monarch who encouraged his royal gunsmiths to experiment with breech-loading. Even then the advantages of breech-loading were recognized. The principal one, of course, is quicker reloading time. Another is that a soldier or hunter armed with a breechloader can reload his piece without exposing himself nearly so much as with a muzzle loader. Still another is that the shooter can see that his rifle is correctly loaded.

On the whole, however, the Colonel Blimps of the world's armies discounted the advantages of the early breechloaders. The military argued that the rifles were too complicated, and feared that soldiers armed with them would shoot up too much ammunition—the basis of the objections advanced later against the manually operated repeater and also the semiautomatic.

The development of a workable breech-loading rifle was dependent upon the invention of the fixed metallic cartridge which, within a single metal case, contains the projectile, powder charge and primer. Before its invention, gunmakers found it impossible to solve the problem of how to make a breech gas tight when loaded with separate components.

EARLY BREECHLOADERS

The earliest breechloaders varied a great deal in design. Although there were many experiments with this type of rifle, none of the resulting models were successful enough to be put into use widely. One model had a hinged barrel that dropped down at right angles to the breech; another one opened for loading as the barrel swung

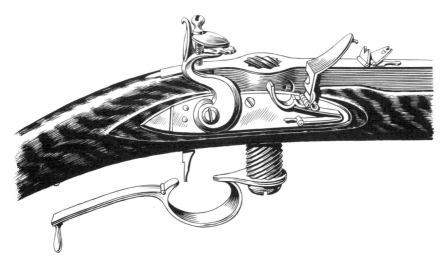

The Ferguson breechloader was used to a limited extent in the Revolutionary War. Its multiple-thread breechblock opens by revolving the trigger guard counter-clockwise.

out to the side. A third type contained a rotary breechblock that opened or closed as it was revolved. Others had threaded breechblocks that were unscrewed to open the breech.

A famous breechloader employing a threaded breechblock was invented by Major Patrick Ferguson of the British Army in 1776. The Ferguson action was opened by revolving the trigger guard counterclockwise. This lowered the breechblock down through the receiver, exposing the chamber. Then the shooter dropped a ball in the chamber, poured powder behind the ball, and turned his trigger guard clockwise to raise the breechblock and seal the charge in the chamber. The Ferguson rifle was used, in limited quantity and with some success, by Ferguson's own regiment in the Carolina campaign during the American Revolution. It was reported to have given good accuracy, but, like other breechloaders of its day, excessive amounts of gas escaped from its breech and its threads quickly became gummed with powder residue, making the weapon difficult to operate.

THE HALL BREECHLOADER

An early and reasonably successful American breechloader was the Hall, an invention of Captain John Harris Hall of Maine. It

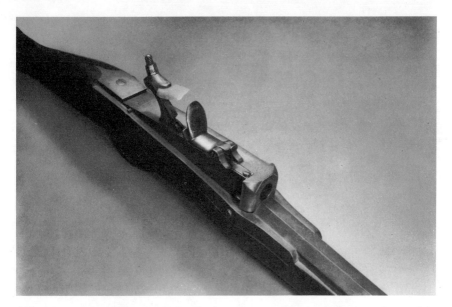

The Hall was the first breechloader to get serious attention from the United States government. Though its loading mechanism was advanced for its day, the gun was still fired by the flintlock method.

was patented in 1811, and eight years later, the federal government commissioned 1,000 of these rifles to be made—the first breech-loading rifles to be used by the United States Army. Early Hall rifles were flintlocks, but many of these were later adapted for use with percussion caps.

A section of the breech at the rear of the Hall barrel rose when a spring was touched. Then powder and ball were inserted into a chamber in the end of the breech section. The seating of the charge was accomplished without the aid of a ramrod and much faster than with a muzzle loader. With the ammunition in place, the breech section was pressed down and locked into position, ready to fire.

The chamber of the breech section was made larger than the bore diameter and the bullets used were oversize for the bore, so that gas would not escape past them. The tight bullet also pushed out a certain amount of black powder fouling ahead of it: hence a Hall could be fired a number of times before the bore had to be cleaned. In early models of the Hall the imperfect joining of the barrel and the breech sections caused large amounts of gas to escape. In a later, improved version, the front end of the breech section was cut on a slant so that the section fitted more closely to the barrel and could be clamped, keeping the escape of gas to a minimum.

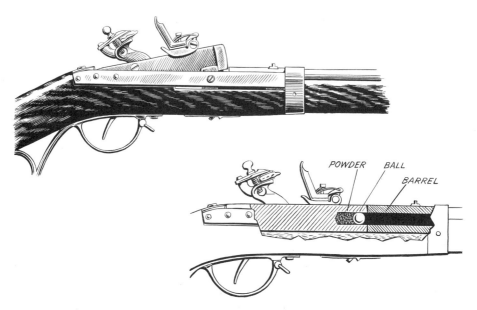

POWDER BALL

BARREL

The Hall breechloader is loaded by opening a section at the rear of the barrel, exposing the chamber for loading powder and ball. Once loaded, the section locks in place, aligning the chamber with the barrel.

Hall was hired by the United States government to work as assistant armorer at Harpers Ferry Arsenal in Virginia. He worked for the government for 21 years, during which time he developed his guns and helped manufacture them. A champion of interchangeable parts and mass production, Hall vigorously fought to see that parts for his rifles made at Harpers Ferry were identical with those made elsewhere. By 1835, about 11,000 Hall rifles had been made by the government. Some were used in the Mexican War and some in the Civil War. The dragoon regiment to which Samuel Chamberlain, author of *My Confession,* belonged during the Mexican campaigns was armed with Hall carbines. Chamberlain records that he thought so highly of the rifle that he detached the chamber portion of his Hall from the carbine and took it with him to use as a pistol when on leave in the tough towns of northern Mexico.

THE SHARPS BREECHLOADER

The most famous and successful breech-loading rifle invented before the development of fixed metallic cartridges was the Sharps. It was the invention of Christian Sharps, a mechanic who had

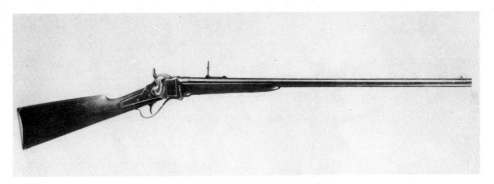

The famous Sharps breechloader was used in the Civil War and later became a popular buffalo gun. *Gun courtesy of Robert Abels, New York.*

worked under Hall at Harpers Ferry from 1830 to 1844. His rifle was patented in 1848, and arrangements to manufacture it in small quantities were subsequently made with several small gunmaking firms, including the Robbins & Lawrence Company of Windsor, Vermont.

The principle of the Sharps was a sliding, vertical breechblock, which was held in a strong metal frame and moved up and down in two vertical mortices cut through the receiver. The block was opened and closed by a lever under the rifle, which also served as a trigger guard. The "falling block" or "sliding breech" principle devised by Sharps is a very sound one that was later used in many famous single-shot rifles such as the Winchester Model 79, the Stevens, the hammerless Sharps-Borchardt and the British Farquharson (see Chapter 4). All of these old actions were strong and are still in demand for conversion by rebarreling to modern high-intensity varmint cartridges. The Winchester and the Farquharson have been used for rifles firing very powerful modern smokeless powder cartridges.

The early Sharps rifles used cartridges with cases made of paper or linen. As the breechblock rose, it sheared off the paper or cloth tail, so the percussion cap could fire the exposed powder charge. Although the Sharps was widely used with these paper and linen cartridges and was considered generally satisfactory, the breech couldn't be made gas tight until it was adapted to the use of metallic cartridges. Some Sharps rifles were altered to take the Maynard tape primer, which in principle worked something like the roll of "caps" in a toy cap pistol. This tape priming mechanism was discontinued after 1859, when a special priming disc magazine was substituted.

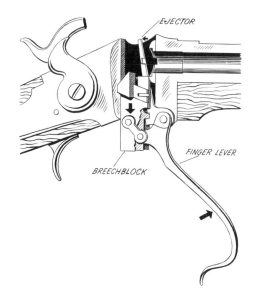

1. To open the simple Sharps action, the shooter pushes the finger lever forward, dropping the breechblock and moving the ejector back, ejecting the empty case.

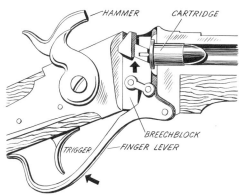

2. The rifle is reloaded by inserting a new cartridge by hand. Then the lever is moved rearward, raising the breechblock and locking the cartridge in the chamber. The trigger is cocked by thumbing back the hammer.

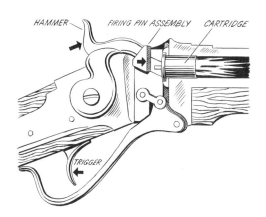

3. Pulling the trigger releases the hammer, which strikes the firing-pin assembly and fires the cartridge.

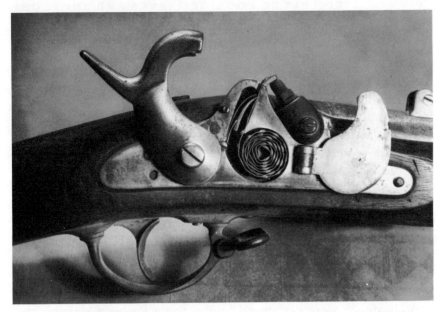

A paper-tape primer was developed by Dr. Edward Maynard, a Washington dentist, in 1850. Working on the principle of today's toy cap pistol, it served up twenty-five primers one by one as the weapon was fired.

Over 80,000 Sharps rifles and carbines were used by Union troops during the Civil War, and the weapon was employed by Colonel Berdan's famous regiment of sharp shooters. This regiment is credited by some military historians with having played a critical part in turning the Battle of Gettysburg into a victory for the North. Its rapid fire held up an advance by Longstreet's corps against one wing of Meade's army. The Sharps was also purchased by anti-slavery groups and 200 of the rifles were used in John Brown's famous raid on Harpers Ferry.

Following the Civil War, the Sharps was chambered for a number of long, straight and bottleneck, large-bore cartridges, with which the rifle became famous as a long-range buffalo gun. One of these cartridges, for example, the Sharps .45/120 (the first figure stands for the bore diameter and the second for the number of grains of black powder used) drove a 550-grain bullet at a muzzle velocity of 1,400 feet per second with 2,390 foot pounds of energy.

Many are the tales told of these old buffalo guns, and some of them are pretty fancy. As passed down in these stories over the years, the ranges at which these old Sharps could make hits get greater and greater. According to the spinners of yarns, the frontiersman thought nothing of knocking off a hostile Indian at 600 yards or a buffalo at 800. Nevertheless, despite the relatively low velocity of the Sharps cartridges and their rainbow trajectories, there can be no doubt that the plainsmen were able to score fatal hits from distances that were then considered extremely long. This was accomplished in part by the use of forked sticks and other types of rests, and many of these big Sharps rifles were equipped with high-powered telescopic sights.

THE PEABODY BREECHLOADER

Another important early breechloader was the Peabody rifle, patented in 1862 by Henry L. Peabody of Boston, Massachusetts. The outstanding feature of this weapon was a dropping breechblock, hinged at the rear in a metal breech-frame or shoe, that connected the barrel to the stock. Because of this breechblock, some of the early Peabodys were designated by the name Peabody-Martini, and the term "Martini" for a dropping breechblock is still used today.

The big advantage of the Peabody dropping block was that its point, which described an arc, moved clear of the base of the cartridge at the moment it was depressed so that it was impossible for the block to become jammed by the expansion of the cartridge at the base. Such jamming sometimes happened in the Sharps, for instance, in which the entire breechblock slid down below the bore. The Peabody's rear-pivoting system also afforded less friction and, consequently, less wear and tear.

The first Peabody actions were chambered for the .58 Berdan cartridge and built into the old Springfield and Enfield muzzle-loaders, thus adapting them to breech-loading. After these transformed muskets proved successful, other Peabodys were produced, including a sporting rifle using the .45 Peabody rimfire cartridge with 26- and 28-inch barrels and a sporting-type stock; the Peabody carbine, which was also chambered for the .45 Peabody rimfire and had a 20-inch barrel, and the Peabody military rifle, which had a full stock and was chambered for the .50/60 Peabody rimfire cartridge. The military rifle was recommended for military service by the United States Army Board in 1865 but was not used by the federal government. It was, however, supplied in large quantities to other countries, including Canada, Switzerland, Roumania and France.

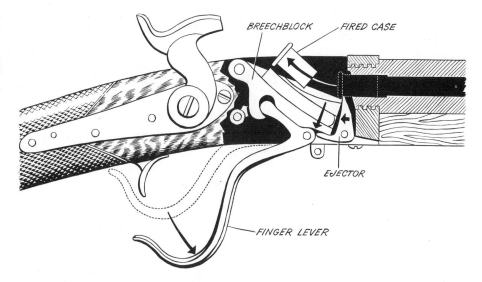

1. The action is opened by moving the finger lever forward, causing the breechblock to pivot downward and strike the projecting arm of the ejector, thereby pivoting the top of the ejector to dislodge the empty case.

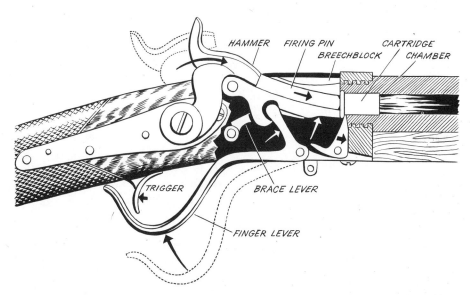

2. A new cartridge is inserted by hand. Then the finger lever is moved rearward to the stock, pivoting the breechblock upward. A spring-loaded brace lever holds the breechblock in position, locking the cartridge in the chamber. The gun is cocked by thumbing back the hammer. The trigger releases the hammer to strike a sliding firing pin which in turn discharges the rimfire cartridge.

PERFECTION OF SINGLE-SHOT BREECHLOADERS

During the years after the Civil War, a few early repeaters were being developed, but this was the time when single-shot actions were being perfected. These single-shot actions, which gun enthusiasts of those days swore by, were very strong. The rifles built around them were highly accurate, and they were available in calibers more powerful than those used by the target shooters and the hunters of big game. They were also adopted by the armies of the world; the Model 1873 "trap door" Springfield, a converted muzzle loader, for example, was used by the United States Army.

The most common and probably the strongest, most widely used type of single-shot action was the falling block which, as we have seen, was the mechanism used in the Sharps. Operated by a lever which was part of the trigger guard, the falling block slid up and down in slots in the receiver, effectively blocking the rear end of the cartridge case. The post-Civil War Sharps single-shots were characterized by outside hammers inherited from the days of the percussion cap. Toward the end of its career, however, the company turned out the famous hammerless Sharps-Borchardt. In this beautiful action, which is still in considerable demand for conversion to single-shot varmint rifles, the hammer and all of its operating action are completely concealed inside the receiver. An indicator on the outside shows whether or not the hammer is cocked.

REMINGTON-RIDER ROLLING BLOCK

An odd but very successful single-shot breech-loading rifle was the Remington-Rider "rolling block," which was invented for Remington by the mechanical genius, John Rider, in 1866. This simple

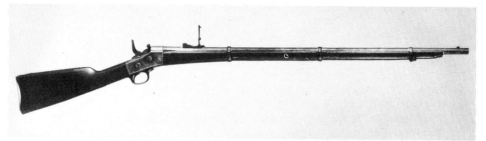

The Remington-Rider rolling block, like the Sharps, was a favorite of buffalo hunters.

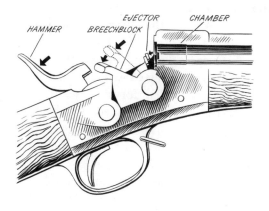

1. To open this famous Remington, the shooter thumbs back the hammer and breechblock separately, exposing the chamber and ejecting the fired case.

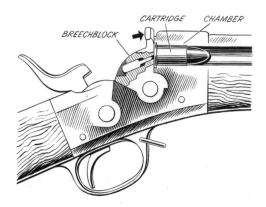

2. The fresh cartridge is inserted by hand and the breechblock is rolled forward to the chamber.

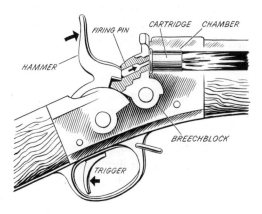

3. Pulling the trigger slams the hammer against the firing pin and presses the block tight against the chamber, locking the cartridge in and detonating the primer.

action was designed for use with the centerfire cartridge. Behind the breech-end of the barrel were the hammer and breechblock, which rotated on heavy traverse pins driven through the receiver. To load the rifle, the shooter thumbed back the hammer to full cock and in the same movement rolled the breechblock backwards, exposing the chamber. The action of rolling back the block caused the ejector to expel the fired cartridge and moved the hammer to half cock. A fresh cartridge was inserted straight into the chamber and the breechblock was then rolled forward, sealing in the new cartridge. The block and the hammer formed, in effect, a solid mass of steel behind the cartridge. When the trigger was pressed, the breechblock was pierced by the firing pin which, in turn, set off the cartridge primer.

Remington rolling block rifles were strong, easy and reliable to operate and fast to load. Although the action was originally designed for black powder and black powder pressures, it was later adapted to smokeless powder. Even today many rolling blocks, chambered for various obsolete black powder cartridges as well as the 7 mm., are sold by surplus stores. The Remington rolling blocks were favorite target rifles and were used by many buffalo "runners" who exterminated the great herds during the eighteen seventies and early eighties.

FOREIGN SINGLE-SHOT BREECHLOADERS

During the Nineteenth Century, developments in breech-loading rifles were taking place abroad as well as in the United States. The French developed the breech-loading *Chassepot*, which in principle resembled Dreyse's Prussian needle gun (see Chapter 3). This French breechloader had a long firing pin, called a needle, enclosed in a hollow bolt that opened for loading. When the trigger was pressed, a spring was released that sent the needle through the cartridge to strike a primer at the base of the bullet.

The British developed a military breechloader, the Snider, and later the Martini-Henry, which were actually refinements of the American Peabody rifle discussed earlier in this chapter.

After Americans developed the art of making cartridges from drawn brass, they furnished vast amounts of single-shot breechloaders and metallic cartridge ammunition to foreign governments. Remington, for example, exported many thousands of the famous

Remington-Rider rolling block military rifles to Sweden, Denmark, France, Prussia, Turkey, Egypt and other countries. Americans also developed rifle-making machinery and gauges which enabled them to make rifles speedily and cheaply and with interchangeable parts, instead of with hand-fitted parts as was the custom in Europe.

EARLY REPEATERS

Although the development of the repeating rifle had to wait until the invention of the metallic cartridge, the Colt Company, as early as 1858, was making cap-and-ball, revolving-cylinder rifles and carbines on the frame of the famous Model 1855 Colt pocket revolver.

Since the Colt handgun action was an outstanding success, it seemed only natural to adapt it for use on rifles. The Colt rifle was basically an oversized revolver action combined with a stock and long barrel. It was made in .44 caliber and, like the revolver, its cartridge chambers were contained in a cylinder which rotated about a central axial pin. By cocking the hammer, the cylinder was rotated through one-sixth of its cycle, aligning a new chamber with the breech-end of the barrel. Because the rifle needed a solid frame to hold the action, the hammer was placed on one side of the frame instead of directly behind the cylinder, as in the revolver.

The rifle was loaded like the revolver; that is, not from the rear, like breech-loading rifles, but from the front of the cylinder as was the case with all of the cap-and-ball revolvers. A combustible paper cartridge containing powder and ball was placed into each chamber of the cylinder. The hammer was half-cocked, and the cylinder rotated, one chamber at a time, until the nose of the bullet was beneath the rammer of the loading lever. A downward pull on the lever, which was located under the barrel, seated the bullet. It was necessary to repeat this operation for each chamber. After a percussion cap was placed on each nipple, the rifle was ready to be fired. If the shooter ran out of paper cartridges, he could substitute loose powder and individual bullets, just as on the revolver.

The Colt system was ideal for handguns, but it was out of its element in weapons of rifle size. The Colt rifles were unsafe to shoot. For safety purposes, all the nipples on the cylinder of the rifle were separated by wide metal partitions to confine each ex-

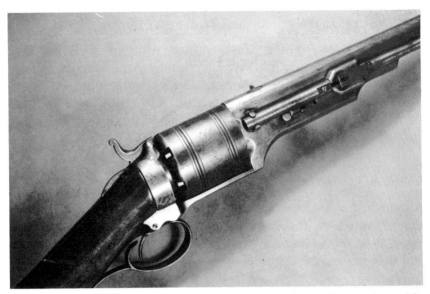

This Colt repeating rifle combines the famous Colt revolver action with a wooden stock and rifle barrel. It works on the percussion cap principle.

plosion and prevent the ignition of more than one chamber at a time. But faulty caps and stray powder grains which often spilled through the rear of the large nipples were a constant danger to the shooter. Then, too, there was always the possibility of all chambers letting go at once. The rifle also leaked gas. So did the revolver, but the two conditions were entirely different. It was not noticeable in the revolver, because in the normal grip the hand was behind the cylinder, and the weapon was not held close to the face. The conditions were just the opposite in a revolving rifle. The cylinder was near the face, and the left arm, which was used to steady the weapon, was near the open end of the cylinder.

The Colt revolving rifle was used in limited quantities during the Civil War; Colonel Berdan's sharpshooters were armed with it before being issued Sharps rifles. In infantry size, the Colt had a cylindrical barrel 31.3 inches long, rifled with seven grooves. The cylinder capacity varied between 5 and 6 cartridges, depending on the caliber of the rifle. The stock was made in two pieces, a buttstock, and a forend which was held to the barrel by two steel bands.

THE NEW ERA OF REPEATING RIFLES

As we have seen, the Sharps and the Colt revolving rifle were employed during the Civil War, but the Henry and Spencer rifles

The Volcanic rifle was one of the earliest repeaters and a forerunner of the Winchester lever action. Its .44-caliber bullet was hollowed out to carry its own firing charge and primer under a cork cover.

were the first magazine repeaters to be used to any great extent by the United States Army during the War. The inventor of the Henry .44 caliber lever-action repeater was B. Tyler Henry of Windsor, Vermont. He apparently had been a machinist early in his career for Horace Smith and Daniel Wesson, mechanics of Norwich, Connecticut.

Smith and Wesson were manufacturing an improved version of the Jennings rifle, incorporating the principles of their breech-loading repeating pistol. In 1855 Smith and Wesson sold their company to a group of New Haven and New York businessmen who incorporated under the name of the Volcanic Repeating Arms Company. When Volcanic failed in 1857, one of the stockholders, Oliver F. Winchester, took it over and formed the New Haven Arms Company. He hired Tyler Henry as plant superintendent.

Henry is generally credited with inventing the first metallic cartridge—a rimfire characterized by a small fulminate primer under the circumference of the rim, and a black powder propelling charge. It contained a .44-caliber, flat-nosed bullet and was the first successful large-caliber rimfire cartridge. Its introduction revolutionized the firearms industry because it was now possible to make a weapon with gas-tight breech, thus opening the door to the

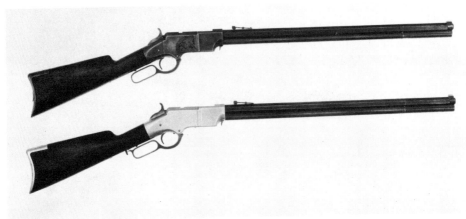

Two Henry lever-action rifles, the top frame made of iron, the other of brass. The Henry's tubular magazine under the barrel holds 15 rounds, which are loaded base first from the muzzle end.

era of repeating rifles. As a tribute to Henry's achievement, the Winchester firm stamped the letter "H" on the head of every rim-fire cartridge they manufactured—a practice the company still follows.

THE HENRY REPEATER

The rifle that Henry developed is the ancestor of the present day Winchester lever actions. The original Henry had an octagonal barrel 24 inches long and a bore diameter of .42 of an inch. The groove diameter was .43. The over-all length of the rifle was 43.5 inches. It had a flat, deep receiver with an exposed hammer behind it. The hinged lever and trigger-guard combination, to which were attached the bolt, locking mechanism and block for lifting cartridges from the magazine to the chamber, was hinged to the frame bottom. The Henry had no forestock. The 15-shot tubular magazine, located just below the barrel and made as an integral part of it, extended from the front of the frame to the barrel muzzle and served as a handgrip.

To load the rifle, the shooter manually depressed a coil spring along the length of the magazine tube, opened the front end of the magazine to one side, and inserted the cartridges, base first. When the shooter swung open the trigger guard lever, the action extracted the empty round, cocked the hammer and placed a live cartridge into position for loading into the chamber. Returning the lever to closed position fed the cartridge into the chamber and locked it up for firing. The Henry had a rate of fire of about 10 shots a minute, and the Confederates called it "that Yankee rifle that can be loaded on Sunday and fired all week." The Southerners thought highly of it and used those they captured.

THE SPENCER RIFLE

The same year that the Henry was invented, another advanced repeating rifle was patented. The invention of Christopher M. Spencer of South Manchester, Connecticut, the weapon was a seven-shot repeater with a tubular magazine running through the center of the stock from the butt to the receiver. It was loaded through the trap in the buttplate.

The action of the Spencer rifle was operated by a trigger guard lever. When lowered, the lever opened the breech, extracted the empty cartridge case and allowed the spring-fed magazine to feed a new cartridge into the chamber. To cock the hammer, it was necessary to thumb it back manually before firing each shot.

The Spencer was made in an infantry model with a 29½-inch barrel and a cavalry model with a 22-inch barrel. The long-barrel model weighed 10 pounds and 8 ounces with the magazine full. The infantry model used a .56/52 rimfire cartridge and the cavalry model used a .56/56.

It would seem logical to suppose that, after the Civil War demonstrated the effectiveness of the Henry and Spencer repeaters, all rifle development would go in the direction of the repeater. Such was not the case. The first breech-loading military rifles were mostly single-shots—English, German, as well as American. Part of the reason was that the single-shot is a stronger and simpler action than the repeater, but another reason was that the military— so influential in firearms development—continued to hold a conservative view.

But the use of the Sharps and various other early breechloaders in the War had convinced American military authorities that the days of the muzzle loader were over. Immediately following the Civil War, gunsmiths began to perfect a breech-loading military rifle. The first was the .50/70 Springfield, turned out at the U.S.

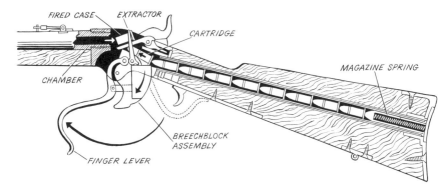

1. As the finger lever is pressed forward, the breech is opened, the extractor removes the fired cartridge case and the breechblock assembly pivots downward to allow a new cartridge, pushed forward by the magazine spring, to move toward the chamber.

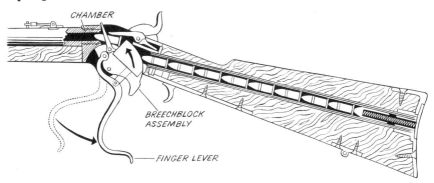

2. Returning the finger lever toward the rear pivots the breechblock assembly upward, pushing the new cartridge into the chamber.

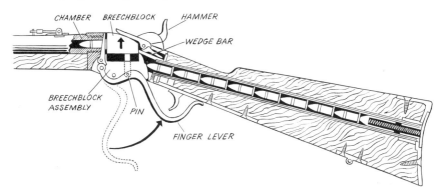

3. As the finger lever moves into "closed" position, the final movement of the lever impels the pin and breechblock straight upward. Note how the wedge bar holds the breechblock tightly against the chamber. The hammer is manually thumbed back and the weapon is ready for firing.

Arsenal at Springfield, Massachusetts, in 1869. A few years later the caliber was reduced to .45, and the famous trap-door Springfield Model 1873 in .45/70 became the standard Army weapon. It was made in an infantry rifle using a 500-grain bullet and 70 grains of black powder and in a cavalry carbine using a 400-grain bullet. It was the standard U.S. military weapon until the adoption of the .30/40 cartridge, which was made with smokeless powder and jacketed bullets. This cartridge was adapted for use with various models of the Krag rifle. Those .45/70 single-shots using black powder were used in combat as late as the Spanish-American War.

CHAPTER THREE

The Forerunners of the Modern Rifle

As we have seen, many types of guns were invented, produced and discarded through the early years of the development of the United States. However, shortly after the middle of the Eighteenth Century one action began to appear in the fields of both battle and hunting that was to emerge heads and shoulders above the rest as the American favorite—the lever action. The Sharps, Spencer and Henry lever-action rifles had been used to a limited extent in the Civil War and afterwards were carried by settlers and hunters across the plains and mountains of the West. The Henry, a relatively modern looking lever-action rifle in its day, was the forerunner of a series of rifles developed by Winchester, a name that to many became synonymous with lever actions.

THE FAMOUS WINCHESTERS

The Winchester Repeating Arms Company was established in 1866 in Bridgeport, Connecticut. The first rifle bearing the Winchester name was the Model 1866—an improved version of the Henry. The 66 was loaded by means of a port on the right side of the frame, and its tubular magazine was unslotted. Otherwise, the Model 1866 was much like the Henry. In fact, it was chambered for the .44 Henry flat and pointed cartridges. The 66 was a popular sporting rifle in this country and it was used as a military weapon in Turkey.

Popular as the 66 was, the rifle that American hunters held in the highest esteem for half a century was the famous Winchester Model 1873, designed to employ the .44/40 centerfire cartridge. The 73 was for a long time the most popular of all deer rifles, and a lot of them are still used to get bucks every year. In fact, the rifle was largely responsible for the decimation of game on the Western plains. More important, the 73 was the rifle with which the pioneers

Winchester Model 1866

Winchester Model 1873

protected their lives and property against attack from hostile Indians. The manufacture of this historically important Winchester model was not discontinued until well into the Twentieth Century.

Although built along the lines of the Henry and the Model 1866, the 73 was stronger. At first its frame was made of brass; later steel was employed. It was made in .44/40, .38/40, .32/20 and also for the .22 short and long rimfire cartridges. All of these cartridges are still on the active loading list. The .44/40 cartridge, incidentally, was also used in the famous single-action Colt revolver, which also appeared in 1873. This enabled the pioneer to interchange cartridges between his rifle and handgun.

Although the action of the 73 was stronger than that of the 66, it was not a very strong one by modern standards. The cartridges for the Model 1873 were relatively weak. Even with today's smokeless powder, the .44/40 uses a 200-grain bullet at a velocity of 1,310 feet per second and only 760 foot pounds of energy at the muzzle. At 100 yards, the energy drops to only 490 foot pounds. Thus, to reach a target 200 yards away, it is necessary for the bullet to rise 15 inches. The degree of the trajectory is about equivalent to that of a modern .22 long rifle cartridge. The .38/40 and .32/20 are even less powerful. The pioneer found that the .44/40 was satisfactory for shooting deer at short range, but that the short, blunt bullet did not shoot "flat" enough for use on such Western plains and mountain

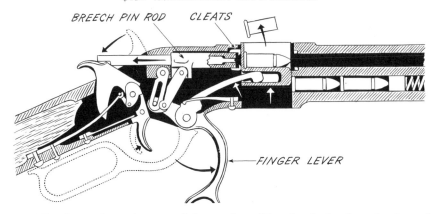

1. The finger lever is pressed forward, pulling back the breech-pin rod, and extracting the cartridge from the chamber. At the same time, the lever action forces the hammer back, cocking the trigger and pressing the carrier block upward, raising a new cartridge to chamber level.

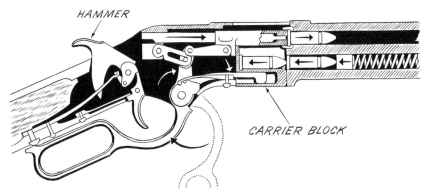

2. Returning the lever to its original position sends the breech-pin rod forward, pushing the cartridge into the chamber and lowering the carrier block to receive a new cartridge.

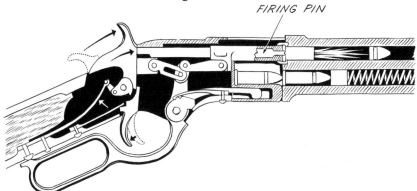

3. Pulling the trigger releases the hammer against the breech-pin rod, causing the firing pin to detonate the cartridge.

game as antelope and bighorn sheep. And the 73 was decidedly not powerful enough for such larger and tougher animals as elk and grizzly bear. As a consequence, many Western hunters used more powerful single-shot rifles like the Sharps and the Remington rolling block. Many hunters, however, liked the idea of a lever-action repeater, but they wanted one with cartridges that would carry more. authority.

Winchester Model 1876

The Winchester Model 1876 answered the hunters' need. An enlarged version of the Model 1873, it was designed to use more powerful, black powder cartridges, which are now obsolete. The first caliber listed was the .45/75, followed by the .50/95 Express, the .45/60, and the .40/60. According to an old Winchester catalog, the .45/75 used a 350-grain bullet with a muzzle velocity of 1,382 feet per second, the .50/95 Express a 300-grain bullet at 1,556, the .45/60 a 300-grain bullet at 1,314, and the .40/60 a 210-grain bullet at 1,532. With the introduction of the 76, there was at last available a lever-action repeater rifle suitable for hunting big game. Even today a 300-grain bullet at over 1,550 would provide formidable firepower at fairly short range.

The manufacture of the Model 1876 was discontinued in 1897. It was superseded by the stronger action Winchester Model 1886,

Winchester Model 1886

developed by the famous gun designer John Browning. The Winchester 86 was chambered for one smokeless powder cartridge—the .33 Winchester—and a variety of black powder cartridges: the .45/70—the government cartridge—.45/90, .40/82, .40/65, .38/56, .50/110 Express, .40/70, .38/70, and .50/100. All the cartridges for the 86 are now obsolete except the old .45/70. The Model 86 got a new lease on life in 1936 when it was chambered for the .348 Winchester, furnished with an action made of heat-treated alloy steels, and renamed the Model 71. It has been recently declared obsolete. The old Model 86 rifle had a very smooth and strong action. Those chambered in .45/70 are still in great demand today by those hunters who believe large, heavy and slow bullets are best for brush shooting.

Other lever-action rifles followed the 86, all of which had the characteristics of a tubular magazine and a loading gate on the right side of the receiver. In 1892, Winchester introduced a model that utilized the same series of cartridges used in the Model 1873.

The greatest Winchester of all was the Model 1894, which is still being manufactured. Over two million of these rifles have been sold since the model appeared. Originally chambered for the black powder .32/40 and .38/55 cartridges, the Model 94 took the world by storm the next year when it came out for the .30/30 and .25/35. In 1902, it was chambered for the .32 Special, a cartridge very similar to the .30/30.

More Model 94 Winchesters have been made for the .30/30 cartridge than for any other. The combination has been so popular through the years because many hunters regard that rifle and cartridge as ideal for deer. In the form of the classic, 20-inch-barrel carbine, the little Model 94 is light, handy, flat and short. It is just right for a saddle scabbard, and it is pleasant to carry in the woods. And the .30/30 with its 170-grain bullet at 2,200 feet per second is adequately powerful to kill a deer at ordinary ranges.

The Model 94, like most Winchester lever actions, has a tubular magazine and a loading gate in the right side of the receiver, a hammer that is on safe at half-cock, and the familiar Winchester loop-lever for operation. It has been made in various models with round and octagonal barrels of various lengths, and with various types of stocks and buttplates. Today it survives only in carbine form and for the .30/30 and .32 Special cartridges.

The Model 95 Winchester employed a box magazine, rather than the tubular magazine of the earlier Winchester lever actions. The

Winchester Model 1895

box magazine made the 95 adaptable to sharp-pointed bullets. Since its action was much stronger than that of the Model 94, it was fairly adequate even for the .30/06. The rifle came out in 1896 chambered for the .30/40 smokeless powder cartridge, the .38/72 and the .40/72 —both black powder cartridges. Later it was made for the .303 British, the .35 and .405 Winchesters, and that first version of the .30 caliber rimless U.S. service cartridge, the .30/03, as well as for the later .30/06. During World War I, many Model 95s were chambered for the 7.62 mm. Russian cartridge and sold to the Russian government.

The Model 95 had its faults. It was neither as strong nor as simple as the Mauser-type bolt action, which is discussed later in this chapter, and its slotted barrel and two-piece stock were not conducive to accuracy. Chambered for the .30/06, the 95 had to be loaded very carefully to prevent jamming. Also, since the breech bolt did not lock at the head, the cartridges stretched at 50,000 pounds pressure, and the actions in .30/06 tended to develop excess headspace. Nevertheless, the Model 95, with its powerful .35 and .405 cartridges, was a favorite with hunters of Alaska brown bear and moose. Many 405s were taken to Africa by such hunters as Theodore Roosevelt and Stewart Edward White, the adventure writer and novelist. In the 1920s, the Model 95 was discontinued in .30/06, following an accident involving the use of 8 mm. Mauser military cartridges. The manufacture of the 95 was discontinued entirely in 1931, and a final clean-up and assembly of parts occurred in 1938. The .38/72 and .40/72 cartridges were never manufactured after the outbreak of World War I, and the .35 and .405 cartridges were declared obsolete in this country a few years ago but are still manufactured in England.

FAULTS OF THE OLD WINCHESTERS

All of these grand old Winchesters have their faults for modern use. For one thing they eject their fired cases straight up and hence are poorly adapted to scope use. For another, their actions do not lock at the head of the breech bolt. Consequently, high-pressure cases fired in them stretch and have to be full-length resized if they are used again. The chambers cannot be made as snug as those of bolt-action rifles because the lever action lacks the camming power to yank out dirty, soft or oversize cases. The barrels, which are slotted for rear sights, and the two-piece stocks are not conducive to accuracy. The strong Model 95 would handle pressures running to 50,000 per square inch, but the Models 94, 92 and 86 should not be used at much over 38,000.

OTHER LEVER-ACTION RIFLES

During the great days of the Winchester, other firms began manufacturing lever-action rifles. Marlin got into the business in 1881 with the Model 81 for .45/70, .45/85, .38/55 and .32/40 Ballard cartridges. In 1888, the company introduced similar rifles for shorter cartridges such as the .32/20, .38/40 and .44/40. These early Marlins were all top ejectors like the Winchesters. The first Marlin with the solid top and side ejection was the Model 1891, made for several black powder cartridges, as well as for the .30/30 and .32 Special cartridges. The present Model 336 Marlin, discussed in the following chapter, is simply a modern version of the Model 1891. The Marlin lever-action rifles, like the Winchester Models 86 and 94, are constructed with tubular magazines.

For a time Stevens also made a line of lever-action rifles similar in appearance to the Marlins. They came out in 1910 and were discontinued in 1918. They were for the Remington rimless line of cartridges: .25, .30, .32 and .35. All except the .35 are now obsolete.

Colt Patent Firearms Company, the world-renowned handgun manufacturing concern of Hartford, Connecticut, introduced in 1883 a lever-action rifle—the Burgess-Colt repeater, which used the .44/40 Winchester cartridge. Its manufacture, however, was discontinued the following year when the company's attention turned to the production of a pioneer pump or slide action—the new Lightning, which appeared in 1885.

The lever action is relatively fast, since it is easy to keep the rifle butt to the shoulder. However, as the right hand moves the lever up and down, it is necessary for the finger to be taken from the trigger. The advantage of a rifle operated by a sliding forend is that it is easy to keep the butt at the shoulder and also that the right hand is at the grip with the trigger finger close to the trigger. The slide or pump action will be discussed more fully in Chapter 4.

There is one more point to be covered before moving on to bolt actions. The lever-action principle has been used in the production of .22s and shotguns, as well as for big-game rifles. Marlin has brought out two lever-action .22s—the famous Model 39, which has been popular for many years, and the Model 56 Levermatic. Winchester's first venture in manufacturing lever-action shotguns was in 12 and 10 gauge in the Model 1887 and in the Model 1901. The latter was made in 10 gauge only, and it was actually a redesigned version of the Model 1887.

THE EARLY BOLT ACTIONS

The principle of using a bolt like a door latch to lock the breech of a rifle is an old one. The first really successful bolt-action rifle was invented by Jean Nicolas Dreyse, who patented his Prussian "needle" gun in 1827. It was put into production in 1838 and adopted by the Prussian army four years later. The breech of this rifle was closed by a sliding bolt that operated on the same principle as the common door bolt. The cartridge used with the Dreyse rifle was unique. The "primer" was attached to the base of the bullet, and the propellant charge of powder was in a papier-mache envelope behind it. When the bolt was drawn back, the bullet and the powder charge were inserted into the open breech. The breech bolt was hollow and inside it a long needle acted as the firing pin. When the trigger was pressed, the needle punched through the powder to the priming compound at the base of the bullet, igniting the powder. Like all breechloaders that did not employ a metal cartridge case, the Dreyse rifle was not gas tight. It is said that German infantrymen fired the needle rifle from the hip instead of the shoulder in order to avoid exposing their faces to smoke and flame.

One of the earliest bolt actions was employed on the so-called needle gun. The firing pin, which gave it its name, is several inches long and protrudes from the rear of the bolt when the gun is cocked.

THE MAUSER ACTION

The next significant event in the history of the bolt action occurred in the 1860s, when the Mauser action appeared. This famous action was developed from the idea of the turning bolt, coupled with the idea of fixed metallic ammunition. The Mauser has proved to be the most successful of all bolt actions. Indeed, most bolt-action rifles made in the world today still employ Mauser ideas. The self-cocking bolt, the long elastic extractor, the camming principle of slowly freeing the expanded cartridge case from its chamber and space-saving rimless ammunition are all distinctive Mauser innovations.

Peter Paul Mauser, a German, invented the action that now bears his name. Assisted by his brother Wilhelm, he developed the first Mauser rifle, a single-shot bolt action which could cock itself by cam action as the breech was opened between shots. Their Model 1871 was adopted by the German army. It was a single-shot for an 11 mm. (.423) cartridge that gave a 386-grain bullet a muzzle velocity of 1,425 feet per second. When the rifle became obsolete in

Germany it was sold all over the world. Ammunition for it was still being manufactured in Canada as recently as 1959, and the rifles are still advertised for sale in the United States.

The more commonly seen Model 71/84 was also chambered for the .43 Mauser cartridge, but it was a repeater holding eight cartridges inserted in the action and pushed forward into a tubular magazine similar to the one developed in the United States for the Henry rifle. The Model 71/84 gave rise to the development of the French Lebel bolt action, which was also a repeater and was chambered for an 8 mm. smokeless powder cartridge. Rifles similar to the 71/84 were made for Turkey, Serbia and other countries. In 1888, the Germans adopted a rifle built on Mauser principles, but which had a clip magazine like the Austrian Mannlicher. The rifle was chambered for an 8 x 57 cartridge, which, except for bullet diameter and weight, is identical to the 8 x 57 cartridge used by many armies today. The old Model 88 cartridge is known as the 8 x 57J (the J designates Infantry); the present cartridge, which came out in 1905, is known as the 8 x 57JS (the S stands for *spitzer*, or sharply pointed). The old bullet had a diameter of .315 of an inch as compared to .323 in the later one.

Although still basically the same, the Mauser action has over the years undergone various refinements. The present box magazine, which holds five cartridges in two rows in most calibers and the bottom of which is flush with the stock, was first seen in the Spanish Mauser of 1892 that was chambered for the 7 x 57 cartridge. A slightly different 7 mm. Mauser—the Model 1893—was used in Cuba during the Spanish-American War. With it, 700 Spaniards inflicted 1,400 casualties on the American force of 15,000 men during the battle of San Juan Hill in 1898.

This Mauser 1893 used smokeless powder ammunition of reasonably high velocity, and was clip loaded. The Americans found this rifle was far superior to the old Model 1873 Springfield using the black powder .45/70 cartridge and the .30/40 Krag-Jorgensen bolt-action rifle, with its box magazine protruding on the right side which had to be loaded one cartridge at a time.

THE MAUSER 1898

Influential as the 1893 was, its importance is slight compared to that of the Mauser Model 1898—probably the most widely used,

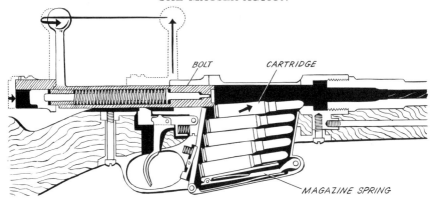

1. The bolt handle is raised and pulled backward, relaxing pressure on the magazine spring which then pushes a cartridge upward into position for loading.

2. As the bolt is moved forward, the end of the firing-pin assembly is engaged by the sear. Moving the bolt fully forward cocks the firing pin and locks the new cartridge in the chamber.

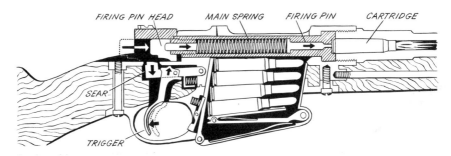

3. Pulling the trigger releases the sear from the notch on the firing-pin head and the main spring drives the firing pin forward, detonating the cartridge primer.

most widely copied and, in many ways, the best bolt action ever developed. It was adopted by the German army in 1898. None of the modified Mauser-type actions which have subsequently been developed has been able to surpass the all-round superiority of the Mauser 98. All contemporary Mauser actions, wherever they are made today, are simply modified Model 98s.

The action of the Model 1898 differs from the Model 1893 in that it cocks on the opening instead of the closing motion of the bolt, and it has a small auxiliary locking lug at the root of the bolt.

There are two large oval cuts through the bolt into the firing-pin space just back of the locking lugs. These conduct escaping gas down the left lug race where it escapes through a deep cut, enabling the shooter to press home a clip of cartridges with his left thumb—a feature not present on the earlier Model 93 or 95 actions. Furthermore, the flanged bolt sleeve tends to dissipate any remaining gas upward, away from the shooter's eyes.

The safety lug on the Model 98 is the best found on any bolt-action rifle. It is small, neat and strong, located just forward of the root of the bolt handle and turns down into a recess in the receiver. The Mauser firing pin is one piece, less liable to break than those on the Winchester Model 54 and the Springfield, and its blow is not cushioned by two-piece construction. Extraction is probably the most positive of any bolt action.

Model 98 receivers are also more durable and better able to stand high pressures. The excellence of the 98 in handling gas, its great strength and the ruggedness of its action make it excellent for cartridges of high pressure. In 1905, the rifle was adapted to the 8 x 57JS cartridge with a .323 sharp pointed bullet weighing 154 grains and having a velocity of 2,870 feet per second with a chamber pressure of around 50,000 pounds. This cartridge influenced the U.S. Army to change the 1903 .30 caliber cartridge with its 220-grain bullet at 2,200 feet per second to the 1906 (.30/06) cartridge with a 150-grain bullet at 2,700.

AN AMERICAN VERSION OF THE MAUSER

After the war with Spain, the United States Army decided that it must have a clip-loaded rifle incorporating Mauser principles. The result was the Model 1903 Springfield, inspired by the 1893 Mauser. It was designed by the government ordnance department and modeled very closely on Mauser principles—so closely that the government had to pay the Mauser concern one million dollars in royalties. The Springfield boasted a few American innovations, however, including a shorter barrel, but essentially it was a Mauser. Even the 7 x 57 Spanish Mauser cartridge was the father of the Springfield's .30/06.

The Springfield was in most ways inferior to the original Mauser, and in spite of excellent American workmanship, the rifle was actually one of the poorest of the "improved" Mausers. It retains the high-swinging bolt handle and safety and the double-stage trigger. Its two-piece firing pin is more liable to break than the one-piece firing pin of the Mauser action. The Springfield's lock-time is slow and it does not handle escaping gas as well as the Mauser. And the action gives less support to the crucial head of the case. The Springfield Model 1903 will be discussed in greater detail in the next chapter.

Rifles patterned after the Model 1893 Mauser have been used by Turkey, Sweden, Brazil, Chile, Uraguay, Peru, China and Serbia, and many obsolete Model 93s are still sold today in the United States.

THE KRAG ACTION

Despite the pre-eminence of the Mauser action, bolt actions of other types have been manufactured. One of the best-known actions of the turn-bolt type in this country is the old Krag, which in .30/40 (also called .30 USA and .30 Army) was the official United States Army rifle from about 1892 until the adoption of the Model 1903 Springfield.

The Krag action had only one locking lug at the head of the bolt; it was not, therefore, as strong as the Mauser with its two lugs. Instead of the centrally located box magazine, made as one piece and incorporating the trigger guard, the Krag employed a box magazine on the side. The Mauser action could either be loaded by putting the cartridges in singly or clip-loaded by stripping five cartridges from the clip with one motion into the magazine, but the Krag had to be loaded one cartridge at a time. This meant that as a battle rifle the Krag did not have the firepower of the Mauser. The Krag action was also employed in army rifles by Denmark in an 8 mm. and by Norway in a 6.5. For many years mem-

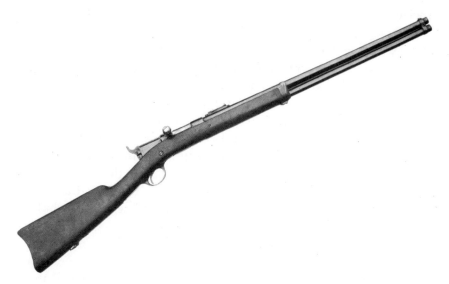

The Remington-Keene bolt-action repeater was produced between 1880 and 1883. It was made with a tubular magazine and round or octagon barrels in .45 through .70 caliber.

bers of the National Rifle Association could buy long-barreled Krags or shortened carbines from the government for a few dollars. Thousands of these old rifles are still being used in the United States. As loaded today with a 200-grain bullet at 2,200 feet per second and a 180-grain bullet at about 2,500, the .30/40 cartridge is a satisfactory one with which to hunt most American big game.

THE REMINGTON-KEENE ACTION

Various other non-Mauser bolt actions have been produced in North America. One, the Remington-Keene, used a tubular magazine and was equipped with only one locking lug, which was located at the root of the bolt. It was chambered for the .45/70 government cartridge and for the rare .40/60 Marlin. It was not successful, simply because it was not a very good action. Also, American rifle shooters of those days were wedded to lever-action rifles, either repeaters or single-shots.

Between 1886 and 1906, Remington manufactured a bolt-action rifle known as the Remington-Lee. It had a detachable box magazine located in front of the trigger guard, and the rifle was furnished with spare magazines. It was variously chambered for cartridges as ancient as the .45/70 and .44/77 Sharps and as modern as the 7 x 57 Mauser and the .405 Winchester. Winchester's first experiment with the bolt-action was the Hotchkiss, a rifle manufactured between 1879 and 1899, and only in .45/70 caliber. The tubular magazine held 6 cartridges and was in the butt. It was on the order of that used on the old Spencer and in some modern .22 caliber autoloaders. The Hotchkiss was made in both military and sporting models and in various barrel lengths. It was purchased in small quantities for testing by both the army and the navy, but it was never adopted by either organization. Since the lever action dominated the sporting field at that time, the Hotchkiss was looked upon with suspicion by American hunters and was not popular.

THE BLAKE RIFLE

The Blake rifle, which was invented by John Henry Blake, made its first appearance in the early eighteen nineties. It was the first American sporting rifle with a central magazine to be put on the market. The Blake employed the Mauser principle of two locking lugs at the head of the bolt turning into recesses into the receiver ring. The rifle's unique magazine was a detachable revolving cylinder holding seven cartridges. The cartridges were contained in a "packet" which was charged into the magazine, located under the receiver and just forward of the trigger guard. As the bolt was operated, the cartridges were fed from the magazine into the chamber one at a time. When the packet was empty the magazine door was opened and the packet dropped out ready to be refilled with new cartridges or replaced by one fully charged. The Blake is the only rifle known to have used this system.

Although the Blake was chambered for such cartridges as the 7 x 57, the .30/40 and the 6 mm. Lee-Navy, rifle fanciers in the United States never did take it to their bosoms.

THE STRAIGHT-PULL ACTION

An interesting variety of the bolt action is the straight-pull, an action in which the bolt is pulled forward and back, not up, back, forward and down as in the Mauser turn-bolt system.

Winchester made such a rifle, the Lee straight pull, from 1895 until 1903. The United States Navy bought 15,000 of these rifles in the 6 mm. Navy caliber, which was one of the very first small-bore high-velocity cartridges and which gave a 112-grain bullet a velocity of 2,560 feet per second. To stabilize the relatively long bullet, the rifling of the barrel had one twist every seven-and-one-half inches.

The most famous of the straight-pull bolt actions was that used in the Ross rifle. Although this rifle sold in large quantities in the United States, it was actually of Canadian origin. The majority of Ross rifles were made at Sir Charles Ross' factory in Quebec. The Ross was chambered for the .303 British and the .35 Winchester cartridges, but what made its reputation was the famous .280 Ross cartridge with its big case, .288 bullet, and high velocity of 3,050 feet per second with the 145-grain copper tube bullet and 2,800 with the 180-grain.

The bolt on the Ross was pulled straight back and thrust forward, and the locking lugs on the front of the bolt rotated in and out of recesses in the receiver ring. The rifles were manufactured with two different types of lugs. One used interrupted screw-type locking lugs on the forward end of the bolt, whereas the other used solid lugs. The Model 1905 with the solid lugs was safe enough, but the Model 1910, which had the interrupted screw, was a bad actor if the bolt was incorrectly assembled. It was possible to fire this model unlocked, and many people were maimed and even killed when the bolt blew back into their faces.

All straight-pull actions lack the camming power of the Mauser turn-bolt action. In addition, the Ross rifles were not satisfactory with over-size or dirty ammunition. These factors, combined with the accidents encountered with the Model 1910, killed it off. The .280 Ross cartridge, however, is still manufactured in England, and occasionally a British gunmaker puts together a rifle for it on the Mauser action.

CHAPTER FOUR

The Basic Facts about Today's Rifle Actions

THE POPULAR RIFLE OF TODAY MAY HAVE A REPEATING OR SINGLE-shot action. It may be operated by a lever, as in the Marlin, Winchester and Savage lever-action rifles. It may have a bolt action, as in all Mauser-type actions, the old Savage sporter actions, the Weatherby Mark V bolt actions and the many seen on .22 rifles. Or it may be operated by a slide handle, as in the Remington line of pump or "trombone" action high-power rifles and in the .22 re-

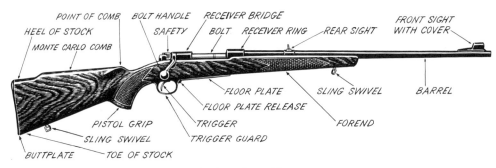

Nomenclature of a modern bolt-action rifle.

peating rifles made by almost all American manufacturers. Or today's rifle may be a semiautomatic, which has a self-loading or autoloading mechanism. To fire this rifle the shooter need only pull the trigger; the mechanism fires the cartridge, ejects the empty case, inserts a new cartridge and cocks the firing pin for the next shot. Let's take a look at each of these actions.

THE SINGLE-SHOT RIFLE

The various large-caliber actions that fire one shot at a time are seldom used today and the only single-shots at present manufactured in the United States are the inexpensive little .22s which lock with the bolt handle turning into a recess in the receiver.

Many custom rifles, however, are made each year in this country and abroad utilizing the good single-shot actions developed in the last half of the Nineteenth Century.

One of the best of all such actions was the famous Winchester Model 1879, an early invention of the American gun designing wizard—John Browning. The 79 had a very strong and simple action that consisted of a falling block with a hammer. It was made in many different styles for a great number of cartridges. The original Winchester announcement reads as follows:

> The Winchester Single Shot Rifle. This gun has the old Sharpe's breech block and lever and is as safe and solid as that arm. The firing pin is automatically withdrawn at the first opening movement of the gun and is held back until the gun is closed. The hammer is centrally hung, but drops down with the breech-block when the gun is opened and is cocked by the closing movement. It can also be cocked by hand. This arrangement allows the barrel to be wiped and examined from the breech.

The Model 1879 was made in many forms—high side, low side, thick wall, thin wall, blued steel and case hardened, for .22 rim-fires and even for 20-gauge shotshells, for black powder cartridges and for high-power smokeless cartridges, as a sporting rifle, a target rifle and a military rifle. Coming right at the end of the single-shot era, it was one of the very finest actions in its class. Even today it is in considerable demand by those who want single-shot varmint rifles, and thousands of old 1879s have been rebarreled and re-stocked to such varmint cartridges as the .22 Hornet, the .218 Bee, and the standard and improved .219 Zipper. One reason the single-shot is well liked is that it can be short over all, yet have a re-spectable barrel length since the barrel is not screwed into a long receiver.

THE FARQUHARSON SINGLE-SHOT

Another single shot-action in great demand is the Farquharson that was developed in England. It has a hammerless falling block that is operated, like the Winchester, by a lever below the trigger. It is a very strong action, so strong that it has been used for cartridges for the very largest game—the .470 Nitro Express, .450/.400 and others. So great has been the demand for this obsolete action that it is almost impossible to find one today in England, because American gun nuts have pretty well cleaned them out.

Until recently the Germans have made single-shot rifles on an action called the Aydt, and single-shot actions are still made in Austria and in Switzerland. However, all have their faults. When used with telescope sights, they are slow and difficult to load. They are also difficult to adapt to modern rimless cartridges, and they lack the extracting power to be completely satisfactory with modern high-pressure ammunition. Their use requires a two-piece stock which does not support barrel and action as does the one-piece stock, and all of them will break firing pins if snapped on an empty chamber. Most American rifle enthusiasts go through a single-shot stage. I did, but I have reformed.

THE DOUBLE RIFLE

Another very old type of rifle action that is still applied to rifles is the double-barreled shotgun action. The manufacture of double-barreled big-game rifles has always been a British specialty, just as the lever-action repeater is an American specialty, and, as we have seen, the Mauser-type bolt action a specialty of the Germans.

The double rifle evolved quite simply. The British just adapted the same types of actions they had developed for their double-barreled shotguns to big-game rifles—side locks and box locks, top levers and under levers, hammerless and hammer, ejectors and non-ejectors. The frames were beefed up, and various devices were used to strengthen the rifles, but basically the double rifle is the breech-loading shotgun with rifled barrels.

The double rifle is a weapon of romance, as are the single-action revolver and the lever-action Winchester carbine. Just as many Americans become Wyatt Earp or Bat Masterson the moment they get a single-action revolver in their hands, so they become Cyril Stokes-Brown, the famous white hunter, once they latch onto a double rifle. The double rifle connotes ivory hunting, long lines of safari porters, drinking sundowners beside a fire of nyombo wood while lions roar on the veldt, affairs of the heart with comely lady leopard hunters.

Romantic notions aside, the double rifle does have its advantages.

The double rifle is a short, fast-handling weapon with a low line of sight for accurate pointing in tight corners.

The author takes a bead with a double rifle, a favorite of African big-game shooters.

For one thing, it is short for its barrel length, because, like the single shot, it does not have the barrels screwed into a long receiver. Because the weight of the rifle rests between the hands of the shooters, it balances well and is generally fast to handle, particularly in the case of a snap shot. Since the double has a low line of sight, it can be pointed more accurately in a tight corner than most repeaters with their higher lines of sight. The double can also be taken down easily and quickly, just as the double-barreled shotgun can, and once taken down it is easily stored and transported in a short case. The double is actually two rifles with two sets of locks on one stock, and, if one set of locks goes bad, the rifle is still usable. In addition, the double is the fastest *powerful* rifle made for two shots. For another thing, it is adaptable to the use of cartridges —for example, the ferocious .577 and .600 Nitro Express cartridges —that are too bulky and too long to work through repeating actions.

But the double has its faults. For one thing, a double is fearfully expensive; in England a good one costs between $750 and $2,000. For another, the ejectors lack the power of the bolt action to toss out oversize, dirty, and corroded cases, or cases that are soft. The locks and the ejector mechanism of the double rifle are relatively fragile as compared to the bolt action, and are easier to put out of commission. A leaf or twig can keep the breech of the double from closing. The most serious drawback of the double is the difficulty of getting two barrels to shoot to the same point of aim with one set of sights. This is a task to try the soul. It is also one reason for the excessive cost of the double. When once sighted in with a particular load, the double is sighted in for no other type of powder and no other bullet weight. Compared to the good single barrel repeater, the best doubles give only fairly good accuracy.

Nevertheless, the doubles do work—even with such high-intensity cartridges as the .300 and .375 Holland & Holland belted magnums and the .270. The ejectors *do* toss out the cases and seem to give relatively little trouble. The most useful of all doubles (and the only double rifles for which there is any real justification) are the ones made for the powerful rimmed big-game cartridges like the .450/.400, .465 and .470. These are usually used when shooting at game at 100 yards or under, when gilt-edged accuracy is not needed. These cartridges develop relatively low pressures and seldom fail to extract. Double rifles are made in many different

The fine engraving and checkering on this beautifully crafted English double is one reason that some cost between $750 and $2000.

A typical double rifle cartridge, the rimless .416 Rigby even dwarfs the .375 Magnum. It's fatal medicine for rhino, elephant and buffalo.

calibers—even for the .22 Hornet, the .22 Savage High Power, and the .257. There isn't anything that such doubles can do that a good bolt action won't do far better. For the big stopping rifle, however, in some such caliber as the .470 or .465, the double has its place; it's the rifle that gives two quick shots with no manipulation of a repeating mechanism.

THE BOLT ACTION

The most universal action today for sporting rifles is the bolt action. This applies not only to rifles mass-produced throughout the world but also to custom rifles built by large and small custom gunsmithing firms. The bolt action has many advantages. It is very strong, simple and easily taken apart. This action has powerful hand leverage to seat and extract dirty and oversize cases. For this reason it is the action for the reloader to use. Cases do not stretch excessively because the bolt is locked at the head. Because of the firm locking and also because the bolt action uses a one-piece stock to support both the barrel and the action as one unit, a good bolt

HOW A MODERN BOLT ACTION RIFLE WORKS ....

(Remington Model 725)

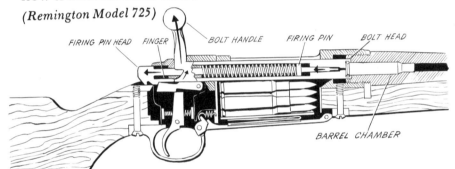

1. Raising the bolt handle unlocks the bolt head from the barrel chamber. At the same time, notch at bottom of the bolt handle catches and pushes up protruding finger of the firing pin head, pushing firing pin to rear.

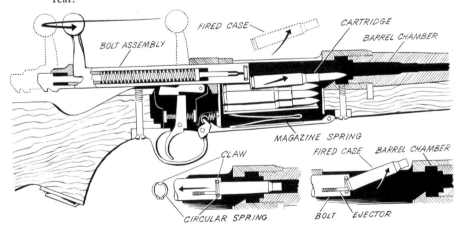

2. Moving bolt assembly back ejects the empty case. A circular spring in the end of the bolt (see detail) exerts pressure on the claw, holding the case tightly. When the mouth of the fired case clears the chamber, the spring-loaded ejector flips the case clear. The pressure of the magazine spring now raises a new cartridge to loading position.

action is generally somewhat more accurate, all things being equal, than rifles with other types of actions.

The typical Mauser action employs two solid locking lugs at the head of the bolt, a box magazine holding the cartridges in staggered rows, large gas escape vents in the bolt, and a one-piece firing pin, which runs through the center of the bolt. This action has been widely copied, but, except for minor details, it has seldom been improved upon.

Mauser rifles and actions are manufactured today in Sweden, Finland, Czechoslovakia and Belgium. The British B.S.A. is a modified Mauser, and the famous London gun makers build their fancy magazine rifles on Fabrique Nationale Mauser actions purchased

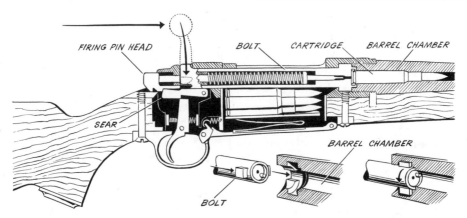

3. Moving bolt handle forward and turning it downward locks the bolt in the chamber and seals in the cartridge. The sear engages notch on firing pin head, cocking the rifle. (Detail shows how bolt locks into barrel chamber.)

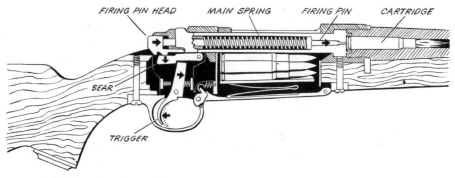

4. Pulling the trigger disengages sear from the notch on the firing pin head. The main spring forces the firing pin forward, detonating the cartridge.

in Belgium and on Brevex Magnum Mauser actions purchased in France.

Before World War II the great Mauser Werke in Oberndorf, Germany, made sporting rifles in many different calibers ranging from 6.5 short to .404 Jeffery on actions of three different lengths. Smallest of these was the short or "K" action suitable for such cartridges as the 6.5 and 8 mm. short, the .250/300 Savage and the .35 Remington. The action of standard length was the sporting version of the regular Model 98. It was used for such cartridges as the 8 x 57, 9 x 57 and .30/06. The long or "Magnum" action was designed for the .300 and .375 H. & H. Magnum cartridges, the .404, the .416 and the .505. All of these actions were made with round and square bridges, with hinged floor plates, some with release lever on the floor plate, some with a release button in the trigger guard, some with pear-shaped bolt-knobs and some with butter-knife flat bolt handles.

In addition, Mauser actions were made by various German arsenals and the German firm of Simson and Kreighoff made Mauser actions for sporting rifles. Thousands of sporting rifles were built on salvaged military actions in Germany between World Wars I and II by various gunsmiths. Because Mauser actions have been made by so many different companies and in so many different countries, they turn up in endless varieties. Anyone who sets himself up as an authority on Mausers is in for some surprises. But any sound Mauser action properly heat-treated and assembled is a good one; thousands of sporters have been built on various sporting and military actions in this country.

THE MANNLICHER ACTION

Besides the Mauser, the principal European bolt-action rifle has always been the Mannlicher, which has been made in both straight-pull and turn-bolt types. The turn-bolt Mannlicher is a strong action, though not as strong as the Mauser. Actions were made with various types of magazines, but the commonest is the clip-type magazine carrying a single row of cartridges and projecting below the bottom line of the stock in front of the trigger guard. The cartridge clip is a functioning part of the magazine. Straight-pull Mannlichers were used by Austria, where the rifles are manufactured, and turn-bolt Mannlichers in 6.5 rimmed were used by

Roumania and Holland. The Italian Mannlicher-Carcano is a modified Mannlicher.

The Mannlicher-Schoenauer is the Mannlicher action with the Schoenauer spool-type magazine. It was used in 6.5 by Greece, and was made in various sporting calibers. The classic Mannlicher calibers were the famous 6.5 x 54 rimless, the 8 x 56, the 9 x 57, the 9.5 x 57. However, in later years Mannlicher-Schoenauers were made in 7 x 57, 7 x 64 and, .30/06, and rifles are today imported into the United States by Stoeger Arms Corporation of New York in .30/06, .270, 6.5 x 68, 8 x 68, .243 Winchester, .244 Remington, 7 x 57, .280 Remington, .308 and .358 Winchester and .458 Winchester Magnum, as well as the classic 6.5 x 54.

The Mannlicher-Schoenauer is generally distinguished by good finish, excellent blue and fine workmanship. It does, however, have a split receiver bridge through which the bolt passes. This prevents the lowest scope mounting, and it also prevents the use of bridge mounts for scope sights. The firing pin fall is slow, but nevertheless it is a satisfactory action.

MODIFIED MAUSER ACTIONS

Marlin, Colt, Sears-Roebuck and Montgomery Ward all produce and sell big-game rifles in various calibers made on Mauser actions imported from Belgium and fitted with American-made barrels, stocks and sights. Browning put on the market in 1960 a Mauser-type rifle made in Belgium. Winchester produces the Model 70, one of the most famous and reliable bolt-action rifles in the world in calibers from the .220 Swift through the .243, .257, .270, .30/06, .300 and .375 Magnum and the .458 African Magnum. The Model 70 was formerly made in .22 Hornet and 7 x 57 Mauser. Two new Winchester short magnum cartridges, the .264 and the .338, have recently been brought out. It is made in featherweight models with 22-inch barrels, and in heavier standard models with 24-inch barrels, in plain and de luxe models, and in special varmint and target models with longer and heavier barrels.

The Winchester Model 70 action is simply a modified Mauser, but it has an excellent single-stage trigger, a bolt and safety adapted to low scope mounting, a different system of gas escape vents, and a magazine separate from the trigger guard. The floor plate is hinged and there is a release forward of the trigger guard. The Model 70 is

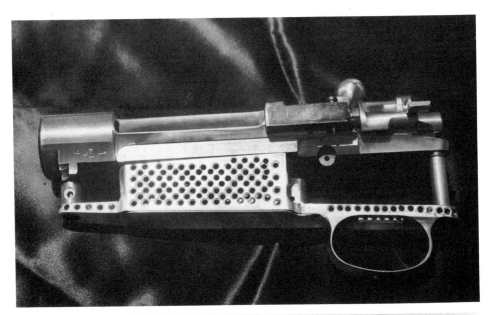

Many modern sporting rifles are built on modified Mauser actions. The skeletonized magazine and floorplate of the Mauser action (above) helps cut down weight. F. N. Mauser action (below) from Belgium is typical of those widely used for custom sporters.

considered by many to be the world's handsomest factory-made bolt-action sporter.

Prior to World War II, Remington had made bolt action big-game rifles based on the Mauser-inspired Pattern 14 British Enfield. This was called the U.S. Model 1917 when it was adapted to the .30/06 cartridge and made in this country during World War I by Remington and others. The first Remington Model 30 was a slightly sporting version of the Model 1917. It was further changed in the Model 30-S and the Model 720.

This Remington bolt action based on the Model 1917 was, however, an expensive rifle to manufacture, and after the end of World War II, Remington brought out the Model 721, a much cheaper rifle to put together. The 721 employs a maximum of manufacturing shortcuts—a tubular receiver broached from round bar stock, rather than machined from a forging, a bolt on which the locking lugs are machined, a stamped trigger guard, and stampings for various other parts.

The Model 721 does not employ the Mauser extractor and ejector. Instead the extractor is a semi-circular device in the bolt face which does not take as large a bite of the rim of the case as does an extractor of the Mauser type. The ejector is of the plunger type. The bolt face is recessed to enclose the head of the case, and the Model 721 action is a very stronge one. The action is made in the long size for such cartridges as the .270, .30/06 and .300 Magnum and in a short size for the .222 Remington, .300 Savage, and the .257.

The Model 725 Remington bolt action is a modified Model 721, with a good side safety, a detachable floor plate and milled (or perhaps cast) trigger guard, and a fancier checkered stock.

Another new bolt-action rifle is the Savage Model 110, which is made in both right- and left-handed models. Like the Remington Model 721, it is a considerably modified Mauser, with a receiver milled out of bar stock, instead of forged, as is the case with the Model 70 Winchester. Like the Remington, the Savage Model 110 has a recessed bolt face, a band-string type extractor, and a non-Mauser ejector. An interesting feature of the action is an extra set of lugs back of the locking lugs. These rear lugs do not lock but act as a gas shield and serve to guide the bolt in the raceways of the receiver. The head of the bolt and the right side of the receiver are vented for gas escape. Resembling the Remington again, the Model 110 is made in a short version for the .308 and .243 Winchester cartridges as well as in a longer version for the .30/06 and .270.

An interesting feature of the Model 110 is that it is available in both right- and left-handed models—and the left-handed job is the only one of its sort in the world. This is a break for one out of fourteen hunters.

As we have seen, the Model 98 Mauser action has been getting a working over from designers and custom gunsmiths during the past few years. Although time tried, this action, like any 60-year-old item, is ripe for a close appraisal of the possibilities for updating modifications. The surprising thing, however, is that over the years it has been so little changed.

The original wing-type safety of the Mauser, which worked left to right and interfered with the low mounting of a scope, has been redesigned for factory rifles and modified on regular 98s by custom gunsmiths for many years. The bolt handles on standard Mausers have been forged either to different shapes or have been cut off and welded on at different angles to permit low scope mounting. On the post-war Mausers, like the FN and the Husqvarna, bolts are factory designed to clear low-mounted scopes.

Many attempts have been made to redesign the essential Mauser action. One famous modification was the Model 1903 Springfield action, a design incorporating Mauser ideas executed by our own ordnance department, probably in the hope of getting out of paying royalties to the Mauser company. But as we saw in the last chap-

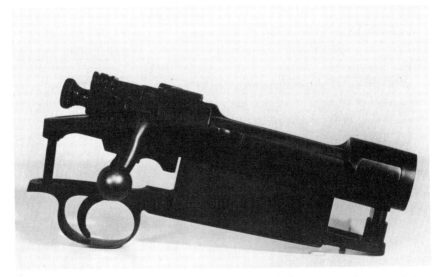

The Springfield 1903 bolt action is a modified Mauser action, retaining the high-swinging bolt handle, safety, and the double-stage trigger.

ter, it didn't work, as the U.S. government had to settle with Mauser for $1,000,000. In spite of excellent workmanship, the Springfield was in most ways inferior to the original Mauser, and it must be rated as one of the poorest of the "improved" Mausers. The high-swinging bolt handle, safety and the double-stage trigger of the Mauser action were retained. The Springfield's two-piece firing pin is more liable to breakage than the one-piece firing pin of the Mauser. Its lock-time is slow, it handles escaping gas less efficiently than the Mauser, and the action gives less support to the crucial head of the case.

THE WEATHERBY MARK V

One of the most recent jobs of redesigning the Mauser is the Weatherby Mark V. It is the creation of Roy E. Weatherby, president of Weatherby, Inc., of South Gate, California, with the assistance of a Weatherby engineer, Fred Jennie.

As any gun nut knows, Roy Weatherby got into the rifle business just after he got out of the Army at the end of World War II by introducing a line of cartridges that were originally wildcats—the .22 Weatherby Rocket (a blown-out .220 Swift), and a .257, a .270, a 7 mm., a .300, and a .375 Weatherby Magnum. The .257, .270, and 7 mm. Magnums were on a shortened, necked-down, and blown-out .300 Magnum brass, and the .300 and .375 were cases that were fire formed by firing in a Weatherby chamber. Later he designed the .378 Weatherby Magnum, a cartridge taking a .375 bullet at high velocity and a case similar to the .416 Rigby except that it has a belt. His latest is the .460 Weatherby Magnum, which is on the same case but is loaded with a .458 bullet.

Weatherby cartridges are based on cases made to Weatherby specifications in Sweden by Norma and then loaded at the factory in South Gate. The ammunition is widely distributed throughout the United States.

The first Weatherby rifles were rechambered Model 70 Winchesters or custom rifles built on Fabrique Nationale Mauser actions. The .378s have been built on Schultz & Larsen actions. These rifles are widely sold by dealers all over the United States and are built for such standard cartridges as the .270, .30/06, .300, and .375 H.&H. Magnum as well as cartridges of the Weatherby series. Custom rifles made to individual specifications are also available.

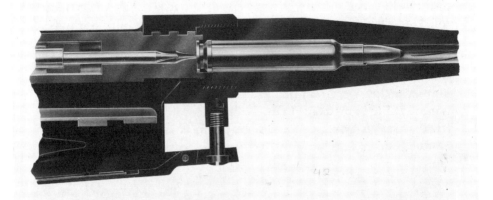

The new Weatherby Mark V bolt action completely encloses the base of the cartridge case within the bolt face.

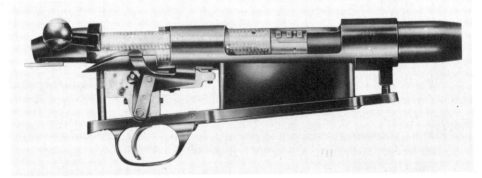

The Weatherby Mark V bolt action is an improved version of the Mauser, with a stronger locking assembly and smoother bolt travel.

The Mark V is the first bolt action to be designed and put into production by an independent American company for over four decades—or since the days of Charles Newton, the brilliant American firearms engineer.

The new Weatherby action is a good-looking, streamlined job. The original Weatherby Mark V actions were produced by the investment casting process and the parts were assembled and adjusted at the South Gate factory. At the present time the actions are made for Weatherby in Germany. Like other designers, Weatherby has attempted to eliminate the obvious faults of the Mauser action—the partially exposed cartridge case, the wobbly bolt travel, the creepy double-stage trigger and the wing-type safety. The redesigned bolt has nine locking lugs in sets of three. The lugs are of the same diameter as the bolt itself, and the bolt is the same diameter as the inside of the receiver. Operation is slick and smooth. The 9 lugs give 50 per cent more shearing area than the conventional 2-lug system of the Mauser.

The bolt face is counterbored to receive and enclose the head of the cartridge case, and the breech end of the barrel is likewise counterbored so as to enclose the portion of the bolt that houses the head of the cartridge case. The brass case, the weakest part of a bolt-action rifle (no action is stronger than its case) is completely enclosed in steel. Bolt lift is 45 degrees, whereas the bolt lift in an action of the conventional Mauser type is 90. The ejector is of the plunger type like that of the Model 721 Remington. Although the extractor doesn't take as much bite as that of the Mauser, it seems to take enough.

The Weatherby trigger pulls cleanly and crisply without any drag or creep. The trigger assembly incorporates the safety, bolt lock, bolt stop and bolt release. Because the working parts are heat treated, they provide long wear.

The bolt sleeve is of one-piece construction with the cocking indicator at the bottom. The gas escape vents are in the bolt. Like the Mauser, the new Weatherby action uses the conventional staggered box magazine. The floor plate is hinged, and the release is forward of the trigger guard. The magazine holds 3 magnum cartridges or 5 cartridges like the .30/06 or .270.

Tested at 60,000 pounds per square inch pressure by using a 180-grain bullet and 82 grains of No. 4350 powder, the Weatherby action provided normal extraction, no primer leakage, and normal case expansion. Results were the same with 84 and 86 grains. According to Weatherby, with 88 grains, case expansion was the same as with 86 grains, but there was some stickage. Even with 92 grains and with pressure that surely must run around 90,000 pounds per square inch, cases could be manually extracted.

The Weatherby action, although essentially a re-working of the Mauser action, also incorporates many ideas that have been tried and found successful on other actions. The multiple locking lug idea is an old device that was used by Newton and on Remington pump and automatic rifles, and by Winchester on its Model 88 lever action. The gas escape vents in the bolt are a feature of the Schultz &

Larsen, and the plunger-type ejector as well as the counterbored bolt face to shroud the head of the cartridge case are used on the Remington Model 721. The counterbored breech is used on the *Arisaka*, the modified Mauser with which the Japanese troops were armed. Adjustable single-stage triggers are standard on most of to-day's bolt-action factory-produced rifles, and the use of fore-and-aft safeties on bolt-action rifles has a history that extends back to the Newton.

Just as the design of the Winchester Model 21 shotgun is a com-bination of time-tried features of earlier American and British double guns, so the new Weatherby action is a fortunate combination of successful ideas.

THE B.S.A. RIFLE

The Birmingham Small Arms Company—a big British arms manu-facturer—has made a bid for a piece of the world's high-power rifle market with well-designed rifles built on modified Mauser actions. B.S.A. rifles are distributed in the United States by J. L. Galef & Son, of New York City.

Produced in 10 different calibers, the Birmingham rifles are avail-able in three action lengths and two different weights. Calibers are .22 Hornet, .222 Remington, 7 x 57 Mauser, .243 Winchester, .257 Roberts, .300 Savage, .308 Winchester, .270 Winchester, .30/06, and .458 Winchester—in other words, the Birminghams are calibered for use on game ranging from jackrabbits to elephants.

Birmingham actions come in three lengths—a long action measur-ing 7.9 inches from center to center between guard screws, with a magazine 3.5 inches long; a medium action measuring 7.1 inches be-tween guard screw centers, with a 3.2-inch magazine; and a short action 6.5 inches between screw centers, with a 2.3-inch magazine.

The B.S.A. actions are modified Mauser actions with dovetails for scope mounts that are integral with the receiver ring and the bridge. The floor plate is made of aluminum alloy; it is hinged at the for-ward end, and it has a release button in the trigger guard like the high-class pre-war Mauser Werke rifles. The safety is a fore-and-aft affair on the order of the one on the Model 1917 Enfield. The trigger is ad-justable, crisp, and light. Nicely shaped, the stock has a good flat cheekpiece, and its dimensions are excellent for the employment of iron sights.

The alloy steel (chrome-molly) barrels are proofed at the Birmingham proof house at 18 long tons per square inch. The two-leaf open sights are dovetailed into lumps on the barrel à la Winchester Model 70. The barrels are 22 inches long on the featherweight models and 24 inches long on the standard weights. The featherweight models have a muzzle brake consisting of seven vertical slots that are milled into each side of the muzzle. The dope is that these conditions reduce recoil 30 to 40 per cent, but that, of course, muzzle blast is increased about the same amount. Take your pick.

Standard weight B.S.A. rifles with long actions and 24-inch barrels weigh 7¾ pounds; with the medium action 7½ pounds; and with the short action 7¼. These figures are, of course, subject to variations depending upon stock densities. The short action B.S.A., in .222 caliber, has been imported for some time, and it is about as neat a little trick as you'll ever see. I have heard fine reports on those in use.

IMPORTED MAUSER-TYPE RIFLES

Many foreign rifles designed after one type of Mauser action or another are imported into the United States from Europe. A few light sporters in 7 x 57 and 8 x 57 came in right after World War II from Czechoslovakia. Modeled on small-ring Mauser actions, they had special safeties, double-set triggers, and flat bolt-handles. The Swedish Husqvarna in .30/06, .270, 7 x 57, and .243 employs a redesigned Mauser action. The great Belgian firearms manufacturing firm of Fabrique Nationale exports to the United States complete rifles in popular calibers, barreled actions, and actions in conventional Mauser type, as well as a redesigned Mauser action called the Series 300. The American importer is Firearms International of Washington, D. C., which also imports the Finnish Sako rifles. Tradewinds, Inc., an importing firm of Tacoma, Washington, is the American representative for the Swedish Husqvarna bolt-action rifles. This company also brings in the Brevex Magnum Mauser action from France, which is a long action of the conventional Mauser type that is suitable for such cartridges as the .300 and .375 Magnum, the .416 Rigby, the .404 Jeffery, and the .505 Gibbs. American custom gunsmiths buy these foreign actions to use as a basis for fine sporters. They also remodel various Mauser Model 98 military actions by altering the bolt handle and the safety, installing single-stage triggers, hinging floor plates and installing release buttons in the trigger guards.

Some of these actions will take more pressure than others. Some are made of better material than others. Some are better designed to handle escaping gas than others, but all of them are adequately strong for cartridges with a mean pressure of no more than 55,000

The lever-action rifle has always been popular because it is a fast-shooting weapon, allowing the shooter to keep the butt at his shoulder while he operates the lever.

The Winchester Model 95, no longer manufactured, was the only early lever action developed for the .30/06 cartridge. In its day, it was one of the most popular rifles for hunting big game in Africa.

pounds per square inch. No cartridge with higher pressures, standard or wildcat, factory made or hand loaded, should be used in *any* action. The actions themselves are not gas tight. Since it is the cartridge case that forms the gas seal, all that the shooter has between his face and hot gas, which can achieve pressures of up to 55,000 pounds per square inch or more, is the relatively soft brass of the case. Brass begins to flow at about 60,000 pounds pressure; therefore it is obvious that the subject of ultra-strong actions tends to be a bit academic.

THE LEVER-ACTION RIFLE

Because the first successful American repeating rifle, the Model 73 Winchester, was a lever action, and because other good lever-action rifles followed it, the American big-game hunter was for many years partial to the lever action. He liked the speed of fire possible with the lever, the exposed hammer which was safe at half cock. The lever-action Model 94 Winchester in .30/30 was the classic American deer rifle, and in that caliber and others has sold over 2,000,000 units.

Lever-action rifles generally can be operated faster than bolt actions but not as fast as pump actions. Since lever actions are thinner than other actions and therefore are well adapted to saddle use, they are the favorites of many hunters who travel on horseback and Western cattle ranchers who carry rifles in saddle scabbards for long periods of time. The Winchester and Marlin lever-action rifles whose safety is locked in place by thumbing the hammer back to half cock are very convenient for the left-handed man, who often finds other types of safeties slow and clumsy.

On the other hand, lever actions have their faults. The breech bolts do not lock at the head and the cases stretch, which means they are not too suitable for handloaders. With the two-piece stocks, the accuracy is not as good as rifles with one-piece stocks. In older types these actions are not strong enough for the 50,000-pound-per-square-inch pressures of modern high-intensity cartridges, and they lack the camming power to extract and seat soft, dirty and oversize cartridges. Modern lever actions, however, are strong enough to handle cartridges of the deer class. Today the shift is to some extent away from the lever action and toward the semiautomatic, the bolt and perhaps to some extent toward the pump.

THE WINCHESTER MODEL 88

The latest of the great Winchester series of lever-action rifles is the Model 88, made for a series of short cartridges based on the new U.S. military cartridge known as the T-65 during the period of its development. Winchester managed to get its name on a sporting version of the cartridge when it brought out the Model 70 feather-weight in that caliber and called it the .308 Winchester. The .358 Winchester cartridge is the .308 necked up to .35 caliber and the .243 is the same case necked down to .23. The Model 88 is a new lever action designed around these short, high-intensity cartridges.

At first glance the Model 88 looks as if a Model 99 Savage had been frightened by a Model 70 Winchester. It has the streamlined receiver of the Model 99, the same curved lever; but the stock and the barrel look like those on the Model 70.

The most interesting thing about the action is that for most pur-poses it is essentially a bolt action. The breech bolt has a separate head with three locking lugs which turn into recesses in the receiver, and which have 30 per cent more locking area than the Model 70 Winchester. This is exactly what gives such bolt actions as the Mauser, the Springfield, the Winchester Model 70 and the Rem-ington Model 721 such a big advantage. In each case the bolt locks

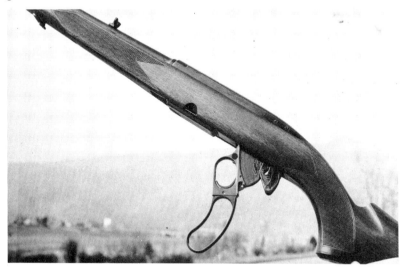

The finger lever of this Winchester Model 88 is in forward position. With the .308 cartridge, this light rifle is a favorite for big game.

at the head and the cartridge cases do not stretch. The breech bolt of the Model 88 has some camming action to get a sticky case going, too. The action is very fast since the lever has a 40 per cent shorter travel than that of the famous old Model 94.

The .308 is a right hot little cartridge, but I had no extraction difficulties. I loaded up some of the fired .308 cases. They seated easily. The Model 88 can be used by the handloader.

The safety is of the trigger-guard, cross-bolt variety and the detachable box magazine is of pressed steel and holds five cartridges staggered as in the Mauser-type magazine. Barrel has a dovetail slot for a folding front leaf sight with white triangle and wide "U". The design is excellent—for an open sight. Light barrel has a forend screw—a pious idea, as those who have jockeyed around with Model 70 Winchesters know. The screw acts like a bedding device and with it tension on the barrel can be increased or slackened off, and by experimenting the rifle owner can tell what degree of tension gives him the best accuracy.

With its front-locking breech bolt, its cam, its one-piece stock, the Model 88 is in effect a bolt-action rifle with most of the advantages of both types. Accuracy has been very good in the two rifles I have shot, and the camming power of the breech bolt makes the rifle useable for full-power handloads. Compared to the sweet simplicity of the best bolt actions like the Mauser and the Model 70, however, the Model 88 is fairly complicated and the trigger pull is on the creepy side. Because of its light weight, its "flatness" (it has no projecting bolt handle), and the advanced cartridges for which it is chambered, the Model 88 makes an excellent woods or saddle rifle and is a worthy successor to the famous Winchesters.

THE MARLIN MODEL 336

The Marlin Model 336 lever action is another famous rifle and a redesign of the earlier Marlin Model 93. Superficially the Marlin looks much like the Winchester Model 94, with its tubular magazine, its loading gate in the receiver, its loop lever, and its hammer. However, the Marlin has a solid top receiver and ejects the fired cases to the side and hence is suitable for low, central scope mounting. The present round breech bolt was designed in 1948 to replace the rectangular breech bolt used in the Model 36 and the earlier Model 93. The Model 336 is made in .30/30, .32 Special, and .35

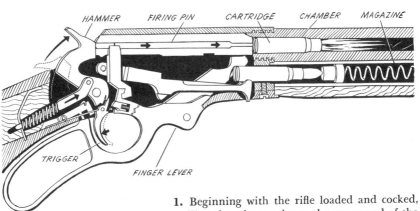

1. Beginning with the rifle loaded and cocked, pulling the trigger releases the upper end of the trigger from notch in the hammer, which springs forward and strikes the firing pin, detonating the cartridge.

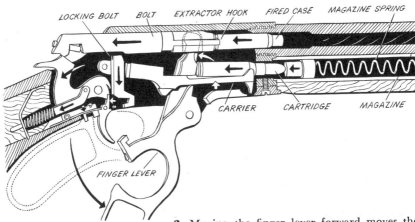

2. Moving the finger lever forward moves the locking bolt downward, disengaging it from the bolt, and the finger lever tip engages slot in the bolt and moves it rearward. As the bolt slides back, an extractor hook pulls the fired case from the chamber and a spring-loaded ejector on the opposite side of the bolt ejects the case. The magazine spring pushes the cartridge onto the carrier and a cam on the finger lever moves carrier upward toward the barrel chamber.

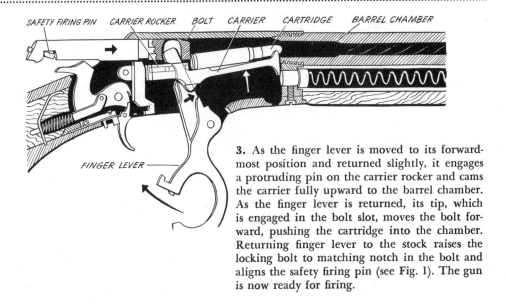

SAFETY FIRING PIN CARRIER ROCKER BOLT CARRIER CARTRIDGE BARREL CHAMBER

FINGER LEVER

3. As the finger lever is moved to its forward-most position and returned slightly, it engages a protruding pin on the carrier rocker and cams the carrier fully upward to the barrel chamber. As the finger lever is returned, its tip, which is engaged in the bolt slot, moves the bolt forward, pushing the cartridge into the chamber. Returning finger lever to the stock raises the locking bolt to matching notch in the bolt and aligns the safety firing pin (see Fig. 1). The gun is now ready for firing.

Remington calibers as well as in the form of a varmint rifle for the .219 Zipper. It is likewise made in various barrel lengths and with straight and pistol grips. It is a favorite for Eastern deer hunting.

THE SAVAGE MODEL 99

The famous Model 99 Savage rifle, of which over a million have been sold, has been around for over half a century. It is a lever action that is quite different from the typical Winchesters with their tubular magazines, top ejection and loading port on the right side of the receiver. The Model 99 employs a spool or rotary magazine similar to that found on the Austrian Mannlicher-Schoenauer. It is hammerless but has a cocking indicator—a little pin that pops up when the rifle is cocked—and a magazine indicator to show how many

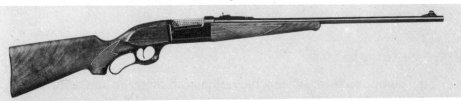

The Savage Model 99 EG is a popular big-game rifle with a strong action and side ejector, which makes it ideal for scope use.

cartridges are in the spool magazine. The magazine is loaded from the top, and the massive breechblock wedges solidly against the receiver. The Model 99 action is a very strong one. Whereas the Winchester Models 94 and 86 were adapted to pressures running only about 38,000 to 40,000 pounds per square inch at most, the Model 99 Savage will take pressures running over 50,000. At the present time it is being made for the hot Winchester .243 and .308 cartridges, as well as for the .250/3000 and .308 Savage cartridges.

The first Savage cartridge for the Model 99 was the .303, which today is loaded with a 180-grain bullet at 2,140, the killing power of which is similar to that of the .30/30. The original cartridge, however, was loaded with a 190-grain bullet at a velocity below 2,000 feet per second. Possibly because of the heaviness of this bullet, it had a reputation for being better for killing animals heavier than the deer.

Over the years, the Savage Model 99 has been made in different models and for many different cartridges. It has appeared with short barrels and long ones, with round barrels and octagonal barrels, in solid frame models and take-downs, in featherweight models and heavy models, in plain and fancy models, with straight loop-levers and grips and with curved loop-levers and pistol grips. Among the cartridges for which it has been chambered are the .25/35, .32/40, .30/30 and .38/55. In 1912, the Model 99 was brought out for the now obsolete .22 High Power. This cartridge, which drove a 70-grain bullet at 2,800 feet per second, was considered for a time as a deadly big-game cartridge. In 1914, the 99 appeared in the fine .250/3000 Savage cartridge, which pushed an 87-grain bullet along at the then sensational speed of 3,000 feet per second. After World War I, the .300 Savage appeared; it used a .30 caliber bullet on a case short enough to work through the Model 99 action and was ballistically comparable to the original .30/06. It became one of the most popular hunting cartridges in the country. The fact that the Model 99 ejects its fired cases to the side makes possible the top mounting of scopes—an advantage top ejecting rifles do not have.

PUMP-ACTION RIFLES

The pump, slide or trombone action, call it what you will, is a peculiarly American institution, and has been widely used in various forms for everything from .22 rimfires to big game cartridges,

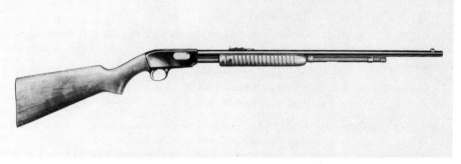

Winchester Model 61 pump action, chambered for .22 Short, Long or Long Rifle cartridges.

in hammerless models and in models with exposed hammers. The pump action is the fastest manually operated action, the easiest action to work from the shoulder, and one that allows the shooter to recock the rifle without taking his finger from the trigger. It is a natural for the man used to a pump shotgun. However, the pump-action rifle with its two-piece stock is generally not as accurate as the bolt action, and the earlier models were not as strong. They did not have the power to eject sticky cases and often the trigger pulls were pretty creepy. The pump action has never been as popular as either the lever or bolt actions.

EARLY PUMPS

Although pump-action rifles were developed by Colt well before the turn of the last century, the action was adapted to relatively low-pressure cartridges. The first successful high-power pump-action rifle was the Remington Model 14, first developed in 1912, which became a favorite for many years with shotgun shooters who were used to the familiar pump guns. The Model 14 was made for the Remington rimless line of cartridges in .25, .30, .32, and .35. These were basically rimless versions of the .25/35, .30/30, and .32 Special. All of these cartridges are now obsolete, with the exception of the .35 Remington.

The Model 14 (later given another stock and called the Model 141) was a strong and simple action characterized by a solid top receiver and a sturdy breechblock which locked up close to the head of the cartridge. Cam action started the cartridges in this action, thus overcoming a previous objection of shooters to the pump action. The rifle used a spiral magazine designed so that the points of the bullets did not rest on the primers of the cartridges ahead of them, a noticeable disadvantage of the tubular magazine. The Model 14 could be taken down. Because of this and the fact that it had a two-piece stock, the rifle was neither as rigid nor as accurate as a good bolt action, but it was a speedy and handy woods rifle.

THE REMINGTON MODEL 760

After the war, the Model 141 was discontinued and replaced by a pump-action Remington, the Model 760, designed for longer, high-intensity cartridges such as the .30/06, .270, .257, and .280 Remington. The breech bolt is locked at the head by rotary multiple locking lugs that turn into recesses in the receiver. The lugs are the interrupted screw type. The magazine is a detachable box holding four cartridges. The Remington Model 760 is chambered for the .257, .30/06, .280 Remington, .270 Winchester, .300 Savage, .35 Remington, .308 Remington and .222 Remington cartridges. The rifle is made in standard and de luxe grades and weighs about 7½ pounds. With its streamlined shape and its slide handle, it looks much like the conventional pump-action shotgun.

Because of the front-locking breech bolt with multiple lugs, the action is a very strong one, but it does not have the camming power of the bolt, and the chamber has to be cut oversize to facilitate extraction. It is a speedy, fast-handling woods rifle with a lot of firepower, but it does not do very well with handloaded ammunition. A good practical hunting rifle, but not for the handloading gun nut.

The Model 760 Remington is the only pump-action, high-powered repeating rifle now being produced in the world. Prior to World War I a Standard rifle calibered for the old Remington rimless cartridges was made for a time, but it was not successful. It was supposed to be convertible from pump to gas-operated automatic, but it was quite unreliable.

Many pump-action small-game and plinking rifles in .22 caliber, generally with tubular magazines, have been manufactured by Colt, Remington, Winchester, Savage and Stevens, and Marlin. The most famous ones have been the old Remington Model 12 (hammerless) and the Winchester Model 61 (hammerless) and the Model 62 (with hammer).

HOW A MODERN PUMP ACTION RIFLE WORKS
(Remington Model 760)

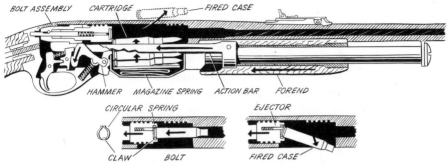

1. Moving the forend rearward pushes back the action bar and the bolt assembly, which in turn moves the hammer downward and ejects the empty case. Ejection is accomplished by a circular spring in the end of the bolt (see detail, showing top view) with a claw which hooks under rim of the cartridge and pulls it out of the chamber. When the case clears the chamber, the ejector spring in the bolt flips the case out. Then the magazine spring moves a new cartridge upward.

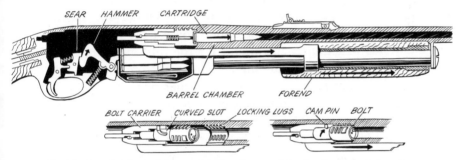

2. Moving the forend forward locks the cartridge in the barrel chamber. The notch in the sear holds the hammer so that the rifle is cocked. As the bolt carrier is moved forward, the threads on the bolt contact the locking lugs (see detail). Continued movement of the bolt carrier causes the cam pin on the carrier to engage a curved slot in the bolt, turning the bolt and threading it into locking lugs.

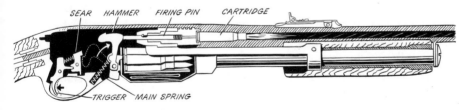

3. Pulling the trigger disengages the sear from notch on the hammer. The main spring forces the hammer against the firing pin, detonating the cartridge. The safety lock and a disconnecting device, which prevents the rifle from going off until the action is closed, is not shown to allow maximum clarity.

THE SEMIAUTOMATICS

The dream of a firearm that ejects the fired case, inserts a live cartridge, and cocks itself so that all the man behind it has to do is press the trigger for each shot is an old one. It has been translated into reality, however, and automatic, self-loading or semiautomatic arms have been on the market for around a half century in rifles, shotguns, and handguns.

Such actions have advantages, as well as disadvantages. The principal advantage, of course, is firepower, and the principal use is in combat—either war or self-defense by police officers. The history of military firearms has been one of continual striving toward greater firepower, as we have seen—from the muzzle loader to the single-shot breechloader, from the breechloader to the repeater, and from the repeater to the semiautomatic. Now, the tendency is to adapt infantry wapons to fully automatic fire, so that the soldier only has to press the trigger to send a stream of bullets toward the enemy.

A semiautomatic action is also useful for the bird and waterfowl hunter, as his "automatic" shotgun will deliver from two to five shots with that many trigger pulls and no other work on his part. Such an action is less useful to the big-game hunter. He needs accuracy more than firepower. He is not confronted with the necessity of cutting down platoons of charging lions or grizzly bears. If he is a skilled shot, he seldom needs more than two or three shots for an animal, and often only one. Generally the semiautomatic is not as accurate as the bolt action, and the violence of the action not only is hard on cartridge cases, but it often throws them so far they are difficult to find. The semiautomatic is no weapon for the reloader, no weapon for the long-range mountain hunter. For big-game hunting it is most useful in brush and forest shooting where there is a good chance that the first shot may be deflected by brush and limbs. Then it is a great advantage to be able to throw in a second shot immediately and hope for the best.

Two sources of power are available to the designer of semiautomatic arms. One is the *recoil* and the other is the *force of the expanding powder gas.* All semiautomatic systems employ one or the other.

THE RECOIL ACTION

The simplest form of semiautomatic action is a recoil action called the *blow-back*, which is used for handguns, .22 rimfire rifles, and centerfire rifles using cartridges developing low pressures. The breechblock is not locked, but is held against the head of the case by spring pressure. When the cartridge is fired, the bullet goes one way, the breechblock the other, but the bullet goes faster because it is lighter and is not held by a spring. As the block moves to the rear against inertia and spring tension, it ejects the fired case. Then the spring brings it forward again. It cocks the action and picks up another cartridge on its way back.

The blow-back works nicely with .22s, handgun cartridges, and with a heavy breechblock and cartridges of low power like the old .351 and .401 Winchester self-loading centerfire cartridges. If weight were no object it could be used even with the .30/06 but it is calculated that if it was, the breechblock alone would have to weigh 27 pounds.

When some means of slowing down the recoiling breechblock is used it is called the *retarded blow-back system*. One way to do this is to employ a breechblock in the form of a toggle. Another is to employ lugs at the head of the breechblock cut at an angle like screw threads. Such retarded blow-back actions have been used in submachine guns.

In the *short recoil system* the breech bolt is locked to the barrel, and barrel and bolt slide back together on firing, compressing a recoil spring. When the barrel has traveled a short distance to the rear and the bullet has left the barrel, the barrel stops and is unlocked from the breechblock. Residual gas pressure and momentum continue to carry the breechblock to the rear until it is stopped by a buffer. Then a spring moves the block forward. It picks up another cartridge, locks against the barrel and is again ready to fire.

The Johnson semiautomatic rifle, used to some extent in the last war, employed the short recoil system and a rotary bolt that unlocked while the barrel was traveling only $\frac{3}{8}$ inch. The short recoil system has also been used in various semiautomatic pistols and on the Browning double automatic shotgun.

In the *long recoil system* the barrel and breechblock are locked together and recoil for several inches. Then the breech bolt is held back while the barrel goes forward. As the barrel starts to return to its original position, the fired case, which has been held to the breechblock by the extractor, is ejected.

When the barrel returns to its original position, it strikes a lever that makes a latch drop. The breechblock comes forward and feeds in a new cartridge.

The long recoil system has been in use for half a century or so and is a good reliable system. However, the recoiling barrel adds to the recoil against the shoulder, and many shooters find the double jolt annoying.

This type of system is used in the Savage, Remington Model 11, the Browning automatic shotguns (with the exception of the short-recoil Double Automatic), and the Italian Breda and Franchi. The system was also used in the now-obsolete Remington Models 8 and 81 big-game rifles for the .25, .30, and .35 Remington centerfire cartridges in which the barrel recoils in a sleeve.

Remington brought out the very successful Model 8 autoloader in 1906. It was designed by John Browning, and it used a breech bolt that locked up close to the head of the case—a more satisfactory arrangement than the blow-back principle of the Winchester self-loaders. It was made for the same line of Remington cartridges as the Model 14 pump—.25, .30, .32, and .35 Remington rimless, and later the .300 Savage was added to the line. The rifle employed a detachable box magazine, and the barrel recoiled in a long outer tube or sleeve, which gave rise to the myth that the hunter could unscrew the barrel and use the sleeve for 12-gauge shotgun cartridges. Like the Model 14, the Model 8 was a take-down.

GAS-OPERATED ACTIONS

The self-loaders that operate with *gas power* are something else again. A hole is drilled in the barrel of the firearm and just after the bullet goes zipping by, some of the gas goes into the hole and into a gas-piston below the barrel. The piston pushes an operating rod that unlocks the lugs of the breech bolt, then drives the bolt on back to eject the fired case and cock the firing pin. The counter recoil spring then moves bolt, rod, and piston forward at the same time picking up a new cartridge.

Most famous example of a gas-operated semiautomatic is the M-1 or Garand, in which the gas is taken off near the muzzle. Used with

HOW AN AUTOLOADING RIFLE WORKS
(Remington Model 742)

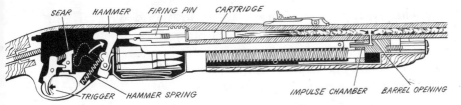

1. Beginning with rifle loaded and cocked, pulling the trigger disengages the sear from notch on the hammer. The hammer spring forces the hammer against the firing pin, exploding the cartridge. After the bullet passes the port, residual gases are metered downward through the barrel opening into the impulse chamber in the forend.

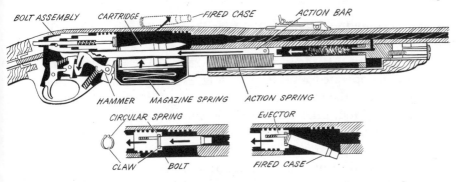

2. Gases force the action bar and bolt-assembly rearward, compressing the action spring, pushing down the hammer and ejecting the empty case. Further rearward travel of the bolt permits the next cartridge to raise into the path of the returning bolt. The ejection mechanism (see detail, showing top view) is the same as in the pump action.

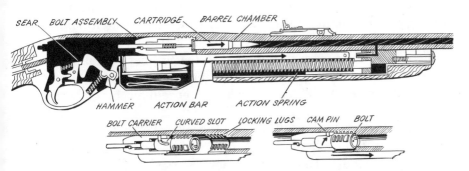

3. Compressed action spring moves the action bar and bolt-assembly forward, causing multiple lugs to lock the bolt into place (see detail also), sealing the cartridge tightly in the barrel chamber. The notch in the sear holds the hammer in cocked position. Pulling the trigger sets the weapon in motion as in the first diagram. The safety lock and a disconnecting device, which prevents the rifle from going off until the action is closed, is not shown to allow maximum clarity.

deadly effectiveness by American troops in World War II, the Garand made all manually operated military rifles obsolete. The new American rifle for the 7.62 mm. NATO cartridge is simply a lighter and somewhat smaller Garand for a cartridge shorter and better designed for automatic actions than the .30/06. The M-1 carbine, which was used in the last war and designed by Winchester, is also gas-operated, as is the High Standard automatic shotgun, the Remington Model 740 big-game rifle, the Remington Model 58 shotgun, and the new Winchester Model 100 rifle in .308 caliber.

A GAS-OPERATED SEMIAUTOMATIC SPORTER

The new Remington Model 740 "Woodsmaster," which replaced the earlier self-loader, then called the Model 81, is chambered for some pretty potent cartridges—the .30/06, .280, .244 Remington, and .308. It is a gas-operated repeater which takes the gas off forward of the receiver under the forend where a gas piston furnishes the power for the operating rod. Like the Model 760 pump, it employs multiple locking lugs of the interrupted screw type and has the same ejector and extractor. In appearance the two rifles are much the same. The receivers are identical in outside contour, and wherever possible the same parts are employed. The magazine used is a four-shot detachable clip, as in the Model 760, and the Model 740 has a cross-bolt safety in the rear of the trigger guard.

The action is a very strong one, and, of course, the rifle has a great deal of firepower. However, some functioning difficulties have been encountered with it in .30/06, possibly because of the lack of seating and extracting power with cases of other than Remington make. It was not made in the popular .270 caliber, probably because oversize cases were encountered in that caliber and also because .270 pressures run a bit higher than those of the .30/06. Those who own the rifle in .308 say they never encounter functioning difficulties.

Like the Model 760, the 740 is a good woods rifle, and, for some reason which I can't explain, the ones I have shot for group do better than the Model 760. The self-loader, however, is no rifle for the hand loading experimenter and gun nut. The cases undergo rough treatment when they are yanked out of the chamber by the gas-powered mechanism and often get mangled. They are also tossed a short city block and are often difficult to find. Like the chambers of the Model 760, those of the self-loader have to be cut large, and the cases have to be resized. This is poison for cartridge cases. But for most non-reloading deer hunters this is neither here nor there; they find the Model 740 an excellent, quick-pointing, fast-shooting hunting rifle.

CHAPTER FIVE

The Rifle Barrel

WHEN THE FIFTEENTH CENTURY GUNSMITHS CRAFTED THE EARLY shoulder firearms, they were faced with the problem of how to make a long hollow tube for the barrel. Because there were no boring machines in those days, barrel makers could not drill a hole through a solid bar of iron. They were forced to solve the problem in another way. They used an iron bar mandrel, heated a flat strip of iron, and welded it around the mandrel to form the desired tube. When the metal cooled, they removed the mandrel.

Generations of gunsmiths have used this traditional method of welding a barrel. Eliphalet Remington in 1816 welded his first barrel in essentially the same way, except that he used the twist method, which was popular in the Nineteenth Century. Remington crafted his barrel from a bar of iron which he heated and pounded into a long strip $\frac{1}{2}$ by $\frac{1}{2}$ inch around. He twisted this hot strip of iron around his mandrel, spiral fashion, welding as he went. When he finished, Remington had a solid iron tube, but the bore had to be reamed and rifled by a gunsmith.

By the eighteen fifties, the Springfield Armory in Massachusetts was turning out musket barrels in quantity, still using the wrap-around welding method. The Springfield gunsmiths didn't twist their barrels, though. Power-driven hammers pounded a flat strip of iron around the mandrel. When the mandrel was removed, the barrel was bored with a succession of augers to the correct bore diameter. After the bore was finished, the barrel was turned on a lathe to approximate outside diameter. Then, to remove lathe marks and polish the outside it was ground and polished to final dimensions on huge grindstones.

The Springfield barrels were straightened by finding the kink and striking the spot with a lead hammer. This process is still used by small gunsmiths. For a long time, straightness was determined by suspending a small weight through the barrel on a thread and rotating the barrel but later the shadow method was used. That is the barrels were inspected for straightness by looking through them at a straight line inscribed on a window pane and watching the shadow that is cast in the bore. This method is still used.

Barrels were also inspected for welding flaws and for cinder holes and small cavities left by bubbles in the iron. Then the barrels were proof tested with heavy charges of black powder.

Rifle barrels were made by the same method. The extra step was the rifling. These early rifle barrels, which were made of soft iron, performed satisfactorily with the low heat and pressures of black powder cartridges and with soft lead bullets. When smokeless powder came in it was another story, but more of that later.

During the Nineteenth Century premium barrels were made of some form of "twist," generally a combination of iron and steel rods twisted together and welded around a mandrel. The combination of iron and steel resulted in the twists and whorls characteristic of "damascus" barrels because the metal and the alloy each took the bluing differently. Depending on the figure, the combination of iron and steel, and the method of manufacture, these combination barrels were variously known as twist, skelp, damascus, rose damascus, laminated, and so on.

Although twist barrels were seldom used for rifles manufactured in the United States, they were widely used in American-made shotguns because such barrels were considered stronger than those of iron or mild steel made by the wrap-around welding method. From the eighteen seventies until the late nineties, a "figured" or twist barrel was considered to be the mark of a fine shotgun, even after modern barrel steels of superior strength had been developed and methods of deep-hole drilling a bar of steel had been perfected.

The partially finished shotgun barrels or "tubes" of damascus steel used in the manufacture of American double-barreled shotguns were for the most part imported from Belgium and England. Later some excellent American shotguns were made with tubes that had been imported from the Krupp works in Germany and were so marked.

Barrels made from twisted strips of metal were differentiated from those made by drilling and reaming steel barrel "blanks" by designating the latter type as "fluid" steel barrels. Although this term is over 75 years old, it is still used. A pioneer in the development of this much stronger barrel material was Sir Joseph Whitworth, an

English mechanical engineer and inventor, whose fluid steel barrels were used on fine British and American shotguns manufactured during the eighteen eighties and nineties.

Today both rifle and shotgun barrels are made from steel-bar "blanks" that are drilled and reamed. Those intended for rifles must also be "rifled." Some experimenting has been done with seamless steel tubing for shotgun barrels, and some rifle barrels have been made from aluminum tubes around a steel liner. Strong aluminum alloys have also been used experimentally for shotgun barrels, but I know of no production barrels made of that material.

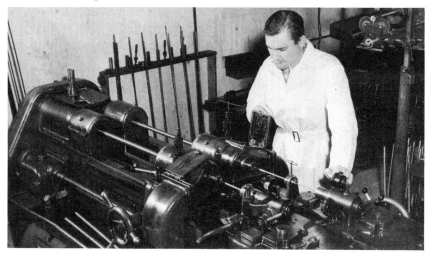

Modern machines like this one at the Weatherby plant are used today for deep-hole drilling of barrel blanks. Afterward, the barrel will be reamed to bore diameter.

MATERIAL FOR MODERN RIFLE BARRELS

In the days of black powder, rifle barrels, as we have seen, were made of iron or soft carbon steel, since breech pressures were only 25,000 pounds per square inch or less. Also, only lead bullets were used. The advent of smokeless powder made it necessary to make barrels of better steel, because these new cartridges employed propellants that burned at higher temperatures and gave higher pressures, and incorporated lead bullets jacketed with cupronickel, gilding metal or mild steel.

A carbon steel called *ordnance* steel was introduced at the turn of the century. It served for many years as the standard material of barrel makers, because of its greater tensile strength and durability.

In addition, ordnance steel is easily machined. It was used for the barrels of the American Model 1903 Springfield and for the high-power rifle barrels made by Remington and other manufacturers.

Nickel steel was used by Winchester for many years, and the barrels made of this material were so marked. I understand that it is still widely used in England. Although nickel steel is more difficult to machine than ordnance steel, it resists erosion better and consequently gives longer barrel life.

Most barrels for high-power rifles produced in the United States today are made of chrome molybdenum steel. Winchester pioneered its use when nickel steel barrels proved unsatisfactory for high-intensity cartridges like the .220 Swift and the .300 Magnum. Generally called chrome molly, these barrels are superior to those of both nickel and ordnance steel for hot cartridges.

Even harder and more erosion resistant are the so-called "rustless steels," which, I understand, are actually a high-chrome iron. In the form of Poldi "Anticorro" and Boehler "Antinit" steels, they were used for premium rifle barrels in Europe as early as World War I, and some blanks were imported by American custom rifle makers. Winchester has supplied these high-chrome barrels in .220 Swift and .300 Magnum calibers. Some of these steels can be blued, although the job is a difficult one, since bluing is a rusting process. The Winchester stainless steel barrels, for instance, are so rust-proof that they cannot be blued. They have been "blued" by painting them with a blue-black lacquer, or by iron-plating them, and then bluing the iron.

The small gunsmith who fits barrels to actions buys barrel blanks from various suppliers. He then turns each blank on a lathe to the contour he wants, threads the breech end to fit the threads of the receiver, cuts an extractor slot if the action requires it, and chambers the barrel for the cartridge desired. Prior to about 1940, the suppliers generally furnished the rough cylindrical blank already drilled, reamed and rifled, but otherwise just as it had come from the steel supplier. In recent years, however, suppliers generally turn the barrels to approximate contour before drilling. Although the warping of barrels in the turning is not as common as it used to be in the days of "normalized" blanks, barrels are still generally inspected and straightened by the use of an overhead clamp or by putting the barrel between two blocks and tapping the kinks out with a hammer, just as was done 100 years ago.

RIFLING

It is not known precisely who first got the notion of putting spiral grooves in the barrel of a firearm and created the rifle. But whoever he was, we all owe him a debt. Without rifling, a barrel-firing weapon is so inaccurate that it is hardly worthy of sights. With rifling of the proper sort, however, it becomes a precision instrument.

Within the past few years, the way in which rifling is put into barrels has undergone a revolution. After drilling a hole through the piece of steel called a barrel blank and reaming the hole to bore diameter, which in the finished barrel is the distance from land to land, the conventional method of rifling was to cut the grooves to proper depth in the barrel by means of a hook or scrape cutter. In a .30 caliber barrel chambered for cartridges such as the

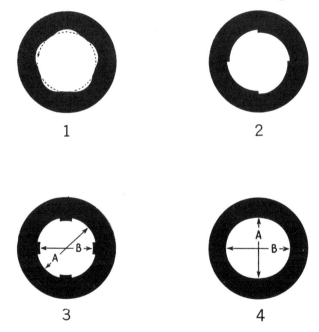

Types of Rifling: 1. SEGMENTAL, originated by Metford in England. Its five grooves are segments of a circle. Cuts are very shallow. 2. PARABOLIC, a modification of segmented types, was used in some Newton rifles produced right after World War I. 3. FOUR-GROOVE, the so-called Enfield type. A is groove diameter; B is bore diameter. 4. OVAL BORE, dimensions are for .30 caliber. A is .300 inch across; B is .310 inch across.

.30/06 and .300 Magnum, for example, the bore diameter is .300 of an inch, while the groove diameter (the distance from the bottom of one groove to the bottom on the opposite one) is .308 of an inch. Each groove, then, is cut to a depth of .004 inch. That's the American practice. In England and on the Continent, the custom is to cut deeper grooves. Americans like the groove diameter and the bullet diameter to be the same; Europeans like the bullets to be smaller than the groove diameter so they will "upset" or expand to fill the grooves. Americans claim better accuracy; continentals claim less pressure, higher velocity with the same powder charge and also longer barrel life.

Over the years, rifling has taken many different forms. The *Metford* system, which was widely used in England during the black powder days, featured grooves and lands that were rounded to facilitate cleaning out the rather formidable black powder fouling that collected. When one looks through such a bore, he is apt to think it is completely worn out. Another interesting type of rifling is the Lancaster oval bore that was used in England and also in this country in some of the rifles turned out by Charles Newton. The oval form of the bore turns as it progresses down the barrel and imparts a spin to the bullet. A person looking through such a barrel for the first time is apt to think it is a smooth bore.

MODERN RIFLING METHODS

The form now most widely used is the so-called *Enfield* rifling which has square-cut grooves and lands. The number of grooves varies from two, which are found in some barrels made for Model 1903-A3 Springfields and in replacements made during World War II for old Model 1917 Enfields, to 16 shallow grooves such as those found in the Marlin Micro-Groove system. Original barrels for the famous Model 1903 Springfield for which the great .30/06 cartridge was developed have four narrow lands and four wide grooves. The original barrels of the Model 1917 Enfield have five grooves. Some barrel makers have experimented with three-groove barrels but have found no particular advantage in this system. Most barrels are cut with either four or six grooves. Many factory-produced high-power rifle barrels are cut with four, many with six. If four-groove barrels have any advantage over six-groove barrels or vice versa, I have yet to see it. However, two-groove barrels are said to run up pressure and to be somewhat less accurate because of bullet deformation. One type of eight-groove barrel with narrow lands had the reputation of giving short barrel life. How deserved it was I cannot say.

During World War II and since that time, a good deal has been done to speed up barrel manufacture. Conventional rifling methods that cut one groove at a time are pretty slow and leave tool marks. But about the time World War II began, barrel makers started to use broaches for rifling. In this system, a series or "gang" of broaches, each a bit larger than the other and taking a deeper cut, is pushed or pulled through the barrel. This innovation enabled all the grooves in a barrel to be cut in a single operation, a much faster method than the old one of cutting one groove at a time. Right after the war Smith & Wesson was broaching all its barrels and so were other manufacturers. Among custom rifle builders, Weatherby was broaching his barrels by 1950. The disadvantages of using broaches, I understand, are that they are expensive and easily damaged.

The rifling is cut into the bore of the barrel on this broaching machine, which cuts the grooves in successive stages.

Still another rifling system, an exceedingly novel one, was used in the United States and Germany during the war. It consists of inserting a mandrel with the reverse impression of the rifling into the bore and then pounding the barrel until the rifling is formed around the mandrel. I understand rifled barrel blanks are now being manufactured to a limited extent by this method in this country and are being offered to the trade.

Still another way of rifling a barrel is by the use of a heated carbide rifling button which "irons" the rifling into the barrel, does all the work at one pass, leaves the barrel smooth and the work hardened. I understand that some barrels supplied to the gunsmithing trade are made with the button rifling system. I have likewise been told that all the rifling of handguns as well as rifle barrels, at the High Standard factory in Hamden, Connecticut is done with the button system. Remington also uses this method, I believe. Button-rifled barrels have been cleaning up in bench rest matches, and the Marlin Micro-Groove barrels have always shot exceedingly well. It would seem logical that barrels produced by this method would be harder, smoother, more uniform and possibly more durable than barrels into which the rifling had been cut rather than ironed.

THE AMOUNT OF TWIST IN THE RIFLE BARREL

A rifle bullet is much like a top. It has to be spun at a certain rate of speed in order to remain stable and point on. Spin the top too fast and at first it wobbles, before it settles down to a smooth spin. Then as its speed of rotation diminishes, it finally begins to wobble once more. The forward velocity of a bullet, however, diminishes more rapidly than its rotational speed.

The longer the bullet and the slower it leaves the muzzle, the sharper the pitch of the rifling must be in order to keep the bullet point on and accurate. A short bullet like the .22 Short, which weighs 29 grains, can be stabilized in a twist having one turn in 24 inches—in other words, 1—24. The longer .22 Long Rifle bullet, which weight 40 grains, needs a twist of 1—16. The twists in barrels chambered for old black powder cartridges, most of which used bullets that were relatively short in proportion to their diameter, were quite slow. The standard twist for the .45/70, for example, was 1—20. The twist for the Winchester .50/95 was 1—60 and for the .50/110 1—54.

When smokeless powder and jacketed bullets came into use, it was found that faster twists had to be used, as early smokeless powder cartridges used relatively long bullets. The standard twist used in Europe for the 7 x 57 Mauser cartridge is 1—8.66, and the twist for the 6.5 Mannlicher-Schoenauer with its 160-grain bullet was 1—7½. The twist for the .25/35 was 1—8 because of its relatively long 117-grain bullet, but that of the .25/20, with its 86-grain bullet, was 1—14.

The standard twist for the .30/30 cartridge has always been 1—12, which is about right for its 170-grain bullet at 2,200 feet per second. On the other hand, the .32 Special, also loaded with a 170-grain bullet, had (and may still have) a twist of 1—16 because it was designed as a compromise cartridge, a smokeless powder job that could be reloaded with black powder. Not a few citizens have noticed that a .30/30 barrel can look like the inside of a smokestack and still shoot pretty well, but that once a .32 Special barrel starts to go, you can't hit the rear end of an obese bull at 32 feet. The reason is that the twist just barely stabilizes the bullet in the first place, and once the rifling starts to go, the bullets wobble.

Many riflemen believe that the most accurate twist is the one which will stabilize the heaviest bullet to be shot through a particular barrel at the longest range at which the rifle will be used. There is much to be said for this theory. The more rapid the twist, the higher the pressure and the more the bullet drifts in the direction of its spin. American barrels with their right-hand twists drift their bullets to the right, just as a baseball with a right-hand spin curves in that direction. Likewise, British barrels with left-hand twists cause their bullets to drift to the left. The rear sight on the Model 1903 Springfield allows for drift. Rifling in Colt revolvers has a left-hand twist, by the way.

Barrels for the .30/06 are made with a twist of 1—10 because the original .30/40 Krag barrel from which it was derived needed a 1—10 twist to spin out its 220-grain bullets at 2,200 feet per second at long range. Many think that a twist of 1—12, which is standard in the .300 Savage and the .308 Winchester as well as the .30/30, is more accurate in .30 caliber, and it is true that a 1—12 will stabilize even a 220-grain bullet to very long range.

Right after World War II, I had Bill Sukalle, the Phoenix, Arizona, gunsmith and barrel maker, put a 22-inch barrel with a 1—12 twist on a Fabrique Nationale action and chamber it for the .30/06.

Al Biesen of Spokane, Washington, stocked it, and consequently I had the best .30/06 Sporter I ever owned—and I have had more than several. Not only did it shoot well with everything from 110-grain bullets to those weighing 220, but it did a pretty good job of putting them to about the same point of impact up to 200 yards. Accuracy was so outstanding for a light .30/06 that I attributed part of the credit to the 1—12 twist.

Some time later I got hold of a Springfield action and had George Schielke of Washington Crossing, New Jersey, put on a war-surplus High Standard barrel. The twist was the standard 1—10. Theoretically, this 1—10 twist should greatly over-stabilize a 110-grain bullet, causing it to wibble and wobble like the top that has just hit the ground and has not settled down to "go to sleep" as the rate of spin decreases. That's the way the theory goes. Then Western Cartridge brought out their 110-grain spire- point bullets for varmints and sent me 200 or so to play with. I loaded them up to about 3,300 feet per second, and the accuracy was sensational. That's enough to destroy a man's faith, but I can only report what happened.

This same rifle likewise gave good accuracy with any bullet up to the 250-grain job by Barnes. The .30/06 with the 1—12 twist, on the other hand, would definitely not stabilize the same Barnes bullet at 300 yards.

Like the .30/06, the factory rifles for .300 H. & H. Magnum cartridge have barrels with a twist of 1—10, which makes no particular sense since all bullets are driven faster in the .300 than in the .30/06. Nevertheless, that is the way she is. Citizens who know more about the .300 Magnum than I do swear that if barreled with a 1—14 twist it will stabilize a 180-grain match bullet to 1,000 yards. I have never tried it. It would seem, though, that with any of the .300 Magnums from the H. & H. to the Weatherby, a 1—12 twist should be ample.

Like the .30/06, the .270 Winchester was standardized with a twist of 1—10. A slower twist probably wouldn't hurt it, but how much good it would do I cannot say—and I have experimented with .270 barrels having twists of 1—10, 1—12, 1—13, and 1—14. A rather heavy .270 with a barrel having a 1—12 twist has probably given me a higher percentage of very small groups than any .270 I have ever played with. However, this good accuracy might be attributed to something else besides the pitch of the rifling. While we are at it, this barrel with the 1—12 twist stabilizes the Canadian Dominion brand load with the 160-grain bullet at 2,800 feet per second. A rifle with a 1—13 twist, which I used in India and Iran, would not stabilize the 160-grain bullet, but shot nicely with the 150-grain round-nose, soft-point bullets made by Hornady and Remington. But the excellent 150-grain Sierra boattail bullet definitely tipped in flight. A .270 barrel with a 1—14 twist I played with at one time shot nicely with anything ranging from 100 to 130 grains, but it wouldn't stabilize anything heavier that I put into it. The 150-grain sharp-pointed bullets would keyhole (enter the target sidewise) at 100 yards.

Shape has much to do with the difficulty of keeping a bullet point on and accurate. Round-nosed bullets are easier to stabilize than those with sharp points because their center of gravity is nearer the center of the bullet. A bullet with a long spire point and a short shank is inherently an unstable form and requires a sharp twist to keep it point on even though it may be light.

I think the danger of "over-stabilizing" bullets has been greatly exaggerated. For every example of a rifle that shot poorly because the barrel had too sharp a twist, I have run into a dozen that shot poorly because the barrel did not have enough twist. If bullets are well made, concentric and uniform in weight, they can be spun very rapidly without affecting accuracy, as shown by my experience with those 110-grain spire-point Western bullets in the 1—10 twist in the .30/06. I remember reading an article in which a writer related that he often got a couple of fliers in each 10 shots with 100-grain bullets out of a .270 with a 1—10 twist. He felt the bullets were over-stabilized. I'd say the answer lay in defective bullets. I have seen too many excellent groups shot in .270s with 1—10 twists using 100- and 110-grain bullets.

It used to be an accepted bit of folklore that the standard 1—14 twist of Model 99 Savage barrel was the reason the .250/3000 cartridge shot so well with 87-grain bullets. I was convinced of it as firmly as I was convinced that the sun rose in the east. Then I got hold of a Fabrique Nationale Mauser barreled action for the .250/3000. I had a custom stock and a good scope put on it. The darned thing shot like a house afire, particularly with the 87-grain bullets. I assumed that the twist was 1—14, but it turned out to be 1—10. The Speers used my rifle for working up the .250 Savage loads that appear in their handbook. The rifle also shot very well with 60-grain bullets.

Winchester brought out their .243 cartridge for use with barrels having a 1—10 twist. I may have had an exceptional rifle, but the featherweight Model 70 they sent me as a sample shot very well, even with bullets weighing 75 grains. The .243 was designed more or less as an all-around cartridge, but when Remington worked out the .244 they had in mind lighter bullets for the varmint hunter. The Model 722 in .244 has a twist of 1—12 that makes stabilizing the heavier bullets a problem. The Speer 105-grain spitzer shot poorly in the 1—12 twist so that to get accuracy with the bullet of that weight, the Speers had to design a round nose. Most citizens now ordering custom rifles in .244 Remington caliber from gunsmiths are specifying a 1—10 twist. They find it handles the light bullets just as well as the slower twist and at the same time shoots the heavy ones well.

The moral of all this would seem to be that if you are in doubt when it comes to specifying the twist in a barrel, pick the sharper twist and you can't go wrong.

Here are some rifling specifications used by a large manufacturer of barrels:

CALIBER	BORE DIAM.	GROOVE DIAM.	WIDTH GROOVES	NO. GROOVES	TWIST
.22 Short	.219	.224	.0688	6	24
.22 L.R.	.217	.222	.0681	6	16
.218 Bee	.219	.224	.074	6	16
.22 Hornet	.217	.222	.0681	6	16
.220 Swift	.2191	.224	.074	6	14
.250/3000	.250	.256	.0785	6	14
.257 Roberts	.250	.256	.095	6	10
.270	.270	.277	.160	4	10
.30/30	.300	.308	.0942	6	12
.30/06	.300	.308	.176	4	10
.32 Special	.305	.311	.099	6	16
.375 Magnum	.366	.376	.115	6	12

CHAMBERING

The chamber of a rifle is the enlarged portion at the breech end of the barrel that holds the cartridge. The chamber is slightly larger than the cartridge, so that the brass cartridge case can expand from the pressure of the gas and then contract for removal from the chamber. The neck of the chamber should be larger than the neck of the case so the latter can expand to release the bullet. If the neck of the chamber is so tight that the bullet cannot be released, the high pressure causes the whole forward end of the cartridge case, along with the bullet, to flow into the barrel.

In all its dimensions, the chamber should be slightly larger than a "maximum" cartridge. Some are not, and that is why it is difficult to seat some factory cartridges in some chambers. The factories in which barrels are made generally use a "roughing reamer" for the first cuts, and then a finishing reamer to complete the chamber. The finishing reamer, however, wears down from use, so that in time it may become so small that the chamber on which it is used is undersize or "tight." Such chambers, particularly if the neck portion is snug, run up pressures. Some gunsmiths use a third or "burnishing" reamer to smooth up the chamber, and all of them polish it with fine emery cloth or some other abrasive substance.

HEADSPACE

It is important that the chamber has the proper dimensions not only diametrically but longitudinally. Because most high-power rifle cartridges are rimless, their progress into the chamber is arrested by the contact of the shoulder of the case with a shoulder in the chamber. The distance between the rear of the cartridge and the face of the bolt is called *headspace*. If the shoulder in the chamber is too far forward a condition called *excess headspace* exists, and the case when fired has a tendency to stretch and to pull itself in two near the head of the case where the brass becomes thin.

In the process of cutting the chamber when making a new rifle, the manufacturer regulates the depth of the chamber by using what is known as *headspace gauges,* steel plugs the size and shape of a .30/06 cartridge case without the neck. When the chamber of a .30/06, for example, is finished the breech bolt should close on a 1.940 inch (or minimum) gauge. If it will not, the chamber is too short and some cartridges will be difficult or impossible to chamber. It should not close on a 1.946 (or maximum) gauge. There is another .30/06 gauge called a field gauge which measures 1.950 inch. If the bolt will close on this gauge the rifle is unsafe and should not be put into service. This 6/1000-inch leeway is standard with chambers of high-power rifles with pressures running up to 55,000 pounds per square inch. Pressures in shotguns and most revolvers are much lower (generally 10,000–15,000 pounds per square inch) so that headspace is not nearly so critical a factor. With most revolvers it is possible to rattle the cartridges after filling the chambers—a condition indicating very generous headspace. The body length and the shoulder slope of .30/06 and .270 cartridges are exactly the same, incidentally, and .30/06 headspace gauges and .270 gauges are identical. Gauges for the .257 Roberts and the 7 x 57 Mauser are also identical. Good gunsmiths have maximum and minimum gauges for all calibers for which they fit barrels. Attempting to gauge chambers by employing factory cartridges is unsatisfactory, as there is too much variation.

When other than rimless cartridges are employed, headspace is determined not by the cartridge shoulder but by other parts of the cartridge. With belted cartridges, such as the .300 and .375 Magnum, headspace is determined by the belt, and the entrance of the case into the chamber is stopped by the forward surface of the belt. In rimmed cartridges, such as the .22 rimfires, the .30/30, .30/40, .219 Zipper, shotgun shells and revolver cartridges, headspace is determined by the thickness of the rim. In some cartridges, the entrance of the cartridge into the chamber is stopped by the mouth of the case coming in contact with a shoulder in the chamber. The .45 auto cartridge and the M-1 carbine cartridge are examples of this.

Correct headspace is important but not as critical as might be believed. For instance, if a cartridge that closes on a 1.950 gauge is fired from a .30/06, it does not necessarily follow that the cartridge case is going to pull in two or that the rifle is going to blow up. For one thing, brass is tough, and also cartridges themselves vary enormously. Some run much smaller than a minimum chamber, some larger than a maximum chamber. The small cartridges usually expand to fit the chamber without pulling apart, and the maximum cartridges are usually sized down to fit the chamber by the camming power of a good bolt action. A maximum cartridge would give trouble, however, in most lever, pump or semiautomatics.

Two signs of excess headspace are protruding primers and complete or partial head separations. The former is caused when the case does not expand back to occupy the space from the head of the cartridge to the face of the bolt. The latter condition exists when the case has to stretch too much to fill the space between the shoulder in the chamber and the face of the bolt. If a rifle owner notices either of these symptoms, he should immediately have a gunsmith check the rifle with gauges for headspace.

BARREL WEIGHT

A considerable portion of the weight of a completed rifle is in the barrel; thus a light rifle means a light barrel. A heavy barrel will generally give somewhat better accuracy than a light one, but if accurately made and properly bedded, a light barrel will shoot as well as a heavy one under hunting conditions for big game, or even for varmints. The rifle with the light barrel is easier to carry, but the heavy barrel will settle down quicker, is less sensitive to tremors on the part of the shooter and hence can be held steadier. It is also less sensitive to stock pressure and to variations in powder charges. Nevertheless, the trend today is toward lighter barrels because of their better handling qualities.

Bench-rest rifles, from which maximum accuracy is expected and which are shot only from a rest, generally have exceedingly heavy barrels. A completed rifle weighs as much as 20 pounds. Target rifles very often have heavy barrels which bring weight to between $10\frac{1}{2}$ and 12 pounds. Varmint rifles often weigh between 10 and 14 pounds. Rifles that are carried on horseback and for long distances on foot in rough country should be lighter; a completed rifle with scope sight should weigh $7\frac{1}{2}$ to 9 pounds, or from $6\frac{1}{2}$ to 8 pounds without scope and mount.

BARREL LENGTH AND ITS RELATION TO BULLET VELOCITY

Custom has made the standard length of the barrel on the hunting rifle 24 inches in length, probably because that length was adopted as a compromise for both infantry and cavalry use in the 1903 Springfield. Although this was a pretty good compromise, a shorter barrel is handier for saddle or mountain use. A length of 22 inches is becoming popular, and some sporting rifles have barrels as short as 20 or even $18\frac{1}{2}$ inches. However, when a barrel for a cartridge of the .30/06—.270 class is cut below 22 inches, muzzle blast becomes annoying. Rifles for cartridges such as the .300 and .375 Magnums should seldom have barrels below 24 inches in length for that reason.

The hunting rifle should be fast-handling and a bit muzzle light, but the target rifle should be on the muzzle-heavy side so that it "hangs" better and is less affected by the rifleman's jerks and tremors. Target barrels are heavier than sporter barrels and are often from 26 to 30 inches long.

At one time it was a generally accepted rule of thumb that there was about 25 feet per second of bullet velocity loss for every inch cut off a high-power rifle barrel. For example, if a 26-inch barrel was cut down to 24 inches, 50 feet per second would be lost. However, although this estimate often applies it is still only a rule of thumb.

Velocity loss varies with the amount and kind of powder used, the pressure achieved, and other factors. A cartridge using a large amount of slow-burning powder loses much more velocity than a cartridge using a small amount of fast-burning powder. As an example, the .22 rimfire achieves its maximum velocity in about an 18-inch barrel and in some cases in a 16-inch barrel. The same ammunition fired in a 28-inch barrel would actually deliver less velocity than in an 18-inch barrel. A .220 Swift loaded with No. 3031 (a medium-burning powder) would lose less velocity in a 22-inch barrel than the same cartridge loaded with No. 4350, which is slower burning. Factory velocity figures should be taken on occasion with some skepticism. For instance, velocities for the .243 Winchester are taken in a 26-inch barrel. With the 100-grain factory load the velocity is listed as 3,050, but in the popular Winchester Model 70 Featherweight with a 22-inch barrel velocity is 2,925.

BARREL LIFE

One of the questions most often asked a shooting editor is how long a barrel will retain its accuracy life. The only answer to that one is that it depends on many factors.

The first of these, obviously, is the cartridge for which the barrel is chambered. Even a relatively soft barrel will last indefinitely if used with small amounts of cool-burning powder and soft lead bullets. Rifles chambered for the .22 rimfire cartridge have been fired experimentally a half million rounds with no wear that could be detected by a gauge.

The other extreme is the large capacity, high-pressure cartridge that burns a large amount of powder at high temperature and sends a hard-jacketed bullet through the bore at high velocity. Barrels for such cartridges as the .300 Weatherby, which uses around 80 grains of powder, will show wear much quicker than those for the .257 Roberts, which uses around 40 grains. Pressure also adversely affects barrel life. A barrel for a cartridge developing a mean pressure of 52,000 pounds per square inch will have a shorter accuracy life than one made for a cartridge with a working pressure of around 40,000.

Bullets are also a factor in barrel life. A very hard bullet with a boattail, which does not form a good gas seal and lets the gas escape past the bullet, will result in shorter barrel life than a softer flat-base bullet which upsets quickly to fill the grooves and makes a gas-proof seal.

The kind of steel in the barrel is also an important factor. A barrel of soft-carbon steel will show wear much quicker than a hard barrel of chrome molly. Often rifle owners get barrels intended for lead bullets and black powder that have been rechambered for smokeless powder cartridges using jacketed bullets. They are shocked to find out how quickly these barrels wear out.

It is always possible, of course, to ruin a barrel by neglect. A barrel chambered for .22 rimfire cartridges used with greased or waxed bullets is self-protecting, as the grease or wax in combination with the neutral fouling prevents rust. However, barrels used with jacketed bullets should be oiled and cleaned to prevent rust forming in a humid atmosphere, particularly around salt water.

It has been found that properly cared for Springfield .30/06 barrels have a life of about 5,000 rounds for gilt-edged accuracy, and a life of about 10,000 rounds for practical hunting accuracy. When nickel steel was used in barrels, most .220 Swifts would show the effects of erosion after about 1,000 rounds; however, with the stainless steel barrels now used, they generally show little or no erosion at 2,500 rounds. Prior to World War II, I used to see erosion after about 1,000 rounds in ordnance steel .270 barrels used with full-power loads. I have a Model 70 Winchester with a chrome-molly barrel that I have put about 3,000 rounds through, and I can still detect no sign of erosion except a slight rounding of the lands at the throat.

Barrel wear first shows up in the throat just forward of the neck of the chamber. You can see the erosion by looking through the breech at an angle. At first you'll notice that the lands are rounded. Then you'll see a slight frosting. Finally the bore is dark and pitted-looking at the rear end. Sometimes the accuracy will fall off almost as soon as the throat gets this frosted appearance, but now and then a rifle will be found that still shoots well even when erosion extends several inches up the bore.

But let us not fret about barrel wear. Putting 1,000 rounds of factory ammunition through a barrel will cost the shooter around $200 and putting 5,000 through costs around $1,000. A new barrel costs only from $40 to $65.

CHAPTER SIX

The Rifle Stock

DESIGNING THE STOCK FOR A FACTORY-MADE SPORTING RIFLE IS A task difficult enough to drive a strong man to despair. For it is up to the designer to turn out a stock that is suitable for tall men, short men, men with long necks and men with short, men with wide faces and men with thin, men with sloping shoulders and with square shoulders, men with long arms and short.

To further complicate the problem, a commercially made rifle may be used with iron sights, or with a scope, which means the line of sight may be an inch or so higher. Furthermore, the man who buys it may be the type of trained rifleman who gets his head down and his right elbow up in the offhand position, or it may be sold to some beginner who is about as much at home with a rifle as he is with a pair of chopsticks.

FUNCTIONS OF THE STOCK

Let us consider what a rifle stock is supposed to do. It should provide the shooter with a steady hold, enable him to have good trigger control and to take quick aim. It should also minimize the recoil effect as much as possible. If, in addition to this, the stock has graceful lines, then all is lovely.

This sounds like a large order—and it is. But designers of factory stocks have managed to do pretty well at turning out designs that are adaptable to the average human frame. If the shooter isn't too offsize, and if he shoots in more or less the orthodox manner he will find that, as far as the stock is concerned, a rifle taken from its factory carton will generally serve his needs.

Just what is the function of each part of the rifle stock?

The *forend* should be designed so that its size and shape will keep the rifleman's hand away from the hot barrel and provide him with a good means of controlling his weapon.

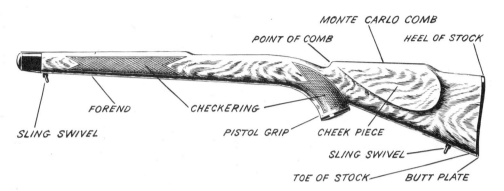

MONTE CARLO COMB
POINT OF COMB
HEEL OF STOCK
FOREND
CHECKERING
SLING SWIVEL
PISTOL GRIP
CHEEK PIECE
SLING SWIVEL
TOE OF STOCK
BUTT PLATE

Nomenclature of a modern rifle stock.

The *pistol grip* should be shaped so the rifleman can steady the butt of the stock against his shoulder, leaving his trigger finger free to squeeze the shot off at the right time.

The *comb* should be high enough and thick enough so that the pressure of the cheek against it steadies his aim and completes the essential pressure triangle of butt, grip, and comb that is essential for steady holding.

The *cheekpiece* should be shaped to give added support to the face and steadiness to the rifle.

The two factors which determine the position of the eye in relation to the sights are the drop at the comb below the line of sight and the thickness of the comb. The comb should be high enough and thick enough to put the eye in line with the sights, whether iron sights or open sights, when the rifleman has his cheek comfortably against the comb. If the comb is too high or too thick so that the rifleman has to crowd down on the comb, his cheekbone will be punished from recoil. The drop at the heel should put the butt comfortably to the shoulder and yet should be at a minimum so recoil effect is lessened. When there is considerably more drop at the heel than at the comb the muzzle of the rifle (and, of course, the comb) rises with recoil and the rifleman is hit uncomfortably on the cheek.

Anyone will do better shooting with a well-designed stock that really fits him. Nevertheless, excellent shooting has been done with some pretty terrible stocks. The original stock for the 1903 Springfield, for example, was far too short for the average man, and it had a straight grip and no comb to speak of. But when shooting, the boys learned to put their thumbs along the side of the grip so they wouldn't get socked in the nose and to adjust their jaws to compensate for the lack of comb height and stock length. Stocks for the older lever-action sporting rifles had combs that were too thin and too low, stocks that were too short, forends that had to be held like a pickle fork. Yet people managed to shoot these rifles.

IMPORTANCE OF GOOD DESIGN

In the last 25 years or so, a lot of thought has been devoted to stock design. The results: some stocks that are handsome and efficient, some that are efficient but not handsome, and some that not only are inefficient but so fantastically ugly as to cause a miscarriage in a lady crocodile.

Many features of design which serve their purpose on bench rest stocks, varmint stocks and target stocks unfortunately have found their way into some sporter stocks.

The forend that is perfectly flat on the bottom is excellent for the stock on a rifle that is to be shot from a rest, but it detracts both from the utility and appearance of a sporting rifle.

Likewise the very sharply curved pistol grip has its place in the target rifle that is shot with deliberation, but not on a sporter that is used to take a fast crack at the south end of a northbound whitetail. The extra-full forend is useful on a target rifle because it keeps the hand away from the barrel that a long string of rapid fire makes hot enough to fry eggs on. On the sporter, it is just more wood to lug around.

The design of stocks for pump, lever and self-loading rifles is a much simpler proposition than for the bolt action. Obviously, the comb on a bolt-action stock has to be low enough so that the bolt can be withdrawn, whereas, with the other types of rifles, the designer can put the comb where it will do the most good. Then you really have a designer's headache if a scope is put on a bolt action rifle so that the line of sight is raised an inch.

American sporter stock design has evolved over a long period of time from two sets of ancestors. Until along in the late nineteen twenties, one source of inspiration for the design of stocks on lever-action rifles was the stock of the muzzle-loading "Kentucky" rifle

The special target stock on this Remington Model 37 .22 target rifle has a sharply curved pistol grip and an extra-full forend.

A completed stock inletted for barrel and action of a bolt-action rifle.

This Mauser .30/06 bolt-action stock has a comfortable pistol grip.

with its short, rather skimpy buttstock, its low thin comb, its excessive drop at the heel, and its rifle buttplate. For example, the stocks on the early Winchester Model 94 lever actions showed a lot of the Kentucky influence. Such stocks were passable for muzzle-heavy rifles with light recoil when fired from the offhand position, but they were poison on a rifle with heavy recoil when fired from prone. It took a long time to design out that excessive drop and those rifle buttplates, and to introduce pistol grips. In my youth, an uncle of mine owned a Winchester Model 95 in .405 caliber. To me it was a romantic weapon of fantastic power, and I often shot it. But when it went off, the excessive drop at heel made the low, thick comb fly up and bust me in the cheek, and the points of that curved buttplate would dig into my shoulder. As I remember it, that old cannon was far more unpleasant to shoot than a modern .458.

The other influence on the design of American sporter stocks has been the classic stock for bolt-action rifles that evolved in the custom gun shops of England and Germany. This type of stock, which has less drop at the comb and heel than the Kentucky, is also characterized by a cheekpiece, a fairly substantial forend, a pistol grip, and a large, flat buttplate of the "shotgun" type that helps to minimize the recoil by distributing it over a large area.

By about 1900, inexpensive factory rifles had just about put the American-born custom rifle makers out of business. Firearms lovers would pay a substantial piece of the folding stuff for a fine custom shotgun, but, as for rifles, they were content with those turned out by mass production. Custom gunsmithing was revived in the United States, however, by a group of European-trained men who started to whittle out sporting stocks for Model 1903 Springfields just before World War I, and who continued the art after the war. This group included Fred Adolph, Hans Wundhammer and August Pachmayr, who were from Germany; the Englishmen, Bob Owen and John

Classic rifle stock with Redfield Bear Cub scope on a Tilden mount on a Mauser rifle made by Al Biesen.

Wright; and Alvin Linden of Sweden. The exceptions were, I believe, Tom Shelhammer and John Dubiel, both native Americans.

These gifted men Americanized the European classic stock in detail by giving it a thicker comb, making it a bit straighter and making the forend fuller. Although there were some excellent stocks for bolt-action sporters with iron sights kicking around during the nineteen twenties, the stocks on the first Model 30 Remington bolt action and the Winchester Model 54 were fearful turkeys because of their excessive drop at comb and heel, poor forends and generally unsatisfactory dimensions. Both the Savage and the Winchester had buttplates that would have been suitable for air rifles, while the Remington had a curved rifle buttplate which made the recoil of the .30/06 rather painful.

Largely because of the squawks of such gun writers as the late Captain E. C. Crossman, *Outdoor Life* columnist, and Colonel Townsend Whelen, who for some years was rifle editor of *Outdoor Life,* gun factories began to redesign their stocks. Consequently, those on the more recent Winchester Model 54s and Model 70s, the Savage Model 40s, and the Remington Model 30s were quite satisfactory. All of these stocks had good wide buttplates, good forends and thick combs.

THE SCOPE PROBLEM

Then the scope sight, with its higher line of sight, came along to complicate the problem. This was a tough nut to crack, since obviously a stock that is right for a rifle with iron sights isn't always right for one with a scope.

This remodeled Winchester 70 has a wide buttplate, full forend and thick comb.

The scope problem has been tackled by two different means. One is by the refinement of the classic stock. That is, by giving it a thicker comb that is high enough so that the bolt can just be withdrawn, and by making the buttstock straight—with the same amount of drop at heel as at comb.

The other method makes use of the Monte Carlo comb. In some cases, this comb is straight from front to rear, dropping off to give the butt an inch or two more drop at heel. A variation of this is the comb that slopes up toward the rear. The idea of the Monte Carlo comb is a fairly old one, since I have seen it on German stocks made during the nineteen twenties. In this country one of the early boosters of combs of this type was Elmer Keith, the gun writer of Salmon, Idaho.

A stock of modern design with a Monte Carlo comb on a Weatherby custom-made sporter.

A Monte Carlo comb supports the face to give steadier aim with scope sights; however, the Monte Carlo that comes straight back doesn't provide any better support than the perfectly straight stock. If the shooter is a stock-crawler who gets right up to the point of the comb, the Monte Carlo that slopes up toward the rear gives him no more support than no comb at all.

The only part of a Monte Carlo that serves any function is the part that supports the face. But many designers bring the Monte Carlo back so far that the buttstock looks like the working end of a canoe paddle. It is a matter of taste, no doubt, but to me such stocks are fearfully ugly.

Preference in stocks as in gals is a personal matter. My own preference is for the simple stock of classic lines. The less difference in drop between comb and heel, the less a rifle kicks. If a rifle recoils in a straight line and the buttplate is large enough to distribute the recoil over a wide area, no one is going to get hurt. The small buttplate that concentrates recoil is poison. So is the crooked stock—with or without a Monte Carlo—since recoil will cause the comb to rise, socking the shooter on the sensitive cheekbone. Some of these stocks are less objectionable than others, but I can take them or leave them alone.

BEST SPORTER STOCK FEATURES

In the sporter, the pistol grip should not be very sharply curved, or what is known as "full." For my hand, I like one that has a forward edge of about 3½ to 4 inches from the center of the trigger and about 1½ inches below the center of the trigger. The best-feeling grips have a slight parabolic curve. Sometimes designers exaggerate this curve, and often they combine it with a very long and flaring grip which strikes my perhaps jaundiced eye as extremely ugly. I believe in small grips for firm and comfortable holding, just as I believe in small handles for baseball bats. For me, a circumference of 4½ inches is about right, and, even for the very largest hands, I doubt if a grip should be over 4¾ inches around. The 5 to 5¼ inch grips seem to me both awkward and ugly.

The comb should rise enough above the upperline of the grip to protect the nose from the thumb, and, on the right side (for a right-handed man), it should be undercut enough to take the fleshy part of the hand at the base of the thumb. I think that the handsomest comb line is a full curve that describes a segment of a circle. The thumb out forward of a comb that dives too far down presents an ugly line. To me the graceful curve of comb and pistol grip are key points in the handsome sporter stock. Trick combs and pistol grips that depart from these specifications generally don't add to the looks of a rifle.

The first cheekpieces on American sporters looked at best like afterthoughts, at worst like limp pancakes. Today the best designers use a modified form of the old Scheutzen cheekpiece, an adaptation from the offhand target rifles used by the Germans. I like a cheekpiece that is rather flat—about ⅝ of an inch thick at the thickest part—so that it supports a considerable area of the face, and that blends forward into a thick, rounded comb. The cheekpieces seen on many European sporters are thin and have sharp forward edges along with thin, sharp combs. These are just about worthless.

The best stocks on sporters have the wood thinned away to the rear of the trigger on the right side so the trigger finger is free. Some pistol grips have a swell on the right side to fit the hollow of the palm but the stocker should not use this device unless he knows just how the shooter holds his rifle. If it is the wrong place for the individual, it is worse than useless. The wood around the action should be left thick enough to give the stock strength, but it should be gracefully contoured to avoid a slab-sided look.

The forend generally should be about 10 inches long from the forward edge of the receiver ring to the end of the forend tip. This seems a graceful proportion for a 22-inch barrel, but could be extended a bit more for a 24-inch barrel. Many excellent forends are just about circular in cross section, but a slight pear shape probably is more comfortable and may give better control.

It is a convention today to tip the forend with black plastic, water-buffalo horn or ebony. This custom started in England and has generally been used on fine custom rifles in the United States. American riflemen are used to the forend tip, but I doubt if it actually adds anything to the looks of the stock. Pistol grip caps are generally made of blued steel, but they are often made of contrasting wood (sometimes with a diamond-shaped inlay to hide the screw), plastic, or even ivory. They add a finished look to the rifle. Some shooters like white plastic spacers between the gripcap and the wood and between the forend and the forend tip. They give me the creeps, but so do strips of chrome plastered on automobiles.

Some stocks have handsome and graceful lines and some do not and why this is so is almost as difficult to explain as the reason why Susie Jones is a rather homely girl but Sally Smith is a lovely dish who draws males' glances and inspires romantic sighs. Both come equipped with the regulation number of eyes, noses, chins, and mouths; but it is a matter of a curve here and a line there that makes the difference. So it is with rifle stocks.

Morgan Holmes, the New Jersey stockmaker, once wrote that the lines of a stock should either be ruler straight or should be segments of a circle. I think he has something; from my experience, his formula checks out. Shadbelly curves and funny angles don't add anything to the looks of a stock.

The proper dimensions for a rifle stock differ among individuals. Length of pull is generally from $\frac{1}{2}$ to 1 inch less than that on the shotgun. For instance, I am a bit over 6 feet tall and wear a 34-inch sleeve. For all-around use, a $14\frac{1}{4}$-inch pull on a shotgun is right for me, whereas I like $13\frac{1}{2}$ to $13\frac{5}{8}$ on a rifle. A very tall man with very long arms might require a 14-inch pull on a rifle. Factory pulls

A standard factory stock. Mass-produced stocks are made of good, plain wood, but they are shaped to fit the average man and may be wrong for the tall or short shooter.

A custom stock is made to the specifications of the hunter.

A target stock is typically long and has a thick forend.

usually run about 13½. The man of average height will do pretty well with a pull of about 13¼ inches and a short man or the average woman with about 13. Pull for a short woman should be about 12¾.

If a rifle is to be custom made, the gunmaker should take into consideration the customer's build and shooting habits. I am tall, have a long neck and square shoulders, and I crawl a stock somewhat. Therefore, I can shoot a rifle or shotgun with a very straight stock. Obviously a short man or woman with sloping shoulders and a short, thick neck needs more heel drop than I do. The shooter with a wide face and thick, high cheekbones would be murdered by the high, thick comb that I find ideal. Because of the way women are constructed (some more so than others) a bit of cast-off (the rifle butt extends a bit to the right of the axis of the bore) puts the butt where it does little harm, but cast-off adds to recoil effect because it tends to push the comb against the cheek. Cast-on (the center of the butt to the left of the axis of the bore) is sometimes justified on a rifle of very heavy recoil, because it tends to push the stock away from the face.

It would be ideal if the man ordering a custom stock would

shoot it before the final shaping and finishing. Often the high, thick comb that sounds and looks so nice is found to be so high it is uncomfortable. It is easier to rasp down an overly high comb to a comfortable height before the finish is added to the stock than afterward.

I have intimated that the factory-made stock is a bit long for the average man (5 foot 8 inches). It is not a difficult trick to get a gunsmith to shorten the stock, either by refitting the factory buttplate, or by putting on a recoil pad. If the comb is too high or thick, it can be whittled down. If one is indifferent to the appearance of a stock, it is not too difficult to. dowel and glue a piece of walnut on and then shape it up into the desired comb. For my taste and for my hand, most factory stocks come with pistol grips that are too large around, and, in general, many factory stocks are a bit long on wood. Many of them can be improved by thinning down and shaping up the grips. Then the grip can be recheckered to match the forend at no great cost.

A more expensive solution for the problem of stock fit is for the shooter to take his rifle and his troubles to some crack stockmaker who has something under the hat as well as in his hands. However, it is well to remember that most beginning rifle shots like stocks longer and more crooked than they do later. It is wise to let the habits form and the tastes jell before investing important money in a fancy stock.

I would rather spend my dough on good wood, precise fitting of barrel and action into the stock, graceful shape, good fit, and plenty of fine, precise checkering. Others like white spacers, inlays of contrasting wood or mother-of-pearl, ivory pistol grip caps and forends, French-skip checkering, carved oak leaves, clusters of grapes, tigers killing water buffalo or mermaids frisking in the waves. I like pistol grip caps and buttplates of blued checkered steel, but I am no more right than the guy who wants his of red, white, and blue plastic. A pal of mine likes stocks of light-colored wood with gold-plated fittings and pearl and ivory inlays. My conservatively shaped, elegantly checkered stocks of dark French walnut sadden and depress him. I don't like his flamboyant stocks, and he wouldn't be caught dead with one of mine.

But that is neither here nor there. What counts is how well the pistol grip fits the hand, how firmly the comb and the cheekpiece support the face, how fast you can get on target and how steadily you can hold when you squeeze off. All else is frosting on the cake.

MATERIALS FOR GUN STOCKS

The classic wood for rifle stocks is walnut, either the thin-shelled European or American black variety, but many other woods have been used—maple, myrtle, apple, cherry, rosewood and even mesquite. Stocks have been made out of various plastics and in 1959 Remington introduced a .22 autoloader with stock and receiver cast of structural nylon. Plastic stocks can be given any color and figure the manufacturer wishes. "Checkering" can be cast into the stock. A structural nylon stock is light, warp-free, and very strong, yet the convention is to make stocks out of wood and the conventional shooter will object to plastic stocks of all sorts for many years.

This is a blank before being cut to shape for a stock. The outline is inscribed carefully to use grain to best advantage.

Whatever sort of wood is used, it takes a long time from tree to rifle stock. It is generally considered the best practice to let the wood that has been chosen for stocks season a couple of years in log form and then an additional two to four years after it has been cut into planks. Then the wood is sawed into "blanks"—long ones for stocks of bolt-action rifles and short ones for buttstocks of shotguns or rifles with two-piece stocks like the Remington Models 740 and 760 autoloading or pump rifles.

Stock blanks for bolt-action rifles should be laid out so that the grain runs parallel to the direction of the grip, and also so that the grain in the forend runs diagonally, not parallel, to the barrel. This lessens the tendency of the forend to warp up or down, changing the point of impact. Crossgrain at the slender grip would, of course, weaken the stock at a crucial point. Before the blank is made into a stock, it should be thoroughly dry. Moisture content is determined by periodically weighing the blank. Theoretically, when a blank no longer loses weight, it is considered dry.

The fanciest figure comes from the portion of walnut trees where the limbs and roots branch off. At that point there is usually grain running in several directions and considerable contrast between light and dark. However, some of this wood never really finishes warping but instead makes minute changes with different atmospheric conditions. It can be used in shotgun buttstocks but never in a rifle stock where the forend would warp against the barrel or warp away from it.

The demand for wood for rifle stocks and other purposes during World Wars I and II greatly depleted the supply of walnut both in Europe and North America. As a result, the price of good wood has risen enormously. In the nineteen thirties it was possible to get a rifle blank of plain, hard, straight grain French walnut for about $5, but a blank like that today costs $20 or more. A really fine one with great contrast between light and dark, with sweeping lines and handsome figure, will sell for from $50 to $100.

EUROPEAN WALNUT

The world's best gun stock material is the European-grown walnut that Americans call "English" walnut. The best wood of this variety grows on rocky hillsides in areas of relatively light rainfall, which causes slow growth. Any variety of walnut that is grown in moist, fertile bottom land where growth is rapid is soft and coursegrained, without much figure.

Because more fine walnut comes from France's Rhone Valley than anywhere else, most European walnut is called "French," despite the fact that good walnut also comes from Italy, England, Spain, Turkey and other countries in Europe. Before World War I, great quantities of fine walnut were exported from the Russian

This fine stock of American black walnut shows a figure called "feather."

province of Circassia; the fanciest of all European walnut was "Circassian walnut." Since the Russian Revolution, however, little wood has come to the West from there.

Fine walnut also grows in the Balkans and in India's Kashmir. I saw numerous groves of beautiful walnut trees in the mountains of northeast Iran when I was shooting there in 1955. In the United States many thin-shelled walnut trees have been planted, but many of them grow in fertile, irrigated soil so that the wood produced has no more figure and character than yellow pine. Some excellent walnut wood, however, comes from California.

The best grade of European walnut is marked, when finished, by great brilliance and contrast of color—a rich light-to-medium brown, often with a reddish cast, offset by long, dark streaks. That cut from where the roots and limbs branch off from the trunk shows a great deal of burl. European walnut is hard, strong, light in weight, but dense. It is also distinctive so that anyone familiar with it can tell a piece of "French" at a glance.

This wood is the stock material for the world's finest guns and rifles such as the $2,000 Purdey double shotguns and the $2,500 Holland & Holland double ejector rifles. "French" walnut is the preferred material for fine rifle stocks made by such crack American stock makers as the late Alvin Linden and Bob Owen, and by Alvin Biesen, Griffin & Howe, Leonard Mews, and other fine stockers who are still practicing their art. It takes and holds fine checkering, and, because of its small pores, walnut has a smoothness and a glitter when finished that few woods can equal.

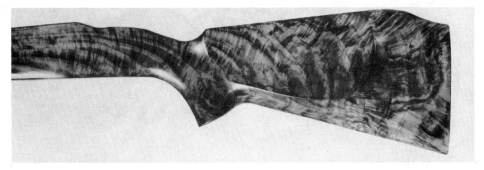

Dark, sweeping lines in the wood are characteristic of a high-grade French walnut stock.

AMERICAN BLACK WALNUT

Gun and rifle factories in the United States almost always make their stocks out of American black walnut, much of which has been grown in the Missouri Ozarks. This variety is somewhat heavier than European walnut, more open grained, softer, and generally lacks contrast. The best is very good stock wood, with some beautiful burl and grain figure, but much of it is only so-so. Because of the great demand for American black walnut, much of it is sawed into planks and kiln dried while the logs are still green and unseasoned. The result is a soft and brittle wood. Although American black walnut does not hold the fine checkering that the best European wood takes, the best American walnut is far superior to the worst European.

OREGON MYRTLE

An interesting gunstock material is the wood of the Oregon myrtle tree, which grows in the coastal mountain ranges of southern Oregon and northern California. This tree is a cone-shaped evergreen, and the ones I have seen from the road while driving through this area looked to be between 30 and 40 feet tall. Cutting the trees, curing the wood, then cutting it up into material for gunstocks or for woodworkers who use it to make fancy bowls or candlesticks is a fairly important local industry.

Myrtle is a hard, close-grained wood that is slightly heavier than French walnut. On the average, it is quite light in color. Some of it is very plain with no more figure than pine, but much of it is marked with long, dark streaks. Sometimes the wood will be streaked with very handsome patterns of yellow, brown and black, and once I saw a rifle stock made from myrtle that, in addition to brown and yellow, had some streaks that finished up green. I have seen myrtle that looked like maple, some that looked like the best French walnut, some a very light yellow and some as dark as light French.

The late Alvin Linden, one of the best stockers that ever practiced the trade, did not care for myrtle and said he had seen few blanks that ever stopped warping. Alvin Biesen says he finds it is too brittle. On the other hand, myrtle is the favorite wood of many stockers, and the one stock I had made out of it was not only exceedingly handsome but entirely satisfactory. If the gun fancier likes light-colored wood, he should make it a point to investigate myrtle.

MAPLE

One of the best of all stock woods is what is called hard maple, rock maple and sugar maple. Although it is often quite without figure, it is also found in birdseye form and in what is called "tiger tail." The weight of hard maple is about comparable to that of black walnut. It is a strong, hard, close-grained wood that takes checkering well. Alvin Biesen says that he finds it more stable than walnut, showing less tendency to warp.

Since it is in less demand than walnut, hard maple is in better supply and is widely used. If a gun fancier likes a light-colored stock, this is his dish, since it finishes up yellow. Those who do

This fine Weatherby .300 Mark V rifle has a stock of tigertail maple.

not like light wood can have it darkened with a suigi finish, which is done by scorching the wood with a blow torch. Alvin Linden used to finish stocks like this and they were very handsome, light and dark brown with a reddish cast. The maple stock also can be given some color by putting a little burnt umber pigment in the linseed oil. The more conventional gun enthusiasts may feel that any maple stock is apt to be on the gaudy side.

OTHER WOODS

I have seen stocks made of apple and pear. Both finish up to an odd brown of a sort of a liverish shade, lacking the warmth and glow of good walnut. However, stocks that I have seen from both woods

This stock of Wisconsin maple is finished with linseed oil, turpentine and burnt umber.

are very hard and dense and take checkering well. The supply of these woods is very limited, but they have possibilities as stock material.

The mahogany I have seen is too brittle and open grained for gunstocks, but I have liked the stocks made of rosewood. This wood is a rich reddish brown that is marked with fine dark streaks. The wood is hard and takes checkering well, but where one can secure it I do not know.

Beech is used for stocks to some extent in Europe. It is light in color, and the beech stocks on Sako sporters would seem to show that it is a hard and close-grained wood.

Within the past 10 or 15 years, some stocks made of screw-bean mesquite wood have come out of California. I can attest that this is a very hard, strong and heavy wood, for I cut and burned tons of it for fuel when I was a lad on the Arizona desert. Mesquite is marked with a grain that runs this way and that, and it is rare to find a blank that doesn't have wormholes in it. The wood finishes up a dead coffee-colored brown, which some like, but which I do not care for.

Mesquite, a dense, hard wood, is used in this big-game Weatherby stock.

This Remington Nylon 66 stock is said to be highly resistant to extreme temperatures, abrasion and the roughest treatment.

FINISHES FOR GUNSTOCKS

There are many ways to finish a stock and each has its devotees. One popular method is the classic London oil finish, which can be used if the wood is very hard and close grained. The first step is preparation of the stock by sanding so it is in the best possible condition to take the finish. The sanding should be done with successively finer grades of sandpaper used on a wooden block or a large artgum eraser so that the sandpaper will not dig down into the softer parts of the wood. Between sandings, the stock should be moistened and then dried by quick heat as over the flame of a gas stove to raise the "whiskers". I like to finish up the sanding with No. 400 and then No. 600 grit wet-or-dry sandpaper, which I use wet. The latter very fine grit actually does more polishing than cutting.

Then if the wood is very close-grained, I like to finish it with ordinary boiled linseed oil. I slop on a coat with the hands or a brush, then set the stock away. If, when I inspect it the next day, there are areas where all the oil has been absorbed, I put on more. The idea is to let the pores of the wood fill clear to the surface so that the finish gums.

When this happens, I cut off the finish clear down to the bare wood with No. 400 grit wet-or-dry sandpaper used wet, and finish with No. 600. When the stock is dry the filled pores shine. Then I put a little oil on my hands, rub it into the stock and polish off all that I can with a dry, clean cloth. A few days later when this coat has thoroughly dried, I repeat the process. By this means many very thin coats of oil are built up on the surface, and the finish has a richness and sheen no other can equal.

If the wood is fairly open grained, I first coat the stock with spar varnish and then let the stock alone until the varnish is bone dry. I then cut the varnish off down to the bare wood with No. 400 grit wet-or-dry sandpaper, and finish with No. 600, both used wet. I then put on thin coats of George Brothers "Linspeed," which I first rub on by hand and then polish with a dry rag.

The twin secrets of a fine finish are (1) the preparation and (2) letting the very thin coats of oil dry thoroughly before others are put on. If oil is put over gummy oil it never dries but piles up in a gummy mess. When this happens, all one can do is take out the sandpaper, the artgum eraser, and the water and start all over again by cutting the finish down to the bare wood.

REFINISHING A FACTORY-MADE STOCK

The average gun fancier probably will never put the original finish on a stock, but he may want to refinish one. Then he should remove the original factory finish by slopping on varnish remover and waiting for the finish to become soft. Then it can be scraped off with a dull table knife or even worked off with a rough piece of burlap. When all the finish appears to be off the stock should be washed thoroughly with alcohol. It should then be thoroughly sanded as described above. If the wood is open and porous, the spar varnish filler method should be used. If not, straight oil is correct.

If the gun owner wants to prevent soft, open-pored wood from becoming very dark with successive coats of linseed, he should use a varnish filler. On the other hand, if he wants to darken a light-colored stock, he should thin the linseed oil with turpentine to get better penetration. Both varnish and linseed oil will darken and oxidize with age. A myrtle stock on which I used nothing but thinned linseed started out almost yellow but finished up a beautiful golden brown.

These are simple and easy ways to finish a stock. There are many others but most of them are more tedious and have no advantages. Most factory-made stocks are finished with a sprayed-on lacquer, some with varnish, a few with oil. A commercially produced stock can generally be improved by the gun nut who has the time, which along with care are two very important factors contributing to a good finish. Time costs factories money and they have to make sparing use of it. On the other hand, putting a beautiful finish on a stock is a labor of love for the gun nut. Anyone who wants to go further into the subject should get a copy of Alvin Linden's *The Finishing of Gun Stocks,* published by Thomas G. Samworth of Georgetown, South Carolina.

FITTINGS FOR THE RIFLE STOCK: BUTTPLATES

Various materials have been used for rifle buttplates—plastic, horn, steel, aluminum and rubber. But for rifles of light and medium recoil the best material is steel, checkered so that the butt will not slip at the shoulder. Generally, horn and plastic are too brittle to be satisfactory for the buttplate of a rifle which will get hard use,

Three types of rubber recoil pads: The soft pad can be used to lengthen the stock as well as soften a rifle's kick. The slip-on goes over the stock like a rubber glove and can be removed at any time. The solid pad, made of tough, hard rubber, usually goes on rifles with elephant-gun recoil.

as often the rifle butt is dug into the ground like an alpenstock as an aid to climbing. Aluminum is too soft. High-grade sporting rifle stocks often have trap buttplates and the recesses in the buttstocks covered by the traps can be used to carry a couple of extra cartridges, a hunting license, a pull-through cleaner, and a little bottle of oil—anything the hunter's heart desires. Such buttplates are made by Al Biesen, the Spokane, Washington gunsmith, and are also imported from Germany. Rifles of heavy recoil such as the .338, the .375, and the .458 should always be fitted with rubber recoil pads and then the shoulder will not be bruised.

SLING SWIVELS

Almost any hunting rifle needs sling swivels, as the sling takes the curse off of carrying a rifle long distances, and the sling is a great aid to shooting. Swivels on most factory rifles are of the fixed type, but detachable swivels are far better. Winchester uses them on deluxe rifles like the Super Grade Model 70 and the now obsolete Model 52 sporter. These can be purchased from Winchester. Smaller and neater detachable swivels are made by Paul Jaeger of Pennsylvania, and Cain of California, and most gun stores and custom gunsmiths stock them. These swivels are no better than the larger swivels but they look neater.

On most sporters it is desirable for the front swivel to be attached to the forend just back of the forend tip or about 15 or 16 inches ahead of the trigger. This allows the hunter who is using a tight sling to get his left hand hard against the front swivel for steady holding. With rifles of very heavy recoil such as the .416 Rigby and the .458 Winchester, the front swivel should be attached to the barrel, either with a band or by seating, ahead of the forend, because when such powerful rifles come back fast a swivel conventionally placed would bruise the hand.

HUNTING SLINGS

In Europe the hunting gunsling is used only for carrying the rifle, but in America the sling is usually designed with a loop for the left arm. (For details on shooting with the sling, see Chapter 19.) Generally slings are from ¾ to ⅞ of an inch wide, and are sometimes made in two pieces like the United States Army sling and sometimes in one. I prefer the one-piece type, which I adjust so that the loop feels right and so the length is also right for carrying.

CHECKERING

Rifle stock checkering, which is done by carving parallel grooves in two directions to form diamond-shaped patterns in the wood, should serve two purposes. The first is to keep the shooter's hands from slipping. The second is to decorate the rifle, along with carving on the stock and engraving on the metal parts.

Unfortunately, much checkering fails to serve both of these purposes. Some is so coarse, slipshod and homely that it decorates a stock about as much as a ring in the nose decorates a pretty woman. Other checkering is so fine or has diamonds so flat on top that, despite its decorative qualities, it doesn't keep the hand from slipping.

Generally speaking, the convention of checkering the forends and grips of rifle stocks is a pain in the neck for gun manufacturers. The best as well as much of the worst checkering is done by hand, and hand labor is expensive today. Even a small amount of coarse checkering adds considerably to the cost of a factory-made rifle or shotgun. Factory hand checkering is usually done on a piece-work basis. If, let us say, the factory pays someone $8 or $10 to scratch

Good checkering not only decorates the stock but keeps the shooter's hands from slipping.

up the grip and forend, the charge will be about $20 by the time it reaches the retail level, and $20 on top of the other costs for a big-game rifle that is to sell for around $125, for example, is a lot of money.

Checkering is increasingly done by machines. The grips of Smith & Wesson revolvers, for example, are entirely machine checkered. The forends of Remington repeating shotguns and pump and semi-automatic rifles are circular in shape so they can be machine checkered. Some custom gunsmiths use electric checkering machines which speed up the checkering process, but which by no means eliminate the hand finishing. A machine that can do perfect checkering from start to finish may some day be worked out, but as far as I know, nothing of the sort is even remotely in sight.

In the factories, checkering is always a specialty done by workmen who do nothing else. Even in the larger custom gun shops that employ several men, those who do the checkering are generally specialists. They often do their work outside the shop on their own time and on a piecework basis. Even a few of the crack stock makers farm out their checkering. The majority of the famous stock makers, however, have always done their own checkering—people like Tom Shelhamer of Dowagiac, Michigan, Leonard Mews of Appleton, Wisconsin, Lenard Brownell of Sheridan, Wyoming, Monte Kennedy of Sun Valley, California, and Al Biesen and Bob Johnson, both of Spokane, Washington. The checkering of a custom stock adds to final costs just as it does to a commercial rifle. A good conscientious checkerer will spend from one day on a simple job to four days on an elaborate one. Many stock makers like to quote the cost of the checkering job separately from the cost of the stock itself. The checkering jobs illustrated and quoted in the Weatherby catalog, for example, run as high as $175.

For many years the checkering on a firearm has been a sort of an index of its quality. Back in the days when many excellent double shotguns were turned out in the United States, the amount, fineness and intricacy of the checkering was an indication of the grade of the shotgun. No better checkering has ever been done anywhere than that on some of the good old American doubles made by Parker, L. C. Smith, Lefever, Ithaca and Baker. Top grade Parkers, particularly, had stocks of figured European walnut and intricate checkering patterns of a fineness and perfection to make the lover of fine workmanship drool.

Good checkering requires not only the skillful hand and the discerning eye of the craftsman, but also good wood that will hold fine, sharp diamonds. The most skillful workman in the world can't do a crack job on soft, spongy wood. Even it it were possible to do really good checkering on such wood, it would not last, because the diamonds would dent and wear off.

Some stock makers, particularly the Germans, substitute carving for checkering and others combine carving with checkering. All of this is a matter of personal taste, and if a man wants his rifle stock carved with oak leaves, grape vines, portraits of leaping stags, slavering hounds and Venus at the bath it is all right with me. It is his dough and his stock. For my money, though, the finest decoration that can be had on a good gun stock is plenty of fine, sharp, precise checkering. Nothing else does as good a job of classing up a

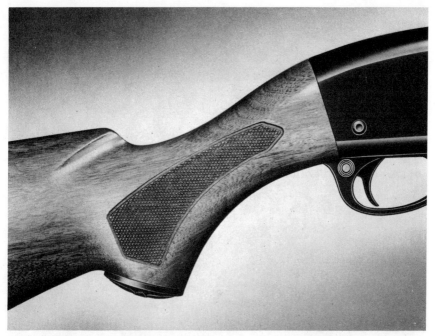

A relatively simple design is this small patch of plain bordered checkering on the grip of a Remington 48 rifle.

The *fleur-de-lis* pattern on the author's Model 70 Winchester extends completely around the grip—a mark of fine checkering.

The forend and pistol-grip on this Model 70 Winchester are both elaborately checkered with a fine *fleur-de-lis* pattern.

An extensive checkering job on a rifle's forend shows how beauty and utility are combined.

stock. Nothing else can quite give it the same appearance of restrained elegance.

Checkering is classified by the number of lines to an inch. The greater the number of lines, the finer the resulting diamonds, and the longer a good job takes to do. Coarse but sharp checkering, with all of the diamonds pointed up sharp with a file, will run from 14 to 16 lines to the inch, but such stuff, even if well done, is no thing of beauty. It keeps the hand from slipping, but it is irritating to anything but a callused palm. Shooting a revolver of heavy recoil that has a grip of coarse, sharp checkering makes the hand feel as if the shooter had just finished giving junior a good tanning.

Checkering that runs about 20 lines to an inch is useful, since it keeps the hand from slipping, and, if well done, it is fairly ornamental. Cleanly cut jobs that go to 22 lines are quite handsome, but on a really fine stock I like checkering that goes 24 to 26 lines to the inch. Checkering finer than 26 lines to the inch begins to lose its usefulness. I have seen some European shotguns checkered 30 lines to the inch, and one intricate checkering pattern I saw that was done by the late Alvin Linden, one of the finest checkering and stock making artists that ever lived, had an interior portion that went about 32 lines to the inch.

Until about 1930 or so, almost all checkering patterns were variations of the diamond, and many still are. Alvin Linden introduced patterns based on the fleur-de-lis, which have become very popular. This pattern is used almost exclusively by Al Biesen, for example. Incidentally, Linden almost never used exactly the same checkering pattern. At one time I had about a half-dozen Linden-stocked rifles, but no two patterns on them were alike.

Checkering patterns are generally laid out on the stocks by means of cardboard or transparent plastic templates. The easiest patterns

Al Biesen, top custom stockmaker, cuts the diagonal lines in the forend of a stock that later will be crossed to form diamonds.

After he shapes the pattern and crosses all the lines, Biesen files diamonds to sharp points. This is the last stage of checkering.

to do are those composed of several separate parts. If the forend checkering, for example, is in two parts, one on each side, the job is much easier for the checkerer than if it is all one piece with long lines that start on one side of the forend and go clear around for several inches to the other side. The longer a checkering line is, the more it can wander and the more cockeyed it can get. Checkering that goes all the way around a pistol grip and meets at top and bottom is tough to execute and really separates the men checkerers from the boy checkerers. On the other hand, a forend pattern composed of, let us say, several small diamonds, each separated from the other, is not as likely to get the less skillful man into trouble. Some of these patterns look very nice, too.

Hand labor costing what it does, gun factories have had to cut down on the amount of hand checkering they put on firearms, even those of the best quality. If you want to see what I mean, take a look at a Winchester Model 21 skeet gun of pre-World War II vintage and then at some recent ones. My wife's Model 21 was purchased in the late nineteen thirties. The price, if I remember correctly, was something less than $130. The checkering is plentiful and of good quality with lines running about 22 to the inch. Postwar Model 21 shotguns that sold for more than three times as much wore course and skimpy checkering.

In fact it is difficult to get a shotgun or rifle anywhere from a large outfit and be sure of having high-class checkering. Some good commercial work is available from England, but also a lot of very sad work. A well-heeled friend of mine owns a .300 and a .375 that were built by a famous London maker. The two of them cost him about $1,000. The checkering on them is lousy. He also has a double rifle which cost him about as much as a new automobile. The checkering is only fair. A pal of mine, who was an officer with the American army in West Germany, had some stocks made there. I regret to say that a good American checkerer could do better with his teeth alone and under water at that. I once bought a pretty, little Spanish 28-gauge double. The engraving is nice, and the well-shaped stock is made from some of the finest wood I have ever seen. But the checkering, it grieves me to say, was only fair. The diamonds were flat, the lines a bit cockeyed and even the borders did not hide the run-overs. I took the gun over to Al Biesen, chained him to his bench, and left him there with a little bread

The unusual French-skip pattern checkers the grip of a Krieghoff scope-mounted three-barrel model.

and water. Now the quality of the checkering is up to that of the wood and the engraving.

What follows is no treatise on how to checker a gun stock, since I have an agreement with the checkerers' guild that if I'll refrain from checkering stocks they won't do any writing. However, here is a brief account of what happens. After laying out his pattern, the stocker cuts two master lines that determine the shape of the diamonds by the angle at which they meet. Then he cuts the other lines by using a spacing tool with two edges so spaced as to give the desired number of lines to the inch. He cuts the next line by following the last one until he has all his diamonds outlined. Then he goes over his pattern several times with a single-edged checkering file to deepen his cuts and point up the diamonds. This is persnickity, painstaking and nerve-wracking work that is very tough on the eyes. Some checkerers wear a 1½X or 2X magnifier. All of them like to work in good strong light, and some even take their work outside into the sunlight when possible.

Most of the best checkering is done without borders. It is not exactly a trade secret that the principal reason for using a border is to hide the runovers that come from hasty and sloppy work. Most crack stock makers do not use borders on their checkering, and they generally finish up their lines with a little V-gouge.

Linden, Biesen and some other talented checkerers have frequently recessed their checkering patterns into the wood about 1/32 of an inch. To me this seems very handsome. So far as I know, this is an American innovation, since I have never seen it employed on a European arm.

There are many checkering patterns, but whatever pattern is used it should bear some relation to the contours of the stock, thus integrating the stock and the pattern into a harmonious whole. The classic patterns based on the diamond don't lend themselves to this as well as patterns with more curves, as in the fleur-de-lis.

Checkering is not permanent. Even that done on the hardest and densest wood will gradually wear down through use and handling. I have seen old trap guns that have been fired many thousands of times on which the checkering had worn down to the bottom of the grooves. An old .270, which Alvin Linden stocked for me over 20 years ago and which I have carried literally thousands of miles on foot and in a saddle scabbard, shows a lot of checkering wear. When this happens, the diamonds can be sharpened up and made as good as new by a half day's work with a checkering file in the hands of a skillful operator.

The life of checkering can be prolonged if the gun owner takes pains not to slop linseed oil into it when he polishes his stock. However, in time the checkering on a gun that is used a great deal will fill up with dirt from sweaty hands, pieces of dead skin, deer blood, and what have you. Then the checkering can be cleaned out with varnish remover and an old tooth brush or a little brass brush such as is used on suede shoes. It is remarkable how much corruption will roll out. But before this operation is undertaken, the checkering pattern should be masked off from the rest of the stock by tape to prevent the varnish remover from acting on the finish of the stock. After it is cleaned out, the checkering should be brushed with linseed oil thinned with turpentine. This will make the pattern, if not too badly worn, look almost as good as new.

Good checkering is cut into a stock after it has been completely finished, and some stockers like to send the completed job to the customer with no oil in the checkering. My own notion is that checkering looks best when lightly oiled. Other gun owners, particularly those who have stocks with light wood like myrtle or maple, like to blacken the checkering pattern with India ink. This seems like a dreary idea to me, but this is a free country.

For the man who'd like to take a crack at checkering himself, there is a whole book on the subject. Written by Monte Kennedy, the California stockmaker, it was published by Thomas G. Samworth of Georgetown, South Carolina. Checkering tools are cheap and easily available, and lads who are good with their hands can build their own checkering cradles—gadgets that are as necessary for checkering as the tools themselves. There is no reason why the man who likes to fool around in his basement while the wife entertains the garden club or the kids watch television cannot checker his own stocks. But whoever undertakes a checkering job should have lots of time and patience.

CHAPTER SEVEN

How Gunpowder and Early Cartridges Developed

THE INVENTION OF GUNPOWDER, AS WE LEARNED IN CHAPTER 1, CAN definitely be traced as far back as the late Middle Ages. For hundreds of years thereafter, the composition of this early powder remained unchanged. All "gunpowder" was black powder, a mechanical mixture of charcoal, sulphur and saltpeter. Now and then I get a request for the exact formula from a lad who wants to cook up a batch in the kitchen some night. Brewing a batch of black powder is a dangerous operation. In the old days the planks on powder-mill walls were nailed on loosely, so that when the joint blew—as it often did—the survivors could simply put the siding back on until the next explosion.

Since all gunpowder was made of the same ingredients, the only way to vary its rate of burning was to vary the grain size. The smallest size (FFFg) was made for handguns, the next largest (FFg) for shotguns and small-bore rifles, and the largest and slowest-burning size (Fg) for big-bore rifles. But in a pinch, I understand, the boys would use any sort of gunpowder in anything. To save a buck, they'd even use blasting powder, which was of approximately the same composition although little if any attention was paid to grain size. Now and then, while they were potting ducks or prairie chickens, one of their old muzzle-loading shotguns would let go, but that was a routine gamble.

Black powder was far from a perfect propellant. For one thing, the smoke sometimes hid the target, and in battle it often became difficult to distinguish friend from foe. Then, too, it took a lot of black powder to give off enough gas to do a job with the bullet. Consequently the old cartridges used on buffaloes and other large game were almost as large as small flashlights. And they kicked like the devil, because not only a heavy bullet but great gobs of soot and clinkers came spewing out of the muzzle to add to recoil. After one shot, a barrel looked like the inside of a smokestack, and to maintain accuracy, it had to be frequently cleaned.

140

Whether confined or unconfined, black powder burns at a constant rate, so to burn a lot of it you had to have a long barrel. Because of this condition, a mistaken idea persists that the longer a shotgun barrel is, the "stronger" it shoots. I am always getting a letter from someone who cherishes an ancient single-barreled shotgun, held together with baling wire and shinglenails. Convinced that a 36-inch barrel will outshoot anything shorter, even to knocking down ducks at 100 yards, he thinks that if he doesn't kill them he must be holding wrong.

There is also a widespread notion that powder is powder, so it must be O.K. to use handgun powder in a shotgun or a rifle. During the war, I remember one chap who somehow had gotten hold of several hundred .45 Colt auto cartridges. He had no .45 pistol, but, being thrifty, he decided to get the bullets out and use the powder for handloads for his old .32/40 rifle. After scaring up some reloading tools, he measured the powder in a .32/40 cartridge, constructed a dip measure to hold exactly that much .45 auto powder, and then loaded up.

On firing, the rifle exploded into several pieces. Since he wore glasses his eyesight was saved, but he spent the next month picking out of his face and neck bits of brass, gunstock, and unburned powder grains.

Another chap got hold of some 37 mm. antiaircraft ammunition and managed to remove the powder. He then ran the stuff through his wife's meat grinder to reduce its grain size. The question was, how much of this hell's brew should he use behind the 180-grain bullet in his .30/40? Luckily, he put that question to me, before experimenting further.

SMOKELESS POWDER

Smokeless powder is now so universally used that not a single commercial cartridge is loaded today in this country with black. Small lots of the stuff are still made, however, partly for export to countries where the natives hunt with crude muzzle-loading gas pipes turned out in Europe, and partly for those Americans who like to put on the coonskin caps and toy with muzzle-loading rifles.

The varieties of smokeless powder are almost endless. They differ in composition, in coating, in grain size, in perforation, and in form. They come in many shapes—rods, disks, balls, square flakes, flat strips, irregular clusters. Some are white, and I've seen others that were pink or orange, but most of the stuff is black. Size varies from grains almost microscopically small to grains as large as ink-wells, for use in big naval and coast-defense guns.

All of these different kinds of smokeless powders are the out-growth of the discoveries of nitroglycerin (an oily liquid formed by the action of nitric and sulphuric acids on glycerin) and of gun-cotton (which is formed by the action of the same acids on any kind of cellulose, including cotton).

DOUBLE-BASE POWDERS

When nitroglycerin and guncotton are mixed, a double-base powder is formed. An early and famous example is Cordite, which is still extensively used in Great Britain and is so called because the powder comes in long, stringy cords that are loaded into the cartridge case before it is necked down.

Double-base powders give relatively high velocity with relatively low pressure, but have the disadvantage of burning very hot. Cordite is really rough on barrels, but the British continue to use it because their double Nitro Express rifles will not take very high pressures. Those big rifles, by the way, are often in beautiful shape after years of use, for the simple reason that they're not fired much. One doesn't go chuck hunting with a rifle with 50 foot pounds of free recoil!

Another famous double-base powder is the excellent American HiVel No. 2, made by the Hercules Powder Company. HiVel No. 2 contains less nitroglycerin than Cordite, and it doesn't burn so hot. It is a bit more erosive than single-base powder, but that's no great drawback, for less of it is needed to attain a given velocity.

SINGLE-BASE POWDERS

Single-base powders are so called because they contain no nitro-glycerin. They are made by dissolving guncotton in a mixture of ether and alcohol. The result is a gluey paste which is squeezed out in strings like macaroni. The diameter of the strings is controlled, of course, by the size of the holes through which the mass is pushed. The length of the strings is controlled by cutting. One powder may be the same as another in composition, coating, and grain size, but different in cut.

The ball powder turned out by Western Cartridge Company is made by an entirely different process, in which balls of powder are formed in water in such a way that their size can be controlled, largely by proper timing, temperature, and speed of agitation.

Modern smokeless powders are specialized. Those used in handguns burn quickly at low pressures. This is because handguns have short barrels, and, since they must be carried and shot in one hand, they cannot be as heavy or strong as rifles. Shotgun powders are made to burn quickly at low pressure and to give relatively little pressure at the muzzle so that the shot pattern will not be blown wide open.

Rifle powders are of many sorts and conditions, and choice is governed by the quantity to be used, pressures wanted, bullet weight and case shape and size. Ideally the powder used in a big-bore, high-velocity rifle should maintain pressure far up the barrel, so that the push behind the bullet will be retained and will cause the bullet to accelerate gradually. Powders which do this are known as progressive or progressive-burning. This effect is achieved by coating the grains so that the powder will burn slowly at first, while the coating is being burned off, and by perforating the grains so they'll burn from the inside out as well as from the outside in— thus increasing the rate of combustion during the latter stage.

POWDERS AND VELOCITY

American powders have led the world, and the only ones that could compare to them were those used by the Germans. New powders have stepped up the velocity of old cartridges. Powder originally used in the .30/30, for example, gave a 160-grain bullet a muzzle velocity of about 1,900 feet per second, whereas modern powders give a 170-grain bullet 2,200 with no higher pressure. Used in the original .30/06 cartridge, the old Pyro DG, a single-base but nonprogressive powder, gave a 150-grain bullet 2,700 feet per second with a mean pressure of around 50,000 pounds per square inch. The much newer government powder, No. 4895, gives the same velocity with about 40,000 pounds, and with other improved powders the same bullet achieves a velocity of more than 3,000 feet per second with pressures comparable to those of the original load.

The success of the .22 Hornet class of cartridges, with velocities in excess of 2,600 feet per second, stems from the development of powders like Hercules No. 2400 and du Pont No. 4227. Similarly, du Pont's great, ultra-progressive No. 4350 made possible such large-capacity big-bore wildcats as the Weatherby and Ackley Magnums.

The shooter who buys factory ammunition need not worry about the safety of the powder used, provided he fires it in a suitable rifle. He should remember, though, that factory cartridges are loaded to velocity and pressure, but not necessarily with any particular kind of powder. Hence two cartridges may have the same bullet weight and muzzle velocity, but if the powder in one burns faster than that in the other, barrel whip won't be the same—and neither will the point of impact.

The more smokeless powders are confined the quicker they burn. If you put a pile of rifle powder on the ground and touch a match to it, it will burn like a celluloid comb or a piece of photographic film. But if you put the same amount of powder in a closed, one-pound powder can and then throw it on a fire, the can will blow wide open. Confinement in a rifle chamber causes powder to burn at an enormously accelerated rate. If powder is over-confined by an oversize or too-heavy bullet, or by an obstruction in the bore, the pressure which shoots up will destroy the weapon.

For potting small game or for mid-range practice with high-velocity rifles, handloaders habitually prepare low-velocity loads with either jacketed or cast lead bullets. A pal of mine, a crack shot and a handloader of many years' experience, is a .257 fan who hunts a great deal in Mexico. He takes along full-power loads for deer and antelope, and low-power loads for quail and rabbits. Last year, in cooking up his low-power load—a 100-grain bullet with a muzzle velocity of around 1,500 feet per second—he absent-mindedly yanked the handle of his powder measure twice instead of once. And when he touched off that particular load, he wrecked his rifle. One charge of No. 2400 was mild and pleasant; two charges raised pressure above the tolerance point.

POWDERS AND PRESSURES

Smokeless powder has doubled shotgun pressures, which in black-powder times ran around 5,000 pounds. Since the average black-powder rifle cartridge gave pressures of about 25,000 pounds and burned at a relatively low temperature, barrels in those days could be made of iron, or iron and soft steel. But the great heat of modern loads will burn out a black-powder barrel in short order, as lads who have rechambered old Winchester .22 single shots to .22 Hornets can testify. This is also true of black-powder rifles used with "low-pressure" smokeless loads. Pressures are safe, but the heat literally melts out the metal at the throat.

POWDERS FOR DIFFERENT PURPOSES

Smokeless powders, as we have seen, are classified by composition —single-base (straight nitrocellulose) or double-base (nitrocellulose mixed with nitroglycerin). They are also classified as to whether or not they are progressive-burning and by their use—in handguns, shotguns or rifles. Use, of course, roughly corresponds to rate of burning.

Shotgun powders such as du Pont Smokeless and Hercules E.C. are "bulk" powders, which can be loaded, volume for volume, like the black powder they replaced. "Dense" shotgun powders are far more concentrated than bulk powders, and cannot be loaded that way. Some dense powders are progressive-burning, some are not. Bulk powder is loaded by the dram (16 drams = 1 oz. avoirdupois), dense powder by the grain (437.5 gr. = 1 oz.), although the finished load will be marked, let us say, "3¾ drams equivalent"—meaning that muzzle velocity will equal that produced by 3¾ drams of bulk powder. Ordinary field and trap loads have bulk and nonprogressive powders; progressive ones are used in wildfowl loads that move heavy charges of shot at high velocity.

Representative pistol powders are Unique, Bullseye (both Hercules, double-base), and du Pont No. 6 (single-base). All burn very fast. Take Bullseye, for example: Only 3½ grains give a 158-grain bullet a muzzle velocity of 920 feet per second in the .38 Special, and only 4.3 grains behind the 230-grain bullet in the .45 automatic give a velocity of 818. These are tiny charges, compared with the great quantity of slow-burning powder loaded in rifle cases—say, 57 grains of No. 4350 behind the 180-grain bullet in the .30/06.

There are many varieties of powders for centerfire rifle cartridges. Small-capacity cases like the .22 Hornet and the .218 Bee call for small-grain, quick-burning powders such as Hercules No.

2400 (double-base) and du Pont No. 4227 (single-base). To show how quick-burning No. 2400 is, it has even been used in powerful handgun loads—the .357 Magnum and the hopped-up .44 Special —and also, I understand, in shotshells. In greatly reduced amounts, it can be used in big-bore rifles for mid-range practice loads.

In HiVel No. 2, Hercules has a grand old double-base powder that burns relatively fast despite its big coarse grains. Its efficiency over a wide range of pressure makes it one of the most versatile of all rifle powders. Using it behind the old 172-grain .30/06 government boattail bullet, for a practice load having a muzzle velocity of about 2,200 feet per second, I got groups that would knock your eye out. It is a good powder for the .257 with the lighter bullets, and it has even been used with the .25/35 and the .35 Remington. With full-power loads in the .30/06, its accuracy is famous. For the .270, though, or for any case with an extreme bottleneck, it burns too fast and is fairly rough on barrels.

No. 4227 has already been discussed; now for du Pont's six other much-used powders (all single-base):

No. 4759, which was developed especially for reduced loads in big-bore rifles, can be used for that purpose in a great variety of calibers.

No. 4198, with its thin, long grains, was designed for small and medium-capacity cases. It can be used for the .25/35 and the .30/30, but it does best in such cases as the 2-R, the K-Hornet, the .218 Bee, and the .219 Zipper.

No. 3031 is another powder with a long, skinny grain. It burns rather quickly and is apparently the best of all powders for the Wasp with its fairly small-capacity case, although it has also been used in everything from the .219 Zipper to the .45/70. I never cared for it for any large-capacity case with a sharp bottleneck—.250/3000, .22/250, .257, .30/06, and .270 included—for, in my hands anyway, it never produced the best accuracy and the slightest overload tended to run pressures way up.

No. 4320 was tailor-made for the .30/06. With it I have gotten the best accuracy with hot, full-power loads with 150- and 180-grain bullets, although with the 180-grain bullet, No. 4064 and No. 4350 have made almost equally good showings. No. 4320 has short, fat grains that measure very accurately in a powder measure, and it is fairly slow-burning. For years my standard .30/06 hunting load has been a good 150-grain bullet with 52 or 53 grains of this powder.

Like No. 3031, it has been used in a whole series of large-capacity cases. It is probably the best choice for .22/250 bullets weighing up to 50 grains and is surely one of the best in the .257, the 7 mm., the 8 mm., and the .30/40. But for the .270 and the .250/3000, I like a powder that burns still a little slower.

No. 4064 is the .270 powder to use with the 100- and 130-grain bullets. With about the same burning rate as No. 4320, and with long, fairly thick grains, it is the usual choice for such cases as the .300 and .375 Magnum and the wildcat .35 Whelen, which have big capacity but are not sharply bottlenecked. A decade ago, I fired about 7,000 rounds of full-power handloads in various .270 rifles in an effort to determine the most accurate loads. I never could find anything better than 49.5 grains of No. 4064 behind the 130-grain and from 49.5 to 54 grains of the same behind the 100-grain bullet. For varmint shooting with the 100-grain bullet I used 49.5 grains of No. 4064, because it was easy on the barrel and flat-shooting, and I killed literally hundreds of jackrabbits and a not inconsiderable number of coyotes.

My two smallest five-shot groups with a .270 at 200 yards measured $1\frac{1}{4}$ and $1\frac{1}{2}$ inches. I was using 49.5 grains of No. 4064 behind a good 130-grain bullet. Smallest group I ever shot with a 100-grain bullet in the .257 was with 38.5 grains of this powder, .046 graphite wad, Winchester No. 120 primer and the prewar .25 caliber Winchester pointed-expanding bullet. While we're at it, I got my smallest-ever .257 group with the old 87-grain soft-point .25/20 bullet with 33 grains of HiVel No. 2. The group measured $\frac{5}{8}$ of an inch. It was an accident I could never duplicate again, with that or any other load.

No. 4350, the newest and slowest-burning powder in this du Pont line-up, has been both useful and misused. To burn efficiently the long, fat grains need great constriction, a very sharp shoulder, a heavy bullet, or they need to be burned in large amounts. A race horse is not versatile; neither is No. 4350. What it's supposed to do, it does superlatively well, but on other jobs it's a very poor performer.

With such cartridges as the .375 Magnum and the .35 Whelen, it isn't particularly good, because the slight shoulder prevents it from working up enough pressure to burn correctly even with heavy bullets. In a short-barreled rifle, No. 4350, used in conjunction with certain case shapes and bullet weights, shoots flame out of the muzzle like a blowtorch and has a muzzle blast that would curdle milk.

But with the right case and a fairly heavy bullet, this powder really goes to town. In the .270, for instance, it gives the long, mean-looking Speer 150-grain spitzer bullet a muzzle velocity that has been chronographed at from 2,925 to 2,960 feet per second, as compared with a standard factory velocity of 2,770 feet per second. In .257 caliber, 44 grains of No. 4350 give the Barnes 125-grain bullet a velocity of around 2,900 feet per second, and 45 grains give the Speer 120-grain bullet not far from 3,000. These two loads put the .257 right on the heels of the .270. With the 220-grain .30/06 bullet, No. 4350 boosts velocity about 150 feet per second more than that obtained with any other powder. The terrific results with the blown-out Weatherby and Mashburn Magnum wildcats would not be possible were it not for this great slow-burning powder.

The government powder No. 4895 was created especially for the M-2 .30/06 load to give the 150-grain bullet a muzzle velocity of around 2,700 feet per second. Efficient, plentiful, and cheap, it has been used in many different calibers. It varies greatly from lot to lot, whereas the commercial canister powders sold to handloaders run surprisingly uniform.

Lot No. 27,277, which I have principally used, burns about like No. 3031, but some lots apparently are slower-burning. It behooves anyone playing with No. 4895 to use No. 3031 loading data, first reducing the recommended charge 10 per cent and then slowly working up.

A seasoned experimenter and accuracy nut wrote me not long ago that he felt that selecting the proper powder for the case shape, capacity, and bullet weight was one of the most important factors in obtaining top accuracy. I agree with him. Now and then the handloader will hit upon a combination that goes together like turkey and cranberry sauce—and then he should stick to it.

Few men who shoot firearms pay any attention to the powder they burn, though it is largely responsible for good patterns in shotguns, and for accuracy and flat trajectory in rifles. There have been many powder improvements—and I think there are more to come. I've heard rumors of an experimental powder, even slower-burning than No. 4350, and of another that will give the 100-grain .257 bullet a muzzle velocity of 5,000 feet per second. If that's true, my lads, we haven't seen anything yet!

CHAPTER EIGHT

The Cartridge

THE WORD "CARTRIDGE" COMES FROM THE FRENCH WORD "CARTOUCHE," which was used as early as the Sixteenth Century in Europe for a roll or case of paper containing powder and shot. The present day cartridge consists of the brass or copper case, the powder charge, the primer and the bullet. As a holdover from black powder days, a modern cartridge is often miscalled a bullet, so that one often hears a customer in a sporting goods store ask for some .22 *bullets* or some .30/06 bullets when he actually should say *cartridges*. During World War II a widely circulated poster said, "A war savings stamp will buy a bullet," but the picture showed a cartridge. Then too, for some odd reason, in the United States a shotgun cartridge is known as a *shell*, although it is correctly called a cartridge in England.

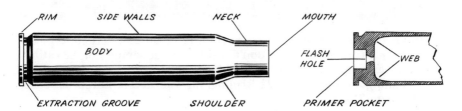

Components of a centerfire cartridge case with cutaway detail (right).

HOW CARTRIDGES ARE CLASSIFIED

Cartridges are classified in many ways. In the trade they are divided into three categories—rimfires, centerfire metallics and shotshells. Rimfires include all cartridges in which the primer is sealed in the rim, not in the center, of the base. The term centerfire metallics takes in all cartridges—rifle and handgun alike—that have primers in the center of the base and have brass cases. Shotshells include all cartridges that contain "shot," or small pellets, instead of a single bullet.

Another way cartridges are classified is by the way in which they are used. For instance, cartridges like the .22 Hornet, the .218 Bee, the .222 Remington, and the .220 Swift that are generally used on small nonedible pests like woodchucks and crows are called *varmint cartridges*. Others like the .30/30, the .32 Special, and the .35 Remington, which are usually used on deer, are loosely called *deer cartridges*. Others that were designed primarily for game larger than deer, although they are often used on deer, are loosely called *big-game cartridges*. A few examples of these are the .30/06, .270, 7 x 57, and .300 Magnum.

Varmint bullets are safest for settled country because bullets go to pieces when they hit the ground and don't ricochet. Some samples of .22 caliber varmint cartridges (left to right): .220 Swift, wildcat .22/.250, .219 Zipper, .222 Remington Magnum, .222 Remington, wildcat 2-R Lovell .22/3000, .22 Hornet, .218 Bee.

Six effective deer cartridges are (left to right) the .25/35, obsolete but still good; the .30 Remington, .30/30, .303 Savage, .32 Special, .35 Remington. The .30/30 has probably killed more deer than any other cartridge.

Some more good deer cartridges (left to right): obsolete .25 Remington rimless, .30/30, .257, and .30/06 with 150 grain Bronze Point for open country.

Strong medicine for moose or grizzly—the .338 Winchester Magnum on left. Other good sheep cartridges: the .270, .30/06 and 7 x 57.

Here's an assortment of power-packing cartridges for the world's biggest game (left to right): the .458 Winchester Magnum, .416 Rigby, .460 Weatherby, .476 Nitro Express, .505 Gibbs, .450/.400, .500 Black Powder Express.

UNTANGLING THE CARTRIDGE NUMBERS

There isn't much rhyme or reason in the naming of cartridges. An early method that is still used to a limited extent is designating the cartridge by the bore diameter of the barrel for which it is chambered, the black powder capacity of the case, plus the weight of the bullet. For instance, the old .45/70 cartridge for the Model 1873 Springfield was called the .45/70/500. Thus the cartridge had a bore diameter of 45 one-hundredths of an inch, carried 70 grains of powder, and a bullet weighing 500 grains. By this method, the .30/06 would be designated the .30/50/180, since a common load for the cartridge is a 180-grain, .30-caliber bullet driven by 50 grains of powder. Cartridges that are still being loaded and named by this method are the old .38/55, the .32/40, the .30/30, and the .30/40.

In the United States, a common practice has been to use the bore diameter of the barrel as the first numeral in the name of a cartridge—sometimes in hundredths of an inch and sometimes in thousandths. The .30 Remington, the .270 Winchester, and the .219 Zipper are named in this way. In recent years, however, many cartridges are named for the diameter of the barrel grooves (see chapter on rifle barrels). Among them are the .308, the .375 Magnum, the new .246 and .338 Winchester Magnums, and the .243 Winchester.

In some cases, the first figure does not correspond to either bore or groove diameter. The .280 Remington, for example, has a bore diameter of .276 and a groove diameter of about .284. All of the .32 handgun cartridges are in reality somewhat oversize .30s. The .38/40 is about a .39, and the .44/40 is about a .42. None of the .38 series cartridges (.38 short and long Colt, .38 Special, etc.) are .38s. They are actually .35s with groove diameters of .357. Only the .357 Magnum, which is an overgrown .38 Special, sails under its true colors—or caliber, rather. The .44 Magnum is about a .42 with a bullet size .431.

The names and figures given after the first numeral of the cartridge designation sometimes give other information about the cartridge besides its powder capacity. The "06" in .30/06 means that the cartridge was adopted in 1906. The "3000" in .250/3000 means that the original velocity of the 87-grain bullet was 3,000 feet per second. Such trade names as Swift, Bee and Zipper are added for sales appeal. The name .257 Roberts says that this is a .25 caliber cartridge designed by a man named Roberts. W.C.F. means Winchester centerfire and W.R.F. means Winchester rimfire. A.C.P. means automatic Colt pistol. The names of the companies that designed the cartridge are generally part of the handle as in .280 Remington, .300 Savage, and .32 Winchester Special. The term "magnum" is applied to a cartridge that is simply a bit faster stepping than most, and does not mean that a cartridge case has a belt as many believe. The .300 Holland & Holland Magnum is a .30 caliber cartridge of high velocity developed by Holland & Holland, the famous British gun and rifle making firm.

SPECIAL CARTRIDGE TERMS

The term "high power" was adopted at the time the first smokeless powder big-game cartridges were coming into being. These gave velocities of around 2,000 feet per second as compared to the 1,500 or so of the black powder cartridges. The term "high-intensity cartridges," which never caught on very well, was used in the United States to designate cartridges with velocities of 2,700 feet per second and upward, in the same way that the British have used the term "magnum." A "wildcat cartridge" is a cartridge that is not in regular factory production but rather has been designed by a gunsmith.

Often if a cartridge case is necked down to another caliber, it bears the name of the new caliber and the old case. The wildcat .25/06 is the .30/06 case necked to .25, just as the .22/.250 is the .250 Savage case necked to .22. The British do it just the other way, so that the .450/400 is not a .45 caliber but instead a .40 caliber on a necked down .45 case. In England the .300 H. & H. Magnum is called the .375/.300 because it is a .30 caliber on a necked down .375 Magnum case. The British term "nitro express" is used to differentiate a cartridge loaded with smokeless powder from one just like it loaded with black powder. For example, the .450 B.P. Express as opposed to the .450 Nitro Express.

On the Continent, most cartridges are named from the bore diameter and the length of the case, both of which are given in millimeters. For instance, the 7 x 57, which we generally call the 7 mm. Mauser; the 8 x 57; the 7 x 64 and the 9.3 x 62. In Continental terminology the .30/06 would be a 7.62 x 63, the .22 Hornet a 5.6 x 35-R, the .25/35 Winchester a 6.5 x 52-R, and the .30/30 a 7.62 x 51-R. "R" stands for *rimmed*. Most rimless cartridges have rimmed counterparts for use in single-shots, double rifles and 3-barrel guns—the 7 x 57-R, the 8 x 57-JR (in this case the J stands for *infantry*, as the 8 x 57 is the German military cartridge). The "S" means that it is the Model 1905 spitzer, which takes a larger bullet than the Model 88 rifle for the 8 x 57J cartridge (.323 as against .318).

As a holdover from the black-powder, muzzle-loading days when any .40 caliber bullet could be used in any .40 caliber rifle, some people today have the notion that smokeless powder cartridges in the same caliber are interchangeable. I get letters from owners of .300 Savages who want to use .300 Magnum cartridges and from owners of .25/35s who think it would be fine to use .257 ammunition. But these are not interchangeable.

EVOLUTION AND TERMINOLOGY

Development of the cartridge goes back to the latter part of the Sixteenth Century. The first crude cartridge of that time was simply a round bullet and the proper amount of powder done up together in a paper packet. Instead of pouring the charge of powder out of a horn into the muzzle and seating the bullet on top, the rifleman opened the packet, poured the powder down the barrel, used the wrapping for wadding, and put the bullet on top. In the next step in the cartridge's development, the paper was nitrated so that it would burn. Still later, linen was used instead of paper. Linen cartridges were used in the early Sharps rifles and proved more durable than paper.

Before the Civil War, Dr. Edward Maynard made a brass case with a small hole in the center of the head to be used in conjunction with his tape primer, discussed in Chapter 2. Another early American brass-case cartridge was the Burnside, developed to be used with the Burnside carbine of Civil War fame. This cartridge tapered from a large, conical-shaped bullet to a smaller diameter at the base, which was perforated by a small flash hole. The cartridge was ignited by external ignition from either a percussion cap or the Maynard tape primer.

Various types of primers have been tried, including the famous pinfire primer which was inside the case and which was ignited by a blow of the pin that projected outside the case. Many old pinfire revolvers are in the hands of collectors in this country, and I am told that pinfire shotgun ammunition is still made in Europe.

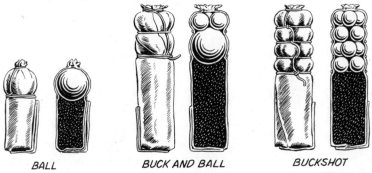

BALL   BUCK AND BALL   BUCKSHOT

The earliest cartridges were simple rolls of paper enclosing one or more round bullets and a powder charge. The hunter tore or bit open the cartridge, poured the powder down the barrel, then rammed the bullet down with the paper wadded on top.

PIN-FIRE   RIMFIRE   BERDAN CENTER-FIRE ANVIL

Early self-exploding cartridges contained the primer in the cartridge itself. The pin-fire had a protruding pin which rested in the detonating compound and fired the powder when struck by the gun's hammer. The early rimfire cartridge held the detonating powder in the rim, as in modern rimfires. The centerfire cartridge had a tiny cup filled with priming mixture in the center of the cartridge base. Berdan's cartridge contained a piece of metal called the "anvil." The firing pin drove the primer against the anvil and exploded the powder.

THE RIMFIRE CARTRIDGE

The first really successful complete cartridge containing a case, bullet, powder, and priming charge in one unit was the rimfire as developed in France by Flobert in his BB caps and further developed by Smith and Wesson as the .22 short in the United States. The priming compound in all rimfires is within the fold of the rim.

The cartridge is fired when the primer is exploded by a blow of the firing pin that crushes the rim. The first "big" rimfire, the .44 Henry for the Henry and Model 1866 Winchester rifles, was simply an enlarged .22 short, and, like the .22, it was made with a copper case.

Rimfire cartridge cases purposely are not very strong, since the firing of the cartridge is dependent upon the rim being crushed by the firing pin. At one time there were many rimfire revolver and rifle cartridges made in the United States, but manufacture of all of them has been discontinued—the .25, .32 and .38 rimfires. One of the most durable was the old .41 Swiss rimfire furnished for the old Swiss Vetterli rifles that were sold by the thousands in this country after they became obsolete in Switzerland. The .41 Swiss rimfire was made here until about 1940.

THE CENTERFIRE CARTRIDGE

With the development of centerfire primers, case heads could be made stronger to stand higher pressures. The Boxer-type primer, as we shall see in the chapter on primers, is used in the United States. It has a single flash hole and an integral anvil. In Great Britain and on the Continent, the Berdan primer, which has twin flash holes and an anvil that is part of the case, is used. Cases using Boxer-type primers are easily decapped by American reloading tools, but this is not true of cases with Berdan primers, which have to be pried out with a little tool resembling an ice pick.

Cartridge cases are made from brass, which is drawn in a series of successive operations. Between operations the brass has to be annealed by heat to soften it since brass is made brittle by working. Proper annealing is an art which requires much skill. If a case is too soft, it clings to the chamber wall and does not eject easily. If it is too hard, it is brittle and may even crack. A properly annealed case expands with pressure to fit the chamber, but as the pressure dies down, it springs back enough so that it can easily be ejected.

Early centerfire cases were rimmed to stop the progress of the cartridge into the chamber, thereby controlling headspace. The development of the Mauser bolt action (see section on bolt actions in Chapter 4) with its staggered box magazine necessitated the rimless case (with the rim the same size as the body diameter of the cartridge). The belted case has a belt just forward of the extractor groove that serves to halt the progress of the cartridge into the cham-

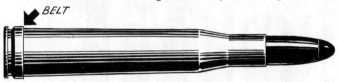

A. Rimmed cartridge is held by forward part of rim.

B. Belted cartridge is held by forward portion of belt.

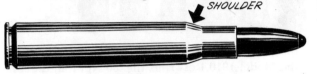

C. Rimless cartridge is held by shoulder.

Points of Headspace: Means Used to Stop Progress of Cartridge into Chamber.

ber and to control headspace. With such a case (the .458 Winchester Magnum, for example), no shoulder at all is necessary. Belted cases, therefore, have some of the virtues of the rimmed case, and, since they work easily through a Mauser-type magazine, they also have the virtues of the rimless case. Some cartridges (the .220 Swift, for example) are semi-rimmed, which means that the rim projects slightly above the extractor groove.

The older centerfire cartridges are nearly all rimmed (the .30/30, .32 Special and .30/40), but of late years all the new cartridges are rimless or belted. All revolver cartridges are rimmed and so are shotshells.

As working pressures of centerfire rifle cartridges have gone up, the brass cases have been made thicker and stronger at the head. The .220 Swift, the .270, .257 and .300 Magnum cases, which are designed for use at pressures of 50,000 pounds per square inch or more, are stronger and heavier at the head, for example, than cases for the .30/30, .25/35 and .30/40, the older cartridges which are made for pressures running from 38,000 to 42,000. Since rifle ac-

Interesting cartridges in the history of cartridge design (left to right): the famous .280 Ross for the Model 1910 Ross rifle, the .30 Newton, the .275 Holland & Holland, the .35 Newton, the .30/40, the 7.62 mm. Russian, the .348 Winchester.

tions are not gas tight the strength of the case is of great importance. It provides the sole protection to the face of the shooter from super-heated gas which may exceed 50,000 pounds pressure. Brass begins to flow at pressures of a bit over 60,000 pounds per square inch. When the primer pocket opens up and the head of the case expands, that means the brass is flowing. If steel cases were adopted, higher working pressures could be used, but steel cases are difficult and expensive to make, and, except for the factor of strength they are not so satisfactory.

Early centerfire cases were straight or had a straight taper. Later, cases were bottle-necked to hold more powder without making the case longer. Various cartridge shoulder angles have been used, and there are many theories about the effect of shoulder angle on powder combustion. Practically speaking, however, a shoulder angle of from 17 degrees, 30 minutes, like the one on the .270 and .30/06, up to one of 30 degrees, found on some wildcats, seems to be all right. A sharper angle is not a good idea, as it tends to run pressures up, and when such a case is reloaded and put back in the rifle, the camming power of the bolt is often not sufficient to size down the cartridge and seat it. The empty cartridge case represents about half the price of a loaded cartridge, and that is why thousands of hand-loaders save their fired centerfire cases, put in new primers, powder, bullets, and fire them again. A good case can be used from 10 to 30 times, depending on the metal, headspace, and other factors.

CHAPTER NINE

The Primer: Sparkplug for the Cartridge

IN CHAPTER 8, WE SAW THAT THE PRIMER MIXTURE OF RIMFIRE cartridges is distributed around the folded rim of the case, and that it is crushed and set off by the blow of the firing pin. Centerfire primers (or "caps" as the English call them) are not made as an integral part of the cartridge in that they can be put in (primed) and removed (decapped). There are two basic types of centerfire primers: the Boxer, which is most generally used in the United States, and the Berdan, which is used in England and on the Continent.

The Boxer primer is composed of a cup, an anvil, a disk, and a primer pellet which does the business. The flame which ignites the primer comes out of a central flash hole at the base of the pocket in the case in which the primer is located. The American cases and primers with the centrally located flash hole are the joy of the hand-loader because removing the primer (decapping) is easy. The European (Berdan) type primer has *two* flash holes and an anvil which is part of the case.

American-type primers as well as American cases have been

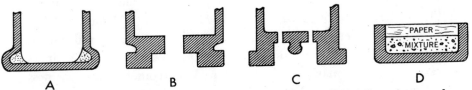

A　　　　　　B　　　　　　　C　　　　　　　D

The priming compound in a rimfire cartridge (A) is distributed around the rim and set off when the firing pin crushes the rim. The case for the American Boxer-type primer (B) has no anvil; a centrally located flash hole makes removal of the primer (decapping) easy. The head of the case for the European Berdan-type primer (C) has two flash holes, and the anvil is part of the case. The Berdan primer (D) has no anvil.

made in Europe, but I understand that they have been manufactured there for the American market.

Except for their ease of decapping, there is, apparently, no particular advantage of one type of primer over the other. American government arsenals have experimented with Berdan-type primers by using them in match ammunition, but no better accuracy was noted than with the Boxer-type, so the Berdan-type was not used.

PRIMERS IN THE UNITED STATES

American primers for centerfire rifle and handgun cartridges are made in two sizes and four kinds—the large rifle and the large pistol, which are .210 of an inch in diameter, and the small rifle and the small pistol, which are .175. The large rifle-size primer is used with the .30/06, .270, .375 and similar cartridges, the large pistol primer for the .45 automatic and .44 Special, among others. The small rifle primers are employed with the .22 Hornet, .222 Remington, and .218 Bee, to name a few, while the small pistol primers are used with the .38 Special, .32 Smith & Wesson, and similar cartridges. Rifle and pistol primers, although they may be the same size, differ in the hardness and thickness of their brass cups. It is not necessary for a revolver's primer cups to be as hard or as thick as a rifle's, since its firing pin packs less punch than that of a rifle. Also revolver pressures run lower than do those of a rifle. Rifle and pistol primers differ, too, in the kind and amount of the primer mixture.

American primers are made at the government arsenals, as well as by independent companies such as Remington, Winchester, and Western. In Canada, primers are manufactured by Canadian Industries of Montreal, and sold under the brand name of Dominion. The Federal Cartridge Company of Minneapolis, Minnesota, perfected an excellent series of primers, which were used in millions of rounds of .30/06 ammunition during World War II. These primers were put on the market after the war. A newcomer in the business is Cascade Cartridge, Inc. of Lewiston, Idaho, a firm started by Dick Speer, brother of Vernon Speer, the bullet maker. Cascade got into the business by making various primers for the government, and now offers the handloader a complete line of primers for shotshells as well as rifle and pistol cartridges.

Here is a primer chart giving the numbers of the different types of primers turned out by the various concerns:

	C.C.I.	WIN.	REM.	FED.	WEST.
Large rifle	200	120	9½	210	8½
Small rifle	400	116	6½	200	6½
Large pistol	300	111	2½	150	7
Small pistol	500	108	1½	100	1½
Shotshell caps	209B	none	none	none	none
	57B	none	none	none	none
Shotshell primers	109	209	none	none	209
	157	none	57	none	none

There are a great many back-fence opinions about primers floating around among handloaders, some of them possibly justified and some not. One article of faith is that Winchester No. 120 and Western No. 8½ primers are somewhat "hotter" than Remington No. 9½ and Federal No. 210 primers and hence are more suitable for large capacity cases like the .375 and .300 Weatherby Magnums. The feeling also prevails that for potency the Cascade primer lies somewhere in between.

One area of general controversy about primers is whether or not the condition of the fired primer tells the loader anything about his pressures. My own notion is that if the fired primer shows the smooth, round indentation of the firing pin and hasn't been flattened out flush with the bolt face the pressures are relatively mild. If, on the other hand, the primer is extruded up around the firing pin, and if the primer has been flattened up against the bolt face, and if the primer pocket has been filled flush, the pressures are high. Something about pressures can be learned by comparing primers of hand loads with those of factory loads. If, on the other hand, a load used in a good case shows a primer leak, it is an indication that pressure ran up around 70,000 pounds per square inch and if the primer is "blown," pressure ran around 80,000 pounds.

If a case shows a primer leak like this one, pressure is up around 70,000 pounds per square inch.

QUALITIES OF THE IDEAL PRIMER

The good primer should above all be reliable, and should perform well even after having been stored for a long time. Even under extremes of atmospheric temperature, it should start the powder burning every time. The fact that this is important is borne out by one laboratory test of primers, which consists of firing them at 100 degrees below zero. The good primer should not contain non-combustible, erosive material such as glass, and when ignited, it should not produce excessive gas. To state it another way, it should not blow the bullet out of the case but rather should ignite the powder and let the powder propel the bullet. Ideally, the primer should ignite the powder by throwing pieces of burning material into the powder

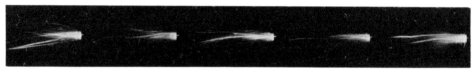

This series of photos shows flashes caused by a fired shot-shell primer.

These are flashes produced by an old Frankfort Arsenal No. 70 corrosive primer.

Flashes from a modern centerfire rifle primer that has a reputation for mildness.

Flashes made by another brand of centerfire rifle primer considered to be "hot."

charge—a process that can be compared to your tossing burning brands into a woodpile. All primers, however, work two ways in that they start the powder off both by hot gas and by burning material. Of course, another requisite of a good primer is that it should not cause rust in the barrel or deterioration of the case.

Although every batch of primers is rigorously tested, every now and then the shooter comes up with a misfire (primer doesn't go off) or hangfire (primer is delayed). How come? One reason is that the priming powder mix may not be absolutely uniform throughout. Batches are made in the form of wet paste in lots of from 10 to 20 pounds, and it is difficult to keep the ingredients uniform throughout. One primer, of course, uses only a tiny amount of the batch—about 1/14,000 of a pound. The handloader himself can cause a misfire. If he should inadvertently load a large pistol primer into a rifle cartridge, the pistol primer would not be hot enough to set the rifle powder on fire. Oil in the primer can also cause a misfire.

MISFIRES AND HANGFIRES

Sometimes the source of a misfire is a mechanical defect in the primer. Primers have been assembled without anvils, with only half an anvil or with an inverted anvil. A primer may not go off unless its crystals of lead styphnate are crushed rapidly and violently. One can be crushed slowly in a vise, for example, without going off. If a firing pin is weak, the blow against the primer may not be violent enough to start things happening. Then, too, a firing pin that is activated by a spring made sluggish because extreme cold has congealed the oil will have the same effect. Excessive headspace in a rifle will cushion the blow of the firing pin, causing misfires.

A hangfire is a condition that results when only a small part of the powder is ignited and has to increase its burning to get hot enough to set the rest of the charge off. Generally the time involved in a hangfire is around 1/10 of a second, but I distinctly remember one hangfire that was so slow that just as I was reaching for the bolt to eject the cartridge, Old Betsy let go. The darndest tale of a hangfire I have ever heard came to me from Dick Speer, president of Cascade Cartridge. He tells me that once a cartridge from a batch being tested in a government arsenal hung fire. It was removed from the rifle and set on a shelf. Fifteen minutes later the thing went off! Interesting and complicated little devices, these primers—as important to the functioning of cartridges as spark plugs are to gasoline motors. The finest powder in the world behind a perfect bullet is worthless, unless you have something to set it on fire and do it right.

BARREL DAMAGE CAUSED BY EARLY PRIMERS

A little over a generation ago anyone who bought a small caliber rifle, such as a .22 rimfire or a .25/20 centerfire, knew that the barrel wouldn't last long. Do what he would, the barrel would soon begin to roughen up and pit and presently lose its accuracy.

Shooters were resigned to the phenomenon. They could no more do anything about it than they could change the weather. Even centerfire rifles of large caliber gave trouble, and it was routine for the much-used old .30/30s and .30/40s one saw around ranches to have barrels so pitted that they'd scratch threads off a flannel patch run through them. Shotguns, although less liable to pitting, were by no means immune, and a great many of the fine old doubles made in the first quarter of this century have pitted barrels.

In the early nineteen hundreds cleaning the barrel of a high-powered rifle was really a production. I went to a high school where military training and target shooting with 1903 Springfields were part of the curriculum. After we shot the rifles, we cleaned them by running through the bores an endless number of patches soaked with a solution of baking soda. We then dried the bores thoroughly with dry patches and oiled them. The purpose of the alkaline baking soda was to neutralize the "acid fouling," which got the blame for all this pitting. In those days, the British cleaned their double rifles by pouring boiling water through the barrels, and most hep users of bolt-action rifles put the muzzles in a can of very hot water, then pumped the water through the bores by means of cleaning patches on rods. All manner of interesting and fragrant light oils called "nitro solvents" were sold in those days. They slowed up but did not stop the pitting. Cleaning with water was such a pain in the neck that many shooters tried to get by with solvents. Their rifles always wound up with rusted bores.

This pitting of barrels was first noticed after the switch from black to smokeless powder, and, as we have seen, the smokeless powder was blamed. It turned out, however, that the villain was the primer composition, and the particular ingredient that caused the trouble was an explosive chemical called potassium chlorate. When it is burned, it turns to potassium chloride, a chemical not unlike sodium chloride or common table salt and with table salt's reaction to water. When a gun was fired the bore became lined with potassium chloride, which mixed with moisture in the atmosphere and caused rust. The man who cleaned his gun with nitro solvents simply slowed up the process of rusting, which under conditions of high humidity would actually form right under an oil film.

The reasons that pitting, for which the smokeless powder was blamed, was not noticed with black powder weapons were that black powder was used in greater amounts and diluted the priming compound more. Also it was common practice to clean out the black powder fouling with water, which dissolved the rust-causing salt. With smokeless powder, the greater concentration of primer salts used, the greater the tendency to pit—and that is why the little cartridges like the .22 rimfire and the .25/20 were more destructive to barrels than the .30/06 or the 12-gauge shotgun.

The corrosive effect of primer compositions was discovered in the nineteen twenties by Dr. Wilbert Huff of the U.S. Bureau of Mines, who published his findings in a work called "Corrosion Under Oil Films."

By modern standards, some of the ingredients used in early smokeless powder primers were pretty villainous. For instance, one arsenal-produced primer, which was used for .30/40 Krag ammunition back in the eighteen nineties, had the following composition, according to E. C. Crossman's "Book of the Springfield":

> Fulminate of mercury 60%
> Potassium chlorate 22%
> Ground glass 16%
> Mealed powder 2%

Outside of the facts that the fulminate of mercury caused the cases to become so brittle they could not safely be reloaded, that the potassium chlorate caused rust and that the ground glass promoted barrel wear and, in turn, metal fouling, this was a pretty good primer. At least, it produced a hot flame and ignited the powder.

In the nineteen twenties, the standard American primer mixture was one that became known as the Frankford Arsenal No. 70, although it was actually worked out by Winchester. Its composition was as follows:

Potassium chlorate 53%
Antimony sulphide 17%
Lead sulpho-cyanide 25%
Trinitrotoluol (TNT) 5%

This formula produced an excellent primer that was the most favored one of handloaders during the nineteen twenties and well into the thirties. It was uniform, efficient and stable. It was the primer used for most American small arms ammunition during World War II, the exception being the M-1 carbine cartridge which was loaded with a non-corrosive primer. Anyone who uses wartime ammunition should not forget this. In those days, priming compounds for .22 rimfires contained the rust-causing potassium chlorate, as well as ground glass.

NON-CORROSIVE PRIMERS

In 1927, Remington hit the market with its Kleanbore priming, a mixture that prevented rusting and "pitting." Since potassium chlorate was not used in this mixture, there was no salt deposit left in the gun barrel to attract moisture. If greased or waxed bullets were used in a .22 rimfire rifle, for instance, it could be left almost indefinitely without cleaning—a pretty hard morsel for the old hot-water school of riflemen to swallow. Shortly thereafter, the other loading companies began to produce non-corrosive primers. All of them contained varying amounts of the same ingredients: fulminate of mercury; barium nitrate; lead sulpho-cyanide; gum, which acted as a binder; and from between 20 to 28 per cent of ground glass.

Although these new primers did not cause rust, they produced other headaches for the handloader. The mercury ruined the cartridge cases, in that it made them brittle, and the ground glass caused excessive barrel wear. Most handloaders stuck to the old Frankford Arsenal No. 70 primer and to hot-water cleaning. The problem now was to find a priming compound that did not cause rust, but also one that would not leave the cases brittle, and yet would still be sufficiently hot, stable and sensitive.

I am told by Dr. Victor Jasaitis, chief explosives chemist for the Cascade cartridge firm, that most non-corrosive and non-mercuric primers, both American and European, are based on an explosive chemical known as lead styphnate. Modern priming mixtures also contain another explosive called tetracene, which makes the primer more sensitive and the burning more uniform. Every primer, he says, must have an explosive, a sensitizer and a fuel, such as antimony sulphide or calcium silicide, plus an oxidizer, such as barium nitrate or potassium nitrate.

Lead styphnate, which is the key chemical of today's priming mixtures, was first used for this purpose during World War I, in Germany, where it was developed as a substitute for fulminate of mercury. Since it is not too difficult for one primer manufacturer to make a spectographic analysis of a primer turned out by another concern, primer composition is not particularly a secret. Although all primers contain these or similar chemicals in varying amounts, I am told that primer composition changes slightly from time to time. For example, a Winchester No. 120 primer or a Remington No. 9½ primer bought today would not necessarily have quite the same composition as a primer of the same make bought five years ago.

Until the advent of the non-corrosive primer, powder companies used to put out dope sheets for handloaders giving quantities of powder charges and their pressures and velocities in various calibers with various weights of bullets. They could do this and get by with it, because at that time the use of the Frankford Arsenal No. 70 primer mixture was just about universal. But as the various non-corrosive primers came into use, the companies discovered that primer A would cause a much different amount of pressure than primer B, so much so that a load that might be entirely safe with one primer would give excessive pressure with another. So the powder companies clammed up, and now the handloader who wants some guidance must get his dope from one of the various manuals that are published by the manufacturers of handloading equipment.

In a recent experiment, Remington made pressure-and-velocity tests in which all the cartridge components were identical except the primer mixtures. Here are the results:

EFFECT OF PRIMING MIXTURES ON BALLISTICS

(Same Bullets, Cases, Powder and Powder Charge)

SAMPLE	PRIMING MIXTURE	AVERAGE VELOCITY	AVERAGE PRESSURE
1	A	2352 fps	53,700 pounds sq. in.
2	B	2316 fps	46,550 " " "
3	C	2311 fps	42,220 " " "
4	D	2298 fps	42,870 " " "
5	E	2229 fps	32,120 " " "

Using the same basic components and simply changing the priming mixture caused a difference of over 120 feet per second in velocity and 21,000 pounds per square inch in pressure. The Remington technicians commented:

"It is only after the most exhaustive, comprehensive, elaborate tests that a priming mixture is admitted to use in production. Even then, powder types and powder charges must be selected specifically for use with the particular primer type being used. The ammunition manufacturer would no more think of using primers of unknown type than he would of using unknown powders. The primer has long since ceased to resemble a match. It is the heart of the cartridge, but a heart whose complexity has increased enormously with time and which must be treated with the respect it deserves."

The primer is, of course, only one of the components of the cartridge that affects pressure, but it behooves the handloader to view a change of primer with caution. Pressure can be hiked up by a tight chamber and bore, as well as by a bullet with a harder than normal jacket or core or more bearing surface, and also by a cartridge case with less than normal powder space. An extra-hot primer added to all these conditions will result in fireworks!

CHAPTER TEN

Bullets for Hunting Game

HUNTERS EXPECT THE LITTLE COMBINATIONS OF LEAD, GILDING METAL or steel that zip out the ends of their rifle barrels to perform a multitude of tasks. They expect them to lay a mighty bull elk low with one well placed hit. They expect them to shoot into a one-inch circle at 100 yards. They expect them to withstand velocities of more than 3,000 feet per second, retain most of their weight and travel the length of a well-nourished bull moose. If a bullet fails to expand properly when shot through the rib cage of a fragile animal like a small deer, the hunter hollers. But if the same bullet blows up when it strikes the heavy shoulder bone of an Alaskan brown bear, he complains even louder.

In addition, hunters expect bullets not to leave metal fouling. They expect the point not to batter in the magazine. And if a limb or two happens to be between the muzzle of a rifle and the game, they expect the bullet to sail right through to the target.

In the past 20 years, American hunters have grown more and more bullet conscious. Handloaders pay premium prices for special bullets, shoot them at targets to see how they group and dig them out of the carcasses of animals to see how they have performed.

This preoccupation with bullets has a lot of good horse sense behind it. A snappy-looking stock with fancy checkering and voluptuous inlays has yet to knock over an animal, and a wicked-looking cartridge case has yet to scare anything to death.

FIVE BASIC CLASSIFICATIONS

If hunters realized that there are really five different classes of game bullets, they would be happier and the designers of bullets would be less harassed. These classifications are: 1. Light, fast bullets for shooting varmints, from ground squirrels to coyotes. These

169

These .30 caliber bullets are made in different shapes, kinds of points and weights (110-220 grain), depending on whether they are going to be used on varmints, heavy game or anything in between.

bullets are designed to go to pieces in small, soft bodies and to disintegrate when they strike the ground, to be safe in settled communities. 2. Bullets that expand rapidly and reliably on small and medium sized "big game," such as antelope, whitetail deer and sheep. 3. All-around bullets that give reliable penetration on heavier animals such as elk, moose and African antelope, and yet expand easily enough to be usable on lighter animals. 4. Bullets for heavy, soft-skinned, dangerous game such as Alaskan brown bear, large grizzlies, lion and tiger. 5. Heavy non-expanding "solids" with power to drive into an elephant's brain or break both shoulders of a buffalo or rhino.

The designer of bullets has many tricks up his sleeve when he sets out to design a bullet for a particular purpose. He can make his bullet light or heavy. He can use a soft core of pure lead or a harder one of alloyed lead. He can make his gilding metal jacket thick or thin, leave it heavy at the base or thin at the point. He can expose a great deal of lead at the nose or simply leave a pin point. If he decides to expand the bullet by means of a hollow point, he can make the opening large or small, the cavity shallow or deep. He can cover the soft lead of the nose with a thin coating of soft metal to keep it from battering in the magazine and to slow expansion, or he can use some mechanical device like a bronze wedge to split the jacket and open up the bullet. He can even retain the ballistic efficiency of the bullet by putting a sharp cap of thin metal over a hollow point so that when the point strikes game it will collapse and air trapped in the cavity will expand the bullet. If he wants the bullet to retain a great part of its weight, he can use one of several devices to stop the mushrooming from one-third to one-half way down the jacket.

PROBLEMS OF BULLET DESIGNING

But with all his wiles, the bullet designer is neither going to be 100 per cent successful, nor is he going to make everyone happy. As we have seen, bullets strike different parts of the animal at different impact velocities and often they do very different things. I once shot a buck mule deer in the ribs at about 125 yards with a 150-grain .30/06 bullet of famous make. It blew up on the surface and made an entrance hole about three or four inches in diameter. The buck's lungs looked as if they had been struck by a charge of shot.

Another time, with a bullet of the same make and weight, I shot a big ram at around 40 yards as he ran from me. The bullet went into the rump, came out of the brisket and didn't expand at all. You explain that one! A good many years had elapsed between those two kills, and I cannot remember another instance when the same bullets did not perform satisfactorily.

The sharp or spitzer point of the bullet helps it get to the target faster and with a flatter trajectory, but once it strikes a game animal it is of no help. Sometimes the sharp point cannot be used at all. In a rifle with a tubular magazine, where the point of the bullet rests on the primer of the cartridge ahead of it, there is danger that the recoil will cause the sharp point of the bullet to fire the primer. For this reason bullets for such lever-action cartridges as the .30/30 and the .348 are always made with round or flat points. A spitzer bullet is deflected badly by brush and in "solid" form it tends to dive and dart when it strikes game, instead of following a straight line. As a consequence, bullets for heavy game like elephants and rhinos are made with round or flattened noses.

The problem of manufacturing game bullets which will make all hunters happy and perform reasonably well on different kinds of game at various ranges is a difficult one. A bullet may strike the soft, water-filled tissue of an animal's abdomen or the relatively thin and brittle rib cage. It may be called upon to drive through heavy rump muscles and watery abdomen up into the lungs, if the hunter takes a rear-end shot, or it may strike the heavy shoulder bones. At 100 yards, a factory-made .270 bullet weighing 130 grains is traveling at 2,850 feet per second, but by the time it reaches 300 yards the velocity has fallen off to 2,320. Obviously, the bullet

that performs ideally at 100 yards may not do too well at 300—
or vice versa. Also, it follows that the bullet that will go to pieces
in the body of a woodchuck or jackrabbit will generally not perform well on moose, or even on deer.

A $100 scope is useful only in that it makes easier the rifleman's
task of putting the bullet where it will do the most good. But the
finest rifle ever made won't shoot well with bum bullets, and even
a well-placed shot is futile unless the bullet is suitable for the job.

IMPROVEMENT OF BULLETS

Widespread interest in bullets, the increase in big-game hunting,
varmint shooting, bench rest experimenting, and the enormous
popularity of handloading since World War II, have all con-
tributed to the design and manufacture of excellent bullets. I don't
think there is any doubt that the most accurate jacketed bullets
and some of the most effective game bullets ever manufactured are
now being turned out in the United States. In good rifles with
suitable powder charges, famous bullets like the 55-grain .224
Sierra soft point, 52-grain Speer .224 open point and 100-grain
.25 caliber Hornady spire point give accuracy that would have
been incredible 20 years ago.

The simplest type of bullet is the plain one of lead slightly alloyed, usually with tin, such as we see used in .22 rimfire and
revolver cartridges. To prevent them from leaving a deposit of
lead in the barrel, such bullets are lubricated with a covering of
grease or wax or are plated with gilding metal as is the case with
.22 bullets. Revolver bullets have grease in their grooves. If bullets
are designed to expand on flesh, they are made with large cavities
in the nose, and, if they are to be driven at much over 1,300
foot seconds, brass cups called gas checks are fitted to the base, so
that the hot powder gases will not fuse the lead bases. Such gas
checks are used in bullets for the new .44 Magnum cartridge, and
on cast bullets used for reduced loads in rifles by handloaders.

Bullets used for target shooting and for varmint and big-game
hunting that are driven at a velocity of 2,000 foot seconds or more
have the lead enclosed in a metal jacket or "envelope," as the British call it. In making the first hunting bullets for rifles with a velocity
in the 2,000 feet per second class—the .30/30, .30/40 and .303, for
example—the British simply left plenty of the lead core exposed

Hunting Bullets

These cross sections of bullets show their unique features of construction (left to right): 1. Remington 180 grain Bronze point .30 caliber; 2. R.W.S. (German) 173 grain boattail bullet for 7 x 64, one of the most elaborate bullets ever constructed. Lead in the base portion is very hard, that forward of the belt is soft. Hollow copper cap gives spitzer shape. 3. 220 grain Remington Core-Lokt .30 caliber; 4. 130 grain Winchester-Western Silvertip in .270 caliber; 5. 175 grain full metal case 7mm round nose; 6. .30 caliber 150 grain Speer spitzer soft point.

at the nose. When the bullet struck game, the soft exposed lead expanded or "mushroomed." If the bullets were intended for military use, or for deep penetration on thick-skinned game, the jacket was simply reversed so that the lead showed at the base of the bullet and the metal jacket covered the nose. The British call these bullets "solids," but in this country we refer to them as either "full metal cased" or "full metal jacketed." Most high-velocity bullets are made with sharp points, because about 50 years ago it was discovered that bullets so shaped retain their velocity better and consequently shoot flatter. Some bullets are made with boat tails or "taper heels" because such bullets are easier to stabilize for long range accuracy. They are also slightly more efficient ballistically, retaining their velocity considerably better at extremely long ranges after velocity has dropped below the speed of sound.

There have been other incidents of this kind of thing. In Africa, I shot a lion and some other game with the 270-grain, soft-point bullet for the .375 Magnum. In every case the recovered bullets looked just like the catalog pictures of perfectly mushroomed bullets. Then in India, I took a crack at a running tiger at about 150 yards. That same bullet killed the big cat with a lung shot, but not before he ran about 125 yards. When the bullet was recovered, it had shed its jacket and otherwise misbehaved. Again, how come?

In order to expand rapidly and go to pieces when they strike, the ground varmint bullets are generally made with relatively thin jackets, soft lead cores and hollow or soft points. Although such bullets have killed deer-sized animals, they are not reliable on such game because they tend to go to pieces too quickly. Their use is not sporting. On the other hand, the use of the heavier, more durable bullets on varmints is unsafe, as the tough bullets tend to ricochet off a flat surface.

With lighter big-game animals, the biggest problem is quick expansion instead of deep penetration. The right medicine is the bullet that expands rapidly and even disintegrates. I have gotten more instantaneous kills on Arizona whitetail deer, which dress out on the average from 90 to 110 pounds, with the Barnes pre-World War II 120-grain .270 bullet than with any other. It had a thin jacket and a soft lead core. When driven at about 3,250 at the muzzle, it was a bomb. I found that a hit anywhere near the heart would almost always rupture the heart with fragments. I never had one of those bullets pass through even a light deer or antelope with a chest shot, and I cannot remember anything but one-shot, instantaneous kills. In fact, I have even seen that bullet stay in the body of a coyote, and I cannot remember hitting a single coyote without killing it instantly.

What Barnes did with a thin jacket and soft lead, the Western Cartridge Company did with a large hollow point in their 139-grain bullet for the 7 mm., 130 for the .270, and 150 for the .30/06. When I used them, the results were wicked. The most successful bullets I have seen on light big game in rifles of the .30/30 class are the old-fashioned soft points with soft cores, thin jackets and plenty of lead exposed. About 20 years ago, I tried loading some 170-grain soft-point .30/30 bullets to about 2,550 to 2,600 in the .30/06; when I scored lung shots with these bullets, the deer dropped as though the earth had been jerked out from under them. Plenty of lead exposed at the nose and thin jackets are good bets for bullets to be used on deer in rifles of the .30/30 class.

A line-up of the flat-shooting, low-recoil .24 and .25 calibers (left to right):
.244 H & H Magnum on necked-down .375 case; .240 belted rimless; .244
Remington seated out for long throat in O'Connor's custom rifle; .275
Roberts; .244 Remington factory load; .243 Winchester; .250/3000.

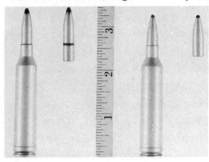

A long-range cartridge for North American big game: the .264 Winchester belted Magnum in two types of bullets—a .140-grain "Power Point"
(left) and the 100-grain soft point.

100-grain Soft Point

500 yards   400 yards   300 yards   200 yards   100 yards   Unfired

140-grain "Power Point"

This is what happens to the two different bullets in the Winchester .264
belted Magnum cartridge upon impact at various ranges.

CONTROLLED EXPANDING BULLETS

Right now the bullets that are getting the biggest play and the most publicity are those designed to control expansion and not blow up. Their points are constructed so as to give quick and reliable expansion, but their bases are supposed to remain intact. The Germans were pioneers in the manufacture of bullets of this sort. A famous one is the DWM strong jacket bullet. It has a boattail with a very heavy base that extends about one-third of the way up the bullet. The forward portion of the bullet has a thin jacket for reliable expansion, and, in various forms, it was available before the last war with a hollow cap of thin metal over an open point, an exposed hollow point and a plain lead nose. Another famous German bullet is the RWS H jacket. The "envelope" is deeply folded approximately halfway up the base in order to stop expansion and keep the rear portion intact. A famous 177-grain 7 mm. bullet made by RWS for the 7 x 64 is the most elaborate bullet I have ever seen. It has *two* types of lead in the core: hard alloyed lead back of the fold in the jacket, soft lead in front. It has a boattail, two-diameter construction and a sharp metal cap over a hollow point. This superb bullet is largely responsible for the excellent record the 7 x 64 has made. British bullet construction has been far more conservative and less imaginative than either German or the American. They have managed to produce a few bullets with metal caps over hollow points, but for the most part their bullets are either soft points or solids.

In the early days, bullet performance was often quite erratic. The old .256 Newton and the .280 Ross gave velocities in excess of 3,000 foot seconds, and, particularly on heavy game, the performance of some of the bullets left much to be desired. Just before World War I, a famous Englishman was killed by a lion that he had hit solidly with the 145-grain bullet of the .280 Ross. This accident was attributed to high velocity, whereas the blame should have been laid to poor bullet construction.

When Winchester brought out the .270 in 1925, they had done a lot of research in order to determine what kind of bullet construction would best stand up under the very high velocity of 3,160 feet per second. The result was one of the finest high-speed bullets ever turned out. One of the original .270 fans who has

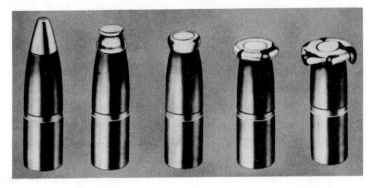

Here's what happens to a 180 grain Silvertip bullet in progressive stages of expansion.

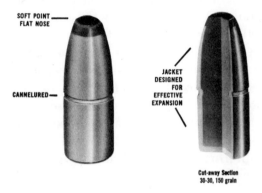

SOFT POINT
FLAT NOSE

CANNELURED

JACKET
DESIGNED
FOR
EFFECTIVE
EXPANSION

Cut-away Section
30-30, 150 grain

A 150 grain .30/30 Core-Lokt bullet designed for reliable expansion at moderate velocity.

used the caliber for 35 years, I have shot game with it as light as 45-pound javelinas and as heavy as 1,400-pound moose. I can testify to its effectiveness. The bullet had a very heavy base and a sharp point of soft lead, protected against battering in the magazine by a thin jacket of tinned copper. Much the same plan is used in the Winchester-Western Silvertip. Its point is soft lead protected by a thin jacket that extends almost halfway back toward the base. Because they are made for most big-game calibers, Silvertip bullets differ in shape of point, thickness of jacket and hardness of core.

Another excellent controlled expanding bullet is the Remington Core-Lokt, which is also made in all calibers. Over the years, it has won an excellent reputation for reliable expansion and deep penetration. Like the Silvertip, the Core-Lokt bullets are made with various types of points, jacket thickness and hardness of core. Those with round noses have the jacket serrated at the point to facilitate expansion; the sharp point jobs like the 130-grain .270 bullet and the 180-grain .30 caliber are made with splits around the points to enable them to open up. Expansion is controlled by a belt of heavy metal about halfway down the jacket.

For hunting dangerous, soft-skinned game, I know of no better bullet for the .30/06 and the .300 Magnum rifles than the excellent and rugged 220-grain Core-Lokt. I shot three grizzlies with the 180-grain pointed soft-point Core-Lokt when, still in the experimental stage, it was called the "Nib Nose." This bullet plows through a big bear's chest cavity from side to side like a hot knife through butter. Because of their good shape and strong construction, the 180-grain .30 caliber and the 130-grain .270 caliber Core-Lokts are excellent for such high-velocity super magnums as the .300 Weatherby and the .270 Weatherby Magnum.

Most of the small bullet makers—Speer, Sierra, Hornady, etc.— use points of unprotected lead and control expansion by jacket thickness toward the base. Speer, however, also makes hollowpoint bullets in .22 and 6 mm. calibers, and an excellent line of open-point bullets is turned out by the Western Tool & Copper Works of Oakland, California. Their 160-grain heavy jacketed job for the 7 mm. magnums and their 150-grain spitzer open point for the .270 have long been famous among the aficionados of these calibers.

The ultimate among the controlled expanding bullets is the Nosler. Unlike other bullets, which have jackets drawn from cups, the Nosler is turned from gilding metal rod, and a solid belt of metal is left between the front and rear portion of the bullet. Reports from the field show that this bullet *always* holds together, even in light forms like the 130-grain .270.

The controlled expanding, all-around bullets will do for any sort of big game, while their heavier forms, like the 220-grain .30 calibers and the 300-grain .375 Magnum bullets, are suitable for even the world's most dangerous soft-skinned animals—Alaskan brown bear, polar bear, lion and tiger. Most controlled expanding bullets, however, do not give as high a percentage of instant kills on smaller, lighter and softer animals like deer, sheep and antelope as do the softer bullets that expand rapidly when they strike and tend to blow up. A friend of mine some years ago switched from a .30/30 to a .30/06 and tried to shoot deer with a well-known 220-

grain controlled expanding bullet. He became convinced that the .30/06 does not kill as well as the .30/30. I'll agree with him if the .30/30 is fed thin jacketed bullets with soft lead cores and the .30/06 is used with rugged, slow expanding 220-grain fodder.

The heavy, full-metal cased or solid bullet has very limited usefulness and should be shot only at the heaviest, most massive animals. But it is a lifesaver when the hunter has to drive the bullet through several inches of bone of an elephant's head to the brain, or to break the heavy shoulders of a rhino or Cape buffalo. Such bullets should not deform at all, and they are best jacketed in steel, have parallel sides, and round or flattened noses. Bullets so designed maintain a straight course to the vital area the hunter wants to strike. They will break massive bones and will penetrate tough hide and muscle. When they strike bone even the heaviest bullets will deform if made with gilding metal or cupronickel jackets. The answer, as we have seen, is steel, which is used in the world's two finest bullets for heavy game—the 410-grain solid for the British .416 Rigby and the 500-grain solid for the .458 Winchester Magnum. If I ever shoot the big stuff again, it will be with these bullets. I once tackled a big Cape buffalo with the 480-grain soft

A Brevex Magnum Mauser action for African big game, chambered for the .416 Rigby (bottom), which is compared here with a .30/06.

point in a .450. The bullet went to pieces on the buff's spine. It put him down for the count, and I thought I had killed him, when he suddenly jumped up and came for us. If I had used a good solid, that bull would never have got to his feet.

There are plenty of excellent bullets on the market, bullets that have been designed after a lot of thought and experimenting. Nevertheless, it is up to the hunter to select the right bullet for the job in hand. It is futile to expect a heavy-jacketed controlled expanding bullet to perform satisfactorily on a 90-pound white-tail as it is to suppose that the 87-grain .250/3000 Savage bullet will give clean kills on moose.

CHAPTER ELEVEN

A .22 for the Beginner

THE FIRST WEAPON OF THE BEGINNING RIFLEMAN SHOULD ALWAYS be a .22 rimfire of some sort. That little cartridge is the one that teaches people to shoot.

Rifles chambered for the rimfire are comparatively inexpensive, and the tiny cartridge has a triple advantage over any other the novice might choose: it's cheap, produces no noticeable recoil, and the report isn't loud enough to disturb the shooter. Thus the beginner with a .22 can calmly concentrate on those things that will make him a good shot with any rifle—proper sight picture, smooth trigger squeeze, and the knack of "calling his shots," which is a matter of co-ordinating sighting and trigger squeeze so that you know where you're aiming at the instant the rifle fires.

Because of their wide use for target and small-game shooting, the .22 rimfire cartridges are highly developed and very accurate. They come in three lengths—Short, Long and Long Rifle. You can get either high or low-velocity loads, solid or hollow-point bullets, and the bullets may be coated with wax, grease or non-fouling copper.

I suggest .22 Shorts for indoor shooting, and they're O.K. for other short-range plinking. The Long Rifles are best for serious target shooting or small-game hunting, and those with hollow-point bullets, which expand on impact, make quicker kills. Any store that stocks ammunition at all is pretty sure to have a good supply of .22 cartridges.

Rifles for the fine .22 cartridges run all the way from inexpensive single-shot models to very expensive and super-accurate match rifles. Prices vary accordingly.

Probably the safest .22 rifle for a youngster (and a good one for any beginner) is a single-shot with bolt action. Since the learner has to insert a cartridge for each shot, he'll always know when the rifle is loaded. Single-shots also teach the novice to make each shot count. The one-shot bolt action is the least expensive of the .22 rifles. Some sell for about $15.

There are also many bolt-action repeaters in .22 caliber, models that chamber a new cartridge from a clip or tubular magazine each time you work the bolt. These repeaters cost more, but quick loading is a convenience most shooters will want sooner or later.

Other types of repeating .22 are the lever action, the "pump" or slide action, and the "automatic," which is more properly called a self-loader or semiautomatic. (A machine gun is a truly automatic weapon; the semiautomatic rifles merely reload themselves after each shot.)

The choice of action in a .22 repeater is mainly a matter of personal preference; there are fine rifles made in each style. Left-handed shooters may find the pump or lever actions more convenient, because standard bolt-action repeaters have the bolt on the right side, whereas slide and lever action are as convenient for one hand as the other. The person who plans to buy a bolt-action big-game rifle some day would be smart to get a bolt-action .22, which would give him practice in the same loading motions he'd need for his big-game rifle.

As for sighting equipment, most .22s leave the factory with iron sights, usually a V-notch rear sight and a bead front sight. Those will do for casual plinking, but they lack the fine adjustment devices needed for precise shooting. A much better rear sight is the adjustable aperture or peep type (you sight through a small hole in a metal disk to line up a front bead with the target). And a good .22 is rifle enough to rate a scope, the best sight of all.

Many of the more expensive .22 rifles sold today are either grooved by the factory to take a scope mount or tapped and drilled for the mounting of a peep sight on the receiver. A quality .22 with scope will use up a $100 bill, but it's a top-notch combination for targets and small game.

THE .22 VARMINT RIFLE

When the .22-trained shooter begins to crave a more powerful weapon, the logical step upward is to acquire one of the long-range varmint rifles. Lots of men have successfully made the jump from .22s to big-game calibers, of course, but middle-ground practice with a rifle firing centerfire varmint cartridges is the finest kind of training for big-game hunting.

Most varmint hunters begin by trying to nail crow, woodchucks or prairie dogs with their .22 rimfires, but they soon learn that it's difficult to hit such small marks at much over 100 yards, even with a top-grade rifle, scope and high-speed ammunition.

What defeats the .22 rimfire is bullet drop. A .22 rimfire bullet will fall a foot or more before it gets to a target 100 yards away. To hit the point of aim at 100 yards, a .22 has to be sighted in so the barrel points slightly upward, sending the bullet toward the target in a long arc. The fast centerfire varmint and big-game cartridges have the virtue of shooting much "flatter" than the comparatively slow .22 rimfires.

The cartridge that really started modern varmint shooting off with a bang was the .22 Hornet, a small centerfire cartridge introduced about 1932. With a scope-sighted rifle chambering the .22 Hornet, a varmint hunter could bowl over woodchucks regularly at around 200 yards. Within the memory of men who still have a few of their teeth, some of their hair and who can navigate without the aid of a wheelchair and a seeing-eye dog, the little .22 Hornet cartridge was about the hottest thing that ever came along. At the time, the public prints were full of its praise. Winchester made the Model 54 for it, Savage the Models 23-D and 19. The famous old de luxe gunsmithing firm of Griffin & Howe adapted many Springfield .22s to it, and various gunsmiths made a myriad of single-shots for the hot little cartridge. Some very fancy and expensive bolt-action rifles in .22 Hornet were imported from Europe.

Now the little Hornet if not a dead duck is at least a dying one. Winchester has dropped it from their Model 70 line, and the only factory-made .22 Hornet I can find listed is the Savage Model 340, which is also made in .222 Remington.

The good little .218 Bee cartridge likewise has the death rattle in its throat. Based on a necked-down .25/20 cartridge, it was originally adapted to the Winchester Model 1892 short lever action, which was designed for such cartridges as the .25/20, .32/20, .38/40 and .44/40. The feeling at Winchester apparently was that there was in this country a hard core of lever-action fans who were fretting for a lever-action varmint rifle. The .218 Bee actually used a bullet of the same size as the Hornet—the .223—but it was named for its bore diameter, rather than its groove diameter. And it had a little more soup than the Hornet—2,860 for the 46-grain bullet instead of 2,650. The Bee was likewise a more satisfactory cartridge to reload as the cases were a bit stronger and had more shoulder. Winchester made the .218 in the Model 43 bolt action, which is now discontinued, as well as in the lever action, and Marlin made a few over-and-under combination guns for it in conjunction with 20-gauge shotgun barrels. Some foreign bolt actions were imported for it, and some single-shots were cooked up. Like the Hornet, the .218 Bee was variously blown out to increase powder capacity, but it was never anywhere as popular as the Hornet, and it is now a pretty dead issue.

The .219 Zipper is another furtive union between a lever-action rifle and a varmint cartridge—in this case the ancient and honorable action used for the Model 94 series of Winchesters with a cartridge based on a necked-down .25/35 case. The .219 delivered a 56-grain bullet at 3,050. The rifle for which it was designed had a long, whippy barrel and a two-piece stock, and as a consequence the combination didn't group too well and fell on its face. In addition the Model 94 action ejects the fired cases straight up, and if a scope is used it has to be offset. If ever there was a curse on a cartridge from the start, it was on the .219.

But in reality, the .219 is a pretty good cartridge, and a lot of fine shooting has been done with it in suitable rifles. My old shooting pal, the late Dr. E. G. Braddock of Lewiston, Idaho, loved fine single-shot rifles and had at least a dozen standard and improved Zippers on Winchester High Side, Sharps-Borchardt and Farquharson actions. I have seen him do some astounding chuck, crow and magpie shooting with them. Because of the limitations of the lever action, the .219 Zipper cartridge as loaded by the factories gave relatively low pressures—around 38,000 pounds per square inch, I understand—and because of the tubular magazine it was loaded with relatively blunt bullets. As a consequence, the bullets lost their velocity rapidly and drifted badly in the wind. Doc used to heat his .219s up to about 45,000 pounds per square inch and push the 50-grain sharp-pointed bullets along at 3,500 or thereabouts. He put even more fire under the improved or blown out, sharp-shouldered versions and got about 3,600. With single-shot rifles, he considered the Zipper the most satisfactory cartridge for serious varmint shooting.

The .220 Swift isn't selling too well today, I am told, even though it has always been a terrific cartridge that at one time had rifle nuts rolling on the floor and crying out in ecstasy. Its velocity of 4,140 with the 48-grain bullet is still the highest of any factory cartridge, and the average over-the-counter Model 70 in .220 Swift is still one of the most accurate factory rifles (if not on the average the most accurate) that one can buy. When I sight a Swift in with factory ammunition to put the bullet 1½ inches high at 100 yards, the bullet hits on the button at 250 and drops only 3 inches low at 300. That is what is known in the trade as a flat trajectory.

I have always thought that the serious varmint hunter who took pride in reaching out 300 to 350 yards for chucks, sitting jack-rabbits, coyotes and other varmints really got his money's worth with the Model 70 Winchester in the .220 Swift. I have had one for some years, and I have shot perhaps a dozen Swifts at bench rests. I have yet to see one that with a little tuning up wouldn't shoot very well, and I have probably killed, with fewer misses, more chucks with the Swift than I have with any other .22 varmint rifle.

About the liveliest .22 caliber varmint cartridge today is the .222 Remington. With its very respectable velocity of 3,200 with a 50-grain bullet, it is the cartridge that did much to put the skids under the milder .22 Hornet and .218 Bee. The .222 is wonderfully accurate and today it holds a good share of the bench rest records. For one thing it is a fine cartridge. For another the report and recoil are exceedingly mild and those who shoot it do not get the flinches. Some very fine rifles have been made for it—the Model 722 Remington, the Marlin Varmint King and the Sako. The other reasons that the .222 shoots well are that the factory ammunition has always been good and that about the time it came out a lot of small bullet-making outfits like Speer, Hornady and Sierra had really learned what it took to make an accurate .22 jacketed bullet. The .222 Magnum, a lengthened version of the regular .222, gives a 55-grain bullet 3,300 feet per second, but it is yet too early to tell how popular it is going to be.

Most of the pioneering .22 wildcats that we developed in the nineteen thirties are pretty well dead. The .22/3000 and its blown out version, the 2-R Lovell, based on the obsolete .25/20 Winchester single-shot case, are no longer heard of, although a few old-timers still swear by them. The .218 Donalson Wasp, which a

The light, accurate Finnish-made Sako rifle, chambered for the lively .222 Remington, is a top combination for varmints. The report and recoil of the .222 are exceedingly mild.

decade ago was the queen of the bench rest shoots, seems to have lost out to the .222. Most younger shooters have never even heard of such cartridges as the .22 Gebby, the .22/4000 Sedgley, the .228 Ackley Magnum and the .22 Neidner Magnum.

In looking over a list of reloading supplies, I see that the handloader can still buy dies for the .218 Mashburn Bee, the .219 Improved Zipper, the .219 Wasp, the K-Hornet and the .220 Arrow, as well as others, but none of them are too popular.

One of the best and most widely used of the wildcats was the .22/250, which is simply the .250/3000 Savage case necked down to .22 caliber and given a 28 degree shoulder. The cartridge is a fine one, probably the most popular wildcat ever designed. The cases are easy to make, and the cartridge is easy to load. Accuracy is

A scope-sighted .22/250 is an accurate varmint weapon. Before the Wasp and the .222 came along, the wildcat .22/250 was cornering most of the accuracy records.

excellent. Before the Wasp and the .222 came along, the .22/250 was the most popular bench rest cartridge. Today, though, even this venerable .22 wildcat is slipping—or so I am told by various custom gunsmiths.

Why have many of the .22s declined in popularity? The .218 Bee and the .219 Zipper fell by the wayside because the rifles in which they were introduced simply were not varmint rifles and would not produce gilt-edged accuracy. If something like the Model 70 Winchester had been available in those calibers, the story might have been different. Marlin has made Model 336 rifles in .219 Zipper with short stiff barrels and side ejection, so that the scope can be mounted low and centrally over the bore. I have never shot one, but I hear they give very respectable accuracy.

But the advent of the .222 with the line of fine rifles to shoot it is what really did more to kill off the Hornet, the Bee and the Zipper than anything else. The report and the recoil of the .222 are not noticeably more severe than that of the Hornet and Bee, and the cartridge is not much more expensive to reload. But its velocity is higher, and its accuracy better.

Another factor is that many of the .22s have suffered a very bad and generally unwarranted press. Many times I have read that the .22 Hornet changed its point of impact. Now if the shooter sticks with the same ammunition, this condition is attributable almost entirely to faulty bedding of the barrel in the stock, not to a malfunctioning cartridge. My own experience with my .22 Hornet (a Model 54 Winchester) was that I had less trouble with it in that respect than with almost any rifle I have ever had.

The great and useful .220 Swift likewise had a very bad press. It was hard to reload, the lads wrote. It was also tough on barrels; and the necks of the cases stretched and thickened. Some of this was true. Pressures of around 54,000 pounds per square inch and velocities in the neighborhood of 4,000 feet per second are not easy on barrels, and some of the early Swifts shot out in a hurry. But great progress has been made in bullet manufacture in the last decade, just as there have been great strides made in barrel steels. In the old days of soft ordnance and nickel steel barrels, some Swifts showed a lot of throat erosion after 1,000 rounds, but, with the hard and tough stainless steel barrel used in the present Model 70 .220 Swift, the erosion problem seems to have been pretty well licked. I have a Swift which I have shot about 2,000 rounds and as far as I can tell it as yet shows no throat erosion whatsoever.

One reason is that I have never tried to get the last few feet of velocity out of it. The load I settled on long ago is 37 grains of No. 4064 with the 55-grain bullet. Velocity is 3,600 feet per second in a 26-inch barrel. Accuracy and barrel life are excellent, trajectory flat. Pressure is probably under 50,000 per square inch and case life uncomplicated. But I wouldn't say that the Swift is the last word in varmint cartridges. If it were being designed today, it would probably have less body taper and a sharper shoulder. Nevertheless, it is a fine cartridge and one that is miles ahead of most wildcats. If there is any difference between the accuracy of a Swift and a .22/250 with equally good barrels, bullets and bedding, I have never been able to find it.

When the Swift first came out it was highly touted as a big-game cartridge, and certainly big game, including elk and moose, was killed with it. However, the results were erratic, and today it is seldom used even on game like deer. I saw some deer killed with it and also some deer that got away, even though well hit, and I lost faith in it for the larger stuff. It is, however, a fine coyote cartridge out to 300 yards, which is as far as I have ever shot one with it. In the Austrian Alps, I am told, it has made a great reputation as a sudden killer on such small-game animals as roe deer and chamois. In Africa it should be just right for small antelope such as the Tompson and Dorcas gazelle, as well as for the numerous small African varmints.

Because of their light bullets driven at high velocity, the .22 varmint cartridges are the safest of all to use in settled country, as the bullets go to pieces when they strike the ground and do not ricochet. The smaller ones are less noisy than the larger calibers and less apt to make the land-owner restless. With varmint bullets the big calibers are safe, too, but people who know little about rifles associate noise with danger. I have known users of .22 Hornets to be permitted to shoot in a certain area, whereas those using .270s and .30/06s were thrown out.

Serious criticism of all the .22 caliber varmint bullets, possibly a reason for their decline in popularity, is their relatively poor sectional density, high rate of velocity loss and wind sensitiveness. A 50-grain .224 bullet has a sectional density of only .142; a 55-grain bullet .157. On the other hand an 85-grain .243 bullet has a sectional density of .205, and a 100-grain bullet of the same caliber a sectional density of .238. Going into still larger calibers, the 87-grain .257 bullet has a sectional density of .188, and the 100-grain .216. The 100-grain bullet of the .270 works out at .186, or better than a 63-grain .224 bullet, and the 130-grain works out at .241. This poor sectional density of the .225 shows up in velocity loss. In traveling 300 yards, for example, the 48-grain .220 Swift bullet, which leaves the muzzle at 4,110 winds up with 2,440, or not much more than the 80-grain .243 Winchester bullet, which starts out at 3,500 and gets to 300 yards with 2,110 remaining. The greater the rate of velocity loss, the more sensitive the bullet is to wind. Any user of a hot-shot .22 has to do some pretty fancy wind doping. Another legitimate criticism of the hot .22s is the deflection of the light bullets. I have had them turned aside by thin grass when shooting at prairie dogs and rock chucks and I have seen them dissolve into blue smoke when they struck a twig in front of a magpie or a crow.

But in spite of their obvious faults the .22s still have their place. For modest ground squirrel shooting at not much over 150—175 yards the little .22 Hornet with its light report, non-existent recoil and sufficiently flat trajectory is just about right. In addition, it is probably the world's best wild turkey cartridge. For more ambitious shooting at longer ranges up to perhaps 225—250 yards, the marvelous little .222 Remington is ideal, and for really serious long range shooting up to 300—350 yards the Swift will still give just about any other cartridge a run for its money—at least on a quiet day.

The .24s and .25s

WAY BACK IN 1914 CAPTAIN EDWARD C. CROSSMAN, THE GIFTED GUN writer and ballistician who wound up his career as a staff member of *Outdoor Life* magazine, defined the ideal all-around rifle for Americans. At the time, the .250/3000 Savage cartridge was brand new. He considered it close to ideal. The perfect cartridge for the average American rifleman, he wrote, would be one that would drive a 100-grain .25 caliber bullet at 3,000 feet per second. He added that it should use a case with a head size like that of the .30/06 and the 7 and 8 mm. Mauser cartridges, so that Springfield and Model 98 Mauser actions could be used. That, of course, was long before the day of the Models 54 and 70 Winchester and the Models 30, 720, 721 and 722 Remington.

The reasons behind Crossman's choice are pretty obvious. Experience had proved that a 100-grain bullet which leaves the muzzle at a velocity of 3,000 feet per second has all the killing power needed for animals of the antelope-deer-mountain sheep class. The trajectory is flat enough so that hits to 300 yards or somewhat over are not difficult. Crossman also recognized the equally important fact that such a cartridge gives a good deal lighter recoil than one like the .30/06.

Some people are born with a lot of built-in recoil tolerance. If a rifle jolts them sharply back, snaps their neck vertebrae and loosens the fillings in their teeth, they don't seem to mind. Most of us, however, can develop such a tolerance to the degree that the kick of a .30/06 doesn't bother us—or bother us consciously anyway. It's even possible to get used to the very potent recoil of something like the .375 Magnum. But most hunters simply do not have the time, the inclination or the opportunity to shoot enough to develop their tolerance to that extent. Probably four out of five .30/06 owners are flustered by recoil to the extent that they flinch, although they wouldn't be caught dead admitting it. These are the lads who would do better shooting and cleaner killing with a rifle of less recoil—Cap Crossman's .25 caliber, for example.

This hypothetical cartridge, with its 100-grain bullet at 3,000 feet per second, would also be an exceedingly fine varmint cartridge, ideal for coyotes and wolves, and excellent, with a lighter bullet (the 87-grain, let us say) at higher velocity, on the smaller varmints. This lighter, faster bullet would also be safer to use in settled areas because it would have less tendency to ricochet.

Four American factory cartridges follow Crossman's specifications fairly closely, and all of them are exceedingly useful all-around cartridges—the old .250/3000, the middle-aged .257 Roberts, the youthful .243 Winchester and .244 Remington. All of them, even the .24s, aren't too far from .25 caliber. Any of them can be loaded to give a 100-grain bullet in the neighborhood of 3,000 at the muzzle. All produce light recoil and give fine accuracy in good rifles when fed good bullets. One of the most pleasant things about them is that special light, short-barreled rifles that shoot accurately and kick lightly can be built for them. Anyone wanting a very light yet reasonably potent rifle for horseback or mountain use wouldn't be making a bad choice in either the .24 or the .25.

DECLINE OF THE .25s

Right now both the .250/3000 and the .257 are in a decline, something which saddens me no end. Let's see how it came about. The .250/3000 was designed especially for the Model 99 Savage rifle by Charles Newton, the famous father of the before-their-time line of Newton cartridges. The cartridge had to be a short one so it would work through the short Model 99 action. Newton cut off the .30/06 case, necked it down to .25 caliber and, for those days, gave it a very sharp shoulder—26½ degrees. He originally designed the little cartridge for a 100-grain bullet at about 2,800 feet per second, but the Savage people, aware that high velocity sold rifles, just as it does now, wanted 3,000. They got it by going to an 87-grain bullet.

About 20 years ago, the original Newton load of a 100-grain bullet at about 2,800 feet per second was introduced, and most .250/3000 users believe that the 100-grain bullet is superior in killing power for deer-size animals. Be that as it may, the original load with the 87-grain bullet was and is a very sudden killer. In his original review of the cartridge, Cap Crossman told how he and another chap had taken a pilot model of the .250 on a northern California deer hunt along with the famous .280 Ross with a 145-grain bullet at 3,050. He wrote that the .250 killed deer just like the .280—instantly. The only difference between the two cartridges was that the .280 blew up more deer. The type of deer he was talking about were Pacific Coast blacktails. Although I have never shot one of these blacktails, I hear they'll average about 100 pounds field dressed.

In those days, the Model 99 Savage action was the strongest existing lever action, and those early .250/3000 cartridges were loaded to give pressures, I understand, slightly above 50,000 pounds per square inch—or to the same pressure level as contemporary .30/06 ammunition. While we are on the subject, Model 99 actions that are made now are even stronger, because of the progress in alloying and heat-treating steel. The Model 99 takes the .243 and the .348 Winchester cartridges without a whimper, and I understand that they are loaded to a mean pressure of about 52,000 per square inch.

The .250/3000 acquired a fine reputation for accuracy and for quick kills on any size game up to deer. The late Jean Jacquot, who was a Yukon outfitter, used one for years and killed many moose and grizzly with it. I wouldn't call the .250 a moose and grizzly rifle by any stretch of the imagination, but I can only report what Jean told me.

The little cartridge was a great success. Winchester chambered the Model 54 and Model 70 rifles for it, and Germany's great Mauser Werke made rifles for it on the short or "K" action. These dainty little jobs, which weighed a little over 6 pounds, were imported into this country before World War II by Stoeger.

But, alas, further ballistic development of the .250 stopped. Although its powders improved, .250 ballistics did not. The velocity with the 87- and 100-grain bullets remained the same as when they were introduced, but pressures have dropped to the neighborhood of 40,000 pounds per square inch.

The .250 has always had a fine reputation for accuracy, even in the lightest of the Model 99s. It was an early favorite of varmint hunters who wanted more bullet weight than could be obtained with a .22 caliber. I have seen several Model 99 rifles that will stay in 1½ inches at 100 yards, and with carefully selected bullets, Fabrique Nationale Mausers and Model 70 Winchesters will shoot into an inch or less.

The handloader can step up the .250 ballistics very easily. A charge of 42 grains of No. 4350 pushes the 87-grain bullet along at 3,145, while 41 grains of the same powder give a 100-grain bullet 3,010. According to pressure tests reported in the *American Rifleman* some years ago, 40.5 grains of No. 4350 with a 100-grain bullet turned up a mean pressure of less than 45,000 per square inch.

For many years .250/3000 rifles were made with barrels having a 1—14 twist, sufficient to stabilize the 87- and 100-grain bullets but no good on anything heavier. About 95 per cent of all the talk about bullets being "overstabilized" is myth. For every barrel that didn't produce because the twist was too fast, I have seen a couple of dozen that had very limited usefulness because the twist was too slow. Some years ago I got an F.N. Mauser barreled action, had it stocked and put a 10X Unertl scope on it. It shot like a dream with a mild load of the 87-grain Speer bullet and 35 grains of No. 4895. I assumed that the twist was 1—14, but lo and behold it turned out to be a 1—10. When the Savage people queried me about the advisability of changing the .250 barrels to a sharper twist, I told them of my experience. Exhaustive experiments at the factory bore me out, and the boys quietly changed over to 1—10 twists at least a year ago.

I, for one, would like to see the fine little .250/3000 cartridge modernized. With its short fat body and sharp shoulder, it is a beautifully designed case. It is easy to load, and it has always had a reputation for accuracy. With a 1—10 twist barrel, there is no reason heavier bullets cannot be used. Volume I of the *Speer Handloaders Manual* lists a load of 44 grains of No. 4831 with the 120-grain bullet for 2,843. I do not know what the pressure is, but I do know that the load was worked up in a Savage Model 99.

STORY OF THE .257

If you think the .250/3000 is an orphan, just listen to the pathetic fate that has overtaken the superb little .257. Before I'm through, I'll have you weeping tears as big as watermelon seeds.

The .257 began life as the .25 Roberts. It was designed by the late Ned Roberts, a long-time gun nut and woodchuck hunter, who wanted a cartridge that would be less subject to wind drift than the hot .22s. It was simply the old 7 x 57 case necked to .25. The Remingtons got interested in it, took it over, changed it a bit and brought it out as the .257 Remington-Roberts. The Model 30 Remington bolt action was chambered for it. Then Winchester countered with the same cartridge called the .257 Winchester Roberts, and they furnished the Model 54 bolt-action rifle for it.

Now the plot thickens. Get out your handkerchiefs and settle back for a good cry.

In their early experiments, Remington found that the best accuracy was obtained with the ballistically inefficient round-nosed bullets, so round-nosed bullets they were. The resulting cartridge has an overall length of 2.75 inches. The magazines of all factory rifles are made short for this stubby factory-made cartridge. While the Winchester Model 70 was still being made in .257, the magazine block could be removed and a .30/06 follower substituted by cutting back the bolt stop. This enables the handloader to load sharp-pointed bullets out to touch the lands of the rifling. Otherwise, the spitzer bullet must be seated deep and take a long jump before it hits the lands—which doesn't improve accuracy. The Remington Model 722 has a short action, and the only way it can be civilized in .257 is to mill out the forward portion of the magazine well back of the lower locking lug recess. This, of course, will weaken the action, but the boys get by with it.

Back in 1934, when the .257 was introduced, du Pont No. 3031 powder was the very latest thing. It was used in the .257, and, although the cartridge was originally advertised to give a 100-grain bullet 3,000 feet per second, pressures were found to be a bit high and the velocity was dropped to 2,900. Powders have improved, and the .257 is seen at its best with the slower burning ones like No. 4350 and No. 4831, but the poor old .257 is still saddled with No. 3031 velocities and the short overall length. As was the case with the .250/3000, velocity remained the same, but as powder improved, pressures went down. One commercial load with the 117-grain bullet gave a mean pressure of only 42,700 pounds per square inch—an exceedingly baffling circumstance when one realizes that no bum .257 factory rifles were ever made.

In rifles with long enough magazines and if it is properly throated, the .257 can be handloaded to be quite a cartridge, one even better than Cap Crossman's ideal American cartridge. It is no trick to get

3,300 in the .257 with 47 grains of No. 4350 and the 87-grain bullet, or 3,100 with the 100-grain bullet and 45 grains of the same powder. For years I used 44 grains of No. 4350 with the 125-grain Barnes bullet for a velocity of 2,900 or thereabouts in a custom-made job on a Springfield action. It was a very wicked, flat-shooting and deadly load on coyotes and deer. Most of my own experience with the .257 has been on varmints, and for this use I long ago stand- ardized on 39 grains of No. 4064 with any good 100-grain bullet. Velocity in a 22-inch barrel is 2,975. Recoil is very mild, accuracy excellent, muzzle blast light. Pressure must be low because I am still using cases I bought years ago and which have been reloaded 30 times and more. I have trimmed the necks, but primer pockets are still tight.

My wife has used a .257 for years, and my sons began their hunt- ing with it. I have been along when they knocked over at least 50 head of whitetail and mule deer, javelinas and antelope, and I cannot recall a single animal that ever got away. Most kills on the small Arizona whitetail deer were made with one shot. Anyone looking for a fine all-around cartridge that gives good accuracy and light recoil can't go wrong on a .257, that is, if he isn't planning to hunt grizzlies, brown bear, moose or elk. It is as good on varmints as it is on bigger game.

THE .243 AND .244

Two new 6 mm. cartridges, the .243 Winchester and the .244 Rem- ington, also come close to the Crossman specifications. Cartridges of .24 caliber or thereabouts are by no means new. The old 6 mm. Lee-Navy cartridge came out in the eighteen nineties, and for many years the British firm of Holland & Holland has featured a .24 caliber belted cartridge with a head-size like the .30/06. The ballistics for this British .24 are nothing staggering—a 100-grain bullet at 2,900. The same firm recently brought out another .24 caliber on the necked down .275 H. & H. case. Apex Rifle Com- pany's .240 Cobra on the .220 Swift case and Fred Huntington's .243 Rockchucker on the .257 case were reasonably popular wildcats.

The .243 Winchester, which is on the same case as the .308 and the .358, is a fine little cartridge. Factory ballistics give the 80-grain bullet 3,500 and the 100-grain bullet 3,070. However, these veloc- ities are taken in a 26-inch barrel; in 22- and 24-inch barrels, velocity is considerably less—about 2,925 for the 100-grain bullet in a 22-inch barrel, for example.

The .243 very quickly gained a reputation for accuracy, and, from all I can hear, it generally shoots very well in Winchester factory rifles. The only rifle I tried it out in was the little featherweight Model 70; with a 6X scope on it, I got groups that averaged only slightly over an inch. A whole flock of rifles are now made for the .243—Model 70s in a lightweight job with a 22-inch barrel, in a standard sporter with a 24-inch barrel, and in a varmint job with a heavy 26-inch barrel. The Model 88 lever action is also chambered for it, as well as the Model 99 Savage, and some foreign imports.

The .244 Remington is based on the .257 case and its powder capacity is slightly greater than that of the .243. As loaded by Remington, the .244 gives a 75-grain bullet 3,500 feet per second and a 90-grain bullet 3,200. Remington barrels for the .244 are cut with a 1—12 twist, and, as a consequence, a 100-grain spitzer bullet will not stabilize in them. Apparently the Remingtons thought of the .244 primarily as a varmint cartridge.

When the two 6 mms. first came out, some pretty fruity stuff was written about them, stuff that I, for one, couldn't swallow. One gun nut friend of mine apparently read all the papers, because he told me with great seriousness that when he sighted in his Model 70 featherweight to put the 100-grain .243 bullet an inch high at 100 yards, he was only an inch low at 300. In my usual tactful manner I told him that since I had chronographed that load in a rifle just exactly like his and had got only 2,925, something was very odd indeed. My only explanation was that Winchester must have hired Anita Ekberg or Marilyn Monroe to breathe softly on each batch of bullets, because his drop figures could not be explained by the laws of physics.

Be that as it may, both cartridges are excellent on varmints and on deer and antelope in open country that is free of bullet-deflecting brush. Les Bowman, a Wyoming big-game outfitter and guide, says that the combination of light recoil, flat trajectory, and adequate killing power makes the two 6 mms. about the most satisfactory deer and antelope medicine that he has ever used.

For some reason, the .244 doesn't have the play that the .243 has, and it is not nearly as popular as its sensational predecessor, the .222. Possibly one reason is that it is used with the short Model 722 action, and that the bullets have to be seated deep in order to work through the magazine. No factory rifle is built for the .244 except the Model 722.

Curious to see what could be done with a gilt-edged .244, I had Al Biesen build me on a short Model 98 type Mexican Mauser action, a .244 with a light 24-inch barrel and a 1–10, instead of the standard 1–12, twist. With the Leupold 8X Mountaineer scope on a Redfield two-piece mount, it weighs eight pounds right on the button.

I latched onto 100 rounds of factory ammunition, some with the 90-grain bullet, some with the 75-grain. Much to my disappointment, though, accuracy was very poor. The chamber has a long throat and possibly one reason the rifle shot poorly was that the bullets had to make a long jump before they hit the rifling. I was about to send the rifle back to Biesen to see what he could make of it when I decided to see what it would do with Speer 90-grain bullets in front of 48 grains of No. 4831. Accuracy was sensational. As yet I haven't had a chance to check with bullets of other makes, but she sure shoots with that Speer 90-grain. The 1–10 twist would stabilize the 100- and 105-grain bullets and with them the .244 should be very effective on the smaller varieties of big game. Except for a sharper shoulder and a slightly shorter case, the .243 Rockchucker is much like the .244, as both are based on the .257 case. The .244 Ackley Improved is simply the .244 Remington case blown out to fit an "improved chamber." It has a 30-degree shoulder instead of the 26 degree shoulder employed on the regular .244. Factory ammunition, of course, can be used in an improved chamber, and ballistics can be improved somewhat by reloading the cases.

But any of these .24s and .25s are fine all-around cartridges for hunting varmints and big game no larger than mule deer. Strictly for varmints, the .24s have the edge because of their factory loads with light bullets at stratospheric velocity. But if the rifleman wants to hunt deer in brush, where bullet deflection is a problem, or if he may want to pot an occasional elk or caribou, the .257 is the cream of the crop when teamed with such heavier bullets as the 117-, 120- and 125-grain. The shot that does the business is the one that hits in the right place, and with these accurate, light-kicking calibers it is easy to put it there.

CHAPTER THIRTEEN

How to Choose Your Deer Rifle

THERE ISN'T ANY DOUBT AS TO THE IDENTITY OF THE NUMBER ONE game animal of the United States. It is the deer. He is the most hunted and talked about animal in this country.

There is good reason why the deer is the principal game animal of a settled and civilized country. Given a little cover and sufficient food, he thrives near civilization and is not bothered by the presence of man. He is intelligent, furtive and wary, and not easy to hunt. In addition, deer begin to breed when they are quite young and they are prolific. All varieties normally produce twin fawns annually. About fifty years ago, deer had just about been killed off in the Eastern states. Since then the animal has made such a remarkable comeback, due to efforts of conservationists, that today there are probably more deer in the United States than were when Columbus discovered America.

VARIETIES OF DEER AND THEIR HABITATS

The deer is generally the animal a hunter has in mind when he chooses his big-game rifle. But writing about deer rifles is a bit formidable because deer vary in size, in habits and in vitality. And the different areas of the country in which they are found vary as much as the animals themselves. I have hunted deer at a few feet above sea-level and above timberline at perhaps 11,000 feet, and I have hunted them where a 75-yard shot was a long one and where a 200-yard shot was a very short one. I have hunted them in country that was as flat as a billiard table, and in country so rough and steep that the deer were right up near those kings of the North American mountains—the Rocky Mountain white goats.

I have seen, but not hunted, the Pacific Coast blacktails in Southeast Alaska, where for days on end the rain pours down and the floor of the forest is as wet as a soaked sponge, and I have shot

many deer in country so dry that the animals live and die without
ever having tasted water. The only moisture these animals get is
from dew and from the sap and juices of their forage.

I have hunted species of deer that are so small that a good buck
probably never dresses out at much more than 50 pounds and others
so large that bucks frequently dress out at over 200 pounds. Now
and then, one of these big fellows turns up weighing over 300 when
field dressed.

I have also hunted deer in areas where there was no other game,
in areas where wild turkey and black bear were also on the menu,
and in other areas where the taking of a deer was incidental to a
hunt for mountain sheep, goats, caribou and grizzly. I have hunted
deer in places where I had an unobstructed shot for as far as I could
see the animal and in country where chances were at least 50-50
that the bullets would encounter brush, twigs or tree limbs on the
way to the target. I have hunted deer in areas where I was the only
hunter in hundreds of square miles and in areas where I saw far
more hunters than deer.

Obviously, then, the term "deer rifle" of necessity covers a lot
of territory, and it doesn't take a genius to realize that the deer
rifle which is excellent, or even adequate, for one set of conditions
wouldn't be too sharp for another.

QUESTIONS TO CONSIDER

To help you narrow down your range of choice, first here are a
few important questions you should ask yourself:

Are you going to hunt deer only? Or are you going to be hunting
in an area where you might run into a grizzly, an Alaska brown
bear, a moose, a wild turkey, an elk, or something else?

Do you plan to use the rifle for varmints as well as deer? Or do
you want to get an all-around big game rifle—one that you can take
deer with at short range and in brushy country, but that you can
also use in Wyoming for antelope or elk and in British Columbia
for moose and grizzlies?

What sort of shots are you going to get? Will you be hunting
in an area where the deer are found in brush and forest, or will
you be hunting in open mountain country where you will have
chances to kill deer at 400 yards?

Will you be hunting in a wilderness area where other hunters are few, or where hunters are more plentiful than deer, where, after being hit, a deer that runs 100 yards is likely to be tagged by someone else?

Your answers to all of these questions should be the basis for selection of your deer rifle. In many areas where the brush is heavy and the deer are small, an old .44/40, for example, with its fat, slow bullet at low velocity, is plenty of rifle, while in others, it is not much better than a handful of rocks. Likewise, in some sections a .270 with the fast-stepping 130-grain bullet and a 6X scope would be a very effective deer outfit, but in others it would greatly handicap the hunter, as we will see below.

DEER IN BRUSH COUNTRY

Of the three species of deer found in the United States—the whitetail, the mule deer and the Pacific Coast blacktail—the whitetail and blacktail are lovers of brush. Consequently, they are generally found in thick country. The ranges for these deer are short and very often the bullet is deflected by brush. Under these circumstances, it is essential for you to have a rifle that enables you, with a minimum of fuss, to throw in a second or third shot, hoping that one of them will get through. Heavy bullets with round or flat points that travel at moderate velocity get through brush a good deal better than light, fast, sharp-pointed bullets. At one time I carried out fairly extensive experiments on the deflection of bullets by brush, twigs and limbs. The conclusion I reached was that the best of all brush-buckers was the heavy, non-spinning, stable rifled slug, and that the poorest was the fast, light, sharp-pointed bullet, such as those used in the .220 Swift and the .24s. I found that the best rifle bullets were those on the order of the 200-grain jobs for the .35 Remington and the .358 Winchester. But the hunter should remember that *any* bullet is liable to be deflected.

A good example of what happens when a bullet strikes brush on the way to an animal is an experience I had when I was hunting in northern Kenya in 1953. I took a shot at a lesser kudu bull through brush so thin I could see the outline of the animal's body. I was using the 220-grain Remington soft-point Core-Lokt bullet loaded down especially for brush shooting to about 2,700 feet per second in a .300 Weatherby Magnum. The bullet plowed through the brush all right, but it was traveling sidewise when it struck the kudu. The entrance wound was a perfect keyhole. If the bullet had been lighter, sharper pointed, faster traveling, or if the kudu had been a bit farther behind the brush, he would not have been struck at all.

On that same trip, I took a shot at a greater kudu bull through brush with the same rifle and the 150-grain Remington bronze point bullet loaded to about 3,400. Apparently all I did was sting the bull with bullet fragments, as he jumped about four feet into the air and took off, leaving no sign of being hit. I have had similar experiences hunting deer in the brush many times.

For brush hunting of deer, I think the best combination is a rifle with a fairly short barrel that has an action capable of fast manipulation, used with a fairly heavy bullet at moderate velocity. The little Model 94 Winchester or Marlin carbines and the .30/30 cartridge are the classic combinations for this work. These rifles are easy to carry around, fast to get the second shot off with, and the 170-grain soft-point bullet in the .30/30 not only has sufficient killing power for deer, but also a sufficiently flat trajectory for shooting to 175 yards or so. Also very good are the Marlin lever actions and the Remington Model 760 pump for the .35 Remington cartridge. Because of its heavier bullet of larger diameter, the .35 Remington is possibly a bit superior in killing power to cartridges of the .30/30 and .32 Special class.

More potent yet are cartridges like the .300 Savage and the .308. The excellent little Savage Model 99-F is available in either caliber.

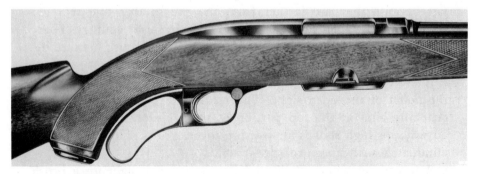

Hunting deer in the brush takes a short-barreled rifle with a fast-working action, and a fairly heavy bullet at moderate velocity. This Winchester Model 88 lever action chambered for the .308 fills the bill.

So is the Remington Model 760 pump. Probably the best bullet weight is the 180-grain. In addition, the .308 is available in the Remington Model 740 autoloader and the Winchester Model 88 lever action.

In heavily hunted areas where a man is liable to find someone else's tag on a deer if it runs very far after being hit, the .358 Winchester with its 200-grain bullet at 2,530 seems to me to be just about ideal. Velocity, shape and bullet weight are such that it gets through the brush well, and it should be a spectacular killer. I have never used the .358 on deer, but I have done some hunting with the 200-grain bullet in the .348, and that really mows them down.

SIGHTS FOR DEER RIFLES

Brush hunting of deer is generally done at short range and often at running animals. It frequently happens that the first shot doesn't get through the brush, but that the hunter's second one does. Such a situation requires not only a fast action but a fast sight. To my mind the finest iron sight for the brush has been allowed to languish. That is the peep sight on a stem, which is mounted close to the eye on the tang of a lever or pump action and on the cocking piece of a bolt action. With one of these sights, the shooter can see all outdoors and shoot very rapidly. The fastest brush rifle I have ever owned was a light 7 mm. Mauser with a Lyman 1-A sight mounted on the cocking piece. Such sights are not easy to adjust and don't give perfect accuracy, but their accuracy is certainly good enough for brush hunting.

Receiver sights are more accurate, easier to adjust, but not as fast because they are farther from the eye so that one sees less through them. Open sights are not so good in bushy country. There is a tendency to shoot over a running deer in the brush because the animal is most conspicuous at the top of his bound. In poor light it is also easy for an excited hunter to fail to get the bead down into the notch of the open sight. The result: he shoots high. Since he generally aims at the top portion of the body on a running deer anyway, his high shot is almost sure to be a miss. This tendency is eliminated with aperture (peep) sights.

A low-power scope (2¼X to 3X) is a very fine sight for a brush rifle because it has a wide field of vision, a conspicuous reticule, and the ability to pick up detail through brush. Many times when I was unable to make out the outlines of a deer's body through the brush with my eye, I could with a scope. For this shooting some like a post. I like a fairly coarse crosswire or a large four- or five-minute dot.

THE RIFLE FOR DEER PLUS OTHER ANIMALS

Many deer hunters, particularly in the Eastern United States, want a rifle they can use on whitetails in the fall and on woodchucks during the summer months. Any such rifle is a compromise; it won't be ideal for deer, and will perhaps leave something to be desired for chucks. However, cartridges like the .243, the .244, the .250/3000 and the .257 used with the heavier bullets will get by on deer and are quite satisfactory for varmints. Although the best compromise scope is a 4X, it has too much power and too small a field to be ideal for brush hunting, and it hasn't enough power to give adequate definition for long range varmint shooting. The various variable powers are better. Outstanding is the Bausch & Lomb Balvar 8, which has the virtue of the same apparent size of the tapered crosswire reticule when set at different powers.

But suppose our deer hunter not only wants to take whitetails in the brush but also wants to come West for long-range shooting of mule deer and antelope or go to Quebec for moose or to New-

A good all-around rifle for deer, antelope and even moose is the author's 7 x 57 built on a Mauser action. It has a mild recoil and flat trajectory.

foundland for caribou. Then he should pick one of the all-around calibers—the .30/06, the .280 Remington, the .270 Winchester, the 7 x 57 Mauser or the .308. For woods hunting, he should select the heavier, slower bullets, and, for open country, the lighter, faster ones with flatter trajectory. He can take his pick of any type of action—lever, pump, autoloader or bolt.

SHOOTING DEER IN THE WEST

In the mountainous West, deer hunting is an entirely different proposition than it is in the wooded East or along the heavily forested West Coast. In the East a 150-yard shot is a very long one. In many parts of the West it is very short.

The mule deer is not only larger on the average than the whitetail, but he also is shot at a greater range. A typical shot at a mule deer, or for that matter, at a Southwestern whitetail, is across a basin or a canyon at from 200 yards on up.

Western country is generally open enough so that the deer can be kept in sight long enough to fire several shots, if necessary. If the first shot misses, subsequent shots must be taken when the deer is on the run, and, for that reason, well-placed shots aren't always the rule.

For such shooting, cartridges such as the .30/30, the .32 Special and the .35 Remington are out of their element. Their curved trajectories make it difficult to score a hit with one of them beyond 200 yards. Furthermore, their low velocity at the long ranges does not give them the shocking power to slow up a deer with a hit in a non-vital area.

For this Western hunting, the best medicine is a rifle in a caliber that moves a fairly light, quick-expanding bullet along at high velocity. In my day I have hunted Western deer with many calibers —the .30/30, .35 Remington, .30/40 Krag, .256 Newton, .35 Whelen, .257 Roberts, 7 x 57, .250/3000, .348, .300 Weatherby Magnum. Of these my long-time favorites have been the .30/06 with the various 150-grain bullets, the .270 with the 130-grain bullet, and the 7 mm., particularly with the now-obsolete Western 139-grain open point at about 2,900 feet per second. The virtue of these cartridges is that when sighted in to put the bullet 3 inches high at 100 yards one does not need to worry about holding high until the game is around 300 yards away. So sighted, the 7 mm. with the 139-grain

Western deer hunting demands high velocity and low trajectory to cope with the wide-open spaces. The .270 Winchester Model 70 with a scope meets these qualifications and is potent medicine for mule deer.

bullet at 2,900, as loaded today in Dominion brand in Canada, or handloaded to that velocity with Speer, Nosler or Sierra bullets of 140-145 grains, is on at approximately 250 yards. So is the 150-grain bullet in the .30/06. The .270 with the 130-grain factory load is on at 275, and such cartridges as the .270, 7 mm. and .300 Weatherby Magnums with the 130-, 140- and 180-grain bullets respectively are on at 300. The trajectory of the .280 Remington with the 125-grain bullet is almost identical to that of the .270 with the 130-grain bullet.

The less the Western deer hunter has to worry about trajectory, the better off he is; the farther he can hit with a dead-on, center-of-the-chest hold, the more deer he is going to kill in open country. It has been my experience that, when I start holding over (aiming above the point I want to hit) to allow for the bullet's drop, I am apt to do some plain and fancy missing, particularly when I also have to worry about lead, that is, shooting ahead of a running animal.

Any of the above-mentioned cartridges will do nicely for antelope and also for the rest of the mountain game, from sheep to timberline moose and grizzly. The recoil from most of these cartridges is light enough so that a man who is used to shooting can do good work with them, whereas he might get the flinches with anything more potent—the .375 Magnum, for example. My recommendation of the 7 mm. Mauser for use on grizzly and moose may surprise some of the heavy bullet enthusiasts, but the late Charles Sheldon shot everything in North America, including many grizzlies and Alaskan brown bears, with the less powerful 6.5 Mannlicher-Schoenauer. Above all things, the long-range deer hunter should avoid overgunning himself. The most important thing is to get the shot in a vital area.

For open-country Western deer hunting, I like a scope of 4X and have never felt that more power was necessary. Some hunters use 6X scopes and swear by them because they say the better definition enables them to see horns and antlers at a greater distance. For my part, I'd rather have more field, even if it means a little less power.

Alongside the moose, the elk, or even the caribou, deer are not large animals. Compare sometime the heavy, massive rib cage of a big bull moose with the relatively thin, fragile one of even a large mule or whitetail deer. With my rifle, camera and binoculars strapped to my person, I once carried a hind quarter of a big buck mule deer in each hand for five miles. Another time, I carried my rifle and the gutted carcass of a large Sonora whitetail about three or four miles to camp. Try that with a moose, elk or caribou.

HARD- AND SOFT-POINTED BULLETS

Because deer are relatively small, frail, soft animals, which are often hit with shots that are not well placed, the best deer bullets are those which open up quickly against fairly light resistance. The bullets that give deep penetration and perform well on heavier game very often do not open up quickly enough on deer, leave a narrow wound-channel, and expend too much energy on the empty air beyond. Some of the 180-grain bullets for the .30/06 that have been designed with larger game in mind don't look very good on the lighter stuff.

For brush shooting in such calibers as the .30/30 and .35 Remington, the old-fashioned soft-pointed bullet with a thin jacket and plenty of lead exposed is a good bet. The Western open-point in 130-grain .270, 139-grain in 7 mm. and 150-grain in .30/06 used to be particular favorites of mine.

A fast-opening bullet will usually kill a deer in its tracks with a lung shot, whereas a slow-opening bullet generally will not. A fast-opening bullet shot into the abdominal cavity will put down or slow up a deer, but a slow-opening bullet may let it get away. It has been my experience that on light animals the faster the bullet sheds its energy, the quicker it kills. On a lung shot, the bullet that stays inside the animal will give a higher percentage of in-the-tracks, one-shot kills than the bullet that goes through.

No one will admit quicker than I will that deer are killed with all sorts of weapons. I know one man who regularly gets his buck with a feeble little .32/20 and another who considers a .375 Magnum about right. An old prospector I knew once kept himself in venison with a single-shot .22 rimfire. Still another tells me he likes to hunt deer in the brush with a .220 Swift and an 8X scope. But generally the more suitable the equipment the better the luck. By and large, the man who chooses the right rifle and sights, shoots the right bullet and practices enough to have some skill won't miss when the big moment comes along.

CHAPTER FOURTEEN

Rifles for Mountain Hunting

IF YOU ARE PLANNING TO HUNT IN MOUNTAINOUS COUNTRY, HERE IS the recipe I recommend for the ideal mountain rifle: A fairly light but well-balanced weapon with a 21- or 22-inch barrel; a reasonably potent, flat-shooting cartridge; a 4X scope on strong, solid mounts; a good gunsling that can be used for both carrying and shooting.

In considering the above ingredients, let's look first at barrel length in the light of an experience I had some 20 years ago. I was hunting sheep one spring afternoon in the Cubaibi mountains just below the Arizona border in Sonora, Mexico. I had decided to try to take a short cut along a ledge overlooking a rocky canyon. At the place where I started out, the ledge was about four feet wide, and the going was easy. But the farther I went, the narrower the ledge became. Below it was a straight drop of about 100 feet.

Finally the ledge got so narrow that I decided to carry my rifle across my back by the sling so that, as I inched along sidewise, I would have both hands free to steady myself against the cliff. But after traveling a few more yards, I discovered that the face of the cliff was beginning to overhang the ledge I was on, and presently I found the muzzle of my rifle hung up against the overhang while I balanced precariously. I was able to free it by wiggling and sidling for a few seconds, but not before I had got a good scare. I was alone and even if I weren't killed by the fall to the rock below, I would never have got off the mountain. After retracing my steps, I took a route that meant more climbing but was safer.

The incident taught me a lesson. At the time I was doing a lot of mountain hunting for sheep and Arizona whitetail deer in very rough country. Since many of the shots were long (particularly at the deer), I had evolved the theory that I could shoot more ac- curately and swing more smoothly if I used a rifle with a fairly long, reasonably heavy barrel that put the weight out in front and made the piece muzzle-heavy. So I had a sporter made with a 26-

208

inch barrel. It weighed about ten pounds after being mounted with a 2¾X Hensoldt scope on the Griffin & Howe side mount. This was it, I told myself. The weight up forward made it swing evenly and settle down quickly. It was a bit awkward to carry in a saddle scabbard, but I felt I was shooting well with it on running game, and it was one of the most accurate .30/06 sporters I have seen to this day. I was in my mid-thirties then, the time of life when a healthy man, although he may not be as fast of foot and as frisky as he was in his twenties, is at the peak of his powers of strength and endurance. The weight of 10 pounds did not bother me. I felt I had the perfect mountain rifle. The incident of the long barrel catching on the overhang, however, had given me a bad time. In addition, a couple of days later along a steep mountainside, I had to go through close-growing stunted trees that are called *sangren grado*. The long barrel of my rifle caught on everything in sight. I came back from the trip exceedingly soured on long barrels for hunting weapons. I had the barrel of the .30/06 chopped off to 22 inches. With the barrel shortened, it was a much handier weapon, and if it shot any less accurately or less flat I was unable to detect it.

THE HEAVY RIFLE

I have read many articles recommending long barrels and considerable weight for the mountain rifle. The articles say the advantages are, of course, greater accuracy, a smoother swing and less weave and wobble if the man behind it is a bit winded. Most of the British writers who have hunted in the high mountains of India's northern frontier have recommended such rifles. The British mountain hunters, however, almost always had *shikaris* (native guides) along to lug their rifles for them; I think anyone will agree that a rifle always weighs less when someone else is carrying it.

The chamois hunters of Switzerland and Austria, some of whom are the world's greatest mountaineers, have always liked shorter and lighter rifles, since in those countries it is customary for the hunter to carry his own weapon, just as it is in North America. The favorite weapons of chamois hunters are the little 6.5 x 54 Mannlicher-Schoenauer carbines with 18½-inch barrels and light Mausers with 20-inch barrels in 7 x 57 and 8 x 57 mm. calibers. Unlike the more conservative British, these hunters almost always use scopes.

Because I am one of the nuttier gun nuts who is always invent-

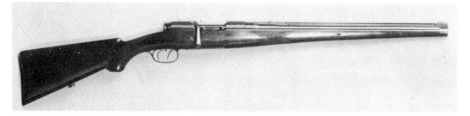

Keeping barrel length down improves maneuverability. The little Mannlicher-Schoenauer carbine, a favorite of European mountaineers, has an 18½-inch barrel and is easy to carry over rugged terrain.

ing an excuse to acquire and use a new rifle, I have experimented with both extremely light and heavy rifles. In spite of its shooting advantages, a heavy, long-barreled rifle is not only awkward when trying to maneuver in very rough country, but it is also burdensome to carry, particularly when the man lugging it is on the wrong side of 40.

Strolling along over level or gently rolling country as one does in many areas when still-hunting deer is one thing. But climbing in steep and rugged mountains is another. Every extra pound the hunter carries in steep, high country drags him down.

THE TOO-LIGHT RIFLE

On the other hand, in an effort to cut down on weight, the mountain hunter should not resort to the ultra-light, short-barreled rifle. It is generally muzzle-light and poorly balanced. This kind of rifle not only is almost impossible to shoot well offhand, but it doesn't swing smoothly and evenly for a running shot. The short barrel gives less velocity, and if it is chambered for a powerful cartridge the muzzle blast becomes decidedly unpleasant. I have done some hunting with a .30/06 with an 18½-inch barrel and with a scope sight. It weighs a shade less than seven pounds. From a bench rest, the little cannon will group surprisingly well, but I have never found it particularly feasible to carry a bench rest around with me while I was hunting sheep. This rifle kicks like three mules, has a muzzle blast that lays the daisies low, and when it is shot in dim light the jet of flame that comes out of the barrel looks like the business end of a blow torch. I can see where such a rifle would be just the thing for the trapper or explorer who has to cut weight to an absolute minimum, yet still needs a powerful weapon. For the hunter, though, it is too much of a good thing. The perfect mountain rifle is a compromise between the two extremes.

I have probably shot more mountain game with an old .270 than I have with any other rifle I own. It was built on a flat-bolt Mauser action with a barrel by Bill Sukalle of Phoenix, Arizona, and a stock of dense Bosnian walnut by the late Alvin Linden of Spokane, Washington. The scope is a 2½X Lyman Alaskan on the very strong, all-steel Noske side mount. The rifle is on its third barrel and its second scope. (The original scope was the now almost forgotten make of Noske.) I have carried this .270 around in mountains from Mexico to the Yukon, and it has been carried many hundreds of miles in a saddle scabbard. But now I seldom use it. The truth is that its weight of nine pounds, for some odd reason, seems heavier to me in 1960 than it did 20 or 30 years ago.

TREND TOWARD LIGHTER RIFLES

Back before World War II, the man who wanted a reasonably light but potent rifle had a pretty tough time securing one. The three most popular American big-game rifles then were the Model 70 Winchester, the Model 30 Remington and the Model 99-R Savage. All had fairly heavy 24-inch barrels, and by the time they were equipped with scopes and mounts they tipped the scales at between 10 and 10½ pounds. All three models also had the habit of becoming pretty heavy if the character carrying one of them was about five hours out of camp and about 4,000 feet above it.

If a mountain hunter wanted a lighter bolt-action rifle, he either had to acquire some import like the little 6.5 Mannlicher-Schoenauer carbine or have a special job made up. In those days, Savage made a dandy little lightweight called the Model 99-T, but it was available only in .250/3000 and .300 Savage and many hunters would settle for nothing less than something of the .270 to .30/06 class.

In 1946 I wrote a piece in *Outdoor Life* pointing out that most factory-made big-game rifles were too heavy by the time scopes were hung on them. It drew a lot of mail from hunters who were in hearty agreement. I have no illusion that the gun and rifle manufacturers hang on my every word or that this piece caused them to revise their specifications and lighten up their muskets. I do think, though, that the piece articulated the feelings of a lot of hunters who had begun to feel that most factory rifles weighed too much and were too long of barrel. A great many smart joes work for the gun companies, and I am sure that they themselves had decided that big-game rifles could do with less beef. At any rate, the Model 721 and 722 Remington rifles which came out shortly thereafter were lighter than the old Remington Model 30 Express or its modification, the short-lived Model 720. The new Remington Model 725 is even lighter.

Winchester followed with the Model 70 Featherweight in .30/06, .270 and .308. Whereas the standard weight Model 70 generally weighed from 9¾ to 10½ pounds when scope-equipped, the featherweight, with its light 22-inch barrel and dural floorplate, trigger guard, and buttplate usually totals up to around eight pounds. With iron sights and right out of the box, it is supposed to weigh 6½ pounds, but depending on caliber and density of wood in the stock the Model 70 may weigh as much as 7 pounds. One in .270, for example, weighed a bit over 6½ but wound up at exactly 8 pounds when equipped with a Buehler mount and a Leupold 4X Mountaineer scope. Rifles in .308 and .30/06, with their bigger bore diameters, are usually a bit lighter because of the larger hole in the barrel.

Just about everyone has jumped on the light-sporter bandwagon. The new Savage Model 110 in .243, .308, .30/06, and .270 weighs about as much as the light Winchester. That is, between 6½ and 7 pounds depending on the caliber and the density of the wood in the stock. Equipped with scope and sling, these models weigh eight pounds or slightly over, and like the Winchester, the Model 110 also has a 22-inch barrel. Even Weatherby rifles in the special Weatherby Magnum caliber have been trimmed down to around eight pounds with scopes.

The Mannlicher-Schoenauer, which is imported from Austria by Stoeger Arms Corporation, is a light rifle, and the Finnish Sako "Forester," which is brought over by Firearms International in .243, .244 and .308, weighs around 6¾ pounds. Imported by Tradewinds, the Swedish Husqvarna weighs even less, and when judiciously scope equipped it will weigh around 7½ pounds. It is available in .270, .30/06, .308 and 7 x 57. All of these foreign jobs are handy ones that won't break down a man's arches. J. L. Galef & Son of New York imports the fine, lightweight B.S.A. (Birmingham Small Arms Company) bolt-action rifles from England in .270,

Another imported rifle suitable for mountain shooting is the light B.S.A., which comes in .30/06, .270 and 7mm.

.30/06 and 7 mm. Scope-equipped, they are right for the mountains.

At this writing, my own two pet rifles for mountain hunting are a pair of remodeled Model 70 Winchesters, one a .270, the other a 7 x 57 mm., which, incidentally, was the last Model 70 in 7 mm. ever put together in the Winchester factory. When I got them, both were standard weight jobs, but I had Al Biesen cut the barrels to 22 inches, lighten them up, smooth up the actions, checker the bolt knobs and then fit fancy stocks of French walnut on them. One wears a Weaver K-4 scope on a Redfield Jr. two-piece mount; the other, a Kollmorgen Bear Cub on a Tilden mount. Each weighs exactly eight pounds.

The old notion that only rifles with heavy barrels shoot well doesn't hold too much water. A heavy barrel heats up more slowly, and it certainly does enable the shooter to shoot smaller ten-shot

One of the author's favorites is this remodeled 70 Winchester .270 with a 22-inch barrel, French walnut stock and Weaver K-4 scope.

Proof of the pudding—the eight-pound Model 70 and a pair of Bausch & Lomb 9 x 35 binoculars accounted for the buck.

groups than a light-barrel job. However, one seldom gets to shoot ten shots for groups on a game animal. Since it is the first shot or two that pays off in the field, a hunting rifle should actually be judged on the basis of whether or not three to five shots heat up the barrel. True, the heavier a rifle is, the more solidly it will settle down, and the harder it is to disturb the aim of a shot if the trigger is yanked slightly, instead of squeezed. A good, precision-made light barrel in a properly bedded rifle, however, affords the means for surprisingly accurate shooting.

TUNING UP YOUR RIFLE

Incidentally, it has been my experience that most light barrels shoot best when the forend exerts just a little pressure upward against the barrel. In a rifle without a forend screw, I like to have the pressure just enough so that when I put my left hand around barrel and forend I can feel them come together with the last half turn of the forward guard screw. That is not a great deal of pressure— a couple of pounds, maybe—possibly three or four. More pressure than this generally causes very erratic shooting. I have cured many a sour-shooting light sporter by simply freeing the barrel channel so that there was no pressure against the barrel whatsoever. Just relieving this excess pressure has often made the difference between a 6-inch group at 100 yards and a 2-inch group. I have also experimented with paper shims of varying thicknesses, placing them in slightly different locations back of the forend tip. The light barrel will almost always shoot best when there is little pressure exerted against it. A man who has mastered the knack of shooting from a bench rest and who used good bullets and a scope of at least 4 power can generally get groups of from 1 to 1½ inches.

Tuning up, such as I have just described, takes more time than gun factories can afford to expend on rifles that are sold to their jobbers for not much more than $75, but that doesn't bother the 20-carat gun nut. To him, tuning up is a labor of love. The owner of a Model 70 that has a forend screw can obtain fine accuracy and the dampening effect by subjecting the screw to different amounts of tension. When I first got my lightweight remodeled .270, it shot best with a very tight forend screw, but some months later when the stock had dried out a bit, I got better groups by backing out the screw about half a turn. It all depends on the individual rifle.

THE IDEAL MOUNTAIN RIFLE

I believe that the light .270 is about the nearest thing to the perfect mountain rifle that I have ever owned. With it, I can shoot on foot factory ammunition, with 130- and 150-grain bullets, and maximum handloads, with bullets of the same weight, so near the same point of impact at 100 yards that a good shot using a sling and shooting from the sitting position wouldn't be able to get better accuracy. The rifle is short enough of barrel so that it doesn't get in the way of overhanging rocks or entangled in brush, yet the barrel is long enough so that the arm balances nicely. The .270 gives no noticeable increase in muzzle blast, and it is handy to carry in a saddle scabbard. Groups average between 1 and 1½ inches, depending on the bullet I use and how well I am shooting. I have shot many groups with it that ran under an inch. I have used it on many trips—both short and long—during which I have used the rifle to bag such diversely sized game as the Dorcas gazelle and the bull elk.

A well-made 4X scope on a good, solid top mount is just about ideal for mountain hunting. For long range shooting of any big game, the 4X affords the shooter sufficient definition generally for him to distinguish the heads of animals, such as sheep, after he has picked them over with his binoculars. A good variable power set at 6X or 8X might be useful occasionally, since animals sometimes change places in a herd between the time the binoculars are put down and the rifle picked up. This happened to me once when I was stalking a herd of bighorn rams in Wyoming. I didn't notice in my 2½X that two rams had changed places, with the result that I shot the wrong ram. At 100 yards the 4X provides a field of view averaging about 30 feet, which is enough for running shooting. A 6X, on the other hand, has less field (about 20 feet generally) and less latitude of eye relief. It isn't nearly as good as the 4X for running shots at short range.

CHOICE OF CARTRIDGE

As for caliber, the mountain hunter can pretty much name his own medicine as long as the bullets step fast enough to give a flat trajectory. If he is hunting nothing larger than sheep or mule deer, he can use a caliber as light as the .243, the .244, or the .257. One of the best sheep hunters I ever knew used a .250/3000 Savage, another one favored a .300 Savage. If the hunter is not recoil sensitive and goes in for power, he can get a mountain rifle in .300 H. & H. Magnum or .300 Weatherby, and I know of one hardy soul who carries a remodeled Winchester Model 70 with a 22-inch barrel in .375 Magnum caliber. He must have nerves of steel. For my part, the thought of a .375 weighing 8 pounds makes my blood run cold.

I think, though, that the most useful mountain cartridges are within the range of the 7 x 57, the .270 Winchester, .280 Remington, .308 and .30/06. All are sufficiently flat shooting for the cross-canyon shots one gets at mule and Western whitetail deer and for the occasional long shot one has to take at sheep or goats. With proper bullets they are powerful enough for the grizzlies one often runs into above timberline on a sheep or goat hunt and for the big mountain moose one also encounters.

Incidentally, one often reads stuff about "long-range shooting at sheep and goats," and those who have never hunted sheep are apt to think that most mountain sheep are shot only at long range. But this has not been my experience—and I have been hunting sheep as a hobby for more than 20 years. Although I have shot a few sheep at over 300 yards, my average shot has been at less than 200. In fact, because both sheep and goats inhabit rough country which enables the hunter frequently to approach behind a ridge, sheep can often be taken at very close range. My first desert sheep was taken at about 75 yards, my most recent one at about 35. The best white sheep I ever shot was killed at approximately 50 yards, and my best bighorn at around 100.

I have used the 7 mm., .270 and .30/06 calibers for most of my sheep hunting. All three of them have been entirely satisfactory. I have generally used the 140-grain bullet at 2,900 in the 7 mm., the 130-grain at 3,140 in the .270 and the 150-grain at 2,940 in the .30/06. If anyone got me down in a hammer-lock, though, I believe I'd confess that I have a slight preference for the .270 because of its somewhat flatter trajectory. The new .280 Remington should rank right up there at the top with the .270.

The choice of caliber, however, varies from hunter to hunter. Don Hopkins, one of the most experienced North American sheep hunters, uses a .285 O.K.H., a wildcat made by necking the .30/06 case to 7 mm., a cartridge not far from being identical to the .280 Remington. Herb Klein and Elgin Gates, both of whom have shot all species of North American sheep, like to use .300 Weatherbys. George Parker, who is probably the best desert sheep hunter in existence, has used a .257, while Colonel Harry Snyder, a Canadian who has hunted all over the mountains of the North, likes a 7 x 64, a cartridge very similar to the .280. Prince Abdorreza Pahlavi of Iran has done most of his sheep hunting for the past several years with a light 7 x 57 with a Weaver K-4 scope. He uses the Canadian Dominion brand ammunition with 140-grain bullets at about 2,900 feet per second. Myles Brown, who has shot all varieties of North American sheep and who was one of the first dude hunters ever to get into the wonderful Stone sheep country around the heads of the Muskwa and Prophet rivers in Northern British Columbia, has used a .30/06 more than any other rifle.

The mountain rifle should be sighted in not necessarily for the traditional 200 yards but for the longest range that will not cause mid-range misses by high shooting. This means that the bullet should land 3 inches above line of scope sight at 100 yards. With the 125-grain bullet in the .280, 130-grain in the .270 or the 180-grain in the .300 Weatherby, the rifle is at point of aim at 275 yards, 2 inches low at 300 and about 5 inches low at 325. So sighted a

The mountain rifle should be equipped with a sling to leave hands free to carry home the game.

.30/06 with the 150-grain bullet is on at 250, 5 inches low at 300 and with the 180-grain bullet, it is on at 225 and 5 inches low at 275. The trajectory of the 7 mm. with the 140-grain bullet in my rifle with a 22-inch barrel is slightly flatter. With the .270 sighted like this, a hold on the top of the shoulder will mean a hit to almost 400 yards.

THE SLING

A sling for shooting and carrying is a must for the mountain rifle. I like the one-piece Whelen-type, because the loop can be adjusted for the individual hunter to use when both shooting and carrying his rifle. Quick detachable swivels are so much superior to fixed swivels that there is no comparison. Without a sling, any rifle is an awkward burden, and anyone who has learned to use a sling knows that he shoots more accurately with one, particularly on a hillside and from the sitting position, which is normal procedure for shooting in the mountains. For more on slings see chapter entitled "Slings and Swivels."

CHAPTER FIFTEEN

The Big-Game Rifle

ONE OF THE OLDEST AND BITTEREST ARGUMENTS AMONG BIG-GAME hunters and rifle fanciers is about the relative virtues of the small bore and the medium bore. In one form or another, the controversy has been raging for well over half a century. Small bores, in this case, generally mean any big-game cartridge with a caliber of .30 or under, and medium bores are those calibers between .32 and .39. For the sake of clarity we'll call anything of .40 caliber or above a large bore.

In the United States, the argument started back in the eighteen nineties. Generally it was between the advocates of the then brand-new smokeless powder calibers such as the .25/35, the .30/30 and the .30/40, and the more conservative hunters who professed that there was surer killing power in black power cartridges of larger caliber such as the .38/55, .38/72 and .45/70. In Africa radical hunters shocked the conservatives by shooting lions, rhinos and elephants with such relatively tiny bullets as the 160-grain for the 6.5 Mannlicher-Schoenauer and the 175-grain used in the 7 x 57 Mauser. The great hunter, D. W. M. Bell, began shooting elephants with a .303 British and a 6.5 but found that the all-around rifle for him was the 7 mm. Mauser. He killed over 1,000 elephants with it.

In the United States the medium-bore advocates reluctantly abandoned their fine old black powder weapons for the .35 Winchester with its 250-grain bullet at 2,160 and the .405 with the 300-grain bullet at 2,220. Now and then, in the days before World War I, 9 x 57 Mausers with a 247-grain bullet at 2,312 were imported. The now-obsolete .35 Newton, with its 250-grain bullet at around 3,000 feet per second, also had its followers.

The United States and North America, however, has not much game that can be called either big or dangerous. Compared to the little deer, the elk is a large animal and the moose is even larger. But by no stretch of the imagination can either be called dangerous, although almost any animal can under some circumstances harm human beings. The grizzly, a tough and unpredictable animal, will on occasion turn the tables on the hunter, and the Alaskan brown bear and the polar bear are also potentially dangerous and should be handled with discretion. But most American "big-game" animals have about as much fight in them as rabbits. The mountain lion or "cougar" may be larger than the African leopard, but the leopard is a feline buzz saw and the mountain lion is a slob.

THE MEDIUM BORES IN AMERICA

This lack of large or dangerous game has been responsible for the American hunter's lack of interest in the medium bores with their heavier bullets which have the power to knock animals flat, and smash heavy bones. The .35 Winchester and the .405 in the Model 95 sold so poorly that rifles to fire them were never manufactured after the nineteen thirties and now the cartridges are obsolete. During the nineteen twenties, however, custom rifle makers like Griffin & Howe, Neidner and Hoffman (the two last firms are no longer in business) made a few .375 Magnums, and there was enough interest in the cartridge to encourage Winchester to bring out the Model 70 in that caliber. Many Americans have taken the Winchester .375 to Africa and Asia, and many have also used it on this continent on brown, polar and grizzly bear.

For the most part, though, the American enthusiasts for the medium bores have turned to wildcats. Griffin & Howe necked down the .375 Magnum case to .35 caliber, creating the .350 G. & H. Magnum with a 275-grain bullet at 2,440. Those rifleman who used it liked the cartridge; however, I have heard little about it in recent years. The last time I saw Phil Johnstone of Griffin & Howe, he was talking about reviving it; undoubtedly with modern powders it would be a real hell-bender. With the Speer 220-grain .35 caliber bullet, for example, 95 grains of No. 4831 will give 3,125, and 91 grains of No. 4350 will turn up 3,210. With the 250-grain bullet, 95 grains of No. 4831 gives 3,085, and 89 grains of No. 4350 gives 3,085. With the original 275-grain bullet, I would anticipate a velocity of around 2,800.

The .35 Whelen with the .30/06 case expanded to take a .35 caliber bullet is another Griffin & Howe production that has had a long, useful, but not particularly sensational life. As originally loaded by Griffin & Howe, it gave a 275-grain bullet 2,250, but with the Speer 220-grain bullet and 60 grains of No. 4320, it will turn up the very respectable velocity of 2,740, and, with the same amount of No. 4064, it registers 2,647. With 59 grains of No. 4320 and the 250-grain bullet, it gives 2,540, as it also does with 58 grains of No. 4064.

The twist of the .35 Whelen is generally 1—14. Because the cartridge has the same overall length as the .30/06, unaltered Model 98 and FN actions can be used for it, as can Model 721 Remington and Model 70 Winchester actions for the .30/06.

The .35 Whelen is a good bet for the reloader who wants to throw a heavy chunk of lead with no more expense than an investment in a new barrel. I once had a .35 Whelen but the largest thing I ever killed with it was a mule deer. I used to buy the old .35 Winchester soft-point bullets and load them to about 2,500 feet per second. The bullets were designed for proper expansion at a muzzle velocity of about 2,200, and at 2,500 they were the most destructive bullets I have ever used on soft-skinned game. I'd hit a buck in the chest with one of these and blow off his far side. A hit in the neck would just about decapitate him. When the .375 factory-cartridge Magnum came out, I felt that there wasn't much excuse for the wildcat .35 Whelen. I got rid of mine and haven't used one since. It is still a useful cartridge for the shooter who is not allergic to wildcats.

Another medium bore that no doubt had its place in the scheme of things was the .348 Winchester. The only rifle made for it was the now-obsolete Winchester Model 71 lever action. Three weights of bullets were used—a 150-grain bullet at 2,890, a 200-grain at 2,530, and a 250-grain at 2,350. It has always been an excellent brush cartridge for anything from deer to grizzly. I had a Model 71, and used it a bit, but I quickly found that it wasn't any cartridge for hunting in the mountainous Southwest. The bullets had to be made with flat noses because the Model 71 used a tubular magazine, and unless the noses of the bullets were flat there was danger that the bullet of one cartridge would fire the primer of the cartridge in front of it. The 150-grain bullet, because of its poor sectional density and ballistically inefficient point, shed its velocity rapidly, and in the open Southwest the slow 250-grain was about as useful as a handful of rocks. The best compromise was the 200-grain bullet which had sufficiently flat trajectory so that hits at 250 yards could be made on large animals like elk without too much

Arkansas elevation. I used the .348 a bit and believe I probably killed the first Arizona whitetail, the first mule deer and the first bighorn ram ever taken with it. I have never had an opportunity, however, to try it out on anything more substantial.

Various gunsmiths have brought out .35 caliber wildcats on shortened .375 Magnum cases with shoulders about like those on the old .35 Newton. My friend Fred Huntington, a big tool and die man, has one and swears by it, but my own experience with any of these wildcats is exactly nil.

I have, however, played with a .33/06, which is the .30/06 necked down to take a bullet measuring .333. Speer makes a 275-grain bullet for it that can be given 2,400 feet per second with 59 grains of No. 4831 or 2,320 with 55 grains of No. 4350. The cartridge has a fine reputation as elk medicine among medium-bore enthusiasts of the Northwest. Fred Barnes makes a 250-grain bullet for it, I believe. Bullet diameter is *not* the same as the American .33 Winchester, but instead it follows the dimensions of the British .333 Jeffery. Like many other cartridges it gets its name from the *groove* diameter.

Elmer Keith used the cartridge under the name of the .333 O.K.H. (which is exactly the same thing) in Africa and reported great success with it. Other hunters have used it on grizzlies and Alaska brown bear. Don Hopkins and his wife Marge, who have spent more time in East Africa and taken more outstanding trophies than any other hunters I can name offhand, consider the .333 on a short belted case the most useful all-around cartridge for hunting in Africa. I do not have the ballistic dope for their .333 Belted, but a similar cartridge, designed by the Luft Brothers, gunsmiths in Spokane, Washington, gives a 275-grain bullet 2,550 with 68 grains of No. 4831 or 2,455 with 63 grains of No. 4350. Don Hopkins imports and loads the British bullets made for the .333 Jeffery in weights of 250 and 300 grains. He says that if he could have but one cartridge for both African and North American shooting, the .333 Belted would be his choice.

EUROPEAN MEDIUM BORES

Because the British in Africa and elsewhere have for the most part shot larger, tougher and more dangerous game than Americans in this country have access to, they have used a considerable variety of medium bores for a long time. Their .333 Jeffery is made in rim-less form for bolt-action rifles and in rimmed (or *flanged* form, as they say) for doubles and single shots. The rimless cartridge gives a 250-grain bullet 2,500 feet per second and a 300-grain bullet 2,200. Velocities and pressures for the rimmed cartridge are slightly lower. Other popular British medium bores are the .369 Purdey with a 270-grain bullet at 2,525 and the .350 Rigby Magnum with a 225-grain bullet at 2,625.

One of the world's most widely used medium bores is the 9.3 x 62 Mauser, which gives a 285-grain bullet the relatively modest velocity of 2,320. It was developed by the world-famous Mauser Company of Germany, and thousands of rifles have been made for it not only in Germany but in Belgium, Austria and Czechoslovakia as well. It has been very popular with the farmer-hunters in south and east Africa, as continental rifles for it were much cheaper than those of British manufacture. The cartridge is a good one for lion, leopard and the larger antelope. In a pinch and with "solid" bullets, it can be used on buffalo, rhino and elephant. Although it is almost unknown in the United States, it is distributed just about everywhere else in the world where big game is shot—in India and all over Africa. When I was in French Equatorial Africa in 1958, I ran into a couple of tough-looking French civil servants who were headed for a big-game shoot with their entire outfit packed in one Land Rover. The two rifles they had with them were both Belgian 9.3 x 62s. Ballistically and in appearance, it is much like our wildcat .35 Whelen.

THE .375 H. & H. MAGNUM

But the queen of the medium bores is the .375 H. & H. Magnum, one of the world's most useful and widely distributed cartridges, and probably the best all-round cartridge ever designed. It was introduced about 1912 by the great London gun and rifle manufacturer, Holland & Holland. Some .375s were made up in the United States along in the nineteen twenties on German Magnum Mauser actions. Even in those days they cost a substantial amount of folding money; the actions alone retailed here for about $100. However, Winchester chambered the Model 70 for the cartridge in 1937, and since then .375s have been within reach of those of moderate means.

Western and Winchester factory-loaded ammunition gives the 270-grain semi-spitzer bullet a velocity of 2,740. The energy at the muzzle is 4,500 foot pounds. The trajectory over 200 yards is slightly flatter than that of the .30/06 with the 180-grain bullet— 2.9 inches midway over a 200-yard range and 7.1 over 300 yards. In comparison, the figures for the 180-grain bullet in the .30/06 are 3.1 and 8.3. The energy of the .375 with the 270-grain bullet at 200 yards is 2,920, or about the same as that of the .30/06 at the muzzle. Sight in a .375 with the 270-grain bullet to group three inches above line of scope sight at 100 yards, and you are on the nose at around 225. That's a very practical trajectory, even for mountain hunting. Even the 300-grain bullet shoots sufficiently flat to make fairly long shots practical. The mid-range trajectory over 200 yards with the 300-grain bullet at 2,550 is only 3.3 inches, and over 300 yards 8.3, or exactly the same as that of the .30/06 with the 180-grain bullet.

My own .375 is a Model 70 Winchester restocked in French walnut by Griffin & Howe and equipped with a Kollmorgen 2¾X Bear Cub scope on the Griffin & Howe side mount. It also has a Lyman No. 48 receiver sight and the factory front sight. If I want to use the scope, I simply slip out the slide of the 48, slip on the scope, and vice versa.

I have no trouble getting groups of 1½ to 2 inches at 100 yards with the rifle, and over the years I have got so I am not bothered by the generous recoil. It has enough power in a pinch for elephants and rhinos, yet it shoots flat enough for mountain hunting. Up to 250 yards, there is so little difference between the point of impact with the two bullet weights that I am not a good enough shot to be able to determine by group which bullet I am shooting.

Incidentally, the published velocity figures for the .375 check out exactly on the chronograph with factory ammunition, which is by no means true of all factory-made cartridges. When I handload, I use 70 grains of No. 4064 behind the 300-grain bullet and 71 grains behind the 270-grain bullet. The points of impact are exactly the same for the factory ammunition. Pressures seem to be O.K., which is verified by the fact that I have some cases that have been loaded five or six times, and the primer pockets are still tight.

My rifle weighs 9 pounds with iron sights, 9¾ with scope and the detachable portion of the mount. I wouldn't have it any heavier, or, for that matter, much lighter. The barrel is 25 inches long, and someday I am going to have another with a 23-inch barrel, which would be a bit handier in the brush.

The .375 is one of my real enthusiasms in big-game cartridges. If I were going to hunt all over the world and could use only one rifle, it would be a .375. If I could have only two, one would be a .375 and the other a .270. I have used the .375 in Africa on two trips, in India, Iran and Alaska, and have shot with it a couple of lions, two Alaskan brown bear and one very large tiger, as well as a slew of the larger African antelope. Both lions and brownies were knocked flat on the first shot, and with one exception all the bullets I have recovered, either in 270- or 300-grain weight, looked exactly like the advertisements showing the perfect mushroom. The exception was the 270-grain bullet I put into the ribs of a running tiger. For some reason, it shed its jacket, and the tiger, though hit hard and square, ran about 150 yards before it uttered its death cry and went down.

Besides the Western factory bullets, Speer makes a .375 semi-spitzer bullet in 235- and 285-grain weight. Fred Barnes makes bullets weighing 250, 300 and 350 grains, and Hornady makes 300-grain bullets in soft point and also in an excellent solid with a *steel* jacket.

As much as I like the .375, I have never seen much use for it in North America, except for hunting the big Alaskan brown bear. However, if anyone wants to use it on elk, moose or grizzly, I am not going to take exception. It is a hard-hitting, flat-shooting cartridge, with which I have scored a higher percentage of one-shot, in-the-tracks kills on medium to large soft-skinned game than with any other cartridge.

THE .338 WINCHESTER

Another cartridge which is going to have the medium-bore aficionados jumping is the new .338 Winchester. It is on a short-belted magnum case with a fairly sharp shoulder and the same size head as the .300 H. & H. case. The overall length is about that of the .30/06, and .338s can be built on slightly altered Springfield and Model 98 Mauser actions as well as on the Winchester Model 70 action. Factory ammunition gives a 200-grain bullet a muzzle velocity of 3,050, a 250-grain bullet 2,750, and a 300-grain bullet

2,400. The 250- and 300-grain bullets are soft points and the 200-grain the Silvertip. Speer Products of Lewiston, Idaho, produces a 275-grain bullet which can be loaded to 2,600 feet per second with 69 grains of No. 4350. Bullet size, incidentally, is the same as that of the old .33 Winchester and not .333 like the British .33s.

The .338 has almost as much soup as the .375 Magnum, and, because of the shorter case, it has the advantage of a shorter bolt-throw. The 200-grain bullet with its high velocity should be very effective for hunting any mountain game, the 270-grain for all-around use and the 300-grain entirely adequate for any of the world's soft-skinned game, dangerous or not. I wouldn't pick the .338 as a mountain rifle, as a .338 weighing less than nine pounds would have a pretty severe recoil, but it is a superb cartridge and one that's going to be used over the world. As a medium bore for Africa, it is on a par with the great .375.

These medium bores with their heavy bullets of fairly large diameter at moderate velocity for the most part have real advantages. The bullets, particularly if round-nosed, get through brush with less deflection than do lighter, faster bullets. The heavy bullets do a more reliable job of breaking heavy shoulder bones, and, all things being equal, do a superior job of getting inside large animals with angling shots. In case the bullet does not come out the far side of the animal, the larger entrance hole that it makes provides a better blood trail in case the animal must be tracked. With the greater momentum of the heavier bullets, the medium bores are more apt to knock an animal down.

But for this continent most hunters don't have much need for them. If the heavy bullets are moved along fast enough for fairly flat trajectory, recoil becomes unpleasant. Rifles likewise have to be relatively heavy to hold down recoil. It takes a seasoned rifle shot to handle them, and most American hunters season themselves by buying a box of cartridges and looking through the barrel to see if it has collected any mice or wasp nests during the off season. No rifle is any more effective than the guy behind it. A bum shot with a .375 is still a bum shot, and a 300-grain bullet in the guts will wound just as ineffectively as a 100-grain bullet in the guts.

Nevertheless, a lot of big-game hunters have done enough shooting so that the recoil of the medium bores doesn't bother them. They derive pleasure and confidence from handling the extra power. And there isn't any doubt that a good big gun is better than a good little gun—if it's properly handled.

CARTRIDGES FOR THE HEAVIEST GAME

Although you might think that the big "elephant" cartridges are only of academic interest to most American sportsmen, there is actually a surprising amount of discussion about them. The only home-grown American cartridge suitable for elephants, rhino and Cape buffalo is the .458 Winchester, and I am told that sales of the cartridge and the Model 70 "African" rifle that fires it have surpassed all expectations. Another surprising fact is that big-bore British double rifles are a hot item on the American market, and almost any old clunker of a British double will fetch a very substantial price.

There is an enormous interest at present in Africa, in African hunting, and in rifles and cartridges for African game. Part of it is due to the fact that since the last war it has been possible for Americans who want to make an African shoot bad enough and who are willing to save for it to actually do it. Not many years ago, an American wanting to hunt in Africa had to take a long, time-consuming trip by sea to England, from where he then had to travel south through the Mediterranean and the Suez Canal to Mombassa on the Kenya coast. Then he would outfit from Nairobi and take off into the bush. For the trip he needed a minimum of six months, but nine months was better. Now relatively inexpensive air transportation and motorized safaris have reduced both the expenditures of time and money involved in an African shoot.

Most experienced white hunters recommend that their clients bring along a "light" rifle like the 7 x 57, .270, .30/06, .280 Remington or .300 Magnum for hunting the various antelope up to the size of the roan (which is as large as an elk) or the eland (which is about the size of the smaller species of moose). Most of the hunting will be done with this weapon. The "medium" rifle should be used on lion, eland, roan, and it can be used on any of the larger antelope such as the greater kudu and the sable. The American-loaded but British-designed .375 Magnum is outstanding in this class, and the new .338 Winchester Magnum would also be excellent. If the African hunter wanted to go light and take but one rifle, he could get by fairly well with only a medium; however, in

Most smaller African game is shot with rifles of around .300 Magnum. This .300 Weatherby Magnum deluxe rifle is a left-handed model with a Weatherby 4X Imperial scope.

Kenya it is illegal to shoot elephant, rhino and buffalo with anything less powerful than a .40 caliber and it is illegal to shoot eland and lion with anything less powerful than the .375. In Tanganyika, the .375 is the minimum caliber for any of the dangerous game.

The "heavy" rifle has limited use and will probably be employed only on elephant, rhino and buffalo, but if the prospective African hunter plans to hunt the big fellows he must include one in his battery. If he wants to go light and cut down on his baggage, he can forget the medium. Instead, he should take a heavy and a light and use the heavy on the larger antelope and the lion.

THE DOUBLE RIFLE

The double rifle is generally thought of as a *must* for this type of hunting. It has the advantage of being available for very powerful cartridges, of having a low line of sight so that in an emergency the rifle can be "pointed" rather than aimed, and of giving two very quick shots. Its disadvantages are great weight and cost. In London a double ejector rifle will cost from $750 to $1,200.

Most of the heavy cartridges for the largest game are British in origin and are descended from the .450 Nitro Express. They were designed when the importing of all .45 caliber weapons was prohibited in India and the Sudan.

All are ballistically similar. They use bullets weighing in the neighborhood of 500 grains at a velocity of around 2,100 to 2,200 feet per second, and their muzzle energy is about 5,000 foot pounds as compared to the 4,000 foot pounds or so of the heavy mediums like the .375 Magnum.

One of the two most popular cartridges in Africa for the heavy doubles is the .465 Nitro Express (also called the .500/.465 because the case is that of the .500 Nitro Express necked down). Developed by Holland & Holland, it uses 73 grains of Cordite to drive a 480-grain bullet at 2,125 feet per second with 4,930 foot pounds of muzzle energy. The other favorite is the .470 with a 500-grain bullet at 2,125 with 5,030 foot pounds of muzzle energy. Used with the full metal-cased bullets which the British call "solids," either caliber will penetrate to the brain of an elephant or smash the heavy shoulder bones of elephant, rhino or buffalo. More important, the big bullets have, particularly when they strike bone, the power to knock a large animal back and turn a charge.

The most powerful of all such cartridges was the .600 Nitro Express, which is now obsolete, but which used a 900-grain bullet in front of 100 grains of Cordite for a velocity of 1,850 and 6,840 foot pounds of energy. The .577, which is still loaded in England, uses a 650-grain bullet at 1,950 feet per second for an energy of 5,500 foot pounds. Other cartridges of this class are the .475, .475 No. 2, .450 No. 2 and .500 Nitro Express, but the bulk of all British doubles of the elephant class are made for the .465 and the .470 and the ammunition is distributed all over Africa.

THE HEAVY BOLT ACTION

If the hunter does not care to go to the expense of buying a double, he can do very well with a bolt action. The obvious choice for an American is the Winchester Model 70 African rifle in .458 Winchester caliber. It has a straight belted rimless case with an overall length about that of the .30/06, but it uses 500- and 510-grain bullets at 2,125 with over 5,000 foot pounds of energy. The ballistics of the .458 duplicate those of the famous .470, and the 500-grain "solid" for the .458, which has a heavy steel jacket, is one of the finest elephant bullets made.

Suitable British bolt-action rifles for the largest game include the .425, the .404 and the .416. The .404 uses a 400-grain bullet at 2,125 with 4,010 foot pounds of energy, the .425 and the .416 drive 410-grain bullets at 2,350 feet per second with a muzzle energy of slightly over 5,000 foot pounds.

Of the two, the best purchase for an American (particularly for the hand-loading gun nut) is the .416, because he can buy .378 Weatherby cases, turn the belts off on a lathe and then run them through a .416 die. He than has reloadable .416 cases which will

The Winchester .458 Model 70 in .458 caliber, such as this one being sighted in at the factory, is a good choice for the American shooter after African big game.

For the big-game hunter who doesn't want to invest in a double rifle, a .416 Rigby on a Brevex Magnum bolt action will stop the big ones.

last almost indefinitely. Incidentally, I load mine with 105 grains of No. 4831 powder behind the 400-grain Barnes .416 bullet. The velocity is 2,450. The energy is considerably above that of the British load. Since World War II, a good many .416 rifles have been built by such custom gunsmiths as Griffin & Howe, Al Biesen and Tom Burgess.

Another good bet for the American rifleman is the .460 Weatherby, which is the .378 Weatherby case necked up to take .45 caliber bullets. With a 500-grain bullet at about 2,800 feet per second at the muzzle, energy is over 8,000 foot pounds, making the .460 the most powerful shoulder arm on earth.

This .416 Rigby is built on a 1917 Enfield action.

Any of these heavy rifles kick like mules, but the recoil of the .416, which, according to my white hunter friends, is adequate for any of the big African game, is less deadly than most. Any of these rifles should weigh at least 9½ pounds and preferably 10 in order to cut down on recoil. My own .416 weighs 10½, and I would not have it lighter.

The use for these cannons is, of course, limited to the very heaviest game, which is found almost exclusively in Africa. They could be used on the Asiatic elephant and on the enormous wild ox, known as the guar, but otherwise there isn't much game in Asia that requires their power and bullet weight.

The favorite tiger cartridges today are the .375 Magnum and the .450/400, which use a 400-grain bullet at 2,150 with a bit over 4,000 foot pounds of energy. It is much like the .404 ballistically, and the energy is not as high as the American-loaded .375 Magnum, which, with the 300-grain bullet at 2,550 feet per second, turns up 4,330 foot pounds.

CHAPTER SIXTEEN

Iron Sights

DESPITE THE FACT THAT TELESCOPE SIGHTS HAVE BEEN GETTING A big play in late years, most gunners still learn to shoot with iron sights. Furthermore, the iron sight is a useful instrument. It has plenty of disadvantages, even in its best forms; but it also has its advantages.

The iron sight is lighter than the scope, less expensive, somewhat more rugged, and less liable to be put out of commission by rain or snow. All this is relative, however. Some iron sights are comparatively fragile, more so than most believe, and are more easily put on the fritz than a correctly mounted scope.

Actually there are four types of iron rear sights. One is the notch, which takes the form of a V or a U cut in a piece of iron. Another is a hole, or "peep." A third form, rarely seen, employs a flat unnotched bar with the center located by a white line or a diamond. Finally, the Patridge type of open rear sight, which, instead of a V or a U, uses a square cut to be employed with a square blade front sight. As we shall see later, the Patridge is the most accurate type of open rear sight.

The use of the open rear sight puts a considerable burden on the human eye. It demands that the user focus on three objects at once—the rear sight, the front sight, and the target. Now the rear sight is about 17 inches from the eye, the front sight between 32 and 38 inches, and the target may be anywhere from a few feet to several hundred yards away. A young man with flexible eyes can make a pretty fair stab at focusing on all three objects simultaneously, but the older man whose eyes have grown less adaptable simply cannot cut it. His rear sight fuzzes up, and he cannot tell how he is holding that front bead in relation to the rear notch. He can still see the front sight and the target but not the rear one. In extreme cases of middle-aged farsightedness, it is sometimes impossible to see even the front sight clearly. In the first

The standard iron rear sights combined with the bead front sight are usually installed at the factory and are hard to adjust.

A better type of rear sight has a flat top and an adjustable V notch.

The most accurate iron sight combination is the peep-type rear sight with the hooded front sight.

case, where only the rear sight fuzzes up, an aperture sight is the only answer. In the second case, the only answer is the scope, because the glass sight puts everything into the same optical plane.

The very essence of the open rear sight is the notch through which the front sight is seen. Anything else is just frosting. The Rocky Mountain buckhorn and semi-buckhorn sights are dearly beloved by those riflemen who don't know much about sights. The "ears" that jut up on these sights do nothing but make game more difficult to see, and, in addition, they blot out light.

Another fallacy commonly entertained about open sights is that the shooter can do better with one that has a narrow rather than a wide V. Actually it is just the opposite. The narrower the V, the more difficult it is to see the same amount of front sight each time. Because it has access to less light, the bottom of the V is darker than the rest. In poor light and under stress of excitement, it is very easy for the shooter to fail to pull the front bead down into the notch. The result is overshooting—and a missed deer. If this narrow V is further complicated by the big, useless, overhanging ears of a buckhorn sight, overshooting is practically certain.

An excellent type of open rear sight is the one Savage used to install on the little Model 99-T. It is a very wide U marked at the center with a white line and used with a red plastic front bead. It makes probably the best type of open rear sight for fast brush shooting.

SHALLOW "V"   BUCKHORN   PEEP

The best type of open iron sight is the Shallow V with a white triangle which hides only half of the animal. The worst iron sight is the buckhorn which hides 2/3 of the animal behind its high wings. With the peep sight the hunter looks through the aperture, puts the front bead where he wants to hit, and shoots.

The British are great believers in open rear sights, usually very shallow V's. They claim that these are the fastest of all sights for brush shooting of large and dangerous game. Whether this is a fact, or simply British conservatism, I don't know.

One of the worst features of most open rear sights is the fact that they are almost impossible to adjust exactly. The typical American open sight has a movable bar with three or four steps cut into it. It is "adjustable" by pushing this bar up under the sight and making the notch higher above the barrel. I continually get letters asking how many yards the second notch on such-and-such a rifle with an open sight will sight in a rifle for. In the old days I used to read hunting stories in which a statement such as this was common: "The buck was 1,000 yards away, so I put the sight in the last notch and killed it."

Now, this kind of statement is based on several misconceptions. In the first place, no one can do much of a job of sighting in a rifle for anyone else, particularly with open sights. In the second place, even at relatively short ranges, a rifle shoots to different points of impact with different loads. In the third place, I don't think those steps have any definite value. I have used sights with steps that gave as little change as four minutes of angle (4 inches at 100 yards), and others that provided as much as eight or ten. The only way anyone can find out about his particular rifle and particular sights is to shoot a group at 100 yards with the rear sight in one notch and then shoot a group under the same conditions with the sight in the second notch. The results give the shooter something definite to go on.

Exact adjustment of the open sight for one load is tough going. It is not uncommon to burn up $10 worth of ammunition to get a $2 sight to put them on the nose. Then if a man wants to change loads, he has to sight in all over again. A cheap nonadjustable sight is the poorest economy I can think of.

Most open rear sights are mounted in a dovetail slot. If the rifle is shooting to the right, the sight has to be tapped a bit to the left, and vice versa. If the rifle is shooting too high with the lowest adjustment, there is nothing to do but file down the notch until she puts them where she looks. If it is shooting low in the first notch, the only thing to do is to hoist her up into the second notch and then file it down, if necessary.

The British ordinarily fit rifles with a whole parade of open rear sights mounted on a short rib. These are presumed to be carefully "regulated" by the maker for various ranges for one certain powder charge and bullet weight, and marked in yards. Maybe all Englishmen see their sights alike, but I know that Americans don't.

Some American firms of custom rifle builders have supplied regulated sights for those who have wanted them. A good many years ago, I dropped in on a custom maker who had just finished up a light .375 Magnum with a 22-inch barrel. It was equipped with a scope on side mounts, and with four leaf sights mounted on a rib. The customer, who was about to take off for an Alaska brown bear hunt, wanted those open leaves adjusted for 100, 200, 300 and 400 yards with the 300-grain Western .375 Magnum load. The barrel and action were still in the white, and the gunmaker slyly asked me how I'd like to go out to the range and file the notches down for the correct ranges so he could finish up the filing, blue the rifle and ship it.

Since it is always hard for me to turn down a chance to shoot for free, I took the job. I used up more than three boxes of ammunition, and I came back full of respect and sympathy for the English rifle makers who do the same job on those ponderous .465, .470 and .600 elephant guns. Presumably my sighting worked out all right, since I heard later that the client got his brownie— and with the open sights.

The receiver sight is more accurate than the open sight, but not as fast as less can be seen through it.

THE APERTURE SIGHT

The peep or aperture sight is a far more logical and effective type than the open rear sight. It is simply a hole to look through. The peep sight works on the optical principle that in looking through an aperture at an object the eye naturally centers the object at the point of strongest light, which is in the middle of the hole.

Most people cannot believe this. They want to draw the bead down "fine" at the bottom of the peep as if it were an open rear sight. The beginner with the peep is annoyed because it looks fuzzy to him. It is supposed to look fuzzy, since the eye does not have enough depth of focus to keep in focus simultaneously both the rear peep close to the eye and the front sight a long way from it. One is supposed to look through the peep, not at it, and to concentrate on putting the front sight on the target.

The beginner with the peep is shocked to find that he can see so much through it. It just doesn't seem right. He rushes off and gets himself a disk with the smallest hole he can find and then he is happy. The disk with the tiny hole is hard to use, which makes everything jake because our shooter probably has the notion that the harder a sight is to use the better it is.

For game shooting, the largest available aperture is the ticket. The Lyman 48 receiver sight comes with a screw-in disk. (I always take it and carefully put it in a box which over the years has been collecting disks until it is practically full.) In some Lyman models there is a little gadget which can be turned up to make the aperture smaller. This I carefully remove and throw away. For target shooting, the small aperture is all right. It sharpens up both front sight and target. For game shooting, however, it is worthless. Actually there isn't much difference between the accuracy obtained with the smallest possible aperture and with the largest. With the disk in a Lyman 48, if a man can shoot a two-inch group at 100 yards, he usually won't do worse than a three-inch group with the large aperture.

Peep sights are mounted in a variety of ways—on the tang (in the case of a rifle of relatively light recoil), on the cocking piece and on the receiver. Because tang and cocking-piece mounted sights are close to the eye, they are very fast. It has been my experience that a big peep is the fastest of all sights—much faster than the open sight and a bit faster than a low-power scope mounted low. For brush shooting in short ranges I know of nothing better. I believe the fastest-handling rifle I ever owned was a seven-pound 7 mm. with a Lyman 1-A cocking-piece sight. The cocking piece, however, always has some wobble in it, and such a sight is not particularly accurate.

The tang sight is easily bent because of the long stem, and in a rifle of heavy recoil it is too close to the eye. With a short stock on a rifle of fairly heavy recoil, an uphill shot presents plenty of chance of putting an eye out. Most tang sights are made with no provision for the adjustment of windage, so that to get one right it is necessary to shim up one side with a piece of paper. Adjustment is made by guess and by gosh.

Today the most popular type of aperture sight is the receiver sight, such as the famous Lyman 48 and the Redfield Series 70. They cost some dough, but they are worth it. Effective, strong and easy to adjust, these are iron sights at their best. With either of them you can shoot a group, measure its distance on the target from where you want it to be, make the adjustments, and your rifle is sighted in. Ordinarily you will save the difference between the cost of an open sight and the cost of a good receiver sight the first time you sight in. It's the difference between burning up six cartridges and burning up 60.

If only iron sights are to be used, the Redfield 70 with the round hunter adjusting knobs can't be beat. It is one of the most rugged sights made. The Lyman 48, however, has one advantage over the Redfield. Its slide can be taken out and put back instantly so there is no change in point of impact; whereas the Redfield slide has to be screwed in and out. If you want to use a receiver sight as an auxiliary along with a scope on a quick-detachable side mount, the Lyman is better because of its instant removal-and-replacement feature. Some receiver sights "click" for $\frac{1}{4}$, $\frac{1}{2}$ and 1 minute of angle. Before sighting in, you should first determine the value of the clicks on your particular sight.

One advantage any iron sight has over a scope is that it is less easily put out of commission by snow or rain. I think that anyone who habitually hunts in wet-brush country or where snow is liable to plop down on him ought to have a quick-detachable scope so that his iron sights will be available in case of need.

Up in northern British Columbia in 1946, I got caught on top of a mountain miles from camp in a rain-snow-sleet storm. My rifle had a permanently mounted scope and no scope covers. When I got back to camp my scope was so waterlogged that it was worthless for several days. Moisture had gotten between the elements of the ocular lens, and every time the temperature changed the scope fogged up so I couldn't see through it. Luckily I had a spare rifle along.

For the very roughest use, auxiliary iron sights are also a good idea. If a scope is hit just right on the ocular, the tube will bend, changing the point of impact.

TYPES OF FRONT SIGHTS

As far as strength goes, the weakest link in the iron-sight system is the front sight. If mounted on a ramp, it is somewhat protected, but the high front sight is really surprisingly fragile, and I have had more trouble with mine than with my scopes. This is particularly true with front sights of ivory and plastic. Since the copper-alloy beads called "gold" are much more rugged, they are generally best for rough usage. In dark woods the ivory bead is the most conspicuous. In good sunlight the red plastic bead seems best. For all conditions, though, gold wins out. The plain flat-topped blade iron sight is the most accurate on the target but hard to see on game.

To some extent, the part of a front sight that looks brightest is likely to be off center, and the rifleman tends to aim with this false center instead of with the whole bead. Thus, if the light is coming from his left, he shoots a trifle too much to the right. This tendency is least marked in the square blade. The worst offender is the shiny gold bead, particularly if it comes to a point in front; shots four inches "off" at 100 yards are not uncommon. The gold bead that is flat on the face is the best type, because it minimizes, although not eliminating entirely, the tendency to shoot away from the light.

Target shots with iron sights always use the blade, usually smoked dead black with camphor or a match. With the six o'clock hold, which has a thin line of white showing between the bull and the top of the blade, this is the most accurate of all front sights.

The six o'clock hold means that if you hold at six o'clock, let us say, the top of the front sight blade touches the bottom of a 12-inch bull at 200 yards, the rifle is sighted in to put the bullet in the middle of the bull, or 6 inches high at 200 yards. Sporting rifles are generally sighted in to put the bullet right where the top of the front bead rests at 200 yards. Therefore, to shoot a good score with a rifle so sighted, one would not hold at six o'clock but try to hold in the middle of the bull.

Front sights take various forms and are found in many sizes. For open country shooting a 1/16-inch bead is all right, but for use under all conditions the 3/32-inch bead is better. A 1/8-inch bead is definitely for quick shooting at short ranges. Foreign gunmakers turn out front sights with auxiliary wide beads, and some American makers have made front sights with as many as three different beads that could be turned into place.

There are many different forms of front sights for target work, including aperture front sights with which aim is taken by centering the bull in the front aperture. The only thing the shooter has to see clearly is the target. Such a sight is great for the farsighted man.

WHEN TO USE IRON SIGHTS

Even with the very best iron sights, the error of aim at 100 yards is about one inch with men with the keenest eyes. Use a 2X scope and that error is cut in half. With a 3X scope it is cut to one-third. All of which explains why the boys in the "any sight" matches always use scopes. This also explains why target shots are going in for scopes of higher and higher power. After all, an X-ring isn't much to hold on. The X-ring, by the way, is a 1-inch ring inside the 2-inch 10 ring. A shot anywhere in the 10 ring counts 10 in small-bore competition but ties are decided by the number of X's or shots within the inner X-ring within the 10 ring.

The varmint shooter has no business with iron sights either, as no iron sight gives good-enough definition to make hits possible at much more than 100 yards even on a fairly large animal like a woodchuck or a jackrabbit. The sure-killing range of an iron-sighted .220 Swift is no better than that of an iron-sighted .22 Hornet, and not much better than that of a .22 rimfire—simply because the rifleman cannot see well enough with iron sights to take advantage of the great accuracy and flat trajectory of the Swift.

Iron sights, then, belong on the big-game rifle that will be used at moderate ranges on large animals. For most deer hunting in woods and brush, the peep with a large aperture and an easily seen front sight are about as good a combination as one can get. Iron sights are also useful on the big-game rifle mounted with a quick-detachable scope so that, under bad conditions, the hunter can fall back on them. Target rifles will continue to be decorated with iron sights for iron-sight matches.

For long-range big-game shooting, for varmint shooting and even for much deer hunting, the scope will give better results. Using the sitting position, a good shot with a big gold-bead front sight and an open rear can just about keep his bullet in an 18-inch circle at 200 yards. With the same front sight and an aperture rear, he can hold in a 12-inch circle. With a low-power hunting scope he can bring the group down to six or eight inches, and with a good 4X scope the group can be cut even more. Plenty of deer are going to be missed at 200 yards with an 18-inch group—and two or three coyotes out of four. The 12-inch group will usually get the deer, but it's likely to miss the coyote. With the $2\frac{1}{2}$X scope and the six-

or eight-inch group, a standing deer at 200 yards is cold turkey, and even out at 300 where the group will open up to between nine and 12 inches, most deer will be hit. With a 2½X scope at 200 yards, I can kill about 50 per cent of the sitting jacks I shoot at. With a 4X scope, I can kill almost all of them. But with a big gold-bead front sight and open rear, killing a jack or a chuck at all at that distance is an accident.

No one can shoot better than he can see, and, in spite of their advantages, iron sights simply do not let the man using them see as well as if he were using glass.

CHAPTER SEVENTEEN

Telescope Sights

IN THE NINETEEN TWENTIES VERY FEW TELESCOPE SIGHTS (SCOPES, FOR short) were in use in the United States, although many were used in Europe, particularly in Germany and Austria. Some target-type scopes were made in this country, and a few German scopes were imported to be used on early American mounts.

A pioneer American manufacturer, the late Rudolph Noske of California, developed a hunting-type scope with internal adjustments for both windage and elevation, and he also developed the first really successful side mount affixed with screws and pins to the side of the receiver of a side-ejecting rifle. German hunting scopes were excellent instruments optically, but they had adjustment for elevation only, and the German mounts were on the whole unsatisfactory. They were difficult to adjust, inexact in adjustment and often did not hold their point of impact. For the most part, the Germans mounted their scopes high enough so that the shooter, if the need arose, could peer at the open iron sights through a tunnel in the scope mount. Since most scopes were mounted on rifles with a high bolt-lift, such as the Springfield and the Mauser, and since gunsmiths had not figured out a way to alter the bolts, most scopes were mounted so high that to see through them the shooter could not put his cheek against the comb of the stock.

Not only did Noske develop the first successful mount, but he also designed a scope with eye-relief long enough that it could be mounted low enough ahead of the bolt-lift to give a line of sight a little higher than that of iron sights.

Then Griffin & Howe, the New York gunsmithing firm, brought out a satisfactory side mount, and W. E. "Bill" Weaver designed the famous Model 330 and 440 scopes, which were simple, inexpensive and optically good. During the nineteen thirties, scopes were beginning to be commonplace. It was not until after World War II, however, that scopes became so much a rule that now most high-quality big-game and varmint rifles are so mounted. Weaver brought out the excellent K series scopes, and Bausch & Lomb went into the scope business. The Lyman Gunsight Co. increased its line, Kollmorgen Optical Co. brought out the superb "Bear Cub" scopes, which are now manufactured by Redfield, and Leupold-Stevens of Portland, Oregon, designed and manufactured the excellent Pioneer and Mountaineer series. In addition to the home-grown product, scopes are imported from Germany, Japan and Austria.

Actually the scope sight for target shooting and hunting is not a new thing, as crude scopes were used as far back as the Civil War on snipers' rifles and on the big black powder rifles used by the buffalo hunters. However, they were very long, optically poor and the mounts were flimsy. The big-game hunting scope as we know it today was developed in Germany and refined in the United States, and today more good scopes are made and used in the United States than in all other countries combined.

CLASSIFICATION OF SCOPES

Scopes are generally classified according to their use. Big-game scopes are generally comparatively small, of relatively low magnifying power, and are designed to be used on rigid mounts. Since these scopes are used on rifles of heavy recoil, they must be built strong, and because they are used on running game they must have wide fields of view—in other words a lot must be seen through them.

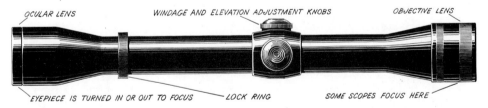

OCULAR LENS   WINDAGE AND ELEVATION ADJUSTMENT KNOBS   OBJECTIVE LENS

EYEPIECE IS TURNED IN OR OUT TO FOCUS   LOCK RING   SOME SCOPES FOCUS HERE

Hunting scope: A scope for the big-game rifle must be sturdy enough to stand the shock of recoil. It should show a sharp, bright image and ample field of view.

Varmint and target scope: This scope is designed for precise shooting at paper targets or long-range varmint hunting.

Varmint scopes are used on rifles designed to take birds, such as crows and harmful hawks, and animals, such as woodchucks and jackrabbits, at long range. Powers run from medium (6X) to high (15X). Some are of the hunting type, with adjustments for windage and elevation in the scope tube, and are of moderate length. Others are of the target type, with no internal adjustments for windage and elevation. They are mounted on micrometer-type mounts which work like micrometers used for measuring tolerances in a machine shop. They "click" for the various graduations—all parts of a minute of angle—½, ¼, ⅛. The minute of angle will change the point of impact 1 inch for each 100 yards of range. That means that a minute of angle has a value of 1 inch at 100 yards, 2 inches at 200 yards, 3 inches at 300 yards, etc.

Target scopes are used in small bore (.22 caliber) shooting and in big bore (.30 caliber) matches. Powers run high, from 10X to 20X, and the scopes have provision for focusing at various ranges: at distances as short as 50 feet for indoor small-bore shooting and as far as 1,000 yards. Many are long and heavy, but that is not a drawback, since target rifles are not carried around. Optical perfection and precise adjustment are the qualities sought. They are always used in micrometer mounts and slide with the recoil.

In addition, many thousands of inexpensive scopes are sold annually which are intended for nothing but .22 rifles. Generally they are not satisfactory for varmint and big-game rifles, because their lenses are not highly corrected, and they are not built to stand the heavy recoil of powerful cartridges.

ADVANTAGES OF THE SCOPE SIGHT

Many believe that the chief advantage of the scope is its magnification. That is one advantage. The principal one is that a scope sight puts the target and the aiming point in the same optical plane. The user of open iron sights has to perform the impossible task of focusing his eye on the rear sight, the front sight and the target, which are all at different distances. Young flexible eyes can make a pretty good stab at it, but older eyes simply are not flexible enough. For the middle-aged man the peep sight makes the task easier because he can look *through* the aperture, put the front sight on what he wants to hit and then shoot. He has only two points to focus on, and since the front sight and the target are near enough in the same optical plane, he is not bothered greatly unless he is extremely farsighted.

But with a scope sight, the aiming point (reticule) and the target are in the same optical plane, and the middle-aged or elderly man can see like a youngster once more. He can also aim with a relatively smaller, more exact device than the large blob of a front sight. With the better definition that the scope affords, the hunter can not only place his shots more exactly but it is easier for him to tell a buck from a doe, or a man in a tan shirt from an elk. Scopes gather light; thus it is possible to make accurate shots under conditions when iron sights would be useless—early or late in the day, by moonlight and by artificial light. In addition, the brightness and good definition of the scope often enable the hunter to see through brush and pick out a deer he could not see to shoot with the unaided eye.

The scope has its disadvantages, but these are outweighed by the advantages. The scope together with its mount is more expensive than iron sights. It is also more fragile. It is more apt to get put out of commission temporarily by rain, snow or wet brush. Finally, it raises the line of sight so that a special stock, although not absolutely necessary, is desirable.

WHAT POWER TO SELECT

In the scope sight, magnifying power comes at a price; the highest usable power is not necessarily the best. All things being equal, the higher the power, the narrower the field of view, the more critical the eye relief and the shallower the depth of focus. A large field is necessary for quick shooting of all kinds and for running shooting. A good $2\frac{1}{2}$X scope has a field of view at 100 yards with a diameter of about 40 feet, but a 4X has a field of about 30 feet and a 6X of around 20 feet. The wider the field, the faster the scope is to "get on with." Any scope used for hunting should have what is known as a "non-critical eye relief." That means that a usable field of view should be obtained at any point from about $2\frac{1}{2}$ inches to 5 inches away from the ocular lens (the lens of the eye piece). If the scope has a critical eye relief, the field grows rapidly smaller if the eye is moved from the point of optimum field, and the field blacks out completely if the eye is too close or too far. This is not important in a target or bench rest scope, because the man behind the scope has all the time in the world, but on a jumping white-tail buck or a galloping jackrabbit it is all-important.

For fast shooting in brush or timber, the hunter needs a wide field, great light gathering power and a non-critical eye relief. A scope of from 2½ to 2¾ is just about ideal. Actually more power is seldom needed for any big-game scope since big-game animals are large and for the most part conspicuous targets. Some of the longest shots I have ever made on antelope, deer, caribou and sheep have been made with low-power scopes. With their satisfactory definition and wide fields, scopes of from 2¾ to 3X are about ideal for all-around use. However, most hunters like a bit more power and the most popular big-game scope is the 4X. It has a bit of the edge on the 3X for plains and mountain shooting and for that purpose it should be chosen. It is also not too bad for medium range varmint shooting. For woods hunting, however, and for the rifle which is to be used both in the brush and in the mountains the 2¾ or 3X scope would be the best compromise. In the brush, the 4X scope is usable with a stock that fits well, but it is inferior to the scope of lower power with its greater latitude and wider field. I have never seen any hunting conditions where more than 4X was needed for big game. Many hunters use 6X scopes for plains and mountains since somewhat more precise aim can be taken with them than with scopes of lower power. Also, details of horns and antlers

Fast Remington Model 760 with a 4X scope is a good combination for brush shooting, although a 2½ or 3X would give a wider field.

The most popular big-game scope is the 4X, mounted here on the author's Winchester Model 70.

can be seen better in case a head is to be picked from a herd at long range. However, the added power is paid for by sacrificing the larger field, shallower focus and the more critical eye relief.

The 6X is seen at its best on a varmint rifle with which shots at small mammals such as woodchucks are not taken over about 250 yards, and when some long-range, running shooting is to be done. The 6X is about right for the coyote and the jackrabbit rifle, and it will get about all out of a .222 that there is in it.

For serious long-range varmint shooting with super-accurate rifles of flat trajectory and great accuracy, powers of from eight to 15 are used in internally adjustable scopes of the hunting type and in target-type scopes on micrometer mounts. For .30 caliber target shooting, the most popular powers are ten and twelve because greater power causes annoying mirage. For small-bore shooting, powers up to 20 are used, and as much as 30X is used by some bench rest shooters.

Since variable power scopes are on the market, at first glance it would seem that with one the shooter could have his cake and eat it too, but in most variable power scopes, the relative size of the crosswire reticule increases with the power. A crosswire that is about right at 4X will be too thin and inconspicuous at 2X and too thick at 8X. An exception is the Bausch & Lomb Bal-8, on which tapered crosswires are etched on glass. With this system, the size apparently remains the same so that at high power the intersection of the crosswires does not blot out small marks.

ADJUSTMENTS

Most hunting-type scopes are internally adjustable for both wind-age and elevation by separate dials with $\frac{1}{4}$-, $\frac{1}{2}$- or 1-minute clicks for both windage and elevation or with graduated dials that do not click. The internally adjustable scope permits a stronger and simpler mount. In most scopes the adjustments are not as uniform and positive as the adjustments in the micrometer-type mount, but they are adequately uniform for all practical purposes. The best practice is to sight in big-game rifles for one load and leave it, checking now and then to see if the rifle and scope are maintaining the point of impact.

Externally adjustable scopes can be made stronger and more nearly dust and waterproof, but the mounts are necessarily more complicated. Take your pick.

RIFLES SUITABLE FOR SCOPES

The older type lever-action rifles that eject the cartridges straight up are not very suitable for scope mounting, as the scopes have to be offset to clear the ejected cases. It is impossible for the man shooting a rifle with an offset scope to get his cheek firmly on the comb and to hold steady. Such rifles include the Winchester Model 94, 71 and 86. On the other hand, Marlin and Savage lever-action rifles, which eject the cases at the side, are suitable for mounting

This Stith scope on a Griffin & Howe side mount is used on an M-1 Garand military rifle.

If the shooter needs to use his iron sights in a hurry, this Weaver Pivot Mount allows him to swing his scope out of the way quickly.

the scopes low and centrally over the bore. Scopes mounted on the old Krag bolt-action rifle likewise have to be offset.

It used to be believed that scopes should not be mounted on rifles with recoil heavier than that of the .30/06, but well-built modern scopes of good quality seem to be able to take almost unlimited recoil. I have used one for many years on a .375 Magnum rifle, and even have one on a .416 Rigby.

Self-loading rifles of the long recoil type, such as the old Remington Model 8 and 81, are hard on scopes because of the jerk and rattle of the recoiling barrel. That applies to a lesser extent to the Remington Model 740 self-loader, which does not have the same type of recoil, since it is gas-operated.

SCOPE-SIGHT RETICULES

Because reticules—the gadgets in telescopic sights by which we aim —are used on all sorts of targets, under many different conditions, and by all sorts of people, they are found in amazing variety. They enable the shooter to aim quickly and accurately. Under some conditions, catching fast aim is more important than precision. Under other conditions, it is accuracy that counts. Some reticules do their job well; others not so well.

In the ordinary type of big-game scope the reticule (reticle, or

Three good reticules: (left) crosswires, (center) flat-top post, (right) dot, suspended on almost invisible crosshairs. Each has special advantages, and there are many variations. In general, the simpler the better.

graticule) is located in a cell which can be pushed up or down, left or right, by means of a couple of screws turning against spring tension. By such adjustments the point of impact of the bullets from the rifle on which the scope is mounted can be regulated. When seen through the scope the reticule looks substantial; actually it is so tiny that in some cases it has to be worked on by the aid of a microscope.

Reticule cells in target-type scopes, which are adjusted by mounts and not internally, are fixed. They are also fixed in some hunting-type scopes, such as the Bausch & Lomb, the old Stith Master line, and one model of Leupold—all of which are designed to be used with adjustable mounts.

The reticule can be located within the scope at any point where an image is formed—either at the plane of the image formed by the objective lens, or at the plane formed after the image has been "erected" (turned right side up) by erecting lenses. In the hunting scope the reticule is usually placed in the focal plane of the objective lens because the adjustment for this mysterious thing called parallax is then independent of focusing for the shooter's vision. (Note: Parallax simply means that the image seen through the telescope and the aiming reticule are not in the same focal plane and that when the head is moved even when the rifle is stationary the reticule will appear to move in relation to the target. This condition is not true when the reticule and the image formed by the objective lens are in the same focal plane.)

If parallax is present, the reticule will appear to move in relationship to the target, so of course accurate shooting cannot be done. It's as if you are looking at two stationary objects—one ten inches from the eye and the other a foot. If the eye is shifted, the nearer object appears to move in relation to the farther object. Parallax is corrected by moving the image to the reticule or the reticule to the image, so they'll both be in the same plane. When this has been done, the shooter can shift his eye up and down, right and left, and the aiming point of the reticule will appear to be pasted to the target.

Reticules are made of many substances. The common "crosshair" reticule is ordinarily made of very fine wire, but the designation "crosswire" has never caught on. The Lee Floating Dot uses for crosshairs the fine, incredibly strong web spun by female blackwidow spiders. Metal posts and crossbars are soldered to the reticule cell. Dots are gobs of shellac, varnish or something of the sort. At various times reticules have been etched on glass. An example of this is the tapered "crosswire" reticule used in the Bausch & Lomb variable power scope.

Once crosshair reticules were actually made of hair. Many years ago I knew a character with a primitive target scope on an old national-match Springfield who claimed he'd plucked a single golden hair from the head of an ash blonde with whom he was in love. Her hair was fine, strong and pliable—precisely right for crosshairs in telescopic sights. He regretted bitterly that some other Romeo had beaten his time, because he didn't know what he'd do if something ever happened to the reticule. He also claimed that he'd tried hairs from brunettes and redheads, but found them too coarse. Some scopemakers have used various animal hairs, such as the long fine ones of the Canada lynx.

Whatever the material, reticules are designed to withstand recoil, but they shouldn't be pushed around. One rifle lover I once knew decided his scope could stand cleaning. He unscrewed the objective and ocular lenses, put the tube to his mouth and gave a hearty blow. To his surprise, he blew the fragile reticule clear out.

Reticules are designed for target, short-range brush and forest shooting on rapidly moving targets, and in 1X shotgun scopes, even for bird shooting. They are also designed for varmint shooting and for long-range use on big game.

Obviously a reticule that covers 6 inches at 100 yards is useless for the man who's trying to stay in a 1-inch X-ring of a 100-yard small-bore target with a match .22 rifle. Likewise the reticule which would enable this target shot to quarter the ten-ring at 100 yards, wouldn't be much use to the deer hunter who wants to catch fast aim on the shoulder of a whitetail tearing through brush at 40 yards in poor light. Then, too, a reticule usable on a snow-white mountain goat standing on a cliff at 500 yards might not even be visible against a whitetail in the Pennsylvania brush.

Many types of reticules have been designed since the telescope sight came into being. For the most part, American scope makers go in for simple reticules, whereas the Germans have always liked them complicated. Fancy reticules fascinate the uninstructed beginner; the old-timer wants them simple.

One of my first scope sights was a German Gerard, a 4X as big as a stovepipe and heavy enough to beat a grizzly's brains out. It had in it the flossiest reticule I've ever seen—four picket posts, a crosshair and a dot. I used to get so interested watching that wonderful reticule that I'd forget to shoot, and when another scope lover put a hammerlock on me and demanded that I part with scope and mount for $30, he didn't have to twist very hard.

Since most scope users have graduated from using the receiver sight, their common choice is some sort of post reticule, since it resembles a front sight seen through the aperture of a receiver sight. Although I swore by the post reticule for a time, gradually I abandoned it for other types.

A flat-top post is best, with the top subtending (covering) from four to six minutes of angle (four to six inches at 100 yards, eight to 12 inches at 200 yards, etc.). Such a post is conspicuous even in poor light, and surprisingly accurate. I used to make up a special target for post reticules—an inverted T with the bars as wide as the amount the flat-top post subtended. Holding so I could just see white at the bottom of the T, I'd shoot groups about as small as I could by quartering a bull with crosshairs.

One enormous disadvantage of the post, however, is that when one must hold over to allow for bullet drop, the post blots out too much target. For that reason it's a poor choice for the varmint hunter—and not too good for the big-game hunter who may have to shoot at long range. It is at its best for brush shooting at relatively short ranges.

Post reticules are often made in combination with a crosswire. The argument for the addition of the crosswire is that it will enable a rifleman to tell if he is canting his rifle. For my part I never pay any attention to the horizontal crosswire but see only the tip of the post. However, some people swear by this combination. The crosswire often confuses the beginner, who doesn't know whether he should aim with the top of the post or with the point lower down where the post and crosswire meet. This uncertainty could be avoided if the top of the crosswire and top of the post were even. But I've never seen such a deal. Because of the way the post-crosswire combination is now made, I prefer the plain post.

About once a week, some chap writes me he has the solution to the post reticule's holdover problem. Put the post in upside down, he says, and you can hold over without blotting out the target. The idea is actually an old one, but it has never caught on.

Less efficient forms of the post reticule are the picket and the blunt post. The sharp point of the picket tends to blend with the target, causing sour shots, particularly high ones. With the blunt post, there is a good deal of lateral error.

One of the most useful reticules of all is the crosswire or crosshair. It is very good, since the eye naturally finds the place where the two wires cross. Fine crosswires or crosshairs can be used for high-power target and varmint scopes, medium for all-around use, coarse for low-power big-game scopes for use in heavy cover. Provided that the "wires" are sufficiently thick, they can be used in very poor light, since it is only necessary to see a section of the wires in order for the eye to locate their intersection point. These reticules are strong and easy to install.

I've seen no mention in print, except by me, of another great virtue of the crosshair reticule: it is excellent for shots at running game. When I lived in Arizona and used to pop away at running jackrabbits and coyotes as well as at running deer, I found the crosshairs far superior to posts for that work.

The lower the power of the scope, the more the crosshair has to subtend in order to be conspicuous. The crosswire in a $2\frac{1}{2}$X hunting scope should cover about $1\frac{1}{2}$ to 2 inches at 100 yards in order to be readily seen under poor light conditions; and in a 4X, about $\frac{3}{4}$ to 1 inch. Obviously, since in most optical systems the reticule is enlarged along with the object at which aim is taken, the higher the power of the scope the finer the crosswires can be and still stand out.

Crosswires in Weaver K-scopes are an excellent compromise. When I was in Africa, I shot a good deal of game with a .257 Weatherby Magnum on which I had mounted a Weaver K-4 scope. The crosswires were just right for the 4X magnification. I had neither any trouble seeing their intersection point in brush at close range, nor in holding high way out at long range. I killed a zebra with one shot at 437 long paces across level ground. I also shot a Roberts' gazelle with the same outfit at about that distance.

For open country the fine crosswire in the scope on my .300 Magnum was excellent, but in the brush it was sometimes hard to pick up quickly against well-camouflaged animals like the kudu, particularly when they were strongly marked with lights and shadows and when there were many small limbs.

Crosswires in the 2¾X on my .375 Magnum were excellent, as were the ones in the Bausch & Lomb 2½X to 4X scope on a .270 when set at 4X. At 2½X they were a bit fine to be ideal. In all variable-power scopes, crosswires stay the same size relative to the target. But they look larger when the scope is set for the higher power. Wire size that is OK for a scope set at 6X, let us say, is pretty skinny when the scope is set at 2¾X.

The dot reticule was popularized in this country by the late T. K. Lee, of Birmingham, Alabama, an accomplished rifle and shotgun shot. Lee dots are suspended on spider-web crosshairs of such amazing fineness that one has to look hard to see them. The dot makes an excellent reticule and in various sizes is suitable for almost any purpose. For the 2½X or 2¾X hunting scope, a reticule subtending four or five minutes is about right. Those who use such scopes exclusively for brush shooting often get six-minute or even eight-minute dots.

For my part, I like a four-minute dot in a 2½X scope and a 2 or 2½-minute dot in a 4X scope. In a 6X scope, a 1½-minute dot is in order, and, for an 8X varmint scope, a 1-minute dot should answer. One great advantage of the single-dot reticule is its speed. There is nothing else in the field to distract the attention. All one has to do is to put the dot in the right place and squeeze off. In the appropriate size, a dot reticule is also a good one for shots at running animals. Most scope makers will furnish Lee or other dot reticules at extra cost.

It's possible to have a whole flock of dots of various sizes strung along the vertical crosshair, each dot being zeroed for a certain range, but they clutter the field, and although they're fine in theory I doubt if they work well in practice. I like the single dot. Probably the best big-game shooting I've ever done was with an old .270 equipped with a 2½X Lyman Alaskan scope with a four-minute Lee dot. I shot that outfit at everything from galloping jackrabbits to Dall sheep and Osborn caribou and got pretty handy with it.

I used to sight in the .270 with the 130-grain bullet, having a muzzle velocity of 3,140 foot seconds, to strike about three inches above the center of the four-minute dot, or about one inch above the top of the dot, at 100 yards. At 200 yards, the bullets struck right where the top of the dot rested. At 100 and 200 yards, I aimed with the top of the dot and had no trouble hitting jacks at 200 yards or so. If an animal was about 300 yards away, I used the middle of the dot as an aiming point, because at factory velocities this bullet drops about 6 inches between 200 and 300 yards. If I thought a standing animal was about 350 yards away, I tried to aim with the bottom of the dot.

If I sighted in to hit at 275 yards, where the center of the four-inch dot rests, at 350 yards the 130-grain .270 bullet, having dropped about 8 inches, would be slightly below the bottom of the dot, which at that distance subtends 14 inches. At 400 yards, the dot subtends 16 inches and the bullet is striking 16 inches low, or half the width of the dot below the bottom edge of it.

Once when hunting elk in Wyoming, I figured that a bull elk was about 600 yards away. I held 1½ widths of the dot over the top of his back—or tried to. Luck was with me. I shot twice, hit the elk twice. He didn't move 20 yards.

Anyone who spends a bit of time with a bullet-drop table can work out some data which will be of great help to him in long-range shooting.

Scope reticules can be used as range finders, if a man has some notion as to the physical dimensions of the game he hunts. From belly line to top of shoulder a coyote, for instance, is generally about nine inches thick. A small deer will measure from 14 to 16 inches, a large deer from 18 to 20, an antelope from 15 to 17, a large mountain sheep or mountain goat from 20 to 22, an elk from 26 to 28, and a bull moose from 34 to 40 inches.

Bill Weaver makes a range-finder reticule for his K-scopes with two horizontal crosswires 6 minutes apart. If we discover, while looking through it, that the chest of a mule deer takes up the whole space between the wires, it's a good guess that he's about 300 yards away. If a big mountain sheep fills that space and a shade more, he's probably around 400 yards away. We can also get some notion of range by comparing an animal's thickness from top of

Range-finding. If deer at left fills 6-minute space between Weaver cross-wires it is 300 yards away. The 4-minute dot at right is on the same buck at the same distance.

shoulder to bottom of brisket with the six-minute flat-top of a post, or with the known value of a dot reticule. These guides help all of us, especially because the deceptive conditions of light and terrain can interfere in judging range.

Another special-purpose reticule is made for use at night. The Germans have made reticules lit by a tiny globe powered by a miniature battery. Another foreign night reticule has four heavy posts with crosswires. But as good as any of these night types is the wide flat-top post reticule. Installed in a good bright scope, it's surprising how well it lets you see to shoot by moonlight.

CHAPTER EIGHTEEN

Mounts for Hunting Scopes

TODAY THERE ARE MANY SATISFACTORY TELESCOPIC SIGHT MOUNTS, some mass-produced, others hand-made in small quantities. There are side-bracket mounts, bridge (or top) mounts, and V-block top mounts, each with advantages and disadvantages which will be discussed later in this chapter.

EARLY SCOPE MOUNTS

German scopes imported into the United States just after World War I were excellent, and the demand they created was responsible for the development of the scope industry in the United States. But German mounts, practically without exception, were terrible. German hunters, who bought scopes in great numbers, evidently never considered the glass anything but an auxiliary sight. Their rifles were stocked for iron sights, and scopes were mounted very high to clear them. And the typical German scope mount was tunneled so that the user could peer through a hole in the mount and aim with iron sights while the scope remained in place.

Most of those mounts consisted of two plates, one on the receiver ring and the other on the receiver bridge. To mount his scope, the shooter slipped a hooked leg into a hole in the front plate by putting it in at an angle. The round rear leg had a notch cut in it, and it was locked by a half-round post turned into position by a lever.

These scope mounts enabled the glass to be taken off and put on very quickly. As we have seen, the scopes were good, and it was great fun to look through them. But they were mounted so high that the shooter's cheek had no support on the comb and it was hard to shoot accurately. Furthermore, the high-mounted scope usually was a heavy one, and its inertia, working against the violent recoil of the rifle, battered the hooked leg, generally made of soft metal, and then the scope would not hold its point of impact. The first hunting scope I ever had was a big German 4X on one of these trick mounts. The scope was a sweetheart optically, but because of the mount it was worthless for shooting.

German scopes were made adjustable for elevation only, and it was necessary for their mounts to provide for the windage adjustment, even though that meant bending the scope with a powerful instrument that looked like a skate key. American scope designers, however, quickly developed scopes with internal adjustments for both windage and elevation. This improvement, pioneered by Rudolph Noske of San Carlos, California, enormously simplified the mount problem. Then Bill Weaver came out with his Models 330 and 440 scopes, which had dual adjustments, and the Lyman Alaskan also made its bow. Now there are many fine American made or designed scopes of the hunting type—Weaver, Lyman, Leupold, Bushnell, Bausch & Lomb, Redfield and Weatherby. Some have dual adjustments and some don't. Magnifying power varies from $2\frac{1}{2}$X to 10X. Nowadays American scopes rank with the top practical hunting scopes in the world, and, in their class, some are the best in the world.

Reams of literature have been written on selecting a scope, but very little on choosing a proper mount. As a consequence, the beginner is often confused. Since the various types of mounts have their faults and their virtues, if you want to buy a scope you should first ask a few pertinent questions.

1. Is the scope to be put on a rifle and left there, or is it to be used in conjunction with auxiliary iron sights?

2. Is the scope to be used on more than one rifle?

3. Is the mount expensive to put on?

4. Do you like the appearance of the mount? And if it is of the quick-detachable type, does the rifle present a clean appearance when the mount is removed?

5. If you have a change of heart, can the mount be removed without leaving the receiver—and perhaps the barrel—full of holes, plus a gaping cut in the stock?

6. Does adjustment require special tools?

7. Will the scope-mounted rifle be carried in a saddle scabbard?

The choice of a scope mount should depend on how these questions are answered. Some mounts can be quickly removed and replaced without affecting accuracy, permitting convenient use of

Two basic types of telescope mounts are the bridge, or top, mount (left) and the side-bracket mount.

auxiliary iron sights. Some mounts give maximum protection to the scope; others do not. Some can be easily and cheaply installed; others require a half day's work by a skilled gunsmith-machinist. And only some mounts facilitate the use of the same scope on more than one rifle.

Although the various makes of mounts differ in detail, actually they fall into a few general types, because there are only a limited number of ways to hang a scope on a rifle.

Side-Bracket Mount. The first satisfactory American scope mount, originated by Noske, was the side bracket. The base portion is a plate screwed and pinned (and sometimes sweated) to the left side of the receiver. The top of the base portion is a male dovetail; the bottom of the removable portion has a female dovetail and brackets for the scope. The two portions are held tight together by various means, including screws and half round posts. Representative mounts of this type are the old Noske, Griffin & Howe and the Jaeger. The Pachmayr Lo-Swing mount is of novel design: its plate is screwed to the left side of the receiver, but the detachable portion—with the rings for the scope tube—swings on male and female cones.

The great advantage of side-bracket mounts is that they permit the scope to be detached quickly so iron sights can be used. An open iron sight can be left in place, or a receiver sight with a quick-removable slide can be used. Then it takes just a moment to remove the scope and slip in the slide of a receiver sight, such as the Lyman 48.

When the scope is removed, the top of the receiver is clear, and, since the base of the mount is inconspicuous, the rifle presents a clean appearance.

A side-bracket mount like the Mykrom permits the scope to be detached quickly so iron sights can be used.

To my way of thinking, this combination of scope and iron sights is the best deal for the man who wants both kinds of sights on his rifle. And that's a good idea when a hunter goes on a long wilderness trip with only one rifle, or hunts in a section where he will encounter rain, snow and wet brush, or when he will, for the most part, carry his rifle in his hands rather than in a saddle scabbard.

When a rifle is stocked with a side mount, however, the wood of the stock surrounds its base. Removing the mount leaves an ugly gap in the stock. That's one disadvantage of the side mount. There

The Pachmayr Lo-Swing side-bracket mount allows scope to be pushed to one side, making iron sights immediately available to the shooter.

Shooter removes his Lyman 48 receiver sight (top) and slips a Stith 4X scope onto a side-bracket Griffin & Howe mount (below).

is another drawback: if a rifle equipped with a side mount is wedged into a too-snug saddle scabbard, some side-bracket mounts may bend under the pressure.

But the side-bracket mount has another advantage: if two rifles are equipped with base portions, a single scope with internal adjustments can be used on both. (Of course, the scope must be sighted in each time it is switched.) This interchangeability is possible in some, but not all, side mounts; there are outfits in which the base and top portions are individually fitted and do not always interchange.

Designed for more permanent scope mounting, the bridge, or top, mount is attached to the receiver bridge and ring. This is a Redfield Jr. Mount with windage adjustment.

A side mount is a good bet for the man who wants both iron and scope sights on a rifle. I have a pair of rifles made especially for far-northern and overseas hunting, one a .30/06, the other a .375 Magnum. I wanted to be able to remove the scopes for shipping the rifles long distances in carrying cases. I also wanted to have good iron sights available if required. Both rifles were equipped with Griffin & Howe mounts and Lyman 48 peep sights. I have carried an ancient .270, fitted with a Noske side mount and various 22 mm. scopes, at least 2,000 miles in a saddle scabbard with no complaints. My feeling is that if a man takes but one rifle on a long trip, it should have a side mount permitting him to use both scope and iron sights.

Bridge (or Top) Mount. Attached to the receiver bridge and ring, this popular type is the one for the man who wants to put a scope on a rifle, sight it in, and leave it there. It is also the mount for the man carrying his rifle in a saddle scabbard who often dismounts, yanks out his musket and takes a shot at something.

Examples of top bridge mounts are the famous Redfield Jr., Buehler, Mashburn, Tilden, Weaver, and Williams. Most of them are relatively inexpensive and easy to mount, since they employ holes already tapped and drilled in the receiver ring and bridge of many rifles. In any case, it is necessary only to tap and drill three or four holes. When the holes are factory drilled and tapped, the Buehler and the Redfield mounts can be put on by anyone who can use a screwdriver. No stock cuts are necessary, and when the base is removed the rifle is as new.

The Redfield Jr. is typical of bridge mounts. Its bases are made to fit various rifles; its rings to fit different scope-tube diameters. The shooter can use the same scope on several rifles, or several scopes on one rifle, provided he sights in each time he makes a change. The standard Buehler employs the same system: a base that is a bar screwed to the receiver and rings for the scope tube. In each, the rear portion of the mount is held to the base with opposing screws which control windage. This feature is very handy when a scope has no windage adjustment within the tube—the old Stith 2½X Bear Cub, for example, and such foreign scopes as those made by

The Stith Streamline is a sturdy bridge mount especially suitable for saddle-scabbard use. Note the scope does not overhang the front of the mount.

Zeiss and Hensoldt. Redfield furnishes rings for most foreign scopes, and you can buy custom rings for the occasional odd one. These mounts are also made with two-piece bases.

An interesting variation of the bridge mount is the Adjusto Mount made for the Leupold 2½X and 4X scopes, which have no internal adjustments. Both the windage and elevation adjustments are entirely within the base of the mount. Consequently, the same scope can be used on as many rifles as one has bases for, once adjustments have been made for each rifle. Scopes with no internal adjustments are cheaper to make, stronger and more nearly waterproof. The Leupold scope and mount form a good outfit, although one needs a special Allen wrench for adjustment. Nevertheless, scopes without internal dual adjustments run into a good deal of consumer resistance, because American rifle users have been pretty well conditioned to demand both windage and elevation in the scope itself. Mounts with both adjustments are also made by Bausch & Lomb and Buehler.

V-Block Top Mount. This type of mount utilizes the V-block principle for bringing the scope back into alignment after it has been removed and replaced. The old Pike mount was of this sort.

The Stith Master Mount and the Bausch & Lomb mount utilize the V-block principle, but the V's are formed by opposing cones on which the scope tube rests. One adjustment knob moves a set of cones right or left for windage; a second knob brings another set together or apart for elevation.

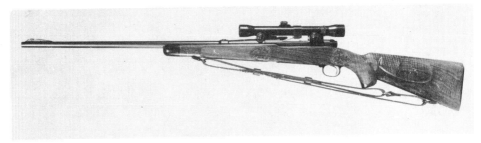

The V-block top mount also has its own adjustments. This Stith Master mount, once it is sighted in can be used for more than one scope.

These two mounts were designed for scopes without internal adjustments—the various types of the Bausch & Lomb, Leupold Pioneer scopes and Kollmorgen scopes. With either mount, the same scope can be used on as many rifles as one has bases for, and no further sighting in is necessary once each base has been adjusted. Another advantage: with either mount, two scopes can be sighted in for one rifle—one by the windage and elevation in the base, the other by the adjustments within the tube. Both mounts have supplementary peep sights that require special high front sights.

Now let's review the advantages and the disadvantages of each type of mount.

Side-Bracket Mounts. Advantages: Best when scope is frequently removed, because it allows the scope to be replaced exactly. Best when auxiliary iron sights are wanted. Only bet when one wants to use supplementary receiver sight.

Best when target scope is also to be used with blocks on bridge and barrel. Adaptable in most cases to use of one scope on two or more rifles, sighting in at each change. Good for the long wilderness trip when only one rifle is to be carried and two sets of sights are desired. Leaves clean appearance when scope is removed.

Disadvantages: Expensive to mount; means drilling holes in side of receiver. Leaves gap in stock when base is removed. Generally not strongest type for saddle and very rough use, because of considerable overhang of scope tube.

Bridge Mount. Advantages: Strong, good for saddle-scabbard use. Takes recoil in straight line.

It's cheap to mount. Leaves receiver clean with no unnecessary holes when base is removed. Some mounts of this type (such as **Redfield Jr.**) lend themselves to use of one scope on two or more rifles, if sighted in at each change. Best when one scope is to be put on the rifle and left there.

Disadvantages: Impossible to use with receiver sights. Should not be chosen if auxiliary iron sights are wanted.

V-Block Top Mount. Advantages: Cheap to mount. Since adjustments are in base, best of all types to choose when one scope is to be used on several rifles. It has very exact adjustments. Receiver looks neat when bases are removed.

Disadvantages: Receiver looks cluttered up when scope is removed but base is left on. And some riflemen dislike the looks of the mount itself. Adjustment knobs may be accidentally turned in saddle scabbard. Mount not good for scope with thin-walled aluminum tube, since a dent could change point of impact. But O.K. with thick-walled aluminum-alloy tube like Bausch & Lomb's, or with steel tube.

Every type of mount, then, has its advantages and disadvantages, and your choice should be made accordingly.

In every case the scope should be mounted as low as possible so the cheek can have maximum contact with the comb. And let the mount buyer beware of anyone who'd sell him the ancient and discredited plan of having iron sights available *under* the mounted scope.

In general, the man who hunts in country of little snow and rain, such as the Southwest, should choose the strongest, simplest type of bridge mount he can get, mount his scope with it and leave it there. This also holds true for the sportsman who does most of his hunting on horseback.

On the other hand, the man who has to hunt in a land of much moisture, such as the rain-forest country of the Pacific Coast, should by all means have a side-mounted scope plus a good receiver sight. Wet brush or rain can put a scope temporarily out of commission. Although he may need an extra sight only once in a blue moon, the combination is a good bet for the wilderness hunter a long way from a gunsmith.

The man who wants to use two scopes (such as a $2\frac{1}{2}$X and a 6X) on one rifle, or the same scope on two or more rifles, is just about limited to such mounts as the Bausch & Lomb or Leupold Adjusto, which also have both windage and elevation in the base.

Each type of mount has its points, so look them over and choose.

CHAPTER NINETEEN

Seven-Lesson Rifle Shooting Course

ONE OF THE FIRST THINGS THAT THE BEGINNER WITH A RIFLE SHOULD realize is that good shots are made, not born. A young man may be descended from rifle-shooting pioneer ancestors on both sides. He may have been born in Texas, Arkansas, Arizona, or some other place reputed to be swarming with good rifle shots. A lad may inherit good eyes and good muscular co-ordination, and if he does, learning to shoot will undoubtedly be easier. But he still will not become a good shot without intelligent practice.

Many men go deer hunting every fall for a lifetime and never become good rifle shots. Most of them do not fire 40 rounds of ammunition a year. Their practice for the big-game season consists usually of going out to a quarry, or some other place where they can shoot safely, putting up a home-made target, and firing a few shots. If one of the bullets hits in or around the bulls-eye, they are happy and ready to take on the biggest elk, bear, or buck in the country.

Some guides are very good shots, some very poor shots. The good shots among guides are those who are interested in rifle shooting and who do a lot of intelligent practice shooting. The poor shots are those who are not particularly interested in shooting and who do little practicing. Many men live in wilderness areas and kill a lot of game and yet are indifferent rifle shots. I have seen men who have made a good part of their living with their rifles but who hadn't the faintest idea of how to sight a rifle in, or what the trajectories of their rifles were.

Many think they are crack rifle shots because they generally kill a deer every season. Actually big-game animals are large targets and more often than not they are shot at close range. Furthermore, these chaps do not count their misses nor the deer they wound. Such "practical" rifle shots often say that they can't hit paper targets but they are poison on anything that runs, flies, sheds feathers, or leaks blood.

Is it easier to hit game than targets? It is not. The black and white target is conspicuous. It is at a known distance, and it stands still. It is far easier to hit than the neutral colored game animal often partially concealed by brush and grass.

Poor rifle shots dislike shooting at targets because they tell them unpleasant stories, just as poor shotgun shots hate to have score kept when they shoot skeet or traps. No one ever becomes a good shot unless he has some way of checking where his bullets hit.

THE BASIC FACTS ABOUT SHOOTING

The elements of good rifle shooting are simple and not very spectacular. They consist of learning to assume the steady and orthodox shooting positions which have been worked out by trial and error by generations of fine rifle shots. To hit any stationary object the rifle must be held as steady as possible. Then the shot must be let off with as little disturbance of aim as possible. This means squeezing rather than jerking the trigger. Then the rifleman must acquire the ability to call his shot—to know exactly where his sights rested when he completed his trigger squeeze.

Just as no one can be a first-class shot unless he can hold his rifle fairly steady and can squeeze his trigger so that the aim is not disturbed, no one can become a first-class shot until he can call his shots.

A rifle firing the .22 rimfire cartridge is the best to begin with, as both report and recoil are light and the beginning rifle shot is spared the jarring recoil and the disturbing report of a more powerful cartridge, such as the .30/06. Another great advantage of the .22 rimfire is that ammunition is relatively cheap, and a great deal of practice can be had at small cost. The .22 rifle chosen by the beginner need not be expensive, but it should have a good trigger pull, and an adjustable rear sight so that the rifle can be accurately sighted in for the individual user. Preferably it should be equipped with a sling, an aid not only to carrying but to accurate holding and shooting.

LESSON NO. 1: AIMING

Let us assume that you, the reader of this book, are a beginner who has never shot a rifle or has done little shooting. First, let us look at the sights. The front sight is affixed to the end of the barrel by some means. Sometimes it is a simple blade, but the sight for hunting is most commonly a bead of some kind—gold, silver, or ivory. The rear sight may be installed about two-thirds of the way back on the barrel—and always, if it is an "open" sight, in the form of a U or a V. It is necessary that open sights be a considerable distance from your eye because both open rear sight and front sight must be seen in fair focus if correct aim is taken.

"Peep" or "aperture" sights are generally installed on the receiver of the rifle, because the closer they are to your eye, the easier they are to see through—just as you can see more through a keyhole when you are close to it. The peep sight need not be seen clearly. You simply look *through* it, put the front sight on what you want to hit, and squeeze the trigger. *The eye naturally centers the front sight in the middle of the aperture.* No effort should be made to center the front sight and no effort should be made to see the rear peep sight clearly.

But remember that correct sight alignment is one of the essentials of good rifle shooting. The shotgun is roughly aligned or "pointed." It is generally used with only a front sight but can be shot well with no sights at all. But with the more precise rifle with its single missile, the sights must be correctly aligned.

As we have seen, you should look *through* your aperture rear sight, paying no attention to centering the front sight in it, and seeing it only as a circular out-of-focus blur. The open rear sight is something else again. The front sight should be seen in the middle of the open U or V and generally the top of the front sight should be level with the top of the rear sight. The same sight picture should always be seen and no attempt made to take a "fine" or a coarse bead.

A   B   C   D

The eye naturally and automatically centers the front sight in the rear peep as at D.

There are three ways of aiming with the front sight. Target rifle-men generally sight in with iron sights to strike the middle of the bullseye with a 6 o'clock hold—the top of the front sight at the bottom of the bull. For game shooting this is not practical because the bullet strikes too far above the sight. For most purposes, you have the choice of aiming either with the center of a bead front sight (having the bullet strike right where the middle of the bead rests) or aiming with the top of the front sight—having the bullet strike where the *top* of the front sight rests. This is generally pre-ferred, as with the center-of-the-bead method too much of the target is covered up.

When aiming, care should be taken to keep the rifle upright. "Canting," which means leaning the weapon to one side, will result in wild shots. Most people cant a rifle to some extent, and if the rifle is always canted the same, pretty good shooting can be done in spite of the fault. However, it is best to start right and not cant. It is

"Six o'clock" hold with Patridge-type sights (left). Proper alignment of U-type rear sight with front bead (center). Proper alignment of V-type rear sight with front bead (right).

"Six o'clock" hold with peep sight (left). Aperture sights (right) can be sighted in so that the point of impact (X) rests in the middle of the front bead, or so the point of impact rests at the top of the front bead. Most shooters prefer the second method.

Drawing too "fine" a bead (left) makes the shot go low. A "course" bead (center) makes the shot go high. "Canting" (right) will throw the shot off.

helpful to have someone stand in front of you and look directly at the muzzle of your rifle when you hold it naturally. He can then detect the cant and tell you so you can correct it.

Most beginners (and many who have been shooting for a long time) close one eye when aiming. This is a habit that should be broken. If you close one eye you lose the advantages of binocular vision. You cut down on what you can see and make it more difficult to judge range. Shotgun shooter, rifleman, or pistoleer—all should shoot with both eyes open.

It is important that you remember to relax. Don't grip your weapon like grim death; rather, hold it firmly but gently. Taut and rigid muscles make for shake and tremor. You should also remember that the work of holding the butt against your shoulder is done with your right hand pressing the piece back and that your left hand (if you are a right-handed shooter) serves merely to steady and swing the piece. In holding the rifle your right thumb should be acrosss the top of the grip and NOT alongside as is often seen. The thumb around the grip gives better control, aids in smooth let-off of the trigger. The thumb-along-the-stock business started because of the too-short stock on the old 1903 Springfield. Your cheek should be against the comb of the stock for steadiness. Your left elbow, under most circumstances, should be under or just about under the forend, and not over to one side, as that promotes shake and tremor.

Correct and orthodox shooting positions will help you hold your weapon with a minimum of sway and wobble, but no one can hold a rifle with absolute steadiness. Even from a bench rest a telescope sight of high power will show a bit of movement.

LESSON NO. 2: SQUEEZING THE TRIGGER

Your first shooting should be from a rest—a bench rest if one is available or if not from the prone position over a padded box, a rolled up bedroll or something of the sort. The reason for this is that you can then concentrate on squeezing the trigger and don't have to worry about holding the rifle steady.

The best way to learn to shoot well is to get into the habit early in the game of squeezing, not jerking or yanking, the trigger. The best practice is to concentrate on the target and increase the pressure on the trigger when the "sight picture" is right and to stop the squeeze when the sights swing off. Theoretically the rifle goes off without your being aware that things are about to pop. This does not give you time to yank or flinch.

In time, however, most shooters learn their pull and know just about when their rifles are going off, but they still complete the let-off with a smooth and even *squeeze*, not a yank. They do this by concentrating on the sight picture.

The whole secret of becoming a good shot is to get good shooting habits so ingrained that you are unaware of them. With thoughtful practice you can learn to squeeze and when the sight picture on target or game looks exactly right the rifle will go off. This business of squeezing so gradually that you presumably don't know the instant before your rifle will go off is called *surprise fire*. Poor shooting generally does not come from inaccurate aiming or from wobble, but from jerking the trigger and flinching the moment before the rifle goes off. Surprise fire is the way to beat this.

Later you can develop the ability to squeeze out the last ounce of the trigger pull as the sights hang just right on the bull or the jumping whitetail buck goes over the log. This is sometimes called a *controlled jerk*, and is the way an experienced rifleman shoots a rifle from offhand.

Often we hear of rifles being held "as steady as a rock," but that is merely a figure of speech as long as there is a human being on the other end of one. We all have muscles that tremble, joints that wobble, blood that courses through our veins, hearts that beat. We are all jittery fellows full of phobias, frustrations and complexes. Just as there is no such thing as absolute darkness or absolute quiet in nature, there is no such thing as holding a rifle absolutely steady, even on a bench rest.

From a good solid rest, an accomplished rest-shooter can hold a rifle relatively steady. In a good prone position, all wrapped up in a tight sling, a good prone shot can hold his rifle almost as steady. The good shot from the sitting position can hold one fairly steady. But the offhand shooter cannot hold his rifle steady at all.

From any position, then, the rifle must be touched off when the sights are right. It takes less skill to do this from a bench rest than from any other way of shooting. And that is why the ideal way for you to start shooting is from a bench rest or, if a bench rest isn't available, from prone position over a sandbag rest. Then you can progress to prone without a rest, to sitting and finally to offhand.

Just before you get ready to squeeze off, take a deep breath. Then let out part of it and don't breathe again until you finish squeezing off your shot. If you still haven't got the shot off when you run out of wind, put the rifle down, take another breath, let some of it out, and start over again. Do NOT yank off the shot just because you want to breathe.

Another thing you should keep in mind is follow-through. Just as in golf the follow-through (the path of the hands and the club head *after* the ball is hit) is important, so it is in shooting. It is important to squeeze off so gently as not to disturb your aim and you should try to keep the sight right on the bull after the firing pin falls. If you let go all holds the instant you fire, the result will be a flinch.

LESSON NO. 3: CALLING THE SHOT

Two things go hand in hand—controlling the trigger and *calling the shot*. As you squeeze the trigger, you should take up, let us say, about three pounds, twelve ounces of your four-pound pull, then when the sights steady for an instant on your target, carefully, quietly, delicately *squeeze* out those extra ounces. Then it is important to form the habit of keeping a mental picture of exactly how those sights were aligned as the rifle recoiled.

In the instant between the time your mind told you to let off the shot and the time when you actually did let it off, the sights may have wandered away a little. But you should know it and have called it. If, let us say, you call a bull but get a three at four o'clock, something is wrong. It is a safe bet that you flinched.

The man trying to master trigger squeeze may not make much of a score, but if his shots are where he calls them he is on his way. The man who cannot call his shots, who does not *always* call his shots as a matter of habit, even under the excitement of big-game shooting, isn't even getting to first base as a rifle shot. He may kill game, but when he does it is more or less of an accident and naturally reflects scant credit upon him.

The man who calls his shots will lose little wounded game because he knows when he ought to hit, just as he knows when he lets one off on the target range that his shot is going to be a five or a very close four at worst.

As an illustration, I once took three shots at a big buck trotting along the opposite side of a ravine in Arizona, not more than 175 yards away. The buck didn't flinch and every time I shot I saw dust swirl up apparently above the buck's back. I wasn't excited. The shots weren't difficult. I was in the sitting position and I was swinging the muzzle just a bit faster than the buck was moving. When the vertical crosshair of the scope was about two feet ahead of the buck's brisket, I touched off. Nevertheless the buck trotted around the point and disappeared.

"Shot right over him every damned time!" said my companion.

"Looks like it," I said half-heartedly.

Something was odd there! I had called those shots. Every one of them should have been in the chest cavity. Unless my rifle had suddenly changed its point of impact or I was unconsciously flinching or stopping my swing, I couldn't dope it out. Across the ravine, about where the buck had run, was a white rock about six inches in diameter. I put the crosshairs on it and squeezed off. The rock shattered.

"Come on!" I said to my guide. "Let's go look for that buck!"

He had traveled about 100 yards after he got around the point, and when we found him he was as dead as Cleopatra with three .30/06 bullets, which for some reason hadn't opened up worth a darn, right through his lungs. They had gone through and kicked up dust on the other side. We had seen dust above the buck and had assumed the shots had gone high.

I got my first moose because I called my shot instead of taking for granted that I missed him when he ran away without faltering. I was hunting alone, and the moose got up in heavy timber around 35 yards away. I shot as he quartered away and called it right against the curve of his paunch and so angled that it ought to drive up into his lungs. Not a drop of blood showed, but I found him within 50 yards of where I had last seen him. He still wasn't dead, but when he got up and took off I put one right through the lungs broadside.

When you have learned to call your shots accurately, when your fours at nine o'clock are fours at nine o'clock and your pinwheel fives are pinwheel fives, you're on your way to becoming a crack shot. From then on you need only practice squeezing off at the right instant. As you practice, your eyes, muscles and nerves will get in tune so that you will acquire the ability to take up the last ounce of pull at exactly the right instant. That comes only with practice.

Since few of us can get out to a range to shoot every day, the thing to do is practice *dry* firing—completing the aim and the trigger squeeze without a cartridge in the chamber of the rifle. Much can be learned about shooting and good shooting habits can become second nature by practicing this way. And the advantage of dry firing is that it can be done in your own home. Place a small bulls-eye target on a wall about ten feet from your shooting position, at roughly the same height your rifle will be when you aim it. If you practice in prone position, place a mat on the floor beneath your elbows to keep them from getting sore. After squeezing off and calling each shot, as described in lessons 1 and 2, take the rifle down from the shoulder and rest a few seconds before taking the next shot.

I keep a small bulls-eye pasted to a filing cabinet in my study, and several times a week I take a rifle out of the rack and practice squeezing off a dozen or so "dry" shots at the bull. If I want to practice with a target at a greater distance, the chimney of a neighbor's house about 100 yards away has one black brick in it. I go out into my back yard with a rifle and practice squeezing off 10 dry ones from offhand and 10 from sitting position at the brick. I call my shots and keep score. Practice is the only way one learns to shoot, and it is surprising how quickly dry firing and shot calling will improve anyone's shooting. Dry firing on an empty chamber should be avoided with a rimfire rifle, but will not hurt most centerfire rifles.

LESSON NO. 4: STEADY SHOOTING POSITIONS

The principles of hitting a stationary object, as we have seen, be it a bulls-eye, a woodchuck, or an antelope are very simple. All one has to do is hold the rifle steady, align the sights correctly, and get off the shot without disturbing the aim by jerking the trigger or flinching.

One of the indications of the experienced shot and a good hunter is that he always takes the steadiest position he can manage, as he wants to place his bullet just right and kill cleanly and humanely. If he can't use a rest or lie down, he'll settle for sitting, and if he can't sit he'll kneel. Only as a last resort will he shoot offhand. If conditions are such, however, that he can shoot prone, prone it should be, because that is the steadiest position of all.

THE PRONE POSITION

Use of the prone position in most big-game hunting is limited, but anyone who takes his shooting seriously should practice it. As you lie down on your stomach and place your elbows on the ground, place your body at an angle of about 45 degrees to the left of your line of sight. These instructions are for a right-handed person, of course; if you're left handed, place your body at 45 degrees to the right of your line of sight. Your legs should be spread apart, as in the illustration. Place your left elbow directly under the barrel, so the rifle is supported by solid bone against solid ground, just as a pillar supports a building. Your right elbow should be sloped outward, so your upper arms and chest form a sturdy "tripod."

But, alas, much of the time prone simply cannot be used in hunting. In flat plains country, grass and low bushes are apt to get in the way. When shooting downhill the position is impossibly awkward,

Fig. 1.

To assume the correct prone position, lie so your body is pointing at an angle of 45° to the right of the line of sight. Spread your legs well apart, turn your feet outward and brace them against the ground.

as no one can shoot with his legs and fanny higher than his head. The use I have found for prone is in hunting mountain game, where the animals are approached by crawling up behind a ridge, often above timberline. The hunter can slide his rifle along ahead of him in the final phases of the stalk, and quickly settle into prone position as soon as the game is in view. Often he can combine the standard prone position with a rest. Many times I have put my 10-gallon hat on a stone or over a solid clump of bunch grass. I know of nothing more comforting, nothing better calculated to head off an incipient attack of buck fever than the sight of the intersection of those crosshairs in the scope resting solid right where you want them.

Fig. 2.

Brace your left elbow directly under the barrel and place your right elbow so it slopes outward, forming a tripod of your upper arms and chest.

Fig. 3.

Curl the fingers of your left hand around the forend of the rifle. Cradle the forend well down into the palm of your hand. Place the thumb of your right hand around the grip, not along the side.

THE SITTING POSITION

In most of the big-game hunting I have done, the queen of all positions is sitting. It puts the line of sight high enough so that it can be used on high grass and low bushes. It can also be used on a hillside. It is much more flexible than prone and can be used nicely for running shots whereas prone generally can not. If used with a sling (which will be discussed in Lesson No. 5), sitting is a very steady and practical position.

The best way to assume this position is to sit facing to the right from the line of aim at an angle of about 45 degrees (to the left if you are left handed), lean way over, so that the flat of the upper arms is against the flat shinbones. Then there is flat against flat and no wobble. The tension of the back muscles will pull these surfaces into close contact, with a resulting steadiness that is the real key to a good sitting position.

Rest the forend of the rifle on the heel of your palm, with the elbow almost but not quite under the rifle. Brace the part of the right arm that's immediately above the elbow against the right leg just below the knee. Spread your feet well apart, for steadiness of tripod effect. On the side of a hill, dig heels into the ground, but on level ground keep feet relaxed as naturally as possible. Trying to dig the heels in on the level results—with me, at least—in a tremor, which doesn't help at all.

A variation of the sitting position is with legs crosssed. I do not use it, but many good shots do. So do teen-agers whose legs have grown faster than their bodies. At 14 I sat cross-legged; the conventional sitting position gave me cramps.

The beginner often makes two grave mistakes in the sitting position. He sits upright and puts his wobbly elbows on his wobbly kneecaps. That way, his position is no steadier than offhand. Bend way over! Get the flat of the upper arm against the flat of the shins. Get the left elbow under the forend with the rifle resting on the heel of the palm!

Sitting is a good steady position, even without a shooting gunsling. With one, and a good loop high and tight on the upper arm, it can be almost as steady as prone and can be used for a long and difficult shot under conditions when getting into prone is impossible.

Fig. 1.

To get into the sitting position, sit facing 45° to the right of the line of sight. Spread your legs well apart to form a steady tripod with your body.

Fig. 2.

As you lean far forward the flat of your left upper arm should rest against the flat of your left shinbone. Cradle the forend of the rifle on the heel of your left palm.

Fig. 3.

Brace your right arm against your right leg, just below the knee. The tension of your back muscles will maintain steadiness if your arms are properly placed.

Fig. 1.

Kneel facing 45° to the right of the target. Sit on your right heel, resting the weight of your body on it. Your left knee should point in the direction of the target.

THE KNEELING POSITION

Kneeling is nowhere near as steady as sitting, but it does have the virtues of being a bit faster to get into and giving a higher line of sight. It also has its advantages when sitting down would fill the shooter's pants full of thorns. To get into the kneeling position, stand facing at about 45 degrees to the right of the target. Then kneel down and sit on your right heel, resting the weight of your body on it. Some shooters like to sit on the side of their foot instead of on their heel—try it and see which you like best. Your left knee should point toward the target. As in the sitting position, avoid putting wobbly elbow on wobbly kneecap; instead, hook your upper left arm over your knee and let the tension of the back muscles do most of the work.

OFFHAND SHOOTING

Offhand is the toughest of all, but under certain conditions it must be used, and anyone who plans to hunt big game should not neglect practicing it. It is *the* position for brush and heavy woods where game is come on suddenly, mostly at close range, and often on the move.

To assume a good offhand position, your right elbow should be about level with your shoulder and the butt of your rifle against

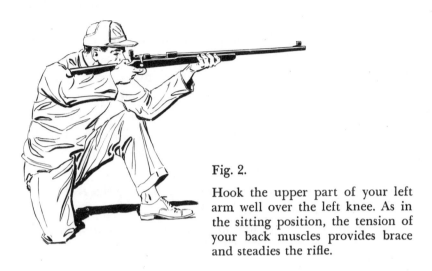

Fig. 2.

Hook the upper part of your left arm well over the left knee. As in the sitting position, the tension of your back muscles provides brace and steadies the rifle.

the pad of muscles formed at the shoulder joint. If the steel butt-plate is farther inside against your collar bone, the recoil is apt to hurt, and if your right elbow is down toward the waist it is difficult to get your right eye in line with the sights with modern stocks. Again, for all shooting remember that the thumb of your right hand should be around the grip and not along side it. With your thumb around the grip you will have more control over your trigger finger and over the rifle.

For fast running shooting your left hand should be moved pretty well out on the forend to give leverage for a fast swing, but for a precise offhand shot your left hand should be farther back toward the receiver and the weight should rest on the heel of the palm with your elbow almost directly underneath the barrel. In this position your left hand merely serves as a support. Your right hand should pull the rifle back against your shoulder and when the sights look right, take up your final ounce of pull.

This is the standard offhand position in military rifle shooting and from it a good shot should be able to keep the majority of his bullets in a six-inch circle at 100 yards or in a 12-inch circle at 200 yards. A bit steadier is the hip-rest position, which is permitted in the standing position in small-bore shooting. The left elbow rests inside the hip and the left hand supports the rifle just forward of the trigger guard.

Now and then a precise and difficult shot must be made from offhand. The hunter may see game suddenly and be afraid that if he moves it will be gone or he may be standing in high grass where any other position would be impossible. It is always easy to forget the misses but I'll never forget the best offhand shot I ever made on a game animal. I was hunting many years ago in northern Sonora, Mexico, when I saw a buck standing under a tree across a canyon. Since the point I was on was covered with waist-high chaparral any position but offhand was impossible. The buck was about 300 yards away, but I decided to try the shot as I had everything to gain, nothing to lose.

As I stood there the intersection of the crosshairs performed a figure 8 but finally it settled for an instant right on top of the buck's shoulder. I took up the final ounce of pull and down the

Fig. 1.

To assume the correct offhand position, stand squarely on both feet, the left side of your body facing the target. Hold your right arm at about the level of your right shoulder, keeping the sights at eye level. As your right hand holds the grip it should press the stock firmly into the muscle pad of your shoulder.

buck went. But this experience was an exception. It isn't once in a blue moon that a 300-yard offhand shot would have to be taken.

But no one should neglect practice in the offhand position, as skill on the hind legs will save the hunter's bacon many a time. It is *the* position for most deer hunting in the brushy East and for the heavy forests of the Pacific Coast. In the open bush of East Africa most game is shot from the hind legs, either from straight offhand or with the aid of the steadying rest from a tree or an ant hill. The last desert sheep I shot was from offhand. I had thought a bunch of rams were on the other side of a saddle, but they had moved, and the first thing I knew I had sneaked right in their midst where they were lying in scattered boulders. The one I killed was on the run and all of 35 yards away.

Any rifleman should learn all the standard positions, how to use them efficiently, get into them quickly.

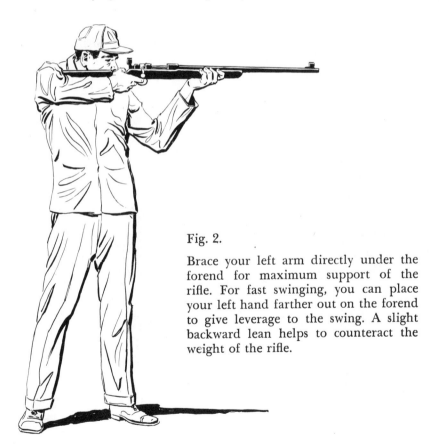

Fig. 2.

Brace your left arm directly under the forend for maximum support of the rifle. For fast swinging, you can place your left hand farther out on the forend to give leverage to the swing. A slight backward lean helps to counteract the weight of the rifle.

LESSON NO. 5: ADJUSTING THE SLING

A good gunsling, properly adjusted, is one of the great inventions of the human race. It is particularly wonderful for the sitting rifleman who wants to polish off a woodchuck perched on a rock at 200 yards, or nail a fine buck poised for flight high on some lofty ridge. Every game shot who takes his shooting seriously owes it to himself to get a good sling, then learn how to adjust it and use it. And never forget that a sling takes the curse off toting a heavy rifle, which otherwise is one of the most awkward burdens known to man.

The best kind of sling for the hunter is the one-piece Whelen type, ⅞ of an inch wide. It's much better for hunting purposes than the 1¼-inch two-piece military and target sling. Normally, the front swivel should be about 15 inches forward of the center of the trigger. Short-armed men want it farther back, and target shooters who use a low prone position want it farther forward. That's why swivels on target arms are adjustable for position.

The sling can be permanently adjusted for use in the sitting position and for carrying. The one-piece sling is a single strip of leather 52 inches long, with a claw hook at one end; holes are

Fig. 1.

How to use a gun sling: Adjust the keepers to suit your build, then slip your left arm through the loop.

Fig. 2.

Push the loop high up on your left arm and draw it tight. Bring your left hand over the strap and . . .

punched into the strap to take the hook. The sling also has two keepers and a stout leather lacing.

The accompanying drawings show you how to get into the Whelen-type sling and use it in the sitting position. The whole key to successful adjustment of the sling for the sitting position is the loop, which is formed when the strap is joined by the leather lacing. I place the lacing 18 inches from the base of the swivel or, with Winchester quick-detachable swivels, about 17 inches from where the sling joins the swivel bow. I put the two keepers on the loop; when both are drawn down against the arm, one helps keep the other in place. Total length of the sling for comfortable carrying is determined by the placement of the claw hook. If, for instance, you want to use both hands for climbing and carry the rifle slung over your back, you can move the claw hook into another set of holes.

No sling without a correctly adjusted loop is worth a hoot. Proper adjustment can be arrived at only by experiment. If the loop is too short or too long, it loses its value and introduces shakes and tremors.

The so-called "hasty" sling, by the way, is a snare and delusion. After years of solitary brooding and endless experiments, I am convinced that the use of the hasty sling is a waste of time and a handicap to the shooter.

Fig. 3.

. . . place it up against the forend swivel, tightening the sling. Bring the butt up with your right hand.

Fig. 4.

Loosened grasp shows how the sling holds the rifle in place, permitting sufficient flexibility for shots at running game.

LESSON NO. 6: SHOOTING MOVING GAME

Hitting moving game with a rifle is much the same thing as break-ing sailing clay targets or downing flying birds with a shotgun. Oddly enough the best way to acquire skill at shooting running game with a rifle is to shoot running game with a rifle. Neverthe-less the swinging, tracking, and shooting of birds and clay targets with a shotgun gives to some extent skill which is transferable to the rifle. Surely it doesn't hurt any.

Riflemen and scattergunners who shoot quickly at moving ob-jects learn the same lesson and that is often a painful one: namely that it is impossible to hit a moving target by shooting right at it with a stationary weapon. They also quickly learn that hitting a running antelope or a flying bird is far easier if the gun is moving. They also pick up from experience the rather sobering informa-tion that even at 100 yards and with a moving rifle it is necessary to lead a running jackrabbit, coyote, or deer. If the rifleman doesn't lead he simply doesn't hit—at least, in the case of the long body of an elk or a deer, where he wants to. This applies even to shooting with fast-stepping cartridges such as the .220 Swift, the 100-grain bullet in the .270, or the 110-grain bullet for the .30/06.

Whether it's flying birds or zipping skeet targets, almost all run-ning game is missed by shooting behind. In my day I have shot at thousands of jackrabbits on the run, and I have missed at least 10 by hitting behind for every one I have shot ahead of. And the same can be said of flying game and sailing clay targets—the misses are usually behind.

And the shotgun shooter can also learn a few lessons from rifle shooting. One is that he cannot flinch and hit anything. Another is that he must have a definite sight picture of muzzle in relation-ship to target, and still another is that if he is to improve his shooting, he must call his shots. By this last I mean that he must retain a mental photograph of precisely where his muzzle was in relation to the bird when the gun went off. If he doesn't do this, he'll never progress. If a gunner is able to knock down a pheasant that flails from under his dog's nose at 10 yards and then an instant later to whirl and dump another cock that flushes wild at 40, it is because he knows just how much to lead because he has killed other birds that looked about that far away with the sight picture he used. The good shot sees his target, swings, and when his sight picture looks just right the gun goes off.

All this simply to say that shooting running game with a rifle and flying game with a shotgun are pretty much the same things, and that a good shot on running game with a rifle is almost always a good wing shot. If he does much rifle shooting the good wing shot is likewise generally a competent hand on running game. In each case the whole point is to shoot with the gun or rifle moving and to point the muzzle ahead of them where they ain't. The only difference is that the rifleman doesn't have the spreading pattern of the shotgun to help him and hence his job requires more care and precision. In each form of shooting, the bugaboos that cause the misses are slowing the swing and stopping the swing an instant before the shot is let off.

Hitting a stationary object with a rifle is enormously easier than hitting it on the move. When you are shooting running game you should take every possible advantage you can of making a good shot. Take a rest if you can. If you can't do that, shoot from sitting or prone. If that is impossible you should kneel, and only when you have no other choice should you shoot offhand. You should likewise bend every effort to try to shoot your game motionless and undisturbed. Not only is the game easier to hit under those circumstances but it is easier to kill with the same placement of the shot. A frightened animal with its body pumped full of adrenaline will carry a lot more lead than one caught unawares.

On the other hand, practice will show you that hitting running game is not as difficult as it might seem and that a running animal at 100 yards offers just as large a target as a standing one. Once you convince yourself of this you will overcome the mental hazard that makes many hunters who are good on standing game simply point in the general direction of a running animal, close their eyes, and yank the trigger.

TYPES OF RUNNING SHOTS

The simplest type of shot on a running animal is, of course, when it is going directly away. Then all you have to do is put the sights where the bullet is to go and squeeze the trigger. But the shot has to be got off *fast*. This is a typical shot at a deer jumped in brush. There is a crash as a buck comes out, and away he goes, presenting a stern or quartering shot. If the country is thick any hesitation is fatal. The thing to do is to throw up, get the sights against the animal's rear end, and shoot instantly.

The next easiest shot is at an animal quartering away. Like the straightaway shot this can be taken with a stationary rifle by shooting to one side of the animal so that he'll run into the bullet. I have killed many deer and a few sheep like that as the animals were climbing out of a canyon on the side opposite me—and I learned how to do it by shooting many dozens of running jackrabbits.

The best spotted Axis stag I got in India came from a quartering shot. He tore out of a little brush patch and took off across an open meadow in a beautiful North Indian jungle. He was quartering slightly and I put the intersection of the crosswires about two feet in front of him, pressed the trigger, and he flipped end over end. The 150-grain, .270 bullet had struck him just behind the shoulder. This is exactly the way I break the Number 1 high house outgoing target at skeet. That baby is traveling directly away from the shooter and dropping. I simply hold about 1 foot under it and shoot fast. It is far easier and less complicated than trying to swing down with the bird. But these straightaway and quartering shots at running game (just like the Number 1 high house skeet target) must be taken *fast*. To dawdle around is to miss your opportunity.

For anything more than a mildly quartering shot, you must shoot with a moving rifle, swinging as if you were shooting a shotgun. And you must keep that musket moving. The tendency of the beginner (and also of the old timer when he gets nervous) is to slow or even stop his swing to assure himself that his sight picture is exactly right. If he does that he will shoot feet or even yards behind.

The fast swing: Start the swing behind the animal, swing rapidly past, and fire when the lead looks right.

Some very fast and superlatively gifted rifle shots tell me that they use on running game exactly the same technique as the fast swinger does with a shotgun. They start their swing behind the animal, swing the rifle apparently faster than the animal is traveling, and then squeeze off when the lead looks right. This is called the *fast swing*. Such lads have very quick-focusing eyes and fast reflexes and they are a joy to watch.

The average hunter would probably do better to hit running game by the process known to the shotgunner as *sustained lead* or *pointing out*. Those who follow this technique swing the rifle along so the sights are moving with the same apparent speed as the running animal. The shooter decides how much lead he wants to give and squeezes the trigger with the rifle still moving ahead of his target. It is precisely like swinging with a duck or using the so-called pointing out method to break the right-angling No. 4 high house target at skeet. The idea is to swing at a smooth, constant speed, and shoot!

When the game is at any great distance the best sight for shooting of this type is a scope of from $2\frac{1}{2}$ to 4 power. The next best is the peep sight with a large aperture, and by far the worst is the incredible Rocky Mountain rear sight with its useless ears sticking up to blot out three-fourths of the view.

And the best types of scope reticules are the crosswire and the dot, with the crosswire having a bit of an edge. For years I used post reticules in hunting scopes because with a post the view through a scope looks like a front sight as seen through a peep. When I switched to crosswires in hunting scopes my average on running jackrabbits jumped about 50 per cent. I quickly learned to drag the horizontal wire along the animal's body to maintain correct elevation and shoot when the vertical wire was the proper distance ahead. With the control afforded by the horizontal wire

The sustained lead: Place the sight the correct distance in front of the game, hold that lead for a few yards, then squeeze the trigger without stopping the swing.

it is much easier to keep from shooting over or under than with the post—or even the dot.

I remember a very pretty (and also somewhat lucky) shot I made like this. I was hunting antelope in Wyoming with Fred Huntington, the big tool and die man, when we spied a buck and his harem of does. They were running at right angles to my left and going at about three-fourths throttle. I slid the horizontal crosswire along the buck's body and squeezed one off when the vertical crosswire was two and a half or three lengths in front of his chest. I heard the bullet strike and an instant after I fired the buck pitched forward on his nose. It turned out to be 285 paces across ground as level as a billiard table. I had been confident that I could cut that buck down before he got out of sight, but I hadn't really thought I'd crack him in the right place the first shot.

A running antelope, by the way, is an easier running target than a deer because he has a smooth, level run, and does not bounce. If the target is bobbing up and down it complicates the elevation problem. In the fall of 1946 when Bill Rae, editor of *Outdoor Life,* Fred Huntington, Red Cole of Cleveland, Ohio, and I were in the Yukon, I nailed a galloping Dall ram with a fine 40¼-inch head at an estimated 250-275 yards. My first shot just clipped the top of his shoulders and sent a shower of white hair into the air. My second broke the skin on the lower part of his chest. I gave him a little more lead on the third shot and broke his jaw. He spun around and stopped and the fourth shot was dead easy. I had the lead for those first two shots just right but the elevation problem was beyond solution because he was bobbing up and down. With a little luck it would have been possible to kill the ram on the first shot and then that would have been a feat to celebrate in song and story. With bad luck I might never have connected. On occasion mule deer, particularly when they are surprised and frightened and are going up and down hill, bounce like so many rubber balls. Then the elevation problem is something to stagger the imagination, and about the only thing one can do is to give the animal what looks like the right lead and hope he runs into a bullet.

The longest running shot (and a very lucky one) I ever made was on a coyote. He had been frightened by another hunter and was running along a grassy ridge below me and far, far away. I was shooting a .270 with the 130-grain bullet. Holding about a foot above his back, I swung the vertical crosswire about 10 feet in front of his nose and cut loose. The bullet hit some four feet behind him. I more than doubled my lead and shot again. The coyote was almost out of the wide field of the scope as the rifle swung when I saw him collapse. He had switched his tail three times before I heard the bullet strike. I would have given a large stack of dimes if one of my hunting buddies could have seen that shot. The only witness, however, was my son, Bradford, who was not the least impressed. He was then in the my-daddy-can-do-anything stage that comes before the my-daddy-is-an-old-fashioned-jerk stage.

The finest practice in the world for learning to hit running game is shooting running jackrabbits, and if I have some small degree of skill in the department I owe it all to the long-eared desert speedster. The jackrabbit hunter will get more practice on running game in a week in good country than the deer hunter will on deer in half a lifetime. On many occasions, when I lived in southern Arizona, I have headed out across the desert with 60 rounds of ammunition with me and returned to the car without one. I wouldn't kill anything like 60 jacks, but I'd generally come fairly close to those I missed. The jackrabbit hunter learns even from his misses— and usually what he learns is that he didn't get far enough ahead! Just as the woodchuck is the teacher of long-range precision shooting, the jack is the professor of skill on the run.

HOW TO PRACTICE

But not everyone has a chance to shoot running jacks, and the days are long past when anyone can acquire this skill by shooting at deer. How, then, can the man ambitious to acquire a modicum of skill on running game go about it?

A good way is to join a club that has a running deer target, something which is not too difficult to construct, as the target can be suspended on ropes or wires between two bicycle wheels put on uprights. Then the "deer" can be given about any speed one would want. Many and painful are the lessons learned from these gadgets. I have often seen people hit five or six feet behind one of these targets at 100 yards, and when the beginner hits the deer at all it is usually too far back. Another way to practice is to shoot at a tire with a target placed inside as it rolls and bounces down an open hillside. Something almost anyone can do is to see that his rifle is empty and then practice swinging along as if to hit the hubcaps of passing automobiles and squeezing off the "shot" with the sights moving the proper distance ahead. Taking running cottontail rabbits with a .22 is also fine practice and more difficult than shooting running jacks.

As is the case with the shotgun, the lead with a rifle depends a good deal on the shooter—on the speed of his swing, the speed of the shooter's reactions, as well as on the velocity of the bullet. The angle at which the animal is running and the animal's speed contribute, of course.

The top speed of a running jackrabbit or coyote is about 30 to 35 miles an hour, but I imagine that when shot at most of them are not going faster than 20 or 25. When a jack is running at right angles about 100 yards away and not going flat out I hit or come very close when I lead about 1½ feet. If he is in the neighborhood of 200 yards away a lead of 3 or 4 feet is required. Since on the average a deer probably runs no faster than a jackrabbit, the average lead for a buck running at right angles would be about one foot in front of the brisket to land the bullet behind the shoulder in the lungs. The lead should be doubled for 200, and if the deer is really flattening out as badly scared whitetails caught in open

A practice deer range can be set up with heavy clothesline strung on pulleys between two trees about 250-feet apart and continued off at an angle to a third tree rigged with a bicycle wheel minus its tire. A cardboard cutout of a deer attached to the line can be moved realistically between the two trees by a man turning the wheel.

An excellent way to develop your aim for shooting running game is to place a target inside an automobile tire and have a partner roll it down a hill.

country often do, still more lead should be given. A very great advantage of shooting in open country is that the bullets kick up dust or rock fragments and if the shot is behind the lead can be corrected.

On occasion it is almost impossible, for me anyway, to give enough lead. Generally mountain sheep are shot on the sit after a long and careful stalk, but I remember trying to hit one thoroughly scared ram that had been spooked after a stalk had gone sour. He was probably over 300 yards away and running faster than any American sheep I have ever seen. I gave him what I thought was a good lead, hit ten feet behind him, swung still farther ahead and just missed his rear end. And then he went around a point and out of sight. Probably the answer was that I was excited and that I tightened up and slowed my swing.

Some of the leads required for running antelope going full speed are fantastic, as a scared antelope can do 60 miles an hour. Many a hunter has swung ahead of the first antelope in a string and has hit the second or third.

But let us forget these most difficult of all running shots, as under most conditions hitting them on the move isn't as tough as it might appear. If the hunter can only overcome his mental block and convince himself that a running buck is just as large as a standing buck and at shorter ranges is not too much more difficult to hit he has come a long way. Then if he can remember to get ahead with a moving rifle and to keep the rifle moving while he squeezes off his shot, he'll probably connect. Swing that rifle, get out in front, and keep it swinging during the trigger squeeze— that's the recipe for hitting them on the move, just as it is for hitting a flying bird.

LESSON NO. 7: SIGHTING IN A RIFLE

Of the several million hunters in the United States, I'd guess that at least half of them are pretty mystified about this business of lining up the sights of a rifle so that they can hit something. I'd also guess that about 50% of all the rifles used in deer hunting are so inexactly sighted that hitting a deer with them at over 100 yards is pretty much a matter of luck.

Surprising thing is how many shooters want some mysterious formula so they can line up the sights without shooting at all— or by shooting only a shot or two. They seem to regard firing a rifle as an evil and unpleasant thing to be avoided at all costs. They do not realize that to do a decent job of sighting in, the hunter has to *shoot*. Many of them would like to check the job of someone else—the gunsmith, the factory. They think it is a mysterious process needing great skill and staggering knowledge, something that requires bench rests and exact measurements. Many feel that if they do not have access to a bench and a target range they are whipped. They do not realize that the job is simple and something best done by themselves. Just because a rifle shoots right for one man is no sign that it will perform properly for another. One man (in the case with open sights) may take a finer bead than another. Ways of holding a rifle differ. Some may cant a rifle to the left, others to the right.

Rifles are sighted in at the factory, but the sad fact is that they are sighted in for 100 yards whereas the hunter may have to take a shot at 200 or 300. They may be sighted in for the bullet weight the hunter wants to use and they may not be. Anyone who simply grabs a rifle out of a factory carton, makes certain that there are no mice or wasp nests in the barrel and goes hunting is taking a chance.

BORE SIGHTING

I may be betraying a trade secret, but I don't think most custom gunsmiths ever fire the rifles they build. Many of them live from 5 to 30 miles from a rifle range, and since most of them do not have an indoor range, they simply bore sight and let it go at that.

And what is this mysterious process called "bore sighting"? Simply this: the lining up of bore and sight so they point at the same spot. Gunsmiths usually put the scope-sighted rifle in a vise after removing the bolt so they can see through the bore. Then they train the rifle so they can see some conspicuous object in the center of the bore. Then they adjust scope or sights so that they point at the same spot.

But bore sighting is no substitute for shooting and no one should ever depend on it except as a preliminary to sighting in. The reason for that is barrel whip. The bore-sighted rifle may put the bullets low, high, right, or left, depending on the vibration of the individual barrel. Now and then shooting will show the bore-sighted rifle right on the button, but this is the rare exception. Once I bore-sighted a .30/06 for a friend and we did not find it necessary to touch the adjustments.

STEPS FOR SIGHTING IN

The easiest method of sighting in is to line up the sight at short range. When you get a new rifle, take it out in deserted country and put up a target against a rise. Pace off 25 yards. Get into the

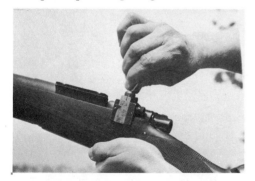

Scope and receiver sights are marked in minutes of angle and, depending on the sight, click in quarter or half minutes.

sitting position, the steadiest of them all, and squeeze off a couple of shots at the bull. Then take a rule and measure the exact distance from the center of impact to the center of the bull.

Scope and receiver sights are graduated in minutes of angle— and a minute of angle has the value of one inch for each 100 yards of range. That means a change of one minute on the sights moves the point of impact of the bullet one inch at 100 yards, two inches at 200 yards, three inches at 300 yards, etc. It also means that the change is ½ inch at 50 yards and ¼ inch at 25 yards.

Suppose the center of impact is five inches right and two inches low at 25 yards. That means that the necessary adjustment is 20 minutes (5 x 4) left and eight minutes up. Shoot two more shots to check and generally (if you have squeezed them off well and if the adjustments are correct) you are at point of aim.

With a scope-sighted rifle 25 yards is best for two reasons. In the first place, it is close enough so that the bullets will generally hit somewhere on the target. In the second place the scope-sighted big-game rifle hitting at point of aim at 25 yards is generally sighted in for the proper distance to be used on big game. But more of that anon. This is strue with the iron-sighted rifle with its lower line of sight putting the bullets right where it looks at 12½ yards.

To bore sight your rifle, cut notches in the end of a wooden box to hold the rifle, as shown above. Place pieces of wood under the box to get the correct elevation. Check to be sure the scope mounts are tight. Remove the bolt and aim at 100-yard target through the barrel. Then center the crosshairs of the scope on the bull, as in drawing at right.

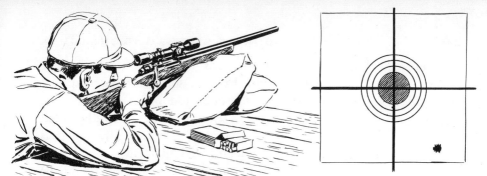

Replace the bolt, load the rifle and fire a shot from the bench. To be sure, you may fire three shots and take the center of the group as the "point of impact." The target at right shows that although the scope crosshairs are lined up on the bullseye, the bullet hit low and to the right.

Place the box back in position, put the rifle back in the notches, then look through the scope at the target and adjust the horizontal crosshair downward with a screwdriver until it is even with the bullet hole.

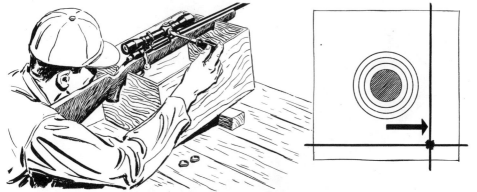

Adjust the windage crosshair to the right with the screwdriver until it is lined up with the bullet hole. Now your scope is sighted in at 100 yards. If your rifle is not the bolt-action type and you can't sight through the bore, set your target at 25 yards to make sure you hit the paper. After adjustments are made at this distance you can sight in at longer ranges.

After adjusting the sights at 25 yards, it is wise to do further shooting at 100 yards with a padded rest of some sort. A good deal is a rolled-up bedroll used from prone, and once on a hunting trip I sighted in a pal's rifle by resting it over his well-padded posterior. If a good bench rest is available, this is gravy, and it is the best of all. But it must be remembered that rifles shoot away from solid objects and whatever the forend rests on should be padded.

Checking at 100 yards is important, because an error made at 25 yards is multiplied by 4 at 100 and any error made at 12½ yards is multiplied by 8.

Sighting in with receiver sights and hunting scopes is an exceedingly simple matter, once you familiarize yourself with your sight. One hunting scope may have ¼-minute clicks, another ½-minute clicks. Still another is marked in five minutes and clicks for one minute. Another is marked in minutes but does not click. Arrows will show in what directions the adjustment dials must be turned to give the desired direction of point of impact. Everyone should familiarize himself with his scope or receiver sight before he starts trying to sight in.

Internally adjustable scopes marked in minutes are easy to sight in. A coin is being used here to change the elevation.

Some scopes do not have internal adjustments for windage and elevation and the adjustments are in the mount. Some mounts have no provision for elevation but have windage adjustment by opposing screws in the bases. Incidentally, if the short-range firing shows the scope much off in windage and the mount incorporates windage, it is smart to use the windage in the mount or else the reticule may be off center once the rifle is sighted in.

In the case of the Redfield Jr., the Tilden, and the Buehler mounts, one loosens the screw on the side toward which he wants point of impact to move, then tightens up on the opposite screw. As a concrete example, let us suppose that shooting at 25 yards shows the bullets striking 8 inches to the right. The thing to do is loosen the left-hand windage screw in the base of the mount about a full turn, then tighten up on the right-hand screw. This moves the rear of the scope (and also the point of impact) to the left. Generally speaking it is best to make these adjustments with a coin such as a 25-cent piece instead of a powerful driver, as it is no great feat to twist the heads off the screws of some mounts if a man is feeling well-fed and frisky. Once the lateral adjustment is about right it can be refined with the internal adjustments.

The target-type scopes are adjusted externally by the mounts, which are marked in minutes and click in quarter minutes.

THE OFF-CENTER RETICULE

If anything is calculated to fill a rifleman's soul with despair it is getting his rifle sighted in and finding that the top of the post or the intersection of the crosswires is out of center—way up in one corner, down at the bottom, in the top fourth of the field, or some place where it doesn't belong. Yet this often happens, particularly with high-powered scopes with small fields. Reason for this is that outside contour of receivers is not uniform from rifle to rifle, that holes are tapped and drilled cockeyed, or that mounts aren't uniformly machined. That can also happen, I am told, if one of the optical elements in the scope is put in cockeyed. Whatever the cause, the out-of-center reticule is enough to make the long-suffering rifleman snarl at the little woman and kick the cat. It can be corrected by a judicious use of brass or cardboard shims under the scope mount base.

This off-center reticule cannot happen with the Weaver K series scopes as the internal adjustments are made without movement of the reticule cell. The Redfield Bear Cub and the Leupold M 7 scopes employ a self-correcting system to keep the reticule in the center of the field. I consider this a very desirable feature in the internally adjustable scope.

Target-type scopes and hunting scopes without internal adjustments for windage and elevation must be sighted in by adjustments in the mounts. Mounts of the target type generally click in quarter minutes of angle, and they are exceedingly reliable.

It should be remembered, before we go further, that the rule in sight adjustment is to move the rear sight the way you want the point of impact to move and the front sight in the opposite direction. If the rifle is shooting to the right, the rear sight should be moved to the left and if it is shooting low it should be moved up. On the other hand, the rifle that is still shooting high with the lowest adjustment of the rear sight needs a higher front sight. The scope is both front and rear sight. The point of impact of the scope-sighted rifle moves in the same direction that the rear portion of the scope tube is moved, but in the opposite direction from the way the reticule is moved.

Factory open sights generally have no provision for windage (lateral) adjustment, but only crude notches for elevation. Generally if a windage change is wanted, the rear sight must be knocked over in the slot. A higher front sight will make a rifle shoot lower; a lower one will make it shoot higher. The task of getting a rifle fitted with open sights only to shoot right on the button is generally a task calculated to drive the finical rifle nut to a sanatorium, but true rifle nuts seldom will be caught dead with such sights.

Some of the worst sights are found on the flossiest rifles. A friend of mine recently got a British double for the .375 H. & H. belted magnum cartridge. One look at it would make a hungry gun lover desert a beefsteak, but the thing shot 18 inches low at 100 yards. All my pal can do is to send to the maker for a couple of lower front sights to try out. About the most expensive luxury I know is a sight which is not readily and positively adjustable. A white hunter friend of mine in Africa had a double .470 by a famous maker that grouped five inches high at 50 yards with the ammunition for which it was supposed to be regulated. At 100 yards it shot, of course, about nine inches high. Since he usually got within 25 yards of an elephant before taking a crack at it, he hadn't been bothered much. If I owned that rifle I'd grab a file and start sawing away at the notch in the rear sight to bring the point of impact down so the bullets would strike on the button at 100 yards and only one inch high at 50. In the heat of battle it is pretty hard to remember to shoot one foot or so low at 100.

SIGHTING IN ACCORDING TO CARTRIDGE

I like to sight in a scope-sighted rifle for open country shooting to put the bullet three inches high at 100 yards. Then such bullets as the 150-grain at 3,190 feet per second in the .300 Magnum, the 180-grain at about the same velocity in the .300 Weatherby, and the 125-grain in the .280 Remington and the 130-grain in the .270 will all be on the button at around 275 yards, slightly low at 300, and will depart no more than four inches at any point in their trajectories between the muzzle and a bit over 300 yards. Long and bitter experience has taught me that the less I have to figure on allowance for bullet drop the better.

Using the same system of putting the bullet from a scope-sighted rifle three inches high at 100 yards will help with the .30/06 with the 150-grain .270 bullet hand-loaded to over 2,900, the 180-grain factory load for the .300 Magnum, and other loads in that velocity bracket.

Bullets that leave the muzzle at around 2,700 feet per second and strike three inches above line of scope sight at 100 yards are at point of aim at about 225 yards. These include the famous 180-grain bullet in the .30/06 and the .308, the 150-grain in the .300 Savage, and the 270-grain bullet in the .375 Magnum.

At a velocity level of about 2,500 such as the 175-grain in the 7 x 57, the 220-grain in the .30/06, the 200-grain in the .308, and the 300-grain in the .375, the bullet is on point of aim at 200 yards.

For brush and forest shooting with the iron-sighted rifle a rise of two inches at 100 yards is about right. With a velocity level of about 2,200 this means that the 170-grain .30/30 bullet and the 200-grain .35 Remington bullet are on at about 150 yards, and the bullet first crosses the line of sight at about 12½ yards.

Heavy rifles used on dangerous game should probably be sighted to hit the point of aim at 100 yards, and since shots are taken at short range at relatively small marks like the brain or the spine, a bullet rise of no more than one inch at 50 yards is desirable.

On the other hand, I think a bullet rise of no more than 1½ inches at 100 yards is the thing for the varmint rifle which is shot at very small targets. If the rise is much more than that it is very easy to overshoot a squatting jackrabbit or a chuck lying on a rock.

So sighted, the .220 Swift with its great velocity is at point of aim at about 275 yards and only two inches low at 300, and cartridges in the 3,500-foot-per-second class like the 100-grain loads in the .270 and the .280 are only one inch low at 250 yards and four inches low at 300. This applies to the 80-grain bullet in the .243 Winchester and the 75-grain bullet in the .244 Remington.

Anyone who would like to know more about the trajectory of his pet load from the muzzle to 500 yards should get a copy of either the Western Ammunition Handbook or the Winchester handbook. Both are free and are mines of general information. Trajectory dope is obtained by using a graph with a transparent overlay. The shooter can use this to determine the point of impact of his favorite load when sighted in either with iron sights or scope at various ranges. Write Western Cartridge Company at East Alton, Illinois, or Winchester at New Haven, Connecticut. The books are free, and anyone who goes over them carefully can set up in business as the neighborhood gun expert.

A careful job of sighting in, periodic checking of point of impact, and some knowledge of trajectory pays off. It is a lot better to use a couple of boxes of cartridges to sight in and practice, then use one cartridge to get the game, rather than use one cartridge for sighting and two boxes shot promiscuously in the direction of the game without a hit.

CHAPTER TWENTY

Use a Rest and Hit

THE MORE EXPERIENCE THE RIFLEMAN HAS, THE MORE SHOOTING HE has done, and the more certain he is to take every advantage he can think of before he touches off a shot. He never shoots offhand when he can shoot kneeling, and never kneels if he can sit, never shoots without a sling if he has time to get into one.

The ultimate, of course, is shooting from a rest—and the ability to take quick advantage of an improvised rest is one of the marks of an experienced and studious rifleman.

BEST POSSIBLE ACCURACY

The use of an improvised rest has enormous advantages for shooting at any kind of game, from ground squirrels to elephants, if nail-driving accuracy is needed and if there is enough time at the disposal of the rifleman. In shooting literature much is written about the accuracy of modern barrels properly bedded into good stocks and used with precision bullets behind the right amount and kind of powder. It is not uncommon these days to find fairly light sporters that will group into an inch or slightly over when the shooter fires from a bench rest and has a good scope to enable him to aim properly. But under field conditions and shooting from conventional positions, taking advantage of such accuracy takes some doing. The world is full of better shots than I am, but I do a good deal of practicing with big-game rifles at a range where the most convenient distance to shoot is just short of 150 yards. Shooting offhand and with a rifle properly balanced for that position, I can generally keep all my shots in a 100-yard small-bore target with about half of them in the 6-inch black. Shooting from the sitting position without a sling, I can keep most of them, say around three-fourths, in the black. With a tight, military-type sling I can generally keep them all within the 6-inch black and now and then, when luck takes a hand in guiding the bullets, I shoot a group that does not compare too unfavorably with one that the rifle would shoot from a rest.

But for consistently hitting small marks at considerable range, there is nothing like a rest of some sort. In actual hunting this "small mark" may be a tiny animal like a Columbian ground squirrel of the Northwest or the heart or neck vertebra of a buck across a canyon. It may be a woodcock at 250 yards or the earhole of an elephant at 50. No matter how good a shot a man is, he who spurns the use of a rest for a difficult shot is gambling. Maybe he isn't taking much of a gamble, but he is still gambling.

I have shot all sorts of odd creatures from rests of one sort or another. When Lee Sproul and I were in India in the spring of 1955, we were out one day with A. D. Mukerji, our outfitter, hunting for crocodiles along the bank of a river where some lived. Presently we saw an enormous one (12 or 14 feet long, Mukerji said) stretched out on a sandbar asleep. He was near as I could figure about 200 yards away and I was elected to take the shot. It would be no trick at all to hit the croc at that distance, but I was told that I must either hit its brain or sever its spine. I elected to take the spine shot because my errors (like those of most riflemen) tend to be horizontal rather than vertical. I could make a horizontal error of several inches but the croc's spine was only a couple of inches through. I rested the .270 on my hand laid over a rock, held what looked like 4 inches under the place where the spine should be, since the rifle was sighted to put the 130-grain bullet 4 inches high at that distance. When I squeezed one off the croc simply quivered for a few seconds and then lay still. The neck vertebra of the great reptile was completely smashed. I could have hit that croc from a sitting position, even from offhand, but I seriously doubt if I could have killed it instantly.

The longest shot I ever made on an elk was from a rest—and this one also with a .270 and the 130-grain bullet. I was hunting out of the Jackson Hole in 1943 with the late Ernie Miller when we spotted the big bull I wanted far down in a basin below us, so far away that under those light conditions I couldn't make out his great antlers through the 2½X Lyman Alaskan I had on my rifle. By comparing the approximate depth of the bull elk's chest with the known size of the 4 minute Lee dot which I had for an aiming reticule, we decided the elk was about 600 yards away.

Figuring it another way, we divided the intervening ground into 100-yard units, and concluded the bull was about 600 yards away.

I sat on one big boulder, rested my rifle on my down jacket laid across another. I held for 600, fired twice, hit the elk both times. He didn't move 20 feet from where he was when I cut loose.

CUSHION THE REST

It is well known that a rifle rested on a hard object shoots away from it. Lay the forend (or, worse, the barrel) on a stone or a log and the rifle will jump away and shoot high. Let the side of the rifle touch a tree trunk and it will shoot away to the left or right as the case may be. Many times I have rolled up a down jacket and used it to pad a boulder when using it as a rest. I have likewise used jackets to help me make improvised rests over clumps of brush, logs, as well as stones.

The advantages of an improvised rest are enormous. Not only does the rest enable you to hold the rifle still but it enables you to concentrate on trigger squeeze, holdover in case of a long shot or holdoff in case of wind and not worry about controlling the wibbles and the wobbles of your weapon. Because your sights lie quietly on your mark, you become filled with confidence and are less apt to flinch or yank the trigger.

What a little excitement can do to marksmanship is a marvelous thing to behold. I have a good friend whose pet story is how he missed a big rhino weighing a ton and a half at less than 50 yards.

An improvised rest, such as this down jacket placed on a boulder, allows the shooter to concentrate on aim and trigger squeeze.

And he missed it clean! He was using a heavy double .470 with which he was not familiar. He came on the rhino suddenly, shot with the barrels settling down. The heavy weapon was moving faster than the light shotguns he was used to, and he probably yanked the trigger a bit to help things along. I also once missed a running rhino as large as a Patton tank at no more than 175 yards at the most. It seemed so utterly improbable that I was actually shooting at one of the prehistoric beasts that when I got my sights on his shoulder I simply stopped my swing. So I, too, belong to the missed-a-rhino club.

USE A REST ANYWHERE

Hunting the rock chuck in the Northwest is in many ways oddly like hunting mountain sheep. A good deal of the time the rock chuck must be stalked from behind a ridge, just as sheep are stalked, and once the hunter is in position he must shoot quickly and with nail-driving accuracy because the rock chuck, like the wild sheep, has wonderful eyes. I always hunt with a binocular and I usually carry it in a case. Because grass is apt to interfere with vision through the scope and with the flight of the bullet, a fairly high prone position is necessary. I have killed several sheep and many dozens of rock chucks by putting my binocular case down, laying my hand on the case, then resting the rifle over my hand.

A binocular case makes a good improvised rest when shooting from prone.

On the plains of Africa, it is rare when the hunter can sit down for a shot. Usually there is a little grass or some brush in the way, and if the hunter sits he loses sight of his game. Even the kneeling position will usually put his line of sight too low. But almost always, our hunter, if he has to make a long shot, can find a spindly thorn tree. Then he will put his left hand against it, rest his rifle over his wrist, and cut loose. Another good rest is that hunter's friend, the termite nest, which usually is from 5 to 10 feet high, but which in some areas ranges from 40 to 50 feet high and has a little forest growing on top. Not only can our hunter use these ant hills for cover as he sneaks up behind them but he can rest his rifle over them—and then drive in a well-placed shot for a quick kill. When I was in Africa in 1953, I sneaked up on my lion from behind an ant hill, took a rest, and popped him in the neck with a .375 Magnum. I made a one-shot kill on a record-class impalla at about 275 yards by stalking from behind an anthill and resting the rifle over it.

Of the several Wyoming antelope I have shot, most of them have been taken while shooting from prone with the rifle rested on a down jacket laid on top of a sage bush.

So don't look down your nose at the use of improvised rests. They're used in the best circles, and they allow the rifleman to take advantage of the fantastic precision built into modern barrels and modern bullets.

If it is necessary to shoot offhand, holding the forend against a tree and using three fingers as a cushion will steady the rifle for accuracy.

CHAPTER TWENTY ONE

Trajectory: The Bullet's Flight

KNOWING A FEW FACTS ABOUT TRAJECTORY CURVES HAS PAID OFF FOR me many times—in picking off meat for the pot at short range and also in making hits at long range on big game. These facts can pay off for any hunter who gives a little thought to them. What is this mysterious thing called trajectory? Let's take a look at it in its simplest form.

When a bullet leaves the barrel of a rifle, it immediately begins to fall from the line of bore, although at the same time it is rising toward the line of sight. All bullets are acted on by the force of gravity. A 130-grain .270 bullet dropped from the hand will hit the ground at exactly the same time as the same bullet fired from a rifle with a muzzle velocity of 3,140 foot seconds, for both are free-falling bodies of the same weight and shape. If the same .270 bullet could be speeded up to 4,000 or even to 5,000 foot seconds it would also hit the ground at the same time. However, the faster the bullet travels the farther it goes in the interval that gravity is acting upon it.

The faster a bullet is traveling, the "flatter" the path of travel—that is, the less it falls for every foot of forward travel. No bullet flies flat, no matter how fast it is traveling, because all the time it is moving forward gravity is also pulling it down.

So the answer to the often-asked question as to how far such-and-such a bullet will travel without dropping is: no distance at all. Even near the muzzle where velocity is high the drop is very slight, but it is there just the same.

Flatness of trajectory depends on three factors: initial velocity, the bullet's shape and its sectional density. A long sharp-pointed bullet loses velocity more slowly than a short round-nosed bullet and hence shoots flatter. And by that last word, I mean more nearly flat, or with a less-pronounced curve. To employ another popular term which doesn't mean much, such a bullet "carries up" better.

To get down to concrete instances, Remington used to load a round-nosed 110-grain bullet in .30/06 caliber at a muzzle velocity of 3,350 foot seconds. In spite of its high velocity, this bullet had a more curved trajectory over 300 yards than the Remington 150-grain Bronze Point bullet, which left the muzzle at a velocity of about 400 foot seconds less. Why? The latter had better shape and sectional density—or, to employ a fancy term, a better ballistic coefficient. This is why using a lighter but faster bullet of the same caliber doesn't always pay off. In a given caliber, the shorter the bullet is the faster it loses velocity, and the more pronounced its trajectory curve is.

The path of a bullet is close to a curve known as a parabola—not the arc of a circle, as is often imagined. Consequently, the high point of a bullet's trajectory over any given range is not halfway but somewhat beyond—about 110 yards over a 200-yard range and 165 yards over a 300-yard. The farther the bullet travels, the greater the drop.

From this technical information, we can deduce three facts: 1. During its flight, a bullet is always falling. 2. Strictly speaking, no rifle is really "flat shooting." 3. High muzzle velocity is just one of the factors contributing to comparatively flat trajectory.

HOW TO BEAT THE PULL OF GRAVITY

In order to compensate for the drop of the bullet, the rear sight of a rifle that's properly sighted in is higher than the front sight, which, in turn, points the bore up. This means that the line of sight is an imaginary line running straight to the target, while the line of bore is another imaginary straight line that intersects the line of sight and continues on. The trajectory curve is the path actually taken by the bullet. Although the bullet crosses the line of sight once near the muzzle and once again at a considerable distance, it never goes above the line of bore because, as we have seen, the bullet starts to fall the instant it leaves the muzzle.

Now and then I get a letter from a reader who wants to know about the value of "bore sighting," which simply means adjusting the sights to line up on an object that can be seen through the bore of a rifle. Bore sighting is a good way of approximately lining up sights. Suppose at 100 yards that the horizontal cross hair of

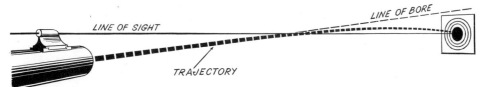

The line of trajectory, which is the path of the bullet, passes through and above the line of sight, but below the line of bore. To compensate for bullet drop, the rear sight must be higher than the front sight, pointing the bore slightly upward.

the scope rests right on the bull, and that the bull can be seen exactly in the center of the bore. The bullet will land somewhere on the target. This is a basis for making further adjustment.

When a rifle has been bore sighted, the bullet will usually land low, because, as we have seen, the path of the trajectory never rises above the line of bore. While the bullet is passing through the bore, however, the barrel vibrates like a trout rod. Consequently, the line of bore when the barrel is at rest is seldom the same line of bore actually determining the path of the bullet.

In bore sighting, you can come fairly near to the final sight adjustment if you point the bore higher than the sights. Once I bore-sighted a .22/250 so that at 100 yards the crosshair intersected the 10-ring of a 100-yard small-bore target, but the bore itself pointed about at the 7-ring directly above the bull. It just happened that with this stiff barrel, this was the medicine; the little rifle shot exactly to the point of aim at 250 yards, or about two inches above the line of scope sight at 100 yards.

If a rifle is fired with its line of bore exactly horizontal, the bullet drop at 100 yards is amazing. Here are some figures: The .22 Long Rifle bullet, at standard muzzle velocity of 1,180 foot seconds, has a drop or total fall below the line of bore of 15 inches. The high-velocity version of the same bullet at 1,375 foot seconds has a total fall of 12 inches. Even the 170-grain .30/30 bullet, which steps along at the much faster rate of 2,200 foot seconds, falls four inches. The 180-grain .30/06 bullet, which is traveling at 2,700 foot seconds when it leaves the muzzle, drops three inches. If the bullet is speeded up to 3,140 (as in the case with the 130-grain .270), the drop is only two inches. Speed it up still more, until it is traveling like the .220 Swift or the 100-grain .270, and the total fall is only

There is a big difference in bullet drop between the .30/06 (a long-range big-game cartridge), the .30/30 (a short-range deer cartridge) and the .22 rimfire (for targets and small game). At 200 yards the .30/06 drops nearly 12 inches, and the .30/30 drops about 30 inches. The .22 rimfire drops so fast that much guesswork is needed in sighting in to hit anything beyond 100 yards.

about an inch. The faster a bullet travels, the less it falls over a given range, because the less time Old Man Gravity has to work on it.

Now let's look at the total fall from line of bore of those bullets over 200 yards. At this distance, the velocity of the bullet really begins to fall off, and the longer distance gives the force of gravity more chance to pull the bullet down.

.22 Long Rifle (standard speed)	55 inches
.22 Long Rifle (high velocity)	50 inches
.30/30 (170-grain)	18 inches
.30/06 (180-grain)	11 inches
.270 (130-grain)	8 inches
.220 Swift (48-grain)	4 inches

TRAJECTORY AND SIGHTING IN

The thing to do in sighting in a rifle, then, is to jockey these figures of total fall, line of sight and line of bore around until we have a useful combination. We can tame this trajectory business by thoroughly learning how to use these figures.

In the case of the .22 with high-speed ammunition, for example, we learn that we tame the trajectory curve a bit by hoisting it above the line of sight, then letting it drop again. In a bore-sighted .22 at only 50 yards the total fall of the high-velocity Long Rifle bullet is three inches, and at that range you'd miss the head of a squirrel; but if you line up its iron sights on a point 50 yards away, the bullet will hit the point of aim—and it will rise only about a half an inch above the line of sight at 30 yards.

Even when zeroed in at 75 yards, the low-velocity .22 Long Rifle bullet from an iron-sighted rifle will cross the line of aim first at ten yards, climb 1.3 inches above the line of sight at 50 yards, cross the line of aim again at 75 yards, (the distance at which it is said to be sighted in for or zeroed at) and fall four inches below the line of sight at 100 yards—a far cry indeed from the appalling total fall of 12 inches at that distance, if the bore were horizontal instead of being tilted slightly up.

At any point between the muzzle and a distance of 85 yards, the bullet would not deviate from the line of sight enough to miss the head of a cottontail—or in most cases, the head of a squirrel.

With the scope-sighted .22 the range can be stretched a bit with the same maximum trajectory height above the line of sight of 1.3 inches. In this case the low-velocity Long Rifle bullet will first cross the line of aim at 12½ yards, cross again at 85 yards and be only two inches low at 100. Even with that sighting, however, the bullet, because of its low velocity, is seven inches low at 125 yards and 15 inches low at 150 yards. All of which explains why the finest scope in the world won't make up for the shortcomings of a .22 Long Rifle on varmints at long range. Gravity simply has too much time to work on the bullet.

To me it seems sheer folly to sight in a rifle for some short distance simply because most game is killed at that range. Not long ago I read a very good hunting tale by a man who used a scope-sighted .270 which he had zeroed for 100 yards because he had it doped out that he would probably shoot his deer at that distance. Now suppose our hunter had got a quick shot at 250 yards and he had held dead on. The 150-grain bullet would have fallen ten inches below point of aim and he probably would have missed his buck.

On the other hand, if he had sighted in for 225 yards, the bullet would have been only three inches high at 100 and 150 yards, and only two inches low at 250. Unless you plan to go around shooting deer in the eye, a three-inch deviation from line of sight surely is not excessive.

A good rule to follow is to sight in modern, high-velocity, flat-shooting rifles for the longest possible distance that will not cause mid-range misses and then never to take a shot where it is necessary to hold above the top line of the animal's back over the vital area.

A scope sighted .30/06 using the factory 180-grain bullet at 2,700 feet per second and sighted to put the bullet three inches high at 100 yards, for example, strikes the point of aim at 225 yards and drops about two inches at 250. With a rifle so sighted, the hunter can ignore trajectory to something over 250 as the bullet will not rise or fall more than 4 inches above or below point of aim up to that point. If the hunter isn't sure about his distance from the game and holds on the top of the back with a rifle so sighted, he will hit the vital area of most animals to a range of from 325 to 350 yards. Cartridges like the .270 Winchester with the 130-grain bullet, the .280 Remington with the 125-grain bullet and the .300 Weatherby Magnum with the 150- or 180-grain bullet have higher velocity, flatter trajectory, and extend the range from 25 to 50 yards.

A high percentage of stories of extra long shots are exaggerations. I know that for my part I have missed far more long shots by holding over and shooting high than I have by holding on and shooting low. Under most conditions, if the animal is so far away that he cannot be hit with the hold I have suggested and with the rifle sighted for his extended range, then it is too far away to shoot at.

This lesson to sight in for the longest possible range that will not cause mid-range misses was impressed on me in Mexico many years ago. I was carrying a .270 zeroed with the 130-grain bullet at the conventional 200 yards. Coming over the rim of a big, open basin, I was just getting set to glass the terrain when a fine whitetail buck got up and took off, traveling around the basin in a semicircle.

I didn't give much thought about the range and didn't hold high. I emptied the rifle, rammed in some more cartridges, and finally knocked him off on the eighth or ninth shot. When I got to him I found four bullet burns on the lower edge of his body. The buck had actually been over 300 yards away. Because of the 200-yard sighting, the drop below line of sight at that distance was eight or nine inches. The high shots in the group had just grazed the buck's chest, and the fatal shot was actually a poorly pulled one that was well out of the group. Since that experience, I have always sighted in a .270 for a much longer range.

With the .270 Winchester-Western factory load with the 130-grain Silvertip bullet, I do the preliminary sighting in at 25 yards and adjust the scope to hit the point of aim at that distance. The bullet then strikes three inches high at 100 yards, four inches high at 150 and 200 yards, at point of aim the second time at 275 and only two inches low at 300. At 325 yards, the bullet is four inches

Knowing how your rifle performs can mean the difference between a hit or miss. At left, a hunter with a .30/30 zeroed at 100 yards is holding dead on a buck 200 yards away. The bullet lands at X, nine inches below point of aim, missing the animal. If he zeroed at 150 yards he would hit the point of aim, and if the deer were 100 yards away he would still connect at Y, as shown at right.

below the point of aim. For shooting big game—even smallish deer and antelope measuring from 14 to 17 inches from top of shoulder to bottom of chest—this is not excessive deviation, and the point-blank range of a .270 so sighted is 325 yards.

Sighted for 200 yards, on the other hand, the point-blank range is only about 260 yards because at that distance the bullet falls four inches below point of aim.

Let's apply the same formula to the scope-sighted .30/06 with the factory 150-grain load at a muzzle velocity of 2,960 foot seconds, sighted in so the path of the bullet first crosses the line of aim at 25 yards and strikes three inches high at 100 yards. At 150 yards the bullet strikes four inches high; at 200 yards it is three inches high; at 250 yards it is at point of aim the second time; and the bullet does not fall more than four inches below point of aim until it has passed the 290-yard mark. Such a sighting makes the .30/06 a pretty good long-range sheep and antelope rifle.

With the slower 180-grain bullet at a muzzle velocity of 2,700 foot seconds and the same formula of the scope-sighted rifle—laying them at point of aim at 25 yards the first time and putting them three inches high at 100 yards—the range is stretched to 225 yards, where the bullet crosses the line of sight the second time. It does not drop more than four inches until it has passed the 260-yard mark.

Now let's take a look at the ordinary deer rifle—say an iron-sighted .30/30 using a 170-grain bullet with a muzzle velocity of 2,200 foot seconds. If you sight one of these babies in for 100 yards, at 200 yards the bullet fall below the line of bore will be about ten inches—enough to miss even a big whitetail buck with a center-of-the-chest hold. On the other hand, if the rifle is sighted in for 150 yards the bullet will fall only five inches at 200 yards, and a hit with no allowance for drop is probable. What's more, at 100 yards the bullet is only two inches above the line of sight, and that is so little deviation as to be negligible. The bullet will cross the line of sight the first time at about 12½ yards, a handy thing to re-member when a grouse perches up in a tree. Substantially the same trajectory applies to any of the other so-called deer cartridges—including the .25/35; .32 Special; .303 Savage; and .30, .32 and .35 Remington.

The iron-sighted rifle using a cartridge with a velocity of from 2,400 to 2,500 foot seconds can well be sighted in for 175 yards. Examples of such rifles include the .30/40 Krag, the .303 British as loaded in Canada and the .300 Savage—all with the 180-grain bullet; also the .348 W.C.F. with the 200-grain bullet, the 7 mm. Mauser with the 175-grain bullet, the .30/06 with the 220-grain bullet and the .22 Hornet. With any of these the bullet first crosses the line of iron sight at from 10 to 12½ yards. At 100 yards it will be 2½ or 3 inches high, at point of aim again at 175 yards and only 2 or 3 inches low at 200 yards.

When such rifles are scope-sighted, the trajectory is apparently flattened out a bit, and they can be zeroed for 200 yards. In that case the bullet will first cross the line of sight at 25 yards. At 100 yards it will be three inches high and at 250 only about five inches low—all of which means that with the 180-grain bullet and a scope sight even the old .30/40 Krag can stretch right out there.

How much mid-range trajectory height above line of sight is allowable? Well, that depends a good deal on the size of the game. The squirrel hunter, for instance, who usually aims at the head, cannot have much more than an inch. The varmint hunter, too, shoots at small targets. In his case, a 2½-inch deviation is the most he can work with.

The hunter of big game, on the other hand, has much larger marks—from the small deer, which averages 14 inches from chest to withers, to the huge moose, which can measure up to 40 inches.

A four-inch deviation is peanuts, even on medium-sized animals like the bighorn ram or the mule deer.

Knowledge of trajectory and the practical application of this knowledge are enormously useful to the hunter. With this background, the hunter can snap off the head of an ugly-looking rattlesnake at 10 feet, knock down a grouse with a big-game rifle at 25 yards or collect the fat buck that is standing and looking at him a good long way across a canyon.

So by all means memorize the trajectory of your rifle. If you don't trust your memory, copy down the dope from the accompanying table on a small piece of paper and affix it to the buttstock of your rifle with Scotch tape. Then it will be right there when it's needed.

UPHILL AND DOWN

When I was a teen-ager I was told that if I were shooting uphill my bullets would strike low and that I should hold high. Likewise I was informed that if I were shooting downhill my bullets would strike high and that to correct I should hold low.

This advice was only about half right, because in either case the bullet strikes higher than it would at the same range when the shooter is on level ground. Generations of hunters have observed that they often overshoot when shooting downhill, undershoot when shooting uphill. How come?

The answer to that one is that when shooting at an animal below you, you aim at the top of his body because that is what you see. If you miss, your shot is usually over. When shooting at an animal above you, you aim at the lower part of the body. In this case, hits are in the lower part of the body and misses generally are low.

The reason bullets fired uphill or down strike higher in each case than they would on the level is that the bullet drop is that of the horizontal range, instead of the greater distance of the slant range.

Let's see how it works out. Suppose you're hunting up in the Yukon. You're sitting high on a steep hillside nursing your weary legs when all of a sudden a big bull caribou comes trotting along through the valley below you headed for a pass. You're armed, let us say, with a .270 or a .300 Magnum sighted to put the bullet on the button at 300 yards. As you look at the caribou, you decide that he is 400 yards away. Knowing that ordinarily the bullet drop at that range will be 12 or 14 inches, you hold six inches or so over the top of the bull's back and cut one loose. Much to your disgust, the bullet is high. You fire another, and once again you just kick up moss and lichens above and beyond the bull. The next time you hold right into the bull's body. We hear the *whump* of the bullet. The caribou staggers. His knees begin to wobble, and he goes down.

The use of a flat-shooting cartridge has taken a lot of thorns out of your problem. Suppose, instead of a .270 or a .300 Magnum, you had used a .30/06 with the 180-grain bullet at 2,700 feet per second sighted to strike the point of aim at 225 yards. Knowing that at 400 yards the bullet drop of your particular .30/06 load is about 24 inches, you held 18 inches high. In this particular instance, however the bullet drop is actually only about 7 or 8 inches; you would be way over. Suppose, on the other hand, that you were using a .30/30 with the 170-grain bullet at 2,200 feet per second. You are sighted to hit on the nose at 150 yards. A quick look tells you your caribou is 400 yards from the muzzle. You decide you need to hold about six feet to allow for the additional drop of 250 yards. With a bullet of that shape and initial velocity, the drop between 300 and 400 is only around 30 inches—so again you would be high.

The more curved the trajectory, the greater the problem. As we have seen, the problem is not too acute with a rifle having a muzzle velocity of 3,000 feet per second or over, but velocities lower than that make it tough for the shooter. Back in the black powder days, the problem was grim indeed.

Dr. C. S. "Chuck" Cummings, Remington's supervisor of fundamental research, has worked out a formula that shows the relationship between the "slant range" (or actual distance over which we shoot) and the "horizontal range" (which governs bullet drop):

ANGLE OF SLOPE (UP OR DOWN)	DIVIDE ESTIMATED RANGE BY
0°	1.0
5°	1.0
10°	1.02
15°	1.04
20°	1.06
25°	1.10
30°	1.15
35°	1.22
40°	1.31
45°	1.41

CHAPTER TWENTY TWO

The Problem of Wind Allowance

MANY A HUNTER HAS MISSED A CHANCE-OF-A-LIFETIME SHOT BECAUSE he failed to allow for the effect of wind, or in some cases, even a slight breeze, on his bullet. The lad who is planning to make a good showing on jackrabbits, chucks, crows, ground squirrels and other varmints should do quite a bit of thinking about the effect of the breeze on bullets.

This problem of wind is one that affects the target shot even more than it does the varmint hunter. If the breeze pushes the varmint shot's bullet way out yonder, he can always make appropriate remarks and just wait for another crow or chuck to show up. The next time he can hold farther into the wind and maybe he'll hit. But not the target shot. Many a citizen who thought he had a match won has been fooled by a puff of breeze that came out of nowhere and blew his critical bullet right out of the bull and into the three-rings or even clear off the target. The 200-yard small bore shooter or the 600- or 100-yard competitor with the .30 caliber rifle may be able to hold like a rock and squeeze them gently, but unless he can read the wind he is sunk.

The hunter of big game in brush and forest where ranges are short doesn't have to worry about wind effect except that it's possible for a breeze to move his rifle or jog his elbow while he is aiming. Once the hunter goes out into the wide open spaces, however, the breeze becomes a real factor affecting accuracy. In that wonderful antelope state of Wyoming, for instance, the wind seems to blow all the time, at least it does when I am there. Since, as a rule, pronghorns are shot at fairly long range, it behooves the hunter to dope out the wind conditions before touching off old Betsy. If he doesn't, he is apt to wonder how come he hit his pronghorn buck in the south end when he held on the north end, or why he made a clean miss with what looked like a perfect hold.

The subject of why and to what extent wind affects the travel of bullets is not too well understood by many shooters. It is commonly believed that the faster the bullet leaves the muzzle the less wind affects it. That sounds reasonable enough but it just isn't true, as thousands found out about 30 years ago when high-speed .22 ammunition came out. It would seem only logical that a 40-grain .22 Long Rifle bullet moving along at 1,335 feet per second would drift less than the same bullet at the standard velocity of 1,145. This is logical theoretically, but it didn't work out that way, since it was quickly found that the high speed stuff drifted more than the low speed.

The answer to this riddle is that drift in the wind is governed not by velocity but "lag," something which erudite ballisticians have known for a long time. This "lag," or delay, simply means the difference in time it would take for a bullet to travel a certain distance in a vacuum and the time it actually takes. A good example is that of the old 150-grain flat base .30 caliber bullet used in a .30/06 rifle with a muzzle velocity of 2,700 feet per second. In a vacuum, theoretically, this bullet takes only one second to cover 900 yards. It actually takes 1.6 seconds; the "lag" or delay accounts for the .6 of a second. A 15 foot-per-second crosswind (10 miles an hour) would drift the bullet 15 x .6, or about 9 feet. That's a lot of drift when you consider that a ten-mile wind is what may be described as a fairly gentle and pleasant breeze that can be felt lightly on the face.

Now the 150-grain spitzer bullet like the one Uncle Sam uses in his M-2 ammo for the Garand and Springfield is a pretty well designed bullet. It could use more sectional density but it has an excellent point and a ballistic coefficient of .387. This term *ballistic coefficient*, by the way, is the ratio between the sectional density of a bullet and its coefficient of form. Sectional density is the weight of a bullet as compared to its cross-section. Put into words of one syllable, all this means that, because of air resistance, a long bullet gets through the air better than a short one with a similar point, and that with two bullets of the same sectional density, the sharp pointed one drifts less than one with a round or flat nose because it loses its velocity less rapidly. For this same reason of air resistance, the bullet of superior ballistic coefficient also shows less drop.

It is because of this tendency to drift in the wind and to shed velocity rapidly that some cartridges, although they might look pretty fancy when muzzle velocity alone is considered, are rather poor at anything except range. An example of such a cartridge is the .219 Zipper, which, because it is used in a lever-action rifle with a tubular magazine, is factory loaded with a round-nosed bullet. The muzzle velocity is 3,110 feet per second, but at only 100 yards, velocity has already fallen off to 2,440, according to Western Cartridge Company figures. At 200 yards it's down to 1,940, and at 300 yards velocity is down to 1,550. On the other hand, the 130-grain .270 bullet with its superior shape and sectional density and about the same muzzle velocity retains 2,580 feet per second at 200 yards and 2,320 at 300. Another sad example is the 110-grain round-nose .30/06 bullet at a velocity of around 3,400 feet per second. Twenty years or so ago when the varmint shooter wasn't as well equipped with special varmint cartridges and special bullets as he is today, varmint shooters used to load up 93-grain Luger pistol bullets and 115-grain .32/20 bullets to high velocities in the .30/06 and use them on jackrabbits and woodchucks. Because of their poor sectional density and poorer ballistic coefficient, any little puff of wind would blow the things into the next county.

JUDGING WIND VELOCITY

In his excellent work, "Small Arms Design and Ballistics," Colonel Townsend Whelen gives the following table for the judgment of wind:

1 mile an hour	Hardly appreciable.
2 to 4 miles an hour	Very light breeze.
10 to 12 " " "	A rather strong breeze.
14 to 18 " " "	Quite a strong wind.
20 to 25 " " "	A hard, strong wind. We pull our hats down and lean against it.
Over 30 " " "	A gale too strong for successful rifle shooting.

At best, the judgment of wind velocity is exceedingly approximate. It used to be a practice in my younger days to put up flags on rifle ranges. By watching them, competitors could tell something of the direction and the velocity of the wind. A 5-mile zephyr barely flutters a flag but a breeze traveling at 10 miles an hour will make it stand out a bit. As the wind increases to 15 miles an hour the flag is out at about 60 degrees. At anything over 20, it is straight out and flapping in the breeze like the traditional shirt-tail.

But unfortunately, the varmint hunter and the long-range big-game hunter don't have the aid of flags. They can guess by the strength of the wind against their faces, by the appearance of the leaves of trees, of grass and weeds, of smoke—in case there is any smoke handy. A wind that will move the grass gently is traveling at about 10 miles an hour. If the grass ripples and dances, the wind is probably pushing along at 15 or so. With a high-powered scope, the varmint shooter can tell something of the direction of the lighter breezes by watching the mirage on a hot day.

Maximum bullet drift comes, of course, when the wind is at right angles—from 9 o'clock or 3 o'clock, to use the term employed in target shooting. As the angle diminishes, the effect of the wind is less pronounced, and winds from 1, 5, 7, and 11 o'clock would require about half the correction needed for a wind of the same speed from 9 or 3 o'clock.

Just how much do bullets drift, then? How much should the innocent varmint hunter allow for a gentle breeze blowing against his left cheek if he plans to knock a crow off a fence post 300 yards away?

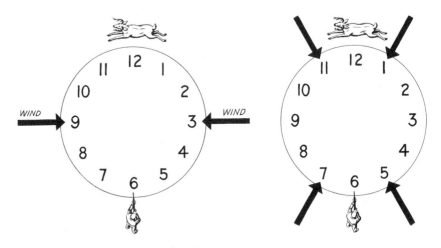

Crosswinds blowing at right angles (9 and 3 o'clock) with your line of aim (left) cause much more bullet drift than winds coming from 1, 5, 7 or 11 o'clock.

In an article published in the *American Rifleman* back in November, 1943, E. Baden Powell, Los Angeles engineer and rifle enthusiast, gave some drift figures for a wind traveling at 10 feet per second, or 6.8 miles an hour. That's not much of a roaring gale by any means:

CALIBER	BULLET	MUZZLE VELOCITY	WIND DRIFT 100 yds.	200 yds.	300 yds.	400 yds.
.219 Zipper	56 gr.	3060 f.p.s.	1.30 ins.	5.21 ins.	11.75 ins.	
.220 Swift	48 gr.	4140 f.p.s.	.66 ins.	2.65 ins.	5.95 ins.	10.60 ins.
.250 Savage	87 gr.	3000 f.p.s.	.62 ins.	2.47 ins.	5.50 ins.	
.270	100 gr.	3540 f.p.s.	.50 ins.	2.00 ins.	5.00 ins.	8.00 ins.
.270	130 gr.	3120 f.p.s.	.45 ins.	1.80 ins.	4.05 ins.	7.20 ins.
.30/06	110 gr.	3380 f.p.s.	1.04 ins.	4.18 ins.	9.40 ins.	

IMPORTANCE OF SHAPE AND SECTIONAL DENSITY

The figures here show conclusively that muzzle velocity does not have much to do with the price of eggs as far as drift is concerned. What does determine wind drift, as we have seen and which is borne out here, is the lag factor. The better the bullet retains its velocity because of the superior ballistic coefficient the less it is affected by wind. Worst of the examples listed are the .219 Zipper and the .30/06 with the 110-grain bullet—in each case because of a short, round-nose bullet at high muzzle velocity. Note that the Swift bullet drifts less than that of the Zipper because of better shape and that because of its superior sectional density the 130-grain .270 bullet is less affected by wind than the faster-stepping 100-grain bullet in the same caliber.

Here are some more figures which further illustrate the effect of shape and sectional density of the bullets on drift in a ten-mile wind at 3 or 9 o'clock.

At 100 yards the old 500-grain bullet of the .45/70 at a muzzle velocity of about 1,200 feet per second drifted 3 inches at 100 yards, 25 inches at 300, 75 at 600, and 220 at 1,000. In case you are interested, 220 inches amounts to approximately 18 feet. The next time you read how the pioneer thought nothing of knocking off buffalo with some old black powder rifle at 1,000 yards, remember the wind drift (and the plains of Wyoming and Montana were windy then just as they are today) as well as the rainbow trajectory he had to use. Then take the tale with a grain of salt.

With its long but round-nosed, 220-grain bullet the old .30/40 Krag army rifle had a drift of 2 inches at 100 yards, 15.5 at 300, 68.5 at 600, and 191 inches at 1,000 yards.

Wind bucking ability of our military cartridge picked up with the adoption of the 150-grain flat-base spitzer bullet of the caliber .30, Model 1906 cartridge, or .30/06 as we know it. The velocity of this cartridge was 2,700 feet per second. Under the same conditions the bullet drifted only 3 inches at 200 yards, 8 inches at 300, 36 at 600, and 115 at 1,000.

The excellent 172-grain M-1 boattail bullet at around 2,700 came out for the .30/06 in the nineteen twenties. It was even better. Drift in a 10-mile wind from 4 o'clock at 200 yards was 2.2 inches, at 300 it was 5.8. Out at 600 yards the bullet drifted only 25.2 inches and at 1,000 only 69 inches. Drift, of course, increases proportionately to the speed of the wind.

All of these figures are from *Military and Sporting Rifle Shooting* by the late Captain E. C. Crossman, who at the time of his death was an *Outdoor Life* gun columnist.

WIND DOPING UNDER HUNTING CONDITIONS

If the figures I have given prove anything, they would tend to show that wind is a pretty serious factor to contend with and that a varmint shot or anyone who plans to do much long-range big-game shooting in windy country should get some notion as to how far off he ought to hold at various ranges and at various speeds.

But at best wind doping is tough, particularly out in the field with no flags to wave, no spotting scope through which to observe mirage, and no coach at the shooter's elbow. The sad thing is that the shooter may be in a sheltered cove unaware that out in the open basin where that big bull caribou is, the wind is blowing a gale. If wind blew steadily all day long, it could be figured out and compensated for; but the darned stuff has a tendency to blow in unpredictable gusts and to shift directions like the "fishtail" wind so loathed by the target shot. Anyone who has done much shooting at small marks like varmints with light, fast bullets has learned that if much of a breeze is blowing, hits are few and far between.

Any fairly serious rifle shot should do some experimenting at various ranges and under different wind conditions with his own rifle. Wind effect dope such as that given above is, alas, not particularly helpful except to show us that any bullet is simply looking for an excuse to get pushed off its path by a vagrant breeze. Distances have to be guessed. So does wind velocity. Breezes have an annoying habit of changing speed and direction.

If much air is moving, long-range hits at small marks become next to impossible. Some years ago a couple of friends and I shot quite a few chucks across a deep canyon at ranges of from 350 to 450 yards. On a still day, and even at the longer ranges, we could hit enough chucks with .220 Swifts to keep us encouraged. We missed a good many, but then again we bowled over a surprising number. But when a breeze was blowing we might as well have stayed at home. I found that I could hit more with a .25/06 with the 117-grain Sierra boattail bullet loaded to about 3,150 than I could with the wind-sensitive Swift. But even with that fine varmint cartridge the wind played hob with my score.

But the chap who has shot his rifle on paper knows all this— and he is saddened by it. It is astonishing how little breeze it takes to put a fast .22 bullet off a crow or a ground squirrel with a center hold even at 150 yards.

The unfortunate thing is there isn't much you can do about it except hold away from the target to compensate for wind. If I can feel a little wind from the left on my whiskers and the crow or chuck is 150 yards or so away, I hold on the left edge of whatever I am shooting at. If I guess the wind is traveling at 10 or 12 miles an hour at that distance I hold off the target and hope for the best. The faster the wind and the greater the range, the more one has to hold off. Windage correction with the scope itself is not practical for the hunter.

To show the effect of wind on a hunter's bullets, here are a couple of examples of big game hits. A few years ago out of Gillette, Wyoming, it came my turn to polish off a big buck antelope at what looked like about 500 yards. A junior-size gale was bellowing in at 10 o'clock, so I held two feet into the wind in front of the animal's shoulders and well over his back. When I shot the buck went down, but instead of having hit him through or behind the shoulders, the 130-grain, .270 bullet had struck him just in front of the hips well below the spine. It turned out that the antelope was just short of 500 yards away, but with that wind I was lucky to hit him even from an improvised rest.

This would be the correct hold on a chuck 300 yards away with a scope-sighted .270 rifle zeroed at 250 yards, if wind is blowing from left at 7 miles an hour.

On another occasion I was trying to polish off a Roberts gazelle up in the northern frontier of Kenya just below the border of Ethiopia. I was using the 87-grain bullet in a beautifully accurate .257 Weatherby Magnum, but the range was around 400 yards. I was resting my rifle on the last available cover, an ant hill that stuck up in an arid plain that had been miserably overgrazed and eroded when Caesar was playing footsie with Cleopatra. I held well into the wind and hit the creature with my first shot. It went down, got up, and started to wobble off. I kept shooting, kept hitting, but the gazelle didn't go down and stay down until I had emptied my rifle and my face was red with embarrassment. I hadn't held far enough into a 25-mile-an-hour wind and all the shots had hit too far back.

But now and then a man will make what looks like an absolutely correct guess. Once in Sonora a good many years ago, I had started out to stalk a fine desert bighorn ram. It was one of those leaden and cold December days when desert and mountain fade into sombre monotone and the wind from the Gulf of California blows sodden gray clouds low across the jagged mountains. I had spotted this ram from a granite ridge across a shallow valley

If there is a gentle breeze and the game is not far away, hold on the windward edge.

With a stiff 3 o'clock wind and the game 300 yards away, a 7 mm. rifle zeroed at 200 yards would make a hit at this hold.

over a half-mile away. He had browsed a bit and had lain down and I thought he'd stay put for some time. To stay out of his sight and to keep the wind right, I made a long circle. I planned to come up on him from behind the ridge and if things worked out I could get close to him.

But things didn't work out. While I had been making my circle he had moved across the ridge and had lain down. The moment I put my head over another ridge about 300 yards away, he must have seen a movement. He jumped to his feet and stood facing me. I can still see him there on the granite boulder, his chocolate brown coat, his slender deer-like neck, his broomed and massive horns, his air of muscular aliveness. He looked to be around 300 yards away and the wind was blowing quite hard from 3 o'clock. I was using a light 7 mm. with an old Noske 4X scope. I knew I'd get only one shot and I had to make it good. I dropped to prone, put my left hand over a rock, rested the forend on it, held the flat-topped post even with his chin and just off his body to the right. The 139-grain Western open point bullet blew his heart to pieces. He made one tremendous leap and that was it. If I hadn't made that all-important allowance for the wind, I would never have hit him.

Quick calculation for a second shot: if the crosshairs are on A and the bullet strikes at B, hold at C to hit.

CHAPTER TWENTY THREE

Placement of Shots for Big Game

THE SHOOTING ABILITY OF THE HUNTER, NOT THE PUNCH OF HIS weapon, is always the determining factor in any hunting situation, especially when he is after big game. It follows, of course, that a good shooter equipped with a good rifle presents a formidable combination. It also follows that *where* a slug is placed is more important than its ballistics. For example, it stands to reason that the hunter who drives a .25/35 bullet into a vital spot, say the heart-lung area of an animal, is more certain of having chops for the frying pan than if he only manages to break its leg with an enormously heavier and more powerful slug, such as the .470 Nitro Express.

Thus a calm, deliberate and accurate rifleman can hunt the largest and toughest of game with a relatively light rifle without ever leaving a wounded animal to bleed to death or fall prey to predators. Yet the same rifle in the hands of a less skillful and level-headed fellow may strew the woods with cripples.

It's this difference in hunters that has led to so much controversy about the adequacy of various calibers. One man, let us say, hunts everything in North America with a 7 mm. and swears by it. Another comes along and declares under oath that the 7 mm. isn't even good enough for sheep or mule deer. The difference, of course, lies not in the rifle itself, but in how it is used, by whom, and under what conditions.

I know a mining man who operates on the desert of northern Mexico. Year in and year out he kills an average of two big mule deer a month for meat. He is not particularly interested in hunting or shooting, and I wouldn't call him a crack shot by any means. When his meat gets low he takes an old Model 94 Winchester .30/30 equipped with a Lyman 1-A tang peep, puts on a pair of basketball shoes for silent stalking, and goes out to some section where deer are plentiful. He hunts with about the same emotion that you and I feel when we buy a rump roast at the corner butcher shop. He never takes a shot at more than 100 yards, and he never takes a running shot. If it is possible, he rests his rifle on the limb of a tree or drops into the kneeling position. He always aims behind the shoulder midway on the animal, giving him a circle of from 14 to 20 inches in which to place his shot. If brush is in the way, he finds an opening, or he doesn't shoot. If the animal is standing in the wrong position for his favorite shot, he either works into a better position or lets the animal shift. If the buck becomes frightened and takes off, he doesn't fire, because he knows that he'll see another deer that day or the next, and he doesn't want to chase a wounded animal or to spook all the deer in the neighborhood with a wild bombardment. When he buys one box of .30/30 cartridges, he is, in effect, buying 20 deer.

Tell that hombre the .30/30 isn't a top deer cartridge under all conditions and he'll think you've lost your mind. In his hands, and under the same conditions, it would also be a good moose cartridge. Which sets up another maxim: if an animal is hit right with almost any fairly adequate cartridge, a kill is the result.

On the other hand, a great deal of vastly unrealistic stuff is written every year about the placement of shots, mostly by people who apparently assume, that nothing but undisturbed deer are hunted, and then only by cool and level-headed marksmen like our miner. These articles always come complete with cutaway diagrams of bucks showing how to reach the vitals from various angles. Such pieces don't do any harm and they may do some good, but they skip lightly over the fact that bucks are often very uncooperative. They don't patiently wait around while someone plinks a bullet into them.

THE BRAIN AND SPINE SHOTS

These experts are fond of pointing out that even a well-placed .22 rimfire will bring home the venison. With that very obvious statement no one can disagree. Consider this, though: under modern hunting conditions, the brain and spine shots which make even a .22 effective are usually almost impossible to make. And this: if those small, vital areas are missed, the result all too often is a wounded animal that escapes.

330 COMPLETE BOOK OF RIFLES AND SHOTGUNS

There is hardly a worse place to shoot a fine game animal than in the head. If the brain is struck, the animal is, of course, killed instantly. But the brain is a small mark. If it is missed, the result may be a broken jaw that dooms the animal to slow death by starvation. And that does happen. Once I found the carcass of a fine buck with the nose and mouth shot away; it had starved to death. Even if you hit the brain and kill the animal in its tracks, the resulting sight is likely to be one to turn your stomach. I once pulled down on the head of a buck about 60 yards away and killed him. The light, high-velocity bullet blew up in the animal's skull. One look at the pulpy, shapeless head, the bulging eyes, the antlers askew—well, I was almost ready to quit hunting deer. A grand animal like a buck deserves a better end.

I cannot get enthusiastic about the neck shot, either. If the spinal vertebrae in the neck are broken, the deer dies instantly. If the spine is missed, however, the neck shot is no more deadly than a shot in any other muscular tissue. I remember seeing a big bull caribou drop after a neck hit—and then get up and run 300 yards before a lung shot brought it down. I once knocked down a fine mule deer with the same kind of shot. He got up and ran. My companion and I tracked him a full half mile. The bullet had severed a big artery, and it seemed incredible that a mule deer could contain all the blood that that one lost.

Head and neck shots are justified at short range and under favorable conditions, particularly by the man who knows his anatomy, and who has to stop dangerous game in an emergency. For ordinary hunting, though, these shots are a long, long way from ideal.

About the only time a shoulder shot is justified is when the hunter wants to disable a potentially dangerous animal like a grizzly or an Alaska brown bear. Broken shoulders will put an animal down and render it helpless without killing it; even with only one shoulder broken, even a grizzly cannot manage a charge on a hillside. For that reason veteran grizzly hunters try to break the shoulder with their first shot. Some men also try for the shoulders on other large animals, like moose, that are hard to kill in their tracks. However, the shoulder shot will wreck a lot of meat by filling it with bone fragments. If the shot goes low it means a broken leg. Then an animal can travel all day, only to be pulled down eventually by wolves.

THE LUNG SHOT

Well, where should you aim? The best place of all is the lung area back of the shoulder. The advantages of this shot are many. A reasonably adequate bullet placed there almost always means a one-shot kill. Death is not always instantaneous, but it is usually quick. The rapid expansion of the bullet tears up the lungs, administers terrific shock to the whole nervous system and very often ruptures

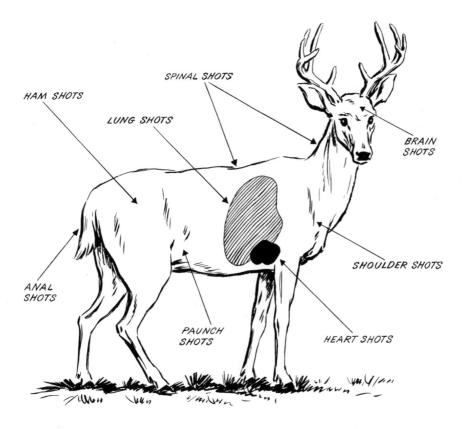

The various areas for placement of shots at deer are indicated here. Avoid the brain, spine and gut shots—the chances of missing or merely wounding the animal are too great. The lung area presents the largest target with the best possibility for a one-shot kill.

the heart or otherwise stops its action. As I write this, the last head of game I shot was a grizzly. He was below me, about 125 yards away, walking slowly across a big, open, timberline basin. The .300 Magnum bullet went high through the left lung behind the shoulder and emerged low through the right lung. The bear fell to the shot, got up, took two steps and fell dead. The only other grizzly I ever saw killed so quickly was one I hit in about the same body area with a 130-grain Silvertip bullet from my .270.

Strangely enough, a shot through the lungs near the heart usually kills more quickly than a shot through the heart itself. The heart-shot animal almost always runs frantically 20 to 200 yards before falling dead. And if it gets out of sight, you may think you've missed completely—as I once did. I was painfully clambering down a high ridge toward camp—beat up, thirsty, and footsore—when a fine whitetail buck came out under the cliffs below and started running up the opposite side of the canyon. I just had time to throw a cartridge into the chamber of my .270, sit down and get off a shot. The buck jumped about five feet in the air, lit and disappeared over the top before I could shoot again.

Well, I knew my cross hairs had been on that buck. Still, I was inclined to believe I'd missed him, probably with a shot that hit a rock and stung him with fragments. But the more I thought about that high and frantic jump, the more convinced I became that I'd hit him. So, tired though I was, I retraced my steps, crossed the canyon and climbed to where the buck had disappeared. There he lay, dead as a mackerel. I discovered then that the bullet had gone in just behind the last rib, ranged forward and blown the heart to pieces.

The lung shot is a quick, if not instant, killer because the ruptured lungs drown the animal in its own blood. The lung area is a much easier target to hit than either the brain or spine because it's larger. Furthermore, this type of shot doesn't destroy any edible meat. If the bullet goes too high, it will break the spine; if too far forward, it may break the shoulders or land in the neck. And even if it lands in the paunch, it may still kill or disable the game if the rifle is a powerful one.

No matter which way the animal is facing, you should try to drive the bullet into this large lung area. You give yourself all the odds on a quick kill, especially if your rifle has more-than-average power.

AVOID GUT SHOTS

Above all, try to keep your shots out of the abdominal area. Now and then a paunch shot—particularly with a light, easily expanded bullet of very high velocity—will result in a quick kill. But all too often a gut-shot animal can run for miles, even when hit with a powerful bullet.

The heart and the lungs are vital organs. Any serious interference with the functioning of either means quick death. But the stomach, intestines, and other abdominal parts are not immediately necessary to life or movement. We have seen that an animal with a pair of broken shoulders cannot travel, and that an animal with a ruptured heart or torn-up lungs dies quickly. But animals have been known to travel a considerable distance with practically all of their paunch organs missing.

Once, in northern Arizona, I took a shot with my .30/06 at a buck running away from me down a hill. The 150-grain Bronze Point bullet struck him high in the left ham and went through, laying open the entire abdominal cavity. The buck went down, but when I got to him, he lurched to his feet and ran with his stomach bouncing along 30 feet behind him. He was practically gutted.

Another time, in Sonora, Mexico, I saw the abdomen of a desert ram ripped open by a 150-grain bullet from a .300 Savage. That ram jumped over a barrel cactus, had its protruding stomach caught on the terrible thorns, and lost every organ in its abdomen. Yet it kept going—and the hunter tracked it a mile before he found it dead.

It is true, of course, that abdominal shots have dropped a lot of game stone-dead in its tracks. Very often, a bullet like the old 139-grain Western open point in the 7 mm. would do it. So would the 87-grain bullet in the .257 or .250/3000, the 130-grain bullet in the .270 and the 150-grain bullet in the .30/06. I have also had many reports of quick-kills with gut shots by the .220 Swift. The point is, though, that sometimes such a shot results in a quick kill, but sometimes it doesn't, even with a rifle of high velocity and rapid bullet distintegration. Dressing an animal that has been gut-shot is always a messy, disagreeable business. The good hunter tries to keep his bullets out of the abdominal cavity if he possibly can.

This is how a deer target should be marked for a hunters' match. Shots in the heart-lung area count 5, hits in the brain or spine 4, and all others minus 5.

ADVANTAGE OF POWERFUL CALIBERS

It is fairly easy to place your shots when game is plentiful and relatively tame, but it's something else again when it is frightened, jittery, hunter-shy or on the move. Half a century ago a famous deer hunter wrote that hitting a running deer anywhere at any distance is not a bad shot. And it's true that in the course of a season, the average hunter in average country doesn't see many bucks, so he'll have to be pardoned for taking his shots as they come. The deer may be on the move, or hind-end to, or partly concealed by bullet-deflecting brush. Under these conditions how many hunters will refrain from shooting? One in ten? I'd say closer to one in 100.

That is why I have always campaigned for the more powerful calibers for modern hunting—bullets that will knock down and disable animals even when poorly placed. You should always try to get your bullet into the heart-lung area. But you should also use a rifle with plenty of power; then, if your shot miscues, it still may kill or disable the animal.

Consider a typical shot—a frightened animal running directly away from the hunter. I have always declined such a chance at elk, moose, or grizzlies, letting these animals go their way unshot but hoping they'll turn. These big animals are just too tough to be put down by hind-end shots with a rifle of the .270—.30/06 class.

On deer-size animals, though, a shot aimed at the center line of the rump will usually kill or disable. I once took such a shot at a buck running away from me, at between 250 and 300 yards. The .270 bullet went right between the hams, through the abdomen and tore up the right lung. The buck traveled no more than 20 yards farther. Later on, I got an identical shot, but at shorter range. This buck—the heaviest Arizona whitetail I have ever shot—ran no more than 10 feet after the bullet connected. If a bullet goes between the hams, it will drive up through the abdomen into the lungs. If it goes high, it will break the spine above the root of the tail. The thing to do is to keep the shot high and center, because if it is low, it will disembowel the animal and the result will be a long chase. If it hits too far on either side it will mess up a ham. At best, you have a lot of spoiled meat; at worst, a wounded animal that may escape and become coyote meat.

In the case of a quartering animal at fairly close range, the hunter should shoot past the hips to drive the bullet at an angle up into the lung area. But such a shot on a running target requires a skill and coolness that I fear too many hunters do not have.

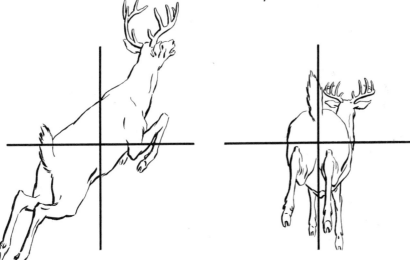

A hunter often has to shoot at a deer which is running away from him. In both cases above, a high-caliber bullet placed where the crosshairs meet will drive through to the lung area.

Such a shot can be tried on an animal the size of deer, antelope or sheep with a .270 or a .30/06. But it should never be attempted with less powerful rifles, even though they may—under ideal conditions and with well-placed shots—lay game of that size out cold.

If a broadside running shot is offered, and the hunter feels he cannot afford to pass it up, he should swing way ahead, since it is far better to miss in front than wound in the gut. Actually, no one should attempt running shots unless he is armed with a rifle with power enough to give him a good chance of disabling the game even with a poorly-placed shot. A fast-opening bullet in the abdominal cavity—from a .270 or a .30/06, for instance—has a very good chance of knocking down the game and paralyzing it long enough for the hunter to get to it. But a shot in the same area from a .25/35, let us say, will mean a wounded animal that keeps on going and escapes to die.

The power of the rifle is a poor substitute for calmness and skill in the placement of shot, but it is to some extent a substitute. In the Canadian Rockies, the hunter usually shoots under very favorable circumstances. The game is in the open, undisturbed, and the hunter can almost always get into a good position, wait until the animal is turned right, and take time to get over his excitement and recover his wind and steadiness.

Consequently, a .270 or .30/06 is plenty of rifle even for moose and grizzly, and, nine times out of ten, a .257 or 7 mm. will be entirely adequate. Yet the .270 and .30/06 are not any too much gun for whitetail deer and antelope, which are much smaller than a moose or grizzly and have but a fraction of their vitality. Why? Simply because modern hunting conditions often make it very tough indeed to place shots properly on a buck that is bouncing through brush on the other side of a ravine, or on a spooked antelope on the opposite hillside.

The idea, then, is to place those bullets as well as you possibly can, to kill as cleanly as you can, and to take advantage of every opportunity for a one-shot kill. But your rifle must have adequate power; then, if a shot is a bit off line, the chances are still good that you'll get the game instead of letting it go away wounded.

CHAPTER TWENTY FOUR

Slings and Swivels

ONE OF THE MOST USEFUL ACCESSORIES ANYONE CAN GET FOR A RIFLE is some sort of a gunsling. Without a sling a rifle is an awkward burden. The hunter can carry it over his shoulder like a soldier on parade. He can let it dangle from one hand, or he can even cradle it in his arms as if it were an infant. When he is approaching game he can hold it across his body in both hands like a quail hunter walking up a bird. But in the long haul any of these methods of lugging a rifle around gets pretty tiresome.

A sling makes carrying the rifle much less of a chore. With it one hand is always free and if the rifle is slung across the back, both hands are free—an exceedingly important consideration to anyone who is scrambling up a cliff, carrying back to camp a sheep head or a quarter of venison, or fighting his way through brush.

Toting a rifle on a sling leaves one hand free, both if rifle is slung across the back.

TYPES OF SLINGS AND SWIVELS

In Europe the sling is a simple strap used only for carrying and generally attached to the rifle with small permanent swivels. Continental hunters use slings on shotguns as well as on rifles, but the British and Americans think slings look like the devil on smooth bores and almost never use them. I have never had a swivel put on a shotgun, but as a guy who often walks 10 or 15 miles a day during the pheasant season I can see that the Continental sportsman has a point. An Idaho skeet-shooting friend of mine had bases for quick detachable swivels put on a Winchester Model 21, 20-gauge shotgun, used a sling in the field, and swears by it.

I don't think permanent swivels improve the looks of any shotgun or rifle, but the quick-detachable swivel is a horse of another shade. With the permanent swivel and most slings, the whole works must be left on either the rifle or the shotgun to nobody's particular benefit. The British often fit rifles with eyes instead of swivels, and the sling is simply narrowed at the ends so that it can be tied into the eyes. Most factory rifles that have any provision for attaching a sling have permanent swivels. The only European or American factory-made rifles I can think of offhand that have come equipped with quick-detachable swivels are the Winchester Super Grades, the Winchester Model 52 sporter, and the Weatherbys.

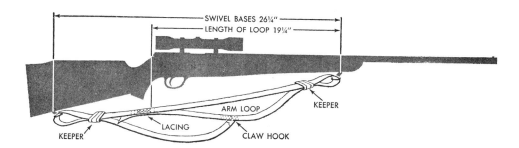

This is a typical one-piece sling. The forward keeper makes the arm loop tight, and the rear keeper holds the claw hook tight. The size of the loop is regulated by the lacings and the hook adjusts the length of the sling.

Quick-detachable swivels were, I believe, originated by Winchester. However, the bases are large, complicated, and not exactly things of beauty. For many years gunsmiths ordered swivels from Winchester and then made up bases that were smaller, neater, and which served just as well. Since the war, however, excellent quick-detachable swivels a bit smaller than those made by Winchester and with simple bases of the type turned out by the gunsmiths have been made by the Cain Products Co., of San Francisco, by Paul Jaeger of Jenkintown, Pennsylvania, by Herter's of Waseca, Wisconsin, and perhaps by others.

The swivels of the quick detachable type have many advantages. The sling can be removed when the rifle is put in the rack or when the hunter is going into thick brush where the sling might catch on twigs and branches. If the bases are the same and the front swivel is the same distance in front of the trigger the same sling can be used on several rifles.

The rear swivel base is simply a metal lump of some sort with a hole in it on the end of a wood screw and it is screwed into the buttstock a few inches in front of the toe of the stock. The front swivel is variously attached. Sometimes the screw portion screws into a shallow hole drilled and tapped into the barrel itself. Sometimes it screws into a nut inletted into the stock below the barrel channel. Other gunsmiths like to fit the nut onto a band around the barrel. In the United States the swivel is generally attached to the forend about 16 inches forward of the center of the trigger.

However, in Europe, where the sling is not used as an aid to shooting, the front swivel base is generally attached to the barrel by sweating or by means of a band. For a gunsling to be used as an aid to shooting this is poison, as the secret of using a shooting gunsling and doing any good with it is to cram the left hand hard against the front swivel. However, the swivel on the barrel does allow the muzzle of the rifle to be carried lower—and this is a very pious idea in heavy brush. This placement of the forward swivel is likewise excellent for a rifle of heavy recoil, as with the conventionally placed swivel the violent recoil of a heavy rifle is apt to skin and cut the shooter's left hand badly, even though the sling is not used as a shooting aid. For this reason the front swivel of the Winchester Model 70 in .458 is up on the barrel where it belongs. With a tight sling and a conventionally placed swivel even a .375 Magnum can hurt the left hand if a glove is not worn.

The base of this swivel goes through the stock and attaches to a band around the barrel.

The swivel on this .458 Winchester is attached to the barrel so the recoil won't injure shooter's hand.

This swivel base screws into a nut in the barrel channel. The band holds the barrel to the forend.

A quick-detachable type swivel (left) is fastened to the forend with a nut in the bottom of the barrel channel. The swivel is easily removed by pressing button release (right).

As far as I know the shooting gunsling is an American invention and first appeared, I believe, on the old .30/40 Krag. I first got acquainted with this wonderful aid to shooting on a then nice new Model 1903 Springfield with the number, believe it or not, of 123456. The regular military sling is of leather, in two pieces, and 1¼ inches wide. The front portion can be formed into a loop into which the left arm is inserted for steady holding. As issued the military sling is excellent for what it was intended for—to lessen the burden of carrying the rifle on long marches and to aid in shooting. For sporting use it is too heavy and too complicated.

THE WHELEN SLING

For those used to the military sling and preferring the two-piece jobs, sporting slings like the military sling but made of lighter and narrower leather straps (⅞ to 1 inch) are available. Still better

Plain swivels (two on left) are suitable if sling is seldom removed. Detachable swivels (two on right) have a spring catch for removing swivel.

is the one-piece sling worked out by Colonel Townsend Whelen, dean of the American gun writers, back before World War I. This one-piece Whelen sling is a strip of leather from ¾ to 1 inch wide and generally about 52 inches long. It has a claw hook at one end and the length for carrying is adjusted by the placement of the claw hook in a series of holes punched in the leather. It likewise has two leather "keepers." The sling is held together and the size of the "loop" is regulated by leather lacings which tie through the holes.

The narrower, lighter edition of the military sling is preferred by many. It is made of two pieces of leather. The forward piece forms the loop into which the upper left arm is inserted for steady holding. It is 45 inches long and has a claw hook and two keepers. The "tail piece" or rear portion is 23 inches long, has a claw hook for adjustment and it is attached to the loop portion with a metal loop.

In addition there are various slings on the market that are made for carrying and for use in the "hasty sling" adjustment. They are one-piece jobs, have no keepers, and are generally adjusted for length by a buckle or something of the sort.

I have used the one-piece Whelen sling for many years and on the whole have found it very satisfactory. I adjust it so that it is of the proper length to carry the rifle with the sling over my right shoulder with the trigger guard forward. I hold the strap with my right hand to steady it. If it is necessary for me to sling the rifle over my back so that I can use both hands for climbing, carrying out a couple of quarters of venison, a sheep head, or some other burden, I simply move the claw hook back to lengthen the sling.

Whelen—a good all-around sling for any hunting rifle.

Military—a fine sling for target shooting, but somewhat heavy for hunting.

Strap—good for packing a rifle, but not much good for sighting.

On a restocked and somewhat remodeled Winchester Model 70 .270 the swivel bases are exactly 27 inches apart. On other rifles in the rack this measurement runs between 26 and 28 inches. Adjusted to be comfortable for carrying as I have described, the sling including detachable Cain swivels is 37¾ inches long. From the forward swivel to the rawhide lacing which controls the size of the loop, the measurement is 20 inches.

SLING WITH THE SITTING POSITION

I adjust the size of the loop to be correct for the sitting position, the most useful of all hunting positions and one of the steadiest. Sitting is far steadier and more reliable than offhand and steadier even than kneeling. It is not as steady as a good prone position but it is seldom possible to use prone in big-game hunting. Too often low bushes and grass are in the way. In hilly and mountainous country much of the shooting has to be done from a hillside across a draw or canyon. Sitting is ideal for this, but prone cannot be used at all. Sitting does not bring the line of sight quite as high as does the kneeling position, but generally it is high enough. The rifleman who is primarily a big-game hunter should do most of his practicing from the sitting and offhand positions—and in sitting he should not neglect the use of the sling.

Getting the "loop" just the right length takes a bit of cut and try. If the loop is too long, it gives little support and is not much better than no loop at all. If it is too short, it makes for cramped and uncomfortable shooting and promotes tenseness and tremor.

To use a loop in a tight sling, one should turn the loop a half turn to the left. He should then thrust his left arm through it until the loop is *high* on his upper arm. He should then pull the keeper tight against the arm. Next step is to reach over the sling with his left hand and put it hard against the front swivel. The sling should be tight enough that it requires a bit of effort to bring the butt up against the shoulder. I like a sling so tight that I have to put the butt against my shoulder with my right hand.

In a good sitting position and with a correctly adjusted tight sling, the rifle holds itself steady. The tension of the upper arm *below* the knee and against the flat shin all held snug by the pull of the back muscles and the tension of the sling make for a wobble-free hold. The left hand does not have to grasp the forend. Ac-

Proper sitting form with the sling: flat of elbow against flat of knee, arm loop as high up on the upper arm as possible and held tight by the metal keeper.

tually it can be open and it makes no difference. The right hand has nothing to do except to grasp the pistol grip lightly and to squeeze the trigger. For more on how to use a sling when shooting, see the Seven-Lesson Shooting Course in Chapter 19.

It is surprising what can be done from the sitting position by a reasonably good shot used to using the sling. I have by this means shot hundreds of jackrabbits at ranges of from 200 to well over 300 yards, dozens of coyotes, several dozen deer, a fair number of sheep, antelope, and elk, as well as various exotic game animals in foreign parts.

After a bit of practice, it is not difficult when shooting from the sit and wrapped up in a sling to keep all shots in the standard 12-inch bull at 300 yards—and that sort of shooting will keep the freezer in meat. The world is full of better shots than I am but once before two witnesses I shot a 5-shot group at 200 yards from sitting with a tight sling that measured $2\frac{1}{2}$ inches center to center of the widest shots. I am not kidding myself that I could do that every day, as that rifle wouldn't shoot any better than that from a bench rest. Lady luck had me by the hand that time and the wibbles must have taken care of the wobbles.

One shot from the sitting position with a tight sling I shall always remember was on the burning plains of India near Merut in 1955. The subject was a little spiral horned antelope known as the black buck, a creature about three-fourths the size of an American pronghorn. He was with a bunch of does and another and somewhat smaller buck and way out yonder, so far that he was a bit apprehensive but not frightened enough to run. I had plently of time to plant my posterior on the bare and sizzling earth and to get into a tight sling. He looked to be something over 400 yards away, so I held the intersection of the crosswires in the Leupold scope over the top of his shoulder, allowed a bit for his leisurely forward travel and squeezed one off. The buck fell on his nose, got up, and started hobbling slowly off while the rest of the herd fled at top speed—and the black buck is one of the world's fastest animals. With my binoculars I could see that the 130-grain .270 bullet had almost shot his left front leg off right where it joined the body. He hobbled over to an acre-sized patch of brush and lay down. We followed him up and got him.

Another shot taken from the sit and with a tight sling that will stay with me was one I made on a magnificent Stone ram with a heavy massive head that looked like that of a bighorn. He and two other rams were on the move. I had seen them first and was able to stay absolutely still, my arm through the loop of the sling, sitting on a hillside and ready to shoot. As I watched the largest ram left his two companions, moved over to a point, stood there wild, alert, tensely alive. I had been a little excited, quite a bit winded, but the use of the sling cut down on my shakes and the picture of those crosswires plastered steady behind the ram's shoulder reassured me. I squeezed off the trigger gently. The ram made a magnificent leap, fell on the talus slope below the point, shot right through the heart.

TARGET SLING

Still another type of sling is used on target shots—if indeed it can be called a sling. It consists of a wide leather band that buckles tight around the upper arm and an adjustable strap that snaps into the front swivel. It is used for shooting only, not for carrying.

Target shots generally wear a heavy shooting mitt on the left hand so that when it is jammed into the front swivel for a long series of shots, the hand will not become bruised from the fairly husky recoil of a .30/06 or .300 Magnum target rifle. For the few shots fired by the big-game hunter this should be no bother with any caliber with less recoil than the .375 Magnum. I can shoot the .375 about ten times with a tight sling and with my bare left hard against the swivel without being bothered, but more shots than that are too much of a good thing. Try the orthodox tight sling with something like a .416 Rigby or a .458, however, and the recoil will about take your left hand off. With rifles of heavy recoil, the forward swivel should be put on the barrel. Since those cannons are shot at short range anyway, the sling is the most useful for carrying, and not once in five blue moons would it be used as an aid to shooting.

HASTY SLING

Many hunters who have never learned the virtue of the conventional tight sling with loop simply use the "hasty sling" position. To get into it the rifleman simply puts his arm through the sling, then back and around, as shown in the illustration. I may be pessimistic and prejudiced, but it is my experience that it is worthless. I have tried shooting offhand at 200 yards with hasty sling and without and almost always I make a better score with no sling at all. However, anyone who feels he gets any benefit from the hasty sling should use it.

Some rifles are so constructed that they are not adapted to a sling. But they are happily in the minority. I'd advise anyone who has a rifle to which a sling can be attached to have one put on—preferably with swivels of the quick-detachable type. If he has a rifle on which permanent swivels have been installed I'd advise him to substitute the more convenient Q.D. jobs. If he has rifles custom-made I suggest that he insist that his rifle maker use his favorite brand of quick-detachable swivels and put the forward swivel base at the most convenient distance forward of the trigger. Obviously the man with short arms will want it farther toward the rear than the chap with long arms and vice versa. Then if on all his rifles the swivel bases fit the same swivels and the front swivels are the same distance from the triggers, he can use the same sling on several rifles with perfect satisfaction.

A handy gadget, this shooting gunsling. If I had to choose between a scope sight and a good sling as an aid to accurate shooting, I'd pick the sling. Swivels and sling together only cost a few dollars but I have seen the time when they were worth their weight in rubies.

The hasty sling without a loop helps steady the rifle somewhat in the off-hand position. In this case the sling is merely slipped *around* the arm, bracing the rifle.

PART 2

CHAPTER TWENTY FIVE

Types of Shotguns

THE SHOTGUN YOU USE TODAY IS A DIRECT DESCENDANT OF THE smoothbore musket. For shotguns are smoothbores by definition, and, as we saw in the early chapters of this book, the development of the old muzzle loader was, in effect, the history of the shotgun until the rifled barrel came into its own.

Probably the oldest bird-shooting gun in existence is a snaphance smoothbore, labeled a "birding piece" and dated 1614. For more than a century afterward, fowling pieces, as they were called, continued to be heavy, long-barreled single guns with a musket-like forend extending to within an inch or two of the muzzle. Some double-barreled guns were designed during this period. The best of these was a light Spanish fowling piece of limited effectiveness.

It wasn't until the early eighteen hundreds that the famous English gunsmith, Joseph Manton, began turning out practical double-barreled shotguns. Americans, used to hunting strictly for food, visited Europe at this time and brought back the novel idea of shooting birds on the wing for sport. They introduced the high-priced Manton guns into the United States. These old flintlock shotguns are still considered masterpieces of workmanship.

By 1850 the muzzle-loading double shotgun had become a moderately efficient game killer, but it was difficult and dangerous to fire. For one thing, the sportsman was loaded down with powder, flasks, shot pouches, wads and percussion caps. He lost many a bird that refused to wait while he tediously loaded his piece, and he occasionally lost a couple of fingers when one of his barrels went off while he loaded the other.

The answer to the hunter's problems—breech-loading—had been tried unsuccessfully over the years. When the French gunsmith, Lefaucheux, brought out a pinfire cartridge in 1850, however, the way was paved for breechloading. Lefaucheux made his own

An early double-barreled shotgun, this Eighteenth Century flintlock has revolving over-and-under 14-gauge barrels that are turned by hand into firing position beneath the flint.

This English side-by-side shotgun, which resembles the modern double, was popular with wealthy sportsmen about 150 years ago. It has 16-gauge barrels and its twin flintlock mechanisms are set off by individual triggers.

breech-loading double gun, and it proved to be a safe and practical weapon. This type of gun, which was refined through the late Nineteenth and early Twentieth Centuries, is the ancestor of our modern shotgun.

TODAY'S SHOTGUNS

Today there are six basic types of shotguns: the single barreled break-open, bolt action, pump action, and semiautomatic; the double-barreled side-by-side and the double-barreled over-and-under. Each has its advocates. Your choice of a shotgun will depend on what kind of shooting you are going to do and how much you want to spend.

THE BREAK-OPEN SINGLE-SHOT

The simplest type of shotgun and one of the cheapest on the market today is the single barrel which fires one shot at a time and breaks open to reload. Sometimes equipped with a hammer and generally equipped with an automatic ejector, the single is obtainable in all chokes from .410 to 12 and with barrel lengths of from 26 to 36 inches.

The single is especially the boys' and farmers' friend, as it is inexpensive, handy for pot shooting and for discouraging a marauding fox or chicken hawk. It is likewise used with buckshot or rifled slugs for deer hunting in heavy brush and woods and often is equipped for this purpose with makeshift iron sights. The single shares one advantage with the double—you can break it open and carry it that way for safety. You can't do this with any of the bolt, pump or autoloading shotguns.

Equipped with a ventilated rib, the single is also used by many crack trap shots. These special trap guns are expensive, nicely adjusted and carefully bored weapons.

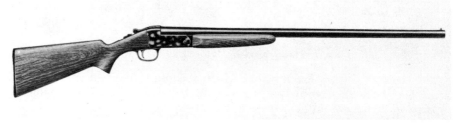

The break-open single-barreled shotgun is a simple, sturdy gun for the beginner or for knockabout use on the farm. This is a Savage Model 220.

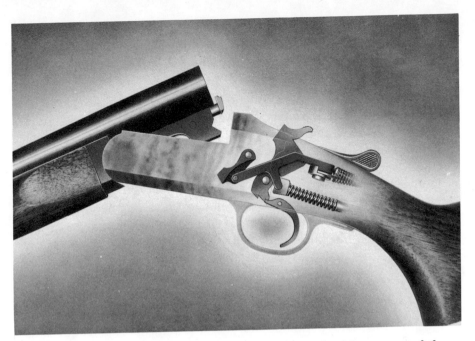

The simplicity of the single-barrel action is shown in this cutaway of the Stevens Model 94 hammer-style shotgun.

THE DOUBLE GUN

The double-barreled shotgun comes in two basic types. The side-by-side double has barrels next to each other and is the traditional upland game and waterfowl gun. The over-and-under double has one barrel on top of the other and as favored by many hunters and skeet shooters because of its single sighting plane. The best doubles are made with selective single triggers that give the shooter the option of firing either barrel first. They also have automatic ejectors that throw out fired shells. The cheaper doubles have two triggers—one for each barrel—or nonselective triggers that always

The classic double-barreled shotgun, the traditional upland game and waterfowl gun, is fast handling, well balanced and safe. This is a Winchester Model 21 with a ventilated rib.

fire the open or unchoked barrel first. Instead of automatic ejectors, they have extractors, and the fired shells must be removed by hand.

Doubles haven't changed much in the past 60 or 70 years. The various types of shotgun actions were pretty well perfected in the eighteen eighties and guns could be had either with hammers or without and with automatic ejectors. The changes that have occured once have been toward shorter barrels and to barrels of fluid steel rather than of those combinations of steel and iron known as twist, Damascus, skelp, and so on. Straighter buttstocks, Monte Carlo combs and beavertail forends have come in, and the single trigger has been perfected. Otherwise, the guns are much the same.

The double presents advantages over other types of shotguns. Besides the single-barrel breakopen, it is the safest of all guns. Break it and you can tell if it is loaded or not. Break it when you cross a fence and it cannot fire. For the same barrel length it is several inches shorter overall than any pump or automatic. It is faster and livelier to handle because the weight is between the hands. It offers quick selectivity to two degrees of choke, which is constriction of a barrel to control the shot pattern. (Generally, of course, the open barrel is fired first, but under many conditions

The safest of all guns, the double can be broken open and carried that way to make sure it's unloaded.

it is best to fire the choke barrel first—at incoming birds, for example.) It is also quick and easy to check the double for barrel obstructions, a desirable attribute when you are shooting in mud or snow.

With the exception of a few foreign guns fitted with Greener side safeties, doubles have their safeties on the tang—the natural, convenient and fast place for the safety to be. Such safeties are much quicker and more convenient to use than the cross-bolt, trigger-guard safeties on pumps or automatics.

A good double should have selective automatic ejection, which means that when the gun is opened only the fired shell is ejected. Likewise it should have a selective single trigger which can be set to fire either the right or left barrel first.

Some of the nicest patterning guns I have ever seen have been expensive doubles, but one cannot count on getting tighter or more even patterns with, let us say, a $1500 Holland & Holland than with a mass-produced pump gun with about as much handwork on it as an automobile axle. Given the same barrel length and boring, the finest double shoots no harder and kills no farther than a farm boy's single barrel with the same load.

The virtues of the double lie elsewhere. Built to the proper specifications it is the queen of upland guns, the best balanced, the fastest to get on with—as well as the safest. Some claim to find the broad muzzles of the side-by-side quicker and easier to point with; others claim they shoot better and point more accurately with the single sighting plane of the pump or automatic. I am inclined to be skeptical of both claims. I shoot both doubles and repeaters and am never bothered by shifting from one type to the other.

On upland game, however, I do my best shooting with a double. One season I killed 23 straight pheasants with a Winchester Model 21 12-gauge with 26-inch barrels, and during another season I killed 21 straight with a 16-gauge that was identical with the 12 except that it was a bit lighter. I have never done that well with any of my repeaters. The good balance, short overall length and lively handling qualities of the double enable the gunner to get on his target faster in the uplands.

I think the fast-handling well-balanced double also has the edge for decoyed ducks. Some may protest that it is better to have the three shots of the repeater than the two of the double. The repeater *is* faster for three shots, but the double with automatic ejectors is faster for four—and likewise for six. For upland shooting the extra shot of the repeater is no advantage as it is very seldom that the average gunner can do anything on upland birds with that third shot.

For pass shooting, the repeater with its greater overall length and greater steadiness of swing is probably superior to the field-type double, and at skeet I can break two or three more targets out of 100 with a pump or automatic, because their relative muzzle heaviness makes it difficult for me to commit my chief error —slowing or stopping my swing. At traps the pump or the single barrel is favored by most, but some like doubles bored modified or improved modified in one barrel and full in the other; they use the more open barrel for 16-yard rise, the full-choke barrel for handicap. For doubles at traps (the toughest of all clay target games) the double is far handier and more deadly than the pump.

For shooting rifled slugs, there is no doubt that the single-barrel gun is superior to the double; even the best doubles tend to crossfire with slugs, the right barrel to the left and the left barrel to the right. Doubles are adjusted to center their patterns at the same spot at 40 yards for one thing, and for another the slugs set up a different set of vibrations than do charges of shot. The repeater also is easier to equip with a receiver sight or a scope for slug hunting.

Right now the over-and-under is a somewhat hotter item than the side-by-side double, and I'd make a guess that this is due to the rifle-mindedness of the American shooting public. The over-and-under has the advantage of the single-sighting plane, recoil that comes back in a straight line and no crossfiring with slugs as

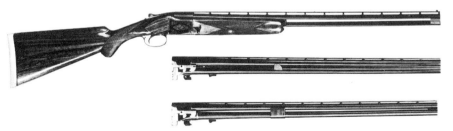

The over-and-under double, such as the Browning 20 Gauge with extra barrels, is favored by some hunters for its single-sighting plane and straight-line recoil.

is the case with the side-by-side. It has the disadvantages of being somewhat more expensive to make, and also of offering more resistance to a side wind—something I'd consider a minor criticism.

Both side-by-side and over-and-under are made in box-lock and side-lock forms. Americans have generally made box-lock guns. The late-lamented Parker was a box lock as is the Winchester Model 21. The side locks have the locks attached to the side plates which in some instances are hand-detachable, and they use flat rather than coil springs. The only American side-lock gun of recent manufacture was the L. C. Smith. Some box-lock guns are made with false side plates. Various types of bolting and rib extensions are used in doubles, including the Greener-type crossbolt, widely used in Spain, and Germany, and the doll's head. The British firm of Westley Richards makes guns with hand-detachable box locks. Actually, there is some question whether the use of an extension rib for bolting shut a double gun is necessary at all. The very strong Winchester Model 21 has none.

Just as the United States is the stronghold of the repeating shotgun, Europe is the home of the double. In Europe it is still the most widely used type of shotgun, so much so that a definitive book on shotguns and shotgun ballistics published in England is almost entirely devoted to the double and mentions other types of shotguns only in passing. Repeating systems were worked out by Americans, the various types of doubles largely by Europeans, although the Browning superposed (over-and-under) was developed by the American John Browning. For the most part, American doubles simply have been refinements of types evolved in England.

Many Europeans are strongly prejudiced against repeating shotguns, considering them for some curious reason "not quite sporting." I know an American who showed up for a grouse shoot in Scotland with an automatic and his host would not have been more shocked if he had come without pants. In East Africa it is illegal to shoot birds with a shotgun capable of firing more than two shots without reloading. The British get around the double's lack of firepower by having their guns built in matched pairs. When the grouse are coming over, the "gun" fires two shots, hands his empty weapon to a loader and grabs another. Some very fast shots are reputed to be able to take two birds from a flock as they come in and two after they have passed!

The doubles with the finest reputations are made in England

by such famous firms as Boss, Holland & Holland, Purdy, and West-ley Richards. The best are works of art with beautiful checkering, chaste engraving, superb polish and, often, gold-plated working parts. The price of these fine guns would startle an American used to paying from $75 to $150 for a repeater. But like the American Parker and the Remington Model 32, fine British guns bought before the war now sell for a good deal more than their original cost. I wouldn't consider an elegant British double an investment to compare with U. S. Steel or American Telephone & Telegraph stock but a man who owns one can always be sure of getting his money back—and more—if he wants to sell it.

Some very fine guns are also made in Belgium, where the city of Liége is one of the centers of the world's firearms industry. Francotte, for example, is a famous Belgian name. From what I have seen of Belgian guns, I'd say that the best of them are equal to the best British weapons; but they don't have the prestige and are not as expensive. Spain produces some pretty sad guns and some very fine ones, with AYA turning out some real works of art. I have a little Spanish 28-gauge double with 25-inch barrels, non-selective single trigger, Holland & Holland hand-detachable side locks, good engraving, and magnificent wood for which I paid less than $200. It was made by Eusebio Arizaga of Palencia de las Armas. Gun-fanciers who have looked it over have guessed the cost at anywhere from $650 to $1500.

The ancient Italian firm of Beretta turns out over-and-unders as well as side-by-sides. They are imported into this country by J. L. Galef & Son, Inc. of New York. Some are good, plain, sound

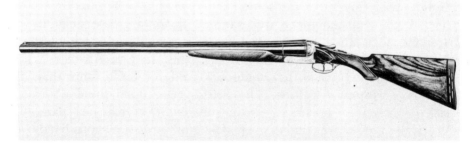

Many fine, expensive doubles are imported from Europe for discriminating shooters. An example is this Italian Beretta.

guns in the moderate-price bracket, but some are beautifully made, fitted and finished, and are expensive. Other famous Italian guns are the Franchi and the Bernardelli. The Sauer and the Simson are famous German guns, and many good-looking doubles are put together in Austria. However, the German guns have never enjoyed the reputation of those made in England and Belgium.

But just because a double is made in Europe is no sign that it is good. One of the worst I ever used was a French shotgun I rented in French Equatorial Africa in 1958. The best European guns would make an aficionado desert his family, but the worst are nothing to rejoice about.

Since the first repeating shotguns came on the market in the United States in the eighteen nineties, the double has been on a constant decline in this country. There are many reasons for this. One, perhaps, is that the rifle training given millions of Americans in two world wars made shooters repeater-conscious and single-barrel-conscious. When they left the service and purchased guns, doubles looked odd to them and they naturally went to repeaters. Also the tendency on the part of many shooters is to think in terms of firepower, and a gun that will shoot three shots or five shots seems like a better bargain than one that will shoot only two without reloading. Perhaps most important of all, the repeating shotgun is much cheaper to manufacture than the double, as it can be put together with a minimum of handwork.

The fine double, on the other hand, requires a great deal of expensive labor. Selective single triggers and automatic ejectors are complicated devices full of delicate parts that must be precisely adjusted. Inletting of buttstock and forend must be carefully done —and by hand.

In spite of these factors, a great many people would like to see something of a double-gun revival in this country. Savage and Marlin turn out knockabout guns that compete in price with repeaters and they take care of a segment of the market. But there are many people who appreciate a luxury item and would be willing to pay for it. I have a hunch that American ingenuity can come up with a double (either over-and-under or side-by-side) that can sell at around $250 with automatic ejection and single trigger. I'd like to see Remington revive the Parker, Savage the high-grade Foxes, Marlin the L. C. Smith, Ithaca make doubles again, and the Winchester Model 21 assembly room hum.

MANUALLY OPERATED REPEATERS

The first really successful repeating shotgun was the Winchester Model 1887, a lever action designed by John Browning. The gun was made in 12 and 10 gauge with 30- and 32-inch barrels and its tubular magazine held four shells. With one shell in the chamber, that made it a 5-shot repeater. Later this lever-action gun was redesigned to handle the smokeless powder loads then becoming popular and was issued, in 10-gauge only, as the Model 1901. Rolled-steel barrels in full choke and 32 inches in length were standard, but Damascus barrels were furnished on special order. The gun was discontinued in 1914.

The lever action is slow for a shotgun. A better type is the pump. The Spencer, a crude and not very successful pump, came out in the late eighteen eighties, but the first one to gain popularity was the Winchester Model 1893. Like the earlier lever action, the new pump was a Browning design. It was a hammer gun operated by a slide handle that made it easy to keep the gun to the shoulder while the mechanism was being worked. It was a slide ejector with a tubular magazine. It was made in 12 gauge only, with 30- or 32-inch barrels. It was manufactured for a relatively short period, and the only one I have ever seen outside of the Winchester museum at New Haven was a rust-covered relic sitting in the corner of a trapper's abandoned cabin beside a lonely lake in the Yukon.

The famous Model 1897 was a revamped Model 1893, and it was manufactured from 1897 until 1957 in both 12 and 16 gauge. It was turned out in barrel lengths of from 26 to 32 inches and in borings from cylinder to full choke, was widely used and almost indestructible, and got the name of the Old Corn Sheller.

The Winchester Model 12, first put on the market in 1913 in 20 gauge with a 25-inch barrel, is still being manufactured, and since it is the oldest hammerless, pump-action repeater continuously manufactured over the years, it is the gun by which all pump guns are judged. It is made in 12, 16, 20 and 28 gauge—and in modified form as the Model 42 in .410 gauge—and in barrel lengths from 26 to 32 inches. The gun with a serial number of 1,000,000 was turned out in 1953 and presented with considerable fanfare to General Hap Arnold. This model has been made as a field gun, trap gun, skeet gun and as a heavy duck gun for the

The Winchester Model 97 pump-action shotgun was the first really successful repeater. This is the short-barreled riot gun model.

The Winchester Model 12 pump has been a favorite since it first appeared in 1913.

3-inch 12-gauge shell. It has been fitted with various types of stocks and forends and in borings from skeet No. 1 to full choke.

The first Remington pump was the Model 10, which was made from 1907 until 1929 and in 12 gauge only. Unlike the Winchester Model 12, it ejected its fired cases from the bottom of the receiver instead of from the side. It was a hammerless. Remington, incidentally, made very fine double-barreled shotguns at one time but discontinued their manufacture in 1910. The Remington Model 1917 was a pump similar to the Model 10 but made only in 20 gauge.

Remington's next pump was the Model 29 made in 12 gauge only and similar to the Model 17. It came out in 1929. It was followed by the famous Model 31, which ejected at the side instead of the bottom of the receiver and which became famous for its smooth, easy action. It was made in 12, 16 and 20 gauge, with various barrel lengths, borings and types of stocks until 1949. It was then replaced by another pump, the currently manufactured Model 870. This is made in 12, 16 and 20 gauge and was designed for labor-saving manufacture. It is one of the slickest, smoothest pumps ever made.

Because the pump shotgun is the dominant type of American shotgun it has been manufactured by various firms. The Ithaca Gun Company, for many years a manufacturer of excellent double-barreled shotguns, went into the making of pumps in the late nineteen thirties with a gun very similar to the Remington Model 17 but made in 12, 16 and 20 gauge. The venture was so successful that after the war Ithaca discontinued the manufacture of doubles and concentrated on pumps. The Savage-Stevens Company has made various models of pumps, and the Model 77 with plain barrel and variable choke device is still in production. The handgun-making firm of High Standard builds a pump under the name "J. C. Higgins," a private brand name for Sears, Roebuck. Marlin has made pump guns, and a new name in the business is the Noble, a hammerless side-ejecting gun turned out in 12 and 16 gauge by the Noble Manufacturing Company in Massachusetts.

The pump gun's popularity is due to its many advantages. For one thing, it lends itself to mass manufacture because it requires

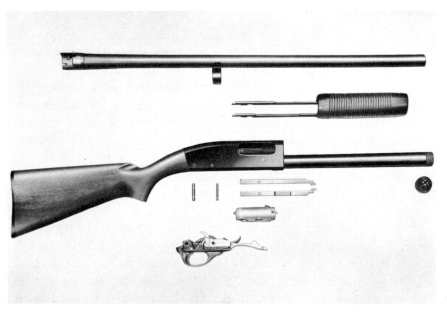

A stripped-down Remington Model 870 pump shotgun. Simplicity of design and smoothness of action have made it popular with shotgun fans.

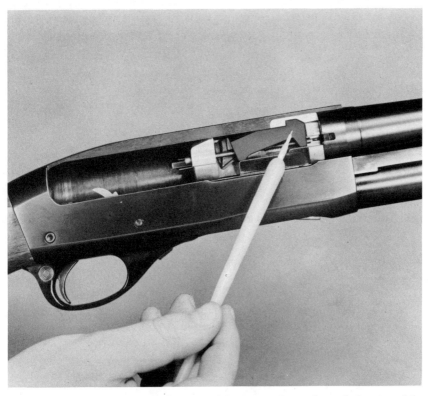

Cutaway photo of the Remington 870 pump shows how bolt assembly locks into the barrel extension, an exclusive feature of this gun.

a minimum of handwork; hence it can be sold more cheaply than a good double. For another thing, many people like its fast, manual action, its three or more shot capacity, and its single barrel. Fitted with a variable choke device, it is about as satisfactory an all-around gun as one can get.

On the other hand the more conservative do not care for the noisy action, excessive length, and tendency to be somewhat muzzle-heavy as compared to the double.

Bolt-action shotguns first made their appearance as modified World War I Mausers under such names as "Geco" at the time of the German inflation after World War I. Since that time, many bolt-action repeating shotguns in various gauges have made their appearance on the American market. They are best used as camp guns, farm guns and guns to be fitted with iron sights to shoot rifled slugs in areas where the use of high-power rifles is prohibited. They are inexpensive, strong and reliable, but they are slower even than the lever action in getting off second and subsequent shots.

The Ithaca fancy-grade pump gun with a ventilated rib.

The Savage Model 77 pump shotgun.

The Noble Model 70 pump shotgun.

HOW A MODERN PUMP SHOTGUN WORKS
(Remington Model 870)

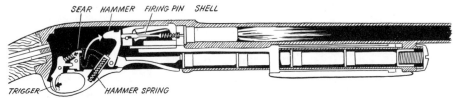

1. Starting with the gun loaded and cocked, pulling the trigger trips the sear, releasing the hammer to strike the firing pin and fire the shell.

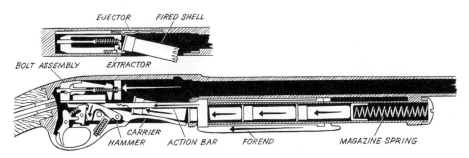

2. Pulling the forend rearward moves the action bar and bolt assembly toward the rear, ejecting the fired shell (see also top-view detail of ejection) pressing the hammer down into cocked position, and moving the new shell onto the carrier.

3. Detail of the carrier mechanism (left) shows how the bolt assembly at its rearmost position engages the carrier dog. As the bolt assembly moves forward (right), it moves the carrier dog downward, pivoting the carrier and new shell up into loading position. At the same time the shell latch moves to the right to hold the remaining shells in the magazine.

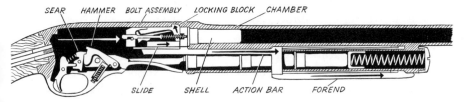

4. As the forend, action bar and bolt assembly continue to move forward, the new shell is pushed into the chamber, and the sear engages the hammer, locking it. At the final movement of the forend, the slide continues forward, pushing the locking block up to lock the action for firing.

THE AUTOLOADERS

The first successful autoloading shotgun—and for many years the world standard—was the famous Remington Model 11 which appeared in 1905. It was an invention of the famous John Browning. It was first offered to Winchester, but when Winchester refused to manufacture the gun on a royalty basis, Browning offered it to Remington. Remington bought the American rights and agreed to pay a royalty. The same gun is manufactured in Belgium by Fabrique Nationale and is marketed in this country under the name of Browning. Since Browning's original patents have long since expired, a very similar gun in various revisions has been made by Savage.

The Model 11 operates on the long-recoil system. Barrel and breech remain locked together to the end of the travel; then the barrel disengages from the breech bolt and in so doing pulls itself away from the fired case. When the case is ejected, the breech bolt moves forward, picks up a new shell from the carrier and inserts it into the chamber. The gun is now cocked and ready to fire.

The kick of the long-recoil shotgun has been called a "double shuffle," as there are two stages of recoil, the initial jar of the fired cartridge and the second impact of the barrel and breech bolt slamming into the receiver at the end of their ride. The speed at which the recoiling elements come back is regulated by springs and friction rings and if this is not properly done, the recoil can be pretty tooth-rattling.

The Browning double automatic (the only 2-shot autoloader) is a short-recoil job and more pleasant to shoot than any long-recoil self-loader. The barrel recoils only about ⅝ inch to start things going and hence does not give the bump of the barrel and breech bolt whanging into the receiver.

The new Winchester Model 50 is another short-recoil job, but in it the recoiling element is a floating chamber. The barrel itself remains fixed. The chamber goes back a little way and shoves a spring-loaded weight down a tube inside the butt. When the weight returns it unlocks the action and the residual gas pressure completes the cycle. It is a pleasant gun to shoot and like the Browning double automatic it doesn't have the somewhat jarring effect of the long-recoil system.

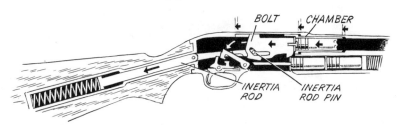

1. Starting with the gun cocked and loaded, squeezing the trigger causes the hammer to hit the firing pin and fire the shell.

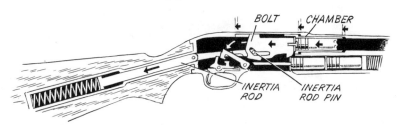

2. Backward force of the recoil moves the chamber and bolt 1/10 inch, kicking the inertia-rod pin so that the rod travels rearward. As it travels backward the inertia rod recocks the hammer.

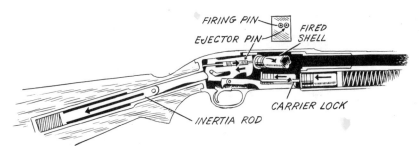

3. Full rearward travel of the inertia rod pulls back the bolt, and the ejector pin throws out the spent shell through the side opening. The carrier lock pivots, admitting a new shell onto the carrier.

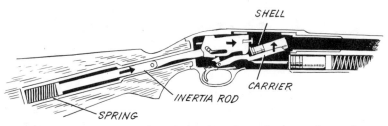

4. The spring at the base of the inertia rod starts the rod returning, moving the bolt forward. As the bolt begins to move, it pivots the carrier, which lifts the new shell into loading position. Full forward movement of the bolt carries the new shell into the chamber.

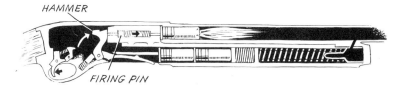

1. Starting with the gun cocked and loaded, squeezing the trigger releases the hammer, which strikes the firing pin and fires the shell.

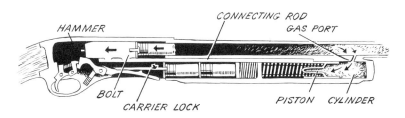

2. The gas generated by the fired shell is metered down through the gas port in the barrel into the cylinder. The pressure of the gas in the cylinder pushes the piston and connecting rod rearward, moving the bolt from the chamber. As the bolt travels rearward it recocks the hammer and opens the carrier lock.

3. Further rearward travel of the bolt ejects the spent shell through the side opening, and the magazine spring pushes a fresh shell onto the carrier.

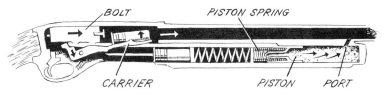

4. The piston spring starts the piston forward, moving the bolt forward, and pivoting the carrier to bring the new shell into loading position. As bolt moves all the way forward, it loads the new shell into the chamber. The spent gas escapes through the port.

The Remington Model 58 and the J. C. Higgins Model 60, which are sold by Sears, Roebuck but manufactured by High Standard, are both gas-operated. They use gas taken off under the forend to operate a piston, which in turn operates the action. Both are pleasant guns to shoot, with minimal recoil.

SHOTGUNS FOR SPECIAL PURPOSES

The vast majority of shotgun shooters own one gun and use it on everything from cottontail rabbits to geese. These gunners have very little knowledge of shotgun ballistics and are not particularly good shots or graceful gun handlers. As a consequence, their "all-around" guns often are not well chosen.

These average shooters think of the shotgun as a long-range weapon and feel that if only they could lead and hold just right they could probably kill a goose at 100 yards with the right load. They are convinced that the longer a gun barrel is the "harder" the gun shoots and the denser the pattern. There is a historical reason for this: In the days before choke boring and smokeless powder, the long barrel did shoot harder. But it is true no longer. With most powders *no* velocity is lost between 30 and 28 inches of barrel length, and so little is lost between 28 and 26 as to make no difference whatsoever. Actually, any velocity lost even in a 22-inch barrel is inconsequential and the density of the pattern is determined by the choke at the muzzle and not by barrel length.

Nevertheless, the average gunner who buys an all-around shotgun selects a pump gun in 12-gauge, bored full choke and with a 30-inch barrel. He has a pretty good gun for 50- to 55-yard pass shooting at ducks or geese, but a very poor gun for almost anything else.

A pump or automatic bored modified and with a 26- or 28-inch barrel would be better. I cannot see the necessity for having a barrel more than 26 inches long on a pump or automatic for *any* hunting, as a repeater with a 26-inch barrel is as long as a double with a 30-inch barrel. Modified boring is the best all-around boring as it throws a wider pattern with better distribution than a full choke, kills at about the same distance and wounds fewer birds. Put a good variable choke device for an overall barrel length of about 26 inches on a 12-gauge pump or automatic and you have a real all-around gun. A 16 gauge is generally a bit lighter than an equivalent 12 and with the heavier loads has adequate range even for pass shooting.

THE UPLAND GUN

The gun to be used for upland hunting should be light, fast to get on with and easy to carry. Often the upland hunter, particularly the man hunting grouse and pheasants, will walk a mile or two for every shot he gets and a heavy gun becomes a burden.

My favorite shotgun for upland shooting is the double. I have a matched trio of Winchester Model 21s—a 12, a 16 and a 20 gauge bored for the 3-inch magnum shell. All have 26-inch barrels, the 12 with two sets: one bored Skeet No. 1 (about cylinder) and Skeet No. 2 (about modified); the other modified and improved modified. The 16 is bored improved cylinder and modified, and the 20 modified and full. The 12 gauge weighs 7½ pounds, the 16- and 20-gauge guns weigh 6¾. I find myself leaving the 12 at home and taking the 16 or 20 when I am following a wide-ranging dog after pheasants. I have a little Spanish Arizaga double in 28 gauge with 26-inch barrels which weighs just a shade under 6 pounds, and I often use it with the 28-gauge magnum load with 1 ounce of shot.

For the uplands I think most people are better off with the 16 or 20 gauge than they are with the 12. The guns are lighter, the ammunition is lighter and at the range at which most upland game is shot, either of the smaller gauges has adequate killing power. Experience has proved that for almost all upland shooting 1 ounce of shot is enough, whether it is fired from a 12, 16, 20 or 28 gauge. In England 12-gauge shells with 2 ounces of shot in 2-inch cases are loaded and used.

Full choke in any gauge is strictly for waterfowl, and no upland single-barreled gun should be bored closer than modified. Most upland shooting is at 30 yards and under, and the man shooting a full-choke gun with its dense pattern not only is apt to chew the birds up but handicaps himself by using a pattern so small that it is difficult to hit with. At 30 yards the entire charge fired from a full-choke gun is contained in about a 26-inch circle, whereas a modified choke gives a spread of about 32 inches and an improved cylinder a spread of 38. A Skeet No. 1 or straight cylinder boring will spread about 45 inches at 30 yards but the pattern is beginning to get pretty thin. The sure killing range of the Skeet No. 1 boring is about 25 yards.

At 20 yards, the distance at which a large proportion of all birds killed over a dog are shot, the full choke spreads only 16 inches, but the improved cylinder spreads 26 inches and a Skeet No. 1 boring about 32 inches. For upland game, particularly quail, woodcock, grouse and rabbits, the single-barreled gun should be bored improved cylinder, and the double, improved cylinder and modified. Pheasants, because they are tough and often flush wild toward the end of the season, generally need a weak modified or quarter choke boring—50%. I often start off the pheasant season shooting either a 12-gauge double bored Skeet No. 1 and No. 2 or a 16-gauge, bored improved cylinder and modified, but I wind up shooting guns bored modified and full.

A 12 gauge, because it generally carries more shot in the "field" or standard loads, can be opened up more than smaller gauges. A 12-gauge, bored improved cylinder, for example, throws about as dense a pattern with $1\frac{1}{4}$ ounce of shot as a modified 20 with 1 ounce of shot.

For the uplands I like 26-inch barrels on a double, and under no circumstances would I shoot a repeater with barrels over that length. In recent years many upland hunters have had variable choke devices fitted to pumps and automatics for upland shooting giving an overall barrel length of 23 and 24 inches. These are fast, nice-handling guns. With $1\frac{1}{4}$ ounce of No. 6, an improved cylinder 12 gives sufficient pattern density to kill pheasants at 40 yards, as does a modified 20 gauge or a quarter choke 16. With the 28-gauge magnum load of 1 ounce of shot, I have repeatedly knocked pheasants cold at between 35 and 40 yards.

Because upland birds are generally rising, a straight-stocked gun that throws the charge a bit high is in order. I like a drop at comb of $1\frac{1}{2}$ inches, drop at heel of 2–$2\frac{1}{4}$, length of pull of $14\frac{1}{4}$, with a pitch down of 1 inch from 26-inch barrels. This is right for me, but some would require stocks a bit crooked or even somewhat straighter.

WATERFOWL GUNS

The special duck gun is just about at the other end of the spectrum from the upland gun. Generally the duck hunter doesn't carry his gun but sits in a blind. He needs an even, steady swing instead of a fast snap shot, and since the majority of his shots are at from 35 to 55 yards he needs plenty of choke. The best gun for ducks, then, is a 12 gauge with 28- or 30-inch barrels bored full choke. This is the gun for pass shooting. For decoyed ducks the upland gun does very nicely as shots are short and action is fast.

Within the past few years, the power of the shotshell has been greatly stepped up and the $2\frac{3}{4}$-inch magnum 12-gauge shells using $1\frac{1}{2}$ ounces of shot are formidable. However, some shooters use guns for 3-inch magnum shells with $1\frac{7}{8}$ ounces of shot and even imported European 10-gauge magnum doubles throwing 2 ounces of shot from $3\frac{1}{2}$-inch cases.

The duck gun should have a more crooked stock than the upland gun because birds aren't always rising, and the stock should be a bit shorter because the duck gunner is generally bundled up in heavy clothes.

TRAP GUNS

There are three separate games in conventional trapshooting— 16-yard rises, handicap, where the competitors shoot at various distances according to their skill, and doubles, where both birds are thrown at the same time.

At 16-yard rise, the average shooter breaks his birds about 32 yards from the gun but for handicap the best shooters have to move back and consequently break them farther away. The targets thrown from the traps are always rising sharply, and trap guns are made with straight stocks so that the pattern flies high for what amounts to a built-in lead. Because the guns are mounted before the bird is called for, trap stocks are longer than stocks for field use. Many are made with Monte Carlo combs so that the eye is always at the same level and a constant elevation is obtained. Since a steady swing is necessary for good trapshooting, barrels are long— 30 and 32 inches generally. At 16-yard rise a modified boring is enough, but for handicap shooting full choke is necessary. For doubles shooting, modified for the first bird and full for the second is about right.

The most popular trap gun is a pump with a special trap stock and fitted with a 30-inch barrel bored full choke. Most trap guns have ventilated ribs to aid in exact aiming. For doubles, over-and-under trap guns with ventilated ribs are very popular, as a double with a single trigger is a shade faster than a pump for the second shot.

A typical stock on a trap gun would have about the following dimensions: drop at comb 1⅜ inches; drop at heel, 1⅝; length of pull, 14½. Because many rounds are fired and the recoil of a light gun makes the shooter tired and jumpy, trap guns should be heavier than field guns. A typical weight is 8–8½ pounds. A trap gun will do fairly well on ducks, but it is no good in the uplands as it is too long and straight of stock, too long of barrel and throws too tight a pattern.

The trap gun is built with a longer stock and barrel than the field gun. This is a Remington Model 870 pump action.

An Ithaca single-barreled trap gun with a ventilated rib.

SKEET GUNS

Skeet is an entirely different sort of a game from traps. Whereas even at 16 yards the trap shot breaks his bird at about 32 yards, the skeet shot breaks his targets at from 3 or 4 yards from the center or No. 8 station to about 20-22 yards at most of the other stations. Trap targets are rising sharply; skeet targets for the most part are flying on a level or falling. Stock dimensions for field shooting are about right for skeet. Barrels should be open bored and short. The most popular skeet guns are automatics and pumps with 26-inch barrels bored about straight cylinder and called Skeet No. 1. Some double-barreled skeet guns are bored Skeet No. 1 and No. 2, but generally the No. 2 boring is about modified and throws too dense a pattern for the skeet field. As is the case with trapshooting, over-and-under shotguns, short of barrel and bored open, are becoming increasingly popular for skeet. Side-by-side doubles are seldom seen on the skeet field; like trapshooters the skeet shots like the single-sighting plane and generally want a ventilated rib to help in exact pointing. For shooting up to 30 yards, most skeet guns do very well for upland game. However, most are too heavy for carrying long distances. There are four classes of competition in skeet: with the 12 or 16 gauge (all-bore); with the 20 gauge; with ¾ ounce of shot (small bore, 28 or .410 gauge), and sub-small bore, the .410 with ½ ounce of shot. Many crack skeet shots get special over-and-under shotguns built with three sets of barrels in 12, 20 and .410 gauge made to give exactly the same balance.

CHAPTER TWENTY SIX

The Shotshell and Its Ballistics

THE SHOTGUN IS CERTAINLY THE MOST VERSATILE OF ALL HUNTING weapons but besides its good qualities it has some built-in limitations. It is necessary for the shooter to know something of the ballistics of his gun in order to know what he can do with it and where he must draw the line.

Shotgun ballistics have not changed much in the last hundred years. A century ago, the shotgun was about a 40-yard weapon, and it isn't much more than that today. A century ago, a charge of $1\frac{1}{4}$ ounces of shot in front of $3\frac{1}{4}$–$3\frac{1}{2}$ drams of black powder was a good, well-balanced load and the same load is efficient in a shotgun now.

This is not to say that there have not been important developments in shotguns and shotgun ammunition. There have been many. Possibly the most important was the invention of the breech-loading gun and the attendant development of fixed ammunition—the shotgun shell. Likewise of great importance was the invention of choke boring. Learning to make shot by dropping it from a tower was a great step forward, and the invention of smokeless powder and its early application to shotshells increased the joy of shooting. Shotguns have become handier and better stocked, and the shotshell is vastly improved over what it was 50 years ago, but since the development of breech-loading, the revisions in shotguns and shotgun ammunition have been in the nature of refinements rather than radical changes. The shotgun is a short-range weapon and there isn't much it can do today that Joseph Manton couldn't do with one of his fine muzzle loaders.

THE SHOTGUN SHELL

The average gunner shoots his shotshell, ejects it and forgets about it. However, the manufacture of the shell is a long, complicated

The components of a shot shell: (top row, l. to r.) powder, wads and shot; (second row) the case and its components; (third row) paper tubing ready to be cut into proper length for case body; (fourth row) components of the brass base.

and delicate operation involving, according to Remington, 14 components, 212 operations and endless inspection. It is said that it costs more to inspect shotshells than to manufacture them. Each batch is tested for pressure, velocity, pattern and functioning.

The shotgun shell is generally made with a paper body, a composition or paper base wad and a thin brass head. Within the past few years some shells have been made of aluminum or plastic. At one time the shells themselves were made of thin brass and were very popular with handloaders. In very wet countries, even the best shotgun shells with waxed paper bodies will swell, and there the brass case continues to be used. They are used in the jungles of South America and I have been told that brass cases loaded with buckshot were furnished for close combat with short-barreled "riot" guns in the jungles of the South Pacific during World War II.

The brass head is stamped out of thin brass stock in much the same way as rifle cases are made. The brass head provides support for the paper case, a pocket for the primer and a strong rim for extraction. All shotshells are rimmed. Generally, shotshell manufacturers use high brass bases for their high-velocity loads with heavy charges of shot; low bases for trap, skeet and field loads carrying lighter charges of powder and shot.

The base wad is made from rolled-up paper. It fits into the end of the paper body of the case and the entire unit of paper tube, brass base and base wad is made secure by stamping canelures in the brass. High base wads are used for "dense" powders which take up but little room. Low base wads are used for "bulk" powders. Sometimes a sheet of thin steel is used to reinforce the shell between the base wad and the brass head.

The length of the shell is the length before crimping, and a $2\frac{3}{4}$-inch shell is not $2\frac{3}{4}$ inches long before it is fired but considerably shorter than that. When the shell is fired it "unwinds" into the chamber and fills the chamber to the end or slightly into the cone.

Shotshells are made in various lengths. In England, for example, one can purchase 12-gauge shotshells in 2-, $2\frac{1}{2}$-, $2\frac{3}{4}$- and 3-inch lengths. However, the standard British chamber is $2\frac{1}{2}$ inches in length and British guns are so made unless they are to be exported to the United States or are specially ordered otherwise. The standard Continental shotgun is made with a 65-millimeter chamber and unless a gun is marked otherwise on the flat under the breech, it can be assumed that the chamber is 65-millimeter or about $2\frac{9}{16}$ inches in length. Continental guns for heavy loads have 70-millimeter ($2\frac{3}{4}$-inch) chambers and are so marked. Usually the Continental gun is marked for gauge (or caliber as it is called over there) and chamber length. For example 16-65, 12-70, etc. Shooting long ($2\frac{3}{4}$-inch) shells in short chambers raises pressures to a high, often dangerous degree because the wads have to be compressed between the mouth of the case and the cone of the chamber. This should be avoided. Long shells fired in short chambers appear frayed at the mouth.

In the United States, standard guns in most gauges have chambers $2\frac{3}{4}$ inches long and most shells (either low base or high base, standard or maximum) have $2\frac{3}{4}$-inch cases. However, many old guns were made with shorter chambers. The old chamber length of the 12 gauge was $2\frac{5}{8}$ inches; of the 16 gauge, $2\frac{9}{16}$; of the 20 gauge, $2\frac{1}{2}$, and of the .410, $2\frac{1}{2}$. Now, however, unless otherwise marked, chambers for 12-, 16-, 20- and 28-gauge guns are $2\frac{3}{4}$ inches long, and chambers for the .410 are 3 inches long. No. 10-gauge guns are being manufactured in the United States at the present time but the old 10-gauge chamber was $2\frac{7}{8}$ inches long. Magnum guns for magnum shells have longer chambers. Before the last war, Parker and Ithaca produced heavy double guns with $3\frac{1}{2}$-inch chambers, and similar guns are today imported from Europe. Repeating shotguns are made today chambered for 3-inch, 12-gauge shells handling $1\frac{7}{8}$ ounces of shot, shells with almost as much killing range as the $3\frac{1}{2}$-inch 10-gauge magnums. Winchester has turned out some 20-gauge Model 21 double guns for the 3-inch magnum shell handling $1\frac{1}{4}$ ounces of shot, and all Browning superposed 20-gauge doubles are now chambered for 3-inch shells.

About the time of World War I, the American standard for the 12-gauge chamber became $2\frac{3}{4}$-inch rather than $2\frac{5}{8}$. The 20-gauge chamber was changed from $2\frac{1}{2}$ to $2\frac{3}{4}$ inches in 1926, and the .410 chamber was changed from $2\frac{1}{2}$ to 3 inches in the early nineteen thirties with the development of the 3-inch .410 shell. All 16-gauge guns were not chambered for the $2\frac{3}{4}$-inch shell until after the last war. I believe all Browning automatic shotguns in 16 gauge were chambered for $2\frac{9}{16}$-inch shells as late as 1939. The 28-gauge chamber was changed from $2\frac{1}{2}$ inches to $2\frac{3}{4}$ inches in 1931.

THE SHOTSHELL COMPONENTS

The primer is pressed into the primer pocket in the head of the shotgun case. Then the powder charge is put in. Powder may be bulk smokeless, which loads bulk, for bulk with black powder, or it may be a "dense" powder, of which a much smaller amount will give the same velocity and pressure as a larger charge of bulk powder. Powder charges are given on boxes of shotshells as "$3\frac{1}{4}$ dram equivalant" for example. That simply means that the powder charge used gives the same pressure and velocity of that amount of black powder. The standard 12-gauge field load contains $1\frac{1}{8}$ ounces of shot and the equivalent of $3\frac{1}{4}$ drams of black powder.

On the charge of powder is placed a cardboard "over powder" wad, and over this a couple of felt or composition "filler" wads. These must seal the bore to prevent gas from escaping into the shot charge and blowing it, and they must be made elastic to take up some of the shock of the fast-burning and sudden acceleration of the powder. Since World War II, cup-shaped wads of plastic or cardboard have been used over the powder to assist in sealing off the gas.

Above the filler wads is the charge of shot. The shell is then usually closed by a cardboard wad over the shot with the end of the shell crimped around it. Because the wad sometimes interferes with the shot pattern when the shot runs into it outside the barrel,

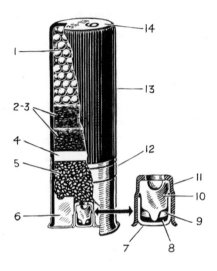

The 14 components of a 12-gauge shotgun shell: 1—Shot pellets, made as round as possible to insure straight trajectory. 2, 3—Felt filler wads keep power behind shot to deliver maximum blow. 4—Over-powder wads—a disk of cardboard ⅛-inch thick. 5—Progressive-burning powder builds up power along gun barrel until charge has left muzzle. 6—Base wad, a tightly-wound strip of paper, strengthens head and primer. 7—Primer cup holds non-corrosive priming mixture. 8—Priming mixture ignites shell. 9—Paper disk is lid on top of priming mixture. 10—Anvil sets off priming mixture. 11—Battery cup holds primer together. 12—Brass shell head, annealed to prevent brittleness. 13—Paper body of shell, corrugated for smoother loading and extraction. 14—Thin, waterproofed paper seal eliminates old "top wad" which often got in way of shot as it left gun, spoiling pattern. Seal also gives load and shot-size information.

many shotshells are now loaded without a top wad but instead with a pie crimp, sometimes sealed with a little paper sticker and sometimes not. One company uses the crimp but employs "frangible" wads of cardboard treated to make them brittle so they disintegrate from the violent push of the shot charge when the gun is fired. The new refinements of gas-seal wads, and pie crimps or frangible wads have resulted in tighter, more even patterns than were common ten or twenty years ago, and many barrels marked modified will now throw full-choke patterns and many marked improved cylinder will throw modified and even tighter patterns.

SHOTSHELL PRESSURES

In recent years the development of special slow-burning powders has enabled the loading companies to step up the amount of shot possible to load in a shell and still give standard velocity and pressure. The maximum amount of shot in a $2\frac{3}{4}$-inch 12-gauge case used to be $1\frac{1}{4}$ ounces; now $2\frac{3}{4}$-inch magnum shells are loaded with $1\frac{1}{2}$ ounces. In $2\frac{3}{4}$-inch cases the 16 gauge has been stepped up to $1\frac{1}{4}$ ounces, the 20 gauge to $1\frac{1}{8}$ ounces, and the 28 gauge to 1 ounce. At one time the maximum load for the 12-gauge 3-inch magnum shell was $1\frac{3}{8}$ ounces, then it was stepped up to $1\frac{5}{8}$ and now to $1\frac{7}{8}$ ounces. As far as shot charges are concerned, all gauges have stepped up a gauge.

Shotgun shell pressures are relatively mild as compared to rifle shell pressures and even the pressures of the hotter handgun cartridges. Pressures must be kept low or the shot pattern is blown to pieces. Pressures of shotshells run between 8,000 and 12,000 pounds per square inch. The 8,000-pound pressure is obtained with the "light" trap load of 3 drams equivalent and $1\frac{1}{8}$ ounces of shot; the 12,000 pounds per square inch is developed with the various maximum loads with heavy charges of shot driven by stiff loads of progressive burning powder. Incidentally the smaller gauges are reputed to develop somewhat higher pressure than the larger ones, with the .410 at the top of the list.

One of the myths believed by shotgun owners is that it is safe to use "low base" loads in ancient shotguns with twist or Damascus barrels. This is not so. The old shotguns were developed to handle pressures of about 4,000-6,000 pounds per square inch, and even the mildest of the modern smokeless powder loads gives pressures of 8,000 pounds per square inch and above.

Velocities delivered by shotshells are not high, and the smaller the gauge the lower the velocity. The muzzle velocity of the 12-gauge "high velocity" load such as Super-X with $3\frac{3}{4}$ drams equivalent and $1\frac{1}{4}$ ounces of shot—the old "maximum" load before the development of the $2\frac{3}{4}$-inch magnum shells—was 1,330 feet per second. The velocity of the similar load in the 16 is 1,240 and in the 20 gauge it is 1,220. The 12-gauge field load with $1\frac{1}{8}$ ounces of shot has a muzzle velocity of 1,255, and the similar 16 has 1,165, and the 20 gauge, 1,155.

The magnum loads in 3-inch cases turn up 1,315 with $1\frac{5}{8}$ ounces in the 12 gauge; the $2\frac{3}{4}$-inch magnum load produces 1,220 with $1\frac{1}{8}$ ounces in the 20 gauge. Because of their poor ballistic coefficient, the velocity of shot pellets drops off rapidly. In the case of No. 4 shot generally used on ducks, it drops to 660 feet per second from 955 feet per second at the muzzle at 60 yards, and in the case of No. 8 shot, in a trap shot, it drops from 870 to 545.

Birds are not killed primarily by the velocity of the shot charge but by the density of the pattern and the penetration of the pellets. It is generally considered that it takes four or five pellets of the proper size striking the body of a bird to make a clean kill—No. 4 for birds the size of mallard ducks, No. 6 for pheasants, and No. $7\frac{1}{2}$ or No. 8 for quail.

The larger the shot size the better it retains its velocity and the harder it hits. The energy at 60 yards of a pellet of No. 2 shot is 5.23 foot pounds, for example, but that of a pellet of No. 8 is .69 foot pounds. On the other hand, the smaller the shot size the denser the pattern, and the proper choice of shot must be a compromise between pellet energy and pattern density.

SHOT

At one time the larger pellets used in shotguns were cast (buckshot) whereas the smaller ones were chopped up by hand from sheet lead. Then someone had the idea of pouring the shot through a perforated pan to allow the drops of lead to form by falling. Shot is still made that way. The molten lead pours through a shower pan from the top of a shot tower of considerable height and then is cooled by falling into water. The size of the shot is controlled by the size of the perforations in the pan.

This is what bird shot looks like in bulk at the factory before it is loaded into shells.

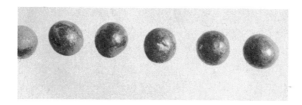

A magnified view of shot shows that most pellets are slightly imperfect and deformed.

No.	12	11	10	9	8	7½	6	5	4	2
Actual Size	•	•	•	•	•	•	●	●	●	●
Diameter In Inches	.05	.06	.07	.08	.09	.095	.11	.12	.13	.15

No.	Air Rifle	BB	No. 4 Buck	No. 3 Buck	No. 1 Buck	No. 0 Buck	No. 00
Actual Size	●	●	●	●	●	●	●
Diameter In Inches	.175	.18	.24	.25	.30	.32	.33

These are the actual sizes of the shot pellets in a shotshell. No. 12 is "dust" shot. No. 00 is buckshot for deer.

Shot is made of lead, as lead is a cheap and heavy metal. The lead contains a small amount of arsenic to aid in the formation of spherical drops as it falls. Drop shot is the pure lead with arsenic added. Chilled shot has been alloyed with a little antimony. Some shot in premium loads has been coated with copper by electro-plating. This makes it harder, more resistant to deformation and less liable to lead the bore.

Chilled and copperized shot give better patterns than drop shot as they deform less—and shot deformation is one of the principal enemies of good patterns. Many quail hunters prefer drop shot, believing that it expands when it strikes a bird. It is doubtful if this is so; the pellets which appear to have expanded probably were deformed in the bore.

CHOOSING SHOT SIZE

Many hunters have their favorite shot sizes and choosing the proper size causes almost as many arguments as choosing the proper calibers for big-game animals. It must be remembered that the greater the surface area of the bird, the larger the shot that can be used and still get the required minimum of four pellets into the body. Likewise the larger the bird the greater the need for the energy and deep penetration of heavy shot.

Geese and wild turkey are generally hunted with No. 2 shot but some hunters like to use the smaller No. 6 and aim for the head and neck. Large ducks like mallard and canvasbacks, and all ducks taken at ranges of over 40 yards, should be shot with No. 4. Decoyed ducks taken at 40 yards and under can be handled with No. 6. Pheasants, grouse, squirrels and rabbits likewise call for No. 6 shot. Small birds like quail and doves should be hunted with No. 7½ or No. 8. Most trapshooters use No. 7½ or No. 8. Skeet shooters use No. 8 or No. 9.

SHOTGUN KILLING RANGE

Commenting on an article I had written about the killing range of shotguns, the late Ken Richards, manufacturer of the Master Choke and long-time experimenter with shotguns, wrote:

"I have determined that for each 5 yards of shot travel, a shotgun loses about 8 per cent of its pattern density. Therefore, if a shotgun shoots a 70 per cent pattern at 40 yards, it can be expected to shoot a 62 per cent pattern at 45 yards and a 54 per cent pattern at 50 yards. Going the other direction, it will shoot a 78 per cent pattern at 35 yards and an 86 per cent pattern at 30 yards, and so on.

"Anyone can figure out just about what percentage to expect at any given distance if he knows what his gun will do at 40 yards, by either deducting 8 per cent for each additional 5 yards beyond 40 yards, or by adding 8 per cent for each 5 yards below 40 yards.

"I have always maintained that at least a 50 per cent pattern is necessary to insure clean kills and that 60 per cent would be even better. I have also maintained that to kill cleanly up to 55 and 60 yards, a gun should be able to throw a 78 per cent pattern at 40 yards for the 55-yard distance, and an 86 per cent pattern for the 60-yard shooting. This is something few shooters ever think about!"

I am heartily in agreement with this. It is illuminating to try patterning a favorite duck gun at 55 yards, at 60 and 65 yards. Then, if you still have the courage, just pattern it at 70 yards. When you look at the pattern, remember how you told the boys that if anything came over within 75 yards you'd knock it over with that new magnum . . .

Richards' figures presumably apply to a 12 gauge with 1¼ ounces of shot. Range would be less with smaller gauges because they throw less shot and thinner patterns and because a higher percentage of what shot they have is deformed because of greater friction on the barrel of the longer shot column. Without having worked it out, I'd say that the percentage of pattern loss would be higher with a 16 than with a 12, higher with a 20 than with a 16. With the .410 it is fantastic. Try patterning a .410 at 25, 30 and 35 yards. You'll find that at the longest distance the pattern is disintegrating.

NUMBER OF SHOT IN AN OUNCE

In order for those who want to pattern their guns to figure percentages easily, the number of shot per ounce in the various sizes is listed below:

SHOT SIZE	NUMBER OF PELLETS PER OUNCE
BB	50
2	88
4	136
5	172
6	223
7	299
7½	350
8	409
9	585
10	868
11	1,380
12	2,385

"HARD SHOOTING GUNS"

There has always been a question as to which gun shoots "harder" —one bored straight cylinder or the one bored full choke? The answer, according to Dr. C. S. Cummings of Remington, is the full choke, but the difference doesn't amount to much. It comes only to one foot per second for each "point" or 1/1000 inch of constriction. That would make only 40 feet per second between the very tightest full choke and the wide-open straight cylinder with no constriction whatsoever, and only about 20 feet per second between the average improved cylinder with around 10 points constriction in 12 gauge and the average full choke with around 30. No practical difference would be noticed in the field either in shot penetration or in necessary lead.

SCATTER LOADS

A stratagem most shotgun users never try and one which many have never heard of, is the use of "brush" or "scatter" loads in full-choke guns to open up the pattern for short-range use. The shot in the shells is loaded with cardboard partitions between portions of the charge. When such a shell is fired in a full choke or modified bore, the pattern will generally be opened up to about improved cylinder. As a general thing patterns are not as even as those thrown by a good improved cylinder barrel and regular ammunition, but they enable the one-gun man with a full-choke barrel to go into the brush for fast, short-range shooting with some hope of hitting.

Remington calls these shells "scatter loads." In Peters brand they are "spreader loads." In Winchester and Western brands they are called "brush loads."

In the old days, when breaking the targets that head right for the skeet shooter at Station 8 was considered a difficult and complicated task instead of being one of the easiest shots on the skeet field, a box of skeet shells contained two of those spreader loads for the two Station 8 targets.

Just to see how well one could do on skeet with a full-choke gun and Remington scatter loads I once shot a round with the combination and broke a 23. Two targets I missed were from carelessness and not from a poor pattern.

HEAT AND SHOTSHELLS

About 90 per cent of all trouble with shotshells comes from overheating, Harold Russell, sales manager of the Federal Cartridge Co., told me on a recent visit to the Federal plant outside Minneapolis, Minnesota. When a shell is subjected to heat that goes over 135 degrees, the wax used to waterproof the cardboard cases liquifies and goes into the powder. This causes a great loss of power.

The next time you hear a shotshell go *poof* when someone fires it, you can assume that it got too hot sometime in its career. Leaving a box of shells on a hot radiator will raise the temperature above the critical 135 degrees. So will storing them in a hot attic. Leaving a box of shells in direct sunlight on a hot, bright day also may make them hot enough to drive the wax into the powder.

If you suspect you have spoiled some shells, you can test them, Russell says, by removing the powder from a shell and pressing the grains hard against a piece of paper. If they make a greasy stain, they have been overheated to the ruinous degree.

SIZE OF SHOTGUN PATTERNS

A true cylinder bore or the skeet boring will usually cover a 32-inch circle at 20 yards, the distance at which most skeet targets should be broken and at which a fast shot kills upland game. The same cylinder bore, however, is no good at 40 yards, as at that distance it will cover about 60 inches and is generally so thin you can throw an Irish setter through it.

The term "improved cylinder" covers a great many different borings. I have seen some barrels so marked pattern like a straight cylinder and others that shot patterns approaching full-choke density. On the average, though, they'll cover about 25 or 26 inches at 20 yards and 50 inches at 50. The man using an improved cylinder boring on skeet instead of cylinder or modifications of it like Winchester Skeet No. 1 is handicapping himself. For most upland shooting, improved cylinder is the best, and the tighter varieties (sometimes called quarter choke) are good on pheasants and decoyed ducks to about 40 yards in a 12-gauge gun.

The most useful, all-around choke is the modified, or half choke. Usually a good barrel will cover an 18- or 20-inch circle at 20 yards and a 45-inch circle at 40 yards. In my experience a modified 12 with 1¼ ounces of No. 6 shot will grass a pheasant to about 45 yards and yet not shoot him to pieces at 20-25 yards. Most gunners will do far better with a modified choke than with a full choke.

The full choke is a one-purpose choke; it is for pass shooting at ducks and doves. Generally speaking, a choke-bored barrel will cover about a 16-inch circle at 20 yards, keep all its shot in a 40-inch circle at 40 yards and from 70 to 80 per cent of its shot in a 30-inch circle at that distance.

Since most upland game is killed under 30 yards and most waterfowl under 40 yards, it can be seen that it is a good idea to spread the shot out a bit.

CHAPTER TWENTY SEVEN

Sorting out the Gauges

FOR MANY YEARS NOW THE VARIOUS SHOTGUN GAUGES HAVE BEEN stepping on one another's toes and right now they are all scrambled up. You can buy 12-gauge shells with the 1-ounce load of the 20, and 16-gauge shells with the 1¼-ounce load of the 12. You can get magnum loads in the 20 for duck shooting and light loads in the 12 for quail and woodcock. I can remember when ¾ ounce of shot in a 2½-inch case was the standard load for the 20 gauge, whereas now the humble .410 will handle ¾ ounce of shot. Today the loading companies are stuffing 1⅛ ounces of shot into the 2¾-inch magnum 20-gauge shells; only yesterday that was the maximum load for the 16 gauge.

It is up to each hunter to decide which of the gauges he wants to use and to give him an educated choice, I am going to try to unscramble some of the facts about them.

EARLY GAUGE NUMBERING

Back when the breechloader was young, in the late eighteen seventies and early eighteen eighties, the 10 bore was the most popular gauge and a load of 1¼ ounces of shot was considered plenty. Actually many 10-gauge users shot 1⅛ ounces and some even shot 1 ounce. In a 10 gauge, mind you!

The 12 gauge, which started replacing the 10 as the Number 1 gauge in this country during the early nineties, used 1 ounce and 1⅛ ounces of shot. In England 1¹⁄₁₆ ounces is still the standard load. In this country, 1⅛ ounces in the 12 has been considered standard for many years, while 1¼ ounces—the old standard load for the 10 gauge with 2⅞-inch case—has been maximum for the 2¾-inch 12-gauge shell case.

Now the 12 with the standard 2¾-inch case will handle 1½ ounces of shot, or almost as much as the maximum 10-gauge load (1⅝ ounces) in the 2⅞-inch case. Just as the 12 is treading on the heels of the 10 gauge, so the 16 is nudging the 12. Not so long ago, the maximum load for the 16 was 1⅛ ounces; now it is 1¼!

The fearsome 10-gauge magnum shotguns using 3½-inch shells, which were made in this country before World War II by both Ithaca and Parker and are still manufactured in Europe, threw two full ounces of shot out of the muzzle—or as much as the fabulous and now illegal 8 gauge did.

LONGER SHOTSHELLS

Not only have shotshells been carrying more shot, but they've been getting longer. The standard 12-gauge shell used to be 2⅝ inches in length before crimping, and 2½-inch (65 millimeter) cases are still standard in all gauges in England and on the Continent. For years now all American 12-gauge shotguns have been chambered for the 2¾-inch shells. With the exception of the .410 with its 3-inch chamber, and the magnums (of which more later), all American shotguns now have 2¾-inch chambers.

The chamber length of the 12s was changed at about the time of the World War I; the 20 gauge was changed from 2½ to 2¾ inches in 1926, and the .410 and the 28 gauge were changed in 1931, I believe.

Before repeaters became so popular, many shotguns were made in various gauges with 3-inch chambers and shells were made to fit them. The 3-inch magnum shells for the 12 gauge were manufactured in limited quantities even before the introduction of the Winchester Model 12 heavy duck gun for shells of that length. The great old double guns such as the Fox, Parker, Ithaca and L. C. Smith were always chambered on special order for 3-inch shell using 1⅜ ounces of shot. That load is still made for 3-inch 12-gauge shells, but it looks like peanuts when we think that they are now putting 1½ ounces in a 2¾-inch 12-gauge case. Maximum amount of shot in the 3-inch case for the 12 has recently been upped to 1⅞ ounces.

In the old days many citizens liked 3-inch 20- and 16-gauge shells with what were then considered heavy loads of shot for duck shooting. Repeaters wouldn't handle the long shells and they died off. In 16 gauge, so far as I know, they have never been revived, but for years various knowledgeable shots around the Winchester and

Western plants were using Model 21 Winchester doubles for 3-inch 20-gauge shells on ducks, and a few years ago these manufacturers put the shells on the open market.

I have a 20-gauge Model 21 for the 3-inch magnum shell and I love it. So far the most shot that has been put into the 20 magnum is 1¾₁₆ ounces of No. 4 and 1⅛ ounces of No. 6. But now that a load of 1⅛ ounces of shot can be had in a 2¾-inch 20-gauge shell, I'd like to bet that the 3-inch 20-gauge get loaded with 1¼ ounces (the old 12-gauge maximum load for the 2¾-inch case).

Not so many years ago, the .410 was made only in 2½-inch cases and with ⅜ ounce of shot. Now the .410 short shells, though still 2½ inches in length, carry a full ½ ounce of shot, while the 3-inch shell, first brought out by Winchester for the Model 42 pump, packs ¾ ounce of shot, or the present load for the 28 gauge and the old load for the 20 gauge. One firm, Federal, now loads 1 ounce of shot in the 28 gauge.

HOW GAUGES WERE NAMED

The gauges were named for the number of balls of their particular size to the pound. Before the days of choke boring, 12 of the round lead balls used in the 12 gauge weighed a pound, as did 16 of those used in the 16 gauge, 20 in the 20 gauge, and so on.

In the days of the muzzle loader, gauges were less standardized. Since the gunner simply poured his powder and shot down the barrel and had his choice of wads, he could also have almost any gauge his heart desired. Many of the old-time guns turn out to be 11s, 13s, 15s or 19s. In Europe, 14-, 24- and 32-gauge guns have been made until recently and may still be made occasionally for all I know. Ammunition is, I believe, still loaded for them.

Actual bore sizes of the six gauges most commonly used in the United States. The 10 gauge is a goose gun; .410 is too small for all-around use.

Guns in 8 gauge were made in the United States until they were outlawed for use on wildfowl just before World War I. I have never seen a breech-loading gun in either 4 or 6 gauge, but I've been told that they have been manufactured here. A British ammunition catalog still lists 4-gauge shells.

As for the .410 "gauge," it is not a gauge at all but a caliber and so is the .36 caliber or 9-millimeter gauge.

Nowadays the round pumpkin balls fired in shotguns are not the gauge size—that is, 12 would not weigh a pound in 12 gauge. The reason is, of course, that the balls have to be made smaller than the bore diameter so they can get through the choke.

RIFLED SLUGS

A very different type of projectile is the rifled slug. It is made of pure, soft lead and has a hollow base which is upset to fill the bore by the blow of the powder gases. It swages down without harming the choke at all when it strikes the constriction toward the muzzle. Those who've done more shooting with rifled slugs than I have tell me the greatest accuracy is obtained with improved cylinder and modified boring, not full choke. The slugs weigh as follows: 12 gauge, 415 grains; 16 gauge, 350 grains; 20 gauge, 282 grains; .410 bore, 93 grains. The velocity of slugs of all gauges is between 1,400 and 1,500 feet per second and their muzzle energy ranges from 1,995 foot pounds for the 12, to 1,600 for the 16, to 1,245 for the 20. The energy of the little .410 slug is only 460 foot pounds. Why it is ever loaded I cannot figure out. It doesn't have enough power for deer even at close range and it isn't accurate enough for varmints.

The slugs of the larger gauges are very respectable killers if the shots can be at all well placed. Even the 20-gauge slug turns up about as much muzzle energy as the .25/35 bullet—and the .25/35 has killed a lot of deer.

The standard bore diameter of the 10 gauge is supposed to be .775 inch, of the 12 gauge .729 inch, of the 16 gauge .552, of the 20 gauge .615, of the 28 gauge .550. The .410 bore is, of course, .410 inch. The Williams Gun Shop, a firm that installs hundreds of choke devices a year and measures hundreds of bores, says that Browning and Winchester diameters for the 12 gauge average about

.725 inch but that Remington bores run larger, or about .730. Ithaca 12-gauge barrels are bored .729 inch.

Bores made by the same company vary somewhat from gun to gun, and since the relationship of muzzle diameter to bore diameter determines the pattern, it can be seen that simply measuring the hole at the end of the barrel isn't necessarily going to tell anyone what kind of patterns he should get.

Williams Gun also says Browning guns, made in Belgium, have more constriction at the muzzle for the various degrees of choke than do American-made guns. That is pretty much true with all European guns, which more or less follow the old classical rule: in 12 gauge, 40 points of constriction (.040 inch) for full choke, 30 points (.030 inch) for three-quarter choke or improved modified, 20 points (.020) for half choke or modified, and 10 points (.010) for quarter choke or improved cylinder.

According to the Williamses, the constriction of the Brownings averages .038, .024, .013. For the three degrees of choke (full, modified and improved cylinder) Remington 12-gauge guns average .036, .018 and .009, and Winchester .031, .016 and .007. Be that as it may, I've seen many a 12-gauge gun throw 70 per cent patterns when it had but .020-inch constriction and according to all rhyme, reason and tradition should pattern about modified or 60 per cent.

In the 16 gauge, the three common degrees of choke are supposed to call for the following amount of constriction: .024, .012 and .005; and in the 20 gauge, .021, .010 and .004.

By far the most popular gauge in the United States is the 12. This is also true in England and probably in Spain; but in France and Germany the 16 gauge leads. Whether the 12 deserves its popularity over the smaller gauges is something that has started many an argument and will doubtless start many more.

The 12 gauge has its disadvantages. Both gun and ammunition are heavier and bulkier than those for smaller gauges. The British make light 12s for short cases and light charges of shot, but the American manufacturer has to consider the fact that any gun he turns out will be fired at least part of the time with very potent loads containing as much as 1½ ounces of shot. Most 12-gauge guns do not have the sleek and racy lines of doubles, pumps and automatics built for smaller shells. Because of the big hole in the end of the barrel, the 12 has a good deal of muzzle blast and in the heavier loadings plenty of recoil.

But the 12 also has its advantages. Because of the larger bore, it will throw a shorter shot column, deform fewer pellets and pattern better than a smaller gauge using the same amount of shot—and in a pinch the 12 can use more shot. Also, a given amount of powder and shot costs less in the 12 than in the 16 or 20.

Few people ever bother to pattern a shotgun—or at least to pattern one thoroughly, correctly and systematically. As a consequence, the myth still floats around that a 16 gauge shoots a smaller pattern than a 12, and that a 20 shoots a smaller pattern than a 16. Often the admirer of the 20 gauge insists that you can kill anything with a 20 as far as you can with a 12 if you point it right.

It pains me to say this, but the same standards hold for 12, 16, 20 and 28 gauges. If a 20 gauge puts 70 per cent of its 1 ounce of shot into a 30-inch circle at 40 yards, it is throwing a full-choke pattern, just like a 16 gauge or a 12 gauge. If it delivers 60 per cent, it is throwing a modified pattern. Patterns run the same size, but those thrown by the smaller gauges are thinner.

Suppose we're using a 20-gauge shotgun with 1 ounce of No. 6 shot. The gun is bored full choke and patterns 75 per cent. We therefore put 75 per cent of the 223 pellets in the charge into that 30-inch circle at 40 yards. That is 167 pellets. If we were shooting a 16 gauge with 1⅛ ounces, we'd wind up with 188 No. 6s in the circle, and if we were using a 12 gauge patterning 75 per cent with 1¼ ounces, we'd have 209 pellets in our circle.

Because the larger hole in the 12 gauge will handle more shot, a 12 will hold sufficient pattern density to longer range than a 16, and a 16 will hold it longer than a 20. The 12 will also throw a better pattern with the same amount of shot because the shot column is shorter. Fewer shot pellets are deformed by friction against the bore and by striking the forcing cone of the choke.

With equivalent loads, velocities are somewhat higher in the 12 than in the smaller gauges. An old Winchester catalog quotes the 12-gauge Winchester Super Speed load with 1¼ ounces of No. 6 shot as having an average velocity over a 40-yard range of 975 feet per second and of the 20-gauge Super Speed load with 1 ounce of shot over the same range having a velocity of 900 feet per second. The velocity of the 16 gauge with ⅛ ounce of No. 6 is a bit higher, or 925 feet per second.

All this sounds as if the 16 and the 20 have no advantages whatsoever. Actually they have some very real ones. Their ammunition is lighter, for one thing. I have just weighed boxes of maximum loads in the three gauges. The box of 12s weighed 3 pounds; the 16s, 2 pounds 9 ounces, and the 20s, 2 pounds 4 ounces. On a long, tough day of shooting every ounce of weight counts.

Guns in the smaller gauges likewise weigh less; and particularly for upland hunting, where the gunner walks long distances and shoots at short ranges, the 16 and the 20 have it all over the 12. Because the lighter gun handles faster, the speed of getting on probably makes up for the thinner patterns.

Difference in range is not as much as many people believe. If a full-choke 20 gauge with a maximum load will kill ducks or pheasants reliably at 40 yards, the full-choke 12 won't kill farther than 50. Actually, in my experience, it is easier to kill a duck or a pheasant at 40 yards with a 20 than it is to knock one off at 50 with a 12.

Guns of the smaller gauges are sleeker and have better lines—if you're interested in looks. Probably their major advantage, though, is that they give less recoil, less report, less muzzle blast; and because they're more pleasant to shoot, people do less flinching with them. A 12-gauge goes BOOM; a 20 goes *crack*.

If very many shots are to be taken at over 40 yards, the 12 gauge should be the choice because of its ballistic superiority. If shots are to be taken at under 40 yards, the 20 is hard to beat. Perhaps the Europeans are right and the 16 gauge is the best compromise.

Just as the 12 throws a shorter shot string and patterns better than a 16, and a 16 is ballistically superior to a 20, the 28 gauge with its ¾ ounce of shot has it all over the .410. I'd call a 70 per cent 28 gauge a practical 37-38 yard upland gun and even a practical gun for short-range shooting on decoying ducks. Because of its very long shot column, its narrow, strung-out shot string, and its great percentage of deformed shot, the .410 with ¾ ounce of shot is only about a 30-yard gun. At greater distances the .410 (although it will kill) wounds too high a percentage of what it is shot at.

CHAPTER TWENTY EIGHT

Shotgun Choke and Pattern

THE PRINCIPLE OF SHOTGUN CHOKE WAS DISCOVERED ABOUT 80 YEARS ago. In this country, it is generally believed that the originator was Fred Kimble, a professional duck hunter, but the English also claim the honor—and probably the French, the Spanish, the Czechs and the Russians.

Shotgun patterns are "choked" or closed up by giving the gun what actually amounts to a slight degree of constriction at the muzzle by one method or another. Sometimes as in "taper choke" or "American choke," this is done by a taper or cone, which instead of being a true straight taper is actually cut with a slight radius. One famous American factory I know of uses this system of choking and all degrees of choke are cut with one reamer, running it in deeper for a modified barrel than for a full-choke barrel, and deeper for an improved cylinder barrel than for a modified barrel.

So-called "standard choke," sometimes called "English choke," is the same as taper choke except that there is a parallel portion or "lede" at the end of the barrel. At least two of our great gun factories use this system.

Swaged choke, used on inexpensive guns, is obtained not by the use of a reamer but by driving the muzzle into a die.

Recess or jug choke is more or less of a makeshift and is not used by any factory I know of. It can be employed when the barrel has been cut down so that all choke is removed, and it can be made to give patterns of up to about 60 per cent. These recesses are cut into the barrel and are from 1 to 6 inches long and from .003 to .008 inch deep. They usually begin about ½ inch from the muzzle. A friend of mine cut a recess into the barrel of an old pump gun that had lost a few inches of muzzle because of mud. He did it by the use of emery cloth on the end of a rod. It was a rough and ready process, but the jug he made rounded up his patterns and brought them up to about 50 per cent.

Various gunsmiths advertise that they can rechoke barrels that have been chopped off. Various methods are open to them. One would be swaged choke in the case of a single-barrel gun or recess choke in the case of a double. Still another method, which is employed by one outfit, is inserting a sleeve in the muzzle and then choking it. For that matter, curing a single-barrel gun that has lost a few inches of muzzle would be very simple by the addition of a choke device such as the Poly-Choke, POWer-Pac, Cutts Compensator, Weaver Choke, Shooting Master, etc.

Another type of choke can be called "bell" or "reverse" choke, and it is designed to throw patterns wider than true cylinder and at the same time more even. I am illustrating a Skeet No. 1 or "Skeet In" choke of that type, the measurements taken from a gun

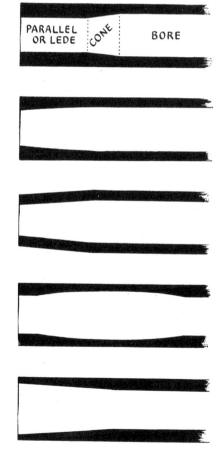

A simplified diagram of the standard or English choke which has a parallel portion at the end of the barrel.

The cone choke, sometimes known as the American or taper choke.

The swaged choke is made by merely tapering the muzzle itself.

The recess or jug choke is usually made by hand with a rod and emery cloth.

The bell or reverse choke is for throwing extra-wide patterns.

of famous make. Not only is this type of choke excellent for the skeet field but it is also very good choke for upland shooting, particularly when the birds are lying close or the hunting is done in the brush. During the last war, a Western air base received 25 pump guns for training personnel in skeet shooting. The rub was that these "skeet guns" all had 30-inch barrels and were bored full choke. They were taken to a gunsmith, who chopped them off to 25 inches and then bored them out to give some reverse choke or "bell," and they served satisfactorily throughout the war.

Choke is measured in one-thousandths of an inch or "points" difference between the bore diameter and the muzzle diameter. In the old days a constriction of .040 (40 points) was considered necessary with a 12-gauge gun to give full-choke patterns. The names one often hears even today—¾ choke for improved modified and ½ choke for modified—come from the fact that improved-modified patterns were usually reached in a 12-gauge gun with 30 points constriction, and modified patterns with 20 points. Likewise the quarter choke (strong improved-cylinder or 50 per cent patterns) were reached with 10 points.

Again to show how little the size of the hole in the end of the barrel means as far as choke and patterns go, we know the standard 12-gauge bore is supposed to measure .729 yet some run as small as .722 and some as large as .747. The tendency these days is for many manufacturers to "overbore" their barrels—make them larger than .729. This is the major reason that you often get contradictory reports on the variable choke devices. If you put a choke device on a .722 barrel and one on a .747 barrel, with the same tube or setting you will get two entirely different amounts of constriction.

The old standard of 40-points constriction for a 12-gauge gun to produce full-choke patterns is pretty well in the discard today, and very few guns, particularly American guns, have that much. Too much constriction can ruin patterns, as many thoughtful owners of guns fitted with a variable choke device have found out. Often the modified tube or setting will throw denser patterns than the full-choke tube or setting. When the user of such a gadget opens up his gun he is relieving the choke, something which the factory gun borer does with his reamer to produce better patterns.

With today's ammunition any gun with much more than 30 points constriction is probably overchoked, and guns marked "full choke" leave the factory with as little as 25 points constriction, and actually full-choke (70 per cent) patterns are often achieved with as little as 14 points constriction.

THE TEST OF A GUN'S CHOKE

I believe we are beginning to see, then, that the hole in the end of the barrel does not have too much to do with the patterns a gun throws, and that even if the gunner had access to an inside microm-eter that would show him the amount of constriction he had, it wouldn't do him much good. The old business of using a dime as a micrometer is particularly silly and valueless. It belongs with the folklore that holds that the long-barrel gun shoots harder than the gun with the shorter barrel; that shotshells a couple of years old lose their strength and merely feather game; that pumps shoot harder than automatics, and so on. The fact that a dime will or will not go down the muzzle of the gun has nothing whatsoever to do with the amount of choke. The average dime runs from .701 to .703 inch in diameter. In a recent orgy of patterning, a friend and I checked all the bores that threw patterns of 70 per cent or more with nice new dimes. About three-fourths of the guns that gave full-choke performance would accept the dimes. So much for folklore.

All of which reminds me of a story. I knew a nice old character who took great pride in an ancient 12-gauge hammer gun with twist barrels. He had killed a lot of game with it and swore it was the "hardest shooting" gun in Arizona. I was always afraid he was going to blow himself up with that venerable musket, so I talked him into getting a new gun. It was a full-choke pump but he claimed it didn't shoot as hard as the old gun, and it did feather and wound a lot of birds. I patterned the two guns. The new pump shot beau-tiful, dense, full-choke patterns, but my friend did not have the skill to hit with them. He struck most of the birds with the thin edge of the pattern, not with the dense center. His old gun, the "hard shooter," had in the course of the years lost all its constric-tion. At 25 yards it shot about a 36-inch pattern. He could hit with it and kill with it whereas he could not with the 20-inch pattern of the new gun.

The test then of the gun is the patterns, and the standard is what percentage of shot in the particular shell the particular gun will average putting into a 30-inch circle at 40 yards. The way to take a pattern is to tack up a sheet of paper about 4 feet square, then

Technicians at the Remington factory count the pellet marks in a shot pattern. The pattern is determined by firing at a paper target at 40 yards (25 yards for skeet loads) and counting how many pellets are grouped within a 30-inch circle.

put a black bull's-eye in the middle of it, aim at the bull's-eye and shoot. Then enscribe a 30-inch circle to enclose the most shot and take the percentage of the shot in that circle as compared to the number of shot in the shell. One should shoot and average at least five patterns; ten patterns would be better.

A little research like this is very interesting and very instructive. It is as important to the shotgun man, be he skeet shot, trapshooter or bird hunter, as targeting a rifle is to the big-game hunter. Often he begins to get some light on his performance in the field. He may find, for instance, that his gun patterns poorly with high-velocity maximum loads of any sort, excellently with standard loads. He may find that his gun does not handle No. 4 worth a hoot but does beautifully with No. 6. Most of the lads who stuff their guns with high-velocity loads and No. 4 shot and then try for ducks at 65 and 70 yards should do some patterning at that distance. Afterward they probably would be much less prone to brag about those occasional long-range kills.

Let's take a look at the patterns the various chokes are supposed to deliver in a 30-inch circle at 40 yards:

Full Choke—70 to 80 per cent
Improved Modified—65 to 70 per cent
Modified (Half Choke)—55 to 65 per cent
Quarter Choke (Strong Improved Cylinder)—50 to 55 per cent
Improved Cylinder—45 to 50 per cent
Skeet No. 2 (Usually delivers modified patterns)
Skeet No. 1 Cylinder—About 35 to 40 per cent

The larger the killing pattern is, the easier it is to hit with since the man behind it is penalized less for his errors in lead and elevation. Let us take a look at the size of the killing patterns that are thrown ordinarily by the various chokes at hunting ranges:

BORING	SPREAD OF SHOT PATTERN IN INCHES AT VARIOUS RANGES IN YARDS:						
	10	15	20	25	30	35	40
Cylinder	19	26	32	38	44	51	57
Improved Cylinder	15	20	26	32	38	44	51
Modified	12	16	20	26	32	38	46
Full	9	12	16	21	26	32	40

Suppose we take 25 yards as the average range at which upland game is killed and then glance at the table. We'll discover that it would probably be a lot easier to hit a bird with the 32-inch pattern thrown by an improved-cylinder boring than with the 21-inch pattern thrown by a full choke.

The deer hunter who embarks on a hunt without shooting his new rifle on paper and then misses his buck because his rifle isn't properly sighted in gets scant sympathy from riflemen. "Got what he deserved!" they say.

NECESSITY OF PATTERNING YOUR SHOTGUN

Yet even very good shotgun shots who shoot a lot seldom bother to pattern their guns. Often this failure results in disappointment and humiliation. A good many years ago I got a new 16-gauge gun bored Skeet No. 1 and No. 2. For two days I hunted quail with it, shooting a well-known make of high-velocity shells with No. $7\frac{1}{2}$ shot. I noticed that I feathered a lot of straightaway birds I should have killed cold. Something was haywire. I patterned the gun and found with that load my right barrel shot about 50 per cent doughnut patterns and the closer I held the more certain I was to miss. I found, though, that the barrel did beautifully with No. 8 traploads. My troubles were over.

The new ammunition which has come out since the war, with the wadless crimps and gas-seal wads patterns much closer than pre-war ammunition and less constriction is necessary to give full-choke patterns. Once a gun that would pattern 75 to 80 per cent was something to celebrate in song and story. With the new ammunition such patterns are a dime a dozen. The new ammunition also accounts for guns patterning closer than they are marked. In a series of tests I made about a year ago, I found that almost all guns patterned closer than expected. Many guns that patterned full choke were marked "modified" and some were even marked "improved cylinder." Here is the record of a barrel marked "improved cylinder." It was purchased for upland hunting and for skeet, and until I patterned it, the owner thought he was actually getting improved-cylinder patterns. Each figure represents the percentage of shot in a 30-inch circle at 40 yards, in an average of 5 patterns: Peters, 1¼ ounces, No. 7—66 per cent; Winchester, 1⅛ ounces, No. 8—71 per cent; Remington, 1¼ ounces, No. 7½—67 per cent. Improved cylinder is supposed to average about 45 per cent, so draw your own conclusions. To show how common very dense patterns are in full-choke guns, here's the record of an over-the-counter pump gun so marked, each figure representing the average of five patterns: 1¼ ounces, No. 7½—78 per cent; 1¼ ounces, No. 6—80 per cent; 1¼ ounces, No. 4—85 per cent.

Actually this business of taking patterns in a 30-inch circle at 40 yards, though useful for purposes of comparison, since the standards are based on it, should not be the sole criterion by which the gun is judged. Most feathered game, even ducks, is shot at *under* 40 yards. Most upland game that is *killed*, not simply feathered or even knocked down, is shot at 30 yards or less. Actually a successful 30-yard shot at a quail, a pheasant or a Hun is a longer than average shot. When the average upland gunner makes a kill at 30 yards, he is apt to think he made it at 40 yards or even at 50 yards. When he does actually make a kill at 40 yards, he will swear he made it at 60. See what those patterns look like at 30 yards!

A score of years ago I used to shoot ducks with a 20 gauge as they flew from one mountain lake to another. My favorite stand was under a tall yellow pine. The birds came in about 10 to 20 feet over the top of the pine. Long practice taught me the necessary lead and my percentage on the birds was good enough so that I gained some slight reputation as a duck shot and my gun became known as the "hardest shooting doggoned 20 gauge in the country." Then a skeptic doped out the height of the pine tree by means of triangulation and figured I was killing the ducks at between 30 and 35 yards away. The gun and I both lost our reputations.

HOW TO SELECT YOUR CHOKE

What the average shotgun owner should think about, then, is not the size of the hole in his barrel, not the way the barrel is marked, not how far he can kill with it, but the sort of pattern his gun throws with the load he uses at the average range at which he shoots.

The hunter who goes after woodcock, ruffed grouse, and Bob White quail in heavy cover, and after rabbits in the brush, needs all the pattern area he can get. He should not use more than quarter choke at the very most and actually he is better off with Skeet No. 1 choke, the spreader tube on a Cutts Comp, Weaver Choke or POWer Pac, or a Poly-Choke set at reverse choke. At 20 yards he can use as much as a 36-inch spread if he can get it.

The man who wants an all-around gun had better shoot for about a 50 per cent pattern in a 30-inch circle at 40 yards. Such a pattern, if even and well distributed, will kill pheasants and ducks at that distance and yet is fairly easy to hit with at 20 yards. Usually these tight improved-cylinder or quarter-choke patterns are achieved with about .008—.010-inch constriction in a 12 gauge.

Let us never forget that the shotgun is primarily a short-range weapon and that most game is killed well within 40 yards. Let us not forget that most hunters are people of short-range skills. The 80 per cent gun is the weapon of the expert. It will indeed kill to 55 to 60 yards but it isn't self-pointing. Most of us no more have the skill to use a gun so bored than we have to drive a race car at 125 miles an hour.

CHAPTER TWENTY NINE

Variable-Choke Devices

ONE OF THE MOST USEFUL IDEAS THAT HAS COME ALONG IN THE PAST half century to benefit the sportsman is that of putting a gadget on the muzzle of a shotgun to vary the patterns the barrel delivers. This gadget is a choke device that can be fitted on a shotgun barrel to allow various choke settings.

The necessity for some such device came into being with the wide-spread popularity of pump and automatic guns with single barrels.

With the double-barrel gun, there is much less necessity for anything of the sort, since the double is generally manufactured with different degrees of choke in the two barrels—modified and full, or improved cylinder and modified, for example. Two triggers give the owner of a double instant selectivity—theoretically, anyway. If he gets a close rise he can use the trigger for the more open barrel; if he gets a distant rise he can press the trigger for the choke barrel. For my part I have found that in using twin-triggered doubles I almost always shoot the open barrel first, come what may. I might also add that all of my doubles are equipped with selective single triggers and when I am in the field I have them set to fire the open barrel first. Then if I have a chance to grass two birds on a rise, I have the closer choke to throw a killing pattern at the greater distance.

It is also enormously difficult to install variable-choke devices on double guns, although it has been done. Somewhere—I think it was either at the shop of Griffin & Howe in New York or at the Winchester plant in New Haven, Connecticut—I once saw a double 12 gauge fitted with a pair of Cutts Compensators. Apparently the experiment was not a roaring success as I have never heard of it being repeated.

There is a great deal of utility in varying the pattern fired by a shotgun. The man hunting Bob White quail, ruffed grouse or woodcock is severely handicapped if his gun throws full-choke patterns. Most of his shots are at 30 yards or less, and with a dense-patterning barrel he either misses his birds or tears them up badly. For pheasant shooting in stubble, where many birds are taken at from 30 to 40 yards, the pattern thrown by a modified choke probably has the most utility. For pass shooting at ducks and geese at ranges from 45 to 55 or 60 yards, the hunter needs as dense a pattern as he can get. One effort to vary patterns with the same barrel is through the use of spreader loads in which the shot charge is separated with cardboard wads. They result in wide, somewhat uneven shot distribution but with them, a full-choke gun will deliver what are approximately improved-cylinder patterns.

There is additional need to vary the degree of constriction at the muzzle of the shotgun in areas where rifled slugs are used on deer. Many tests have shown that the greatest accuracy with slugs is obtained when they are fired in a straight-cylinder bore—and that the more choke the barrel has the worse they shoot. Large buckshot likewise shoot better in barrels of less constriction.

The variable-choke devices have another good feature about which one hears little; that is they can be installed on a pump or automatic to give the gunner the length of barrel and boring he wants. I can see no reason whatsoever for the barrel on a repeater to be over 26 inches long for general use, as a 26-inch barrel on a pump or automatic gives about the same overall length as a 30-inch barrel on a double. But our gunner can no more buy a repeater with a modified or full barrel 26 inches long than he can learn to read and write Arabic over a weekend. The long barrel has real advantages for trapshooting and it is very good for pass shooting on ducks and geese. But for knocking down decoyed ducks or for general upland shooting, the long barrel is relatively slow and unwieldy.

Gunners who are unhappy with the awkward handling qualities of the pump or automatic with 28- or 32-inch barrels can easily change them: All they have to do is get a variable-choke device installed to give them the overall barrel length they want. Over the course of the years I have been advising correspondents to have these devices installed to give them an overall length of from 24 to 26 inches. I have yet to have anyone squawk because his barrel was too short. On the other hand, dozens have written in saying the shorter barrels have improved the speed and accuracy of their pointing. If the choke devices had no other utility, they would still earn their keep by enabling the owner of a long-barreled repeater to civilize it.

MISCONCEPTION ABOUT CHOKE DEVICES

In spite of the fact that choke in the muzzle of a shotgun has been with us for a great many years, the subject is still surrounded by a good deal of mystery and rife with misconceptions. Just as many believe that a full-choke 20 gauge shoots a smaller pattern than a full-choke 12 gauge, and that the longer the barrel of a shotgun the "harder" it shoots. There are also those who believe that if they only knew some magic formula they could tell what kind of patterns their shotguns threw by measuring the muzzle diameter. Then they would not have to bother to pattern their guns.

A couple of years ago an acquaintance of mine came up to my place with a pump gun of well-known make in his hands. His eyes were flashing fire and he was roaring with rage. He had, he told me, purchased this miserable gun in good faith. It was marked "Full Choke," but as soon as he got home he had discovered that a dime would go into the muzzle. It was not, therefore, a full-choke gun, and he had been cheated.

I assured him that whether or not a dime would go down the muzzle of a 12-gauge gun was no test of the choke, and that some dimes would go down the muzzles of certain full-choke guns and some would not. I assured him that dimes differed a bit in diameter and that the muzzles of full-choke guns likewise differed in diameter. I also assured him that there was only one reliable test of the choke and that was the pattern it delivered. If a gun patterned 70 per cent or better it was full choke even if you could throw a Brittany spaniel down the bore; if it didn't pattern 70 per cent it wasn't a full choke even if you couldn't put a shirt button down the muzzle.

We took the gun out to the local gun club, set up a patterning frame and fired ten shots with 1¼ ounces of No. 6 in front of 3¾ drams of powder at a sheet of paper about 4 feet square. Then we drew a 30-inch circle to enclose the most shot possible and compared the number of shot within the circle to the number of shot in a shell. The average in this particular case was 72 per cent, and there was no argument but that with No. 6 shot the gun was throwing full-choke patterns.

When a certain choke device appeared some years ago many purchasers discovered to their horror that dimes would go down the muzzle of the full-choke tubes that came with it. I got a barrage of letters from indignant purchasers—so many that I had to draw up a form letter to answer them. I told them to pattern their guns and then if they were not happy it was time to register their kicks. Actually there isn't anything to the tale that the smaller the muzzle of the gun, the tighter the pattern. It is easy to overchoke a gun—and when that happens the pattern goes to pot. Many a gun has been made to shoot denser patterns by reaming out some of the constriction.

TYPES OF CHOKES

The notion of being able to vary the amount of constriction in the end of the barrel by putting some sort of a gadget on it is quite old. I understand that along in the eighteen nineties, some gunsmiths threaded the ends of barrels for screw-on tubes giving various amounts of constriction and various patterns. Pioneer devices in the field that are still manufactured are the Poly Choke, which was invented by the late E. Field White, and the Cutts Compensator, the invention of the late Colonel Richard M. Cutts of the United States army. The Cutts Comp has been manufactured for many years by the Lyman Gunsight Company. All of the other variable-choke devices on the market are variations of one or the other of these two.

THE INTERCHANGEABLE TUBE CHOKE

The Cutts Comp consists of an enlarged, slotted tube or "cage" which serves as a muzzle brake to divert gasses, lessen the pressure on the shot column and decrease recoil. This is screwed to the barrel of the shotgun. Into the other end of the cage are screwed tubes of various lengths and degrees of constriction giving different patterns and making the same shotgun serve various purposes from skeet shooting at from 5 to 25 yards to pass shooting at waterfowl at 55 to 60 yards.

The Cutts Comp is made in 16, 20, 28 and .410 gauge as well as in 12 gauge. Tubes are made for all kinds of shooting, from the spreader tube, which is presumed to give patterns somewhat wider

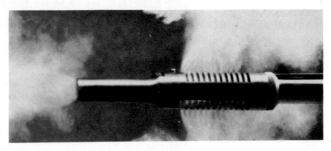

The Cutts Comp variable-choke device screws into the barrel. The forward end receives tubes of various choke sizes. Here the gases can be seen venting through the tube slots as the gun is fired.

than improved cylinder, to full and extra full choke. Tubes giving patterns that are about quarter choke and modified are also listed. For gauges smaller than 12, only the spreader, modified and full-choke tubes are available. An adjustable collet-type tube is also made. Tubes giving different degrees of choke are of different length and, of course, a barrel with an overall length of 25 inches with the spreader tube would be a good deal longer when the full-choke tube was screwed in.

The slotted cage gives considerable recoil reduction, from about 15 per cent with skeet loads to something like 35 per cent with the old maximum 12-gauge loads of $3\frac{3}{4}$ drams of powder and $1\frac{1}{4}$ ounces of shot and likewise with the new $2\frac{3}{4}$-inch 12-gauge magnum loads with $1\frac{1}{2}$ ounces of shot.

The reduction of recoil coupled with the availability of the spreader tube has made the Cutts Comp very popular with skeet shooters. However, the report is high pitched and for that reason it has never been popular with trapshooters because those in the same squad find it annoying.

In theory, the diversion of the gasses before the shot column strikes the constriction of the choke lessens the gas pressure on the base of the shot column and produces more even patterns. I have never made up my mind about this.

Other variable-choke devices of the interchangeable tube type are the Weaver Choke and the POWer-Pac. Each has a ventilated cage and each has screw-in tubes which give various degrees of choke. The POWer-Pac tubes, like those on the Cutts Compensator, are of different lengths, but unlike those of the Cutts and the Weaver Choke, they extend *into* the cage with the result that the barrel has the same overall length no matter what tube is being used. The

PGWer-Pac is made of steel, and the Cutts Compensator can be had with either a steel or an aluminum alloy cage. The Weaver Choke is built of aluminum alloy throughout. Its cage is smaller than those of the other devices of this sort and is vented for gas escape with holes rather than with slots. Many consider that it looks less bizarre on the end of the gun barrel than do the other choke devices in its class.

THE COLLET-TYPE CHOKE

The other type of choke device was originated by E. Field White and the first in the field was his Poly Choke. This is the collet-type choke, which gives different degrees of constriction with the same adjustable tube simply by turning a knurled sleeve. When the sleeve is turned in one direction the fingers of the tube are squeezed in to decrease the diameter of the muzzle; when it is turned in the other direction, the fingers relax to increase the diameter. The Poly Choke can be adjusted for any degree of choke to give patterns of from full choke to reverse choke, which presumably opens up the pattern wider than true cylinder and which, incidentally, is the setting to be used for rifled slugs.

Choke devices of the collet type are the easiest to adjust since all one has to do is to reach up and give the knurled sleeve a twist. With the choke devices of the interchangeable tube type, the extra tubes must be carried along in the pocket and generally screwed

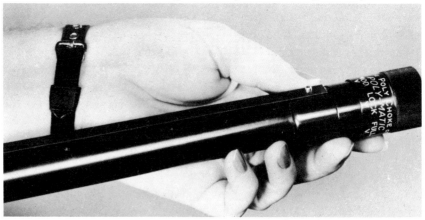

The Poly Choke screws into the barrel and enables the shooter to change the degree of choke by turning the knurled sleeve.

home with a wrench. However, the gunner does not often change his choke setting in the field. Generally, if he is after pheasants, let us say, he will adjust the device for modified and let it stay there.

It behooves any owner of a gun equipped with a variable-choke device to do some patterning to see just what the device is accomplishing. There are a good many reasons for this. One is that generally speaking the pattern delivered is determined by the difference between the bore diameter and the muzzle diameter. The Williams Gunsight Company of Davison, Michigan, which installs many hundreds of choke devices each year makes the following statement in their catalogue: "The best way to determine choke is to measure the amount of constriction in the end of the barrel, skeet boring excepted, and then subtract this figure from the actual bore diameter of the barrel. This will give you the number of thousandths of actual choke in the barrel."

According to the Williams people, 12-gauge bore diameters run from .717 inch up to .750, and obviously a tube or a choke setting that might give a good full-choke pattern with a .717 bore would overchoke a gun with a .750 bore. They likewise say that the bore diameters of Browning 12-gauge guns run about .725 whereas those of Winchester and Remington run .730 and their bores are about the same, or .729. In the 16 gauge, Browning bore diameters run .665, Remingtons .673, and Winchester .664. In the 20 gauge they run .611 for the Browning, .619 for the Remington, and .614 for the Winchester. All of this would tend to show that the man who patterns his variable-choke device with various tubes and settings is acting wisely.

The full-choke standard used to be .040 (40/1000) inch, or 40 "points" of constriction, to employ the gunmaker's term, but with modern ammunition, a gun with that much constriction is overchoked. Most full-choke barrels today have from 28 to 37 points of constriction, and I have seen guns with 22 points constriction that deliver full-choke patterns with certain loads. In the old days, 30 points constriction was supposed to give improved-modified patterns, 20 points (half choke) modified or 60 per cent patterns and 10 points (quarter choke or strong improved cylinder) about 50 per cent.

The Poly Choke is made in three different sizes in 12 gauge so that the proper size can be chosen to give the greatest efficiency with the bore diameter.

The Poly Choke is made in standard and ventilated styles. In the ventilated model the slotted cage which vents gas and acts as a muzzle brake is forward of the knurled sleeve and the constriction. It serves only to reduce recoil and has no effect on the pattern. Lyman makes a collet-type tube for the Cutts Compensator. It screws into the cage just as the non-adjustable tubes do.

Other concerns have begun to manufacture variable chokes. Herter's turns out a device very similar to the Poly Choke. Savage-Stevens installs their Super-Choke on their Model 775 automatic and Model 77-SC pump. The Super-Choke is made with the ventilated cage to the rear of the choking portion of the device. A similar and very good device is the Cyclone Choke put out by the Hartford Choke Company.

Still another choke device is the automatic type. It is the collet tube all fancied up and with machinery installed to vary the degree of constriction and to shoot progressively denser patterns, just as the owner of the double will usually fire his open and then his choke barrel. Years ago I heard that the Poly Choke people were experimenting with such a device, but the first in the field was the Flex Choke made by the Jarvis Manufacturing Company. It is wound up against spring tension by turning the knurled sleeve. The first shot will be at improved cylinder, the second at modified, and the third at full choke. It can also be locked at any of the settings. The gadget is long and heavy but an interesting development. A somewhat similar automatic choke has recently come into the field. It is the Adjustomatic made by the Hartford Gun Choke Company, and since it is of aluminum alloy construction it is lighter than the Flex Choke. So far it is only made in 12 gauge. The device gives an option of seven degrees of constriction. When a gun equipped with it is fired, the ring and outer sleeve of the choke move forward and lock to reduce automatically the diameter of the choke and give the next denser pattern. It can be set, let us say, on cylinder and the second shot will then be improved cylinder. Or it can be set to give improved cylinder and modified or a modified pattern and then full. It also incorporates a short, slotted sleeve for recoil reduction.

So that's the line-up of the variable choke devices: Screw-on tube, ventilated cage with tube, plain collet, collet with muzzle brake and automatic.

I get a great many questions about the devices. Many ask if they can be put on a barrel with any type of choke. They can. Generally the barrel is cut off at a point where all the constriction is removed. If the gun owner wants a longer barrel, all choke can be reamed out and the gadget put right on the end of the barrel. Some skeet-type chokes are bell-muzzled and in these the bell must be cut off before installation of the variable choke.

I am also asked which fundamental type gives the best patterns. Both are entirely satisfactory, but from my limited experiments I have got wider close-range patterns for skeet shooting with the spreader tubes on the Cutts Compensator and the POWer-Pac. A Weaver Choke with a full-choke tube gave me the densest patterns I have ever obtained with No. 6 shot in a 20 gauge; one of the best shooting guns I have ever had was a 16 equipped with a standard Poly Choke set at *modified*.

The greatest recoil reduction is obtained, I believe, with the chokes with the large slotted cages—the Cutts and the POWer-Pac. As far as convenience goes, there is no contest. The quickly adjustable collet-type device like the Poly Choke wins easily.

I can't say that a muzzle device stuck on the end of the barrel adds to the beauty of any gun, but users become accustomed to it. From the aesthetic standpoint, the neatest is the simple collet type like the Poly Choke.

Some gunners try to shoot a shotgun by aiming as if with a rifle. When one of the fatter choke devices is fitted to guns with barrel and receiver in line, these gunners tend to shoot low because the device acts like a higher front sight on a rifle. This tendency can be cured by giving the barrel an upward bend to place the center of impact at the point of aim. The devices should always be installed by men who know their business. Most of the criticism of these devices has been caused by poor installation.

Variable-choke devices have been around in more or less their present forms for close to 30 years. It looks as if they are here to stay and there is no argument that the repeating shotgun equipped with one of them is the nearest thing to a real all-around shotgun.

The Shotgun Stock

THERE IS A LOT OF HOCUS-POCUS AND MISINFORMATION CONNECTED with the subject of stock fit and since the matter is of considerable importance to the shooter, I think we should be as clear about it as possible. For one thing, I am convinced that a lot of the motions the flossier gunmakers go through in fitting a shotgun stock are unnecessary and have little to do with getting the right dimensions. Furthermore, I think there is only one person who can tell if his stock fit is correct and that is the shooter himself. But even he can do it only after he knows enough about shooting and about himself to judge. Some of the most unshootable stocks I have ever seen have been on expensive, custom-made guns.

But comparatively few special stock jobs are done on shotguns. The overwhelming majority of shotgun shooters simply take what the factories give them. Not long ago I dropped in to see a famous stocker and asked him how many shotguns he stocked as compared to rifles. He told me that he does maybe two or three shotgun jobs a year yet does several dozen jobs on fine rifles in the same period and has a miles-long waiting list of rifle owners.

The more one contemplates this circumstance, the odder it seems. Even at its speediest, rifle shooting is deliberate compared to shotgun shooting, and it is far easier to adapt the human body to a poorly fitting rifle than it is to an off-size shotgun stock. Thousands of men of assorted shapes and sizes, for example, have done fine shooting with the miserable stock on the old 1903 Springfield, in spite of the fact that it is a fair fit only for people about 5 feet 2 inches tall.

Whereas the rifle is deliberately aimed, the shotgun is approximately aimed or "pointed," if we want to use that term. The good shotgun shot actually does most of his pointing with the position of his feet and the placement of his head before he brings the gun to his shoulder. Then if his stock is a good fit, he is on target and he shoots. Also, the good and fast shotgun shot has already started his swing by rotating hips and shoulders while he is mounting his gun and before the butt hits his shoulder. As a consequence, the shotgun that doesn't fit handicaps the gunner far more than a poorly fitting rifle handicaps the rifleman. A gun that is muzzle-heavy or muzzle-light, too high or too low of comb, too short, too long or pitched wrong, lets many a bird and many a clay target live to fly another day.

The only scattergunners that pay much attention to stock fit are trapshooters, and most of those I know are constantly fiddling with their stocks. They buy trick buttplates to change drop and pitch; they rasp down combs or build them up. On the other hand most skeet shooters don't worry much about their stocks but simply accept what the factories give them. Maybe this is because skeet shooters are simply a merrier and more carefree lot, but a good guess is that trapshooters worry because they are involved with money. Sometimes a missed target may cost a trapshooter several hundred bucks.

Shotgun shooters weren't always so easy to please. Prior to the big depression, great quantities of fine double guns and classy single-barrel trap guns were made to order by Parker, Ithaca, Lefever, Hunter Arms and Fox, and even field shooters had definite ideas about stock fit and design. When they ordered new guns they wrote detailed specifications. Now the fine old-time shotgun firms have folded, and the only builder of premium-grade doubles in this country is Winchester with its great Model 21.

Try-guns such as these Winchester Models 21 (top) and 12 are a great help in fitting a shotgun stock. They are adjustable for length of pull, drop and pitch.

In England, where only the well-to-do can do wing shooting, the picture is entirely different. Most guns are custom built and fitted and the working out of proper stock dimensions is a complicated ritual that includes the use of a try-gun and trips to the shooting range so that the fitter can ascertain the shooter's habits.

PROPER STOCK DIMENSIONS

Since the fit of the stock is extremely important, I think we should follow the English example and take it seriously.

Let us take a look at stock dimensions. Length of pull is right when the stock is short enough to mount quickly and easily without catching on the clothes at the shoulder, and long enough to keep the thumb of the right hand from bumping the nose. I think

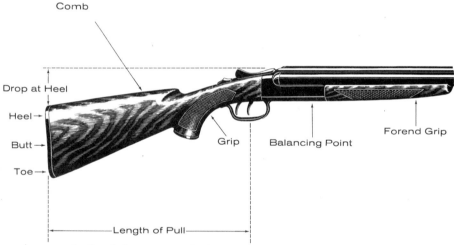

A correctly fitted shotgun stock allows the shooter to raise the gun with a quick, natural motion, and puts his eye instantly in line with the top of the barrel as his cheek rests against the comb.

this business of ascertaining stock length by putting the butt in the crook of the arm with the finger on the trigger is about as sensible as determining the correct length of a stirrup by the length of the arm. These methods might be valid if people shot guns with the butts in the crooks of their arms and rode horses standing on their heads in the saddles, with their hands in the stirrups. But they don't. Trap stocks run longer than field stocks because the gun is at the shoulder when the target is called for. The stocks on wild fowl guns should be comparatively short, as the duck hunter is usually bundled up in heavy clothes.

The comb of a shotgun is in effect the rear sight because it determines the relationship of the eye to the end of the barrel. A high comb makes the gunner shoot high because it raises his eye, makes him see more barrel and point the barrel *up* so that the shot charge flies higher. A low comb has the opposite effect. If it is too low, the gunner not only tends to shoot low, but since the comb does not support his face, he tends to swing his arm instead of his body. It should be remembered, though, that the drop at comb isn't the only factor to be considered; the thickness of the comb influences the sight also. A thick comb will put the eye higher than a low one.

With the fact that the comb acts as a rear sight in mind, the trapshooter looks for a higher comb than the skeet shooter because his targets are rising sharply and he needs a built-in lead so he can shoot *at* a straightaway bird and yet hit it. With a low comb he has to blot out his target in order to hit it, something not conducive to good shooting. A high comb is needed by the upland gunner also, particularly the pheasant shooter, since he too shoots at sharply rising birds.

Drop at heel should be enough so that the butt comes naturally to the shoulder. The amount of drop depends on the shooter's build and on his shooting habits. A square-shouldered man with a long neck who shoots in good form with his head down can use a very straight stock. On the other hand, the short-necked man with sloping shoulders has to have more drop at heel. A beginner usually likes a good deal of drop, but as his skill grows, he generally wants a longer and straighter stock (one in which there is less difference between drop at comb and drop at heel). Anyone should shoot the straightest stock he can because the straighter the stock the easier it is to mount and point and the less the apparent recoil. The straight stock brings the recoil straight back; the crooked stock causes the comb to rise and crack the shooter on the cheek. Because a straight stock lessens recoil and aids fast pointing, it is favored by trapshooters. Likewise, the straighter the stock the less difference in elevation of the shot charge a slight difference in cheek position makes. The reason for this is fairly obvious. If the stock, with, let us say, a 1½-inch drop at comb has much drop at

A Weatherby-stocked Winchester Model 42 in .410 gauge with a Monte Carlo comb has a sharp heel drop, which increases recoil and slows mounting the gun.

heel, it will give a 1⁹⁄₁₆-inch drop a bit farther back, a 1⅝-inch drop still farther back and a 1¾-inch drop beyond that. This is the reason that many trapshooters want Monte Carlo combs which are level and which do not allow changes in elevation with changes in the position of the cheek. For my part, I think Monte Carlo combs are something less than beautiful and I'd rather make do with a little drop at heel.

Pitch is the angle at which the buttplate is set on and it is measured from the muzzle. Its most important function is to keep the butt firmly against the shoulder. If there is too little downward pitch, the butt has a tendency to slip down and the gun to point *up* and throw the shot charge high. If there is too much downward pitch, the stock tends to slip up on the shoulder, make the gunner see the breech rather than the muzzle and shoot low. A shotgun stock takes less pitch than a rifle stock. In the old days many gunners liked zero pitch. I like 1–1½ inches, from 26-inch barrels, but many gunners like more. On the other hand a downward pitch of about 3½ inches from the iron sights about catches one with a rifle. Obviously the more drop there is at heel the greater the downward pitch must be to maintain the same angle of the butt at the shoulder.

Pitch is something the average gunner doesn't bother much about, but it is something that can spoil his shooting. A pal of mine once decided he wanted a recoil pad on his pump gun. He specified length of pull but not pitch and the gunsmith put the pad on to give two inches pitch *up*. All at once my friend's shooting fell off. He tried new glasses, prayers, incantations and sacrifices in the dark of the moon, but he still couldn't hit anything; the butt was slipping down under his armpit and he saw too much barrel and shot over everything. I cured his miseries by loosening the screws on the pad and inserting cardboard shims between the pad and the wood at the heel. Lengthening the stock at the heel makes for more downward pitch, by the way, and at the toe for less. Wrong pitch can make anyone's shooting turn sour.

The average American repeating shotgun has a drop at comb of $1\frac{5}{8}$ inches, a drop at heel of $2\frac{1}{2}$ and a length of pull of 14. Such dimensions do reasonably well for anyone from about 5 feet 7 to 5 feet 11 inches tall and for all-around use. The tall man who does a lot of shooting needs more stock length and less drop at comb and heel. I, for instance, am something over 6 feet tall, have square shoulders, a long neck, and wear a 34-inch sleeve. For all-around use I am best fitted with the following dimensions: $1\frac{1}{2}$ x $2\frac{1}{4}$ x $14\frac{1}{4}$ with a down pitch of $1\frac{1}{2}$ inches from the 26-inch barrels of a double gun.

The tall man can shoot a long stock—$14\frac{1}{2}$ or even $14\frac{3}{4}$ inches; the boy, the woman or the small man needs less length—about $13\frac{1}{2}$ inches, for anyone around 5 feet 4 or 5 feet 5. The point is that the stock should feel right and comfortable. People with very wide cheekbones need less drop at comb. Trapshooters like straight and long stocks because they mount their guns before they call for their birds and because they shoot at rapidly rising targets. Typical dimensions for a trap gun are $1\frac{3}{8}$ x $1\frac{7}{8}$ x $14\frac{1}{2}$. Sixty or 70 years ago people apparently liked to shoot with their heads up, as many old doubles have drops at heel of 3, $3\frac{1}{2}$, or even 4 inches. Such stocks are slow to get on with and kick like the very devil!

The British generally make their stocks with cast-off, which means that for a right handed man the butt is to the right of the line of bore in a single-barrel gun, or to the right of the rib in a double. Sometimes there is more cast-off at toe than at heel, and the whole subject is exceedingly mysterious. Presumably cast-off makes the gun easier to mount, but whether it has much actual effect or not I cannot say. It is seldom used by American stockers, but the British swear by it. Theoretically, cast-off increases recoil effect and has a tendency to drive the comb against the cheek. Cast-on has the opposite effect.

The classic shotgun stock has a straight grip, as it was evolved before the single trigger was invented, and most users of double triggers like to shift the right hand slightly as they go from trigger to trigger. Almost all European shotguns are made with straight

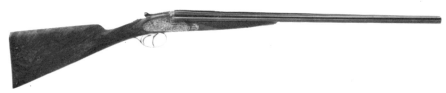

The classic European double has a straight grip, which tends to cramp the wrist and causes the gunner to shoot high.

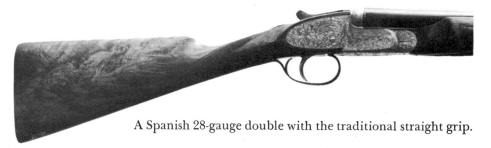

A Spanish 28-gauge double with the traditional straight grip.

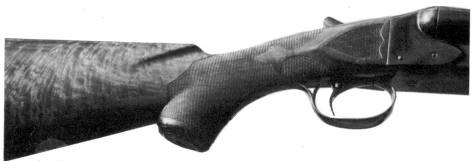

A pistol grip, such as this one on a Winchester Model 21 double, gives better control of the gun.

grips, and many gunners think that the straight grip gives a gun a handsome and racy appearance. However, the straight grip cramps the wrist and slightly decreases the control the shooter has over his gun. For this reason, I think the gun with the straight grip has a tendency to shoot high—or at least to cause an occasional shot to get away high. I have a beautiful little Spanish 28 gauge with a straight grip—otherwise the stock is the same as those on my other doubles, which have pistol grips. With the Federal load of a full ounce of No. 6 the Spanish gun is a lethal pheasant gun, but I have to fight it to keep from overshooting quail.

Most grips on shotguns seem to me to be too large in circumference, some running 5 or even 5¼ inches, and like a baseball bat with a too-large handle, they are clumsy. My own taste runs to about 4½ inches in circumference on a 12-gauge gun. A 20 gauge looks best to me with about a 4-inch grip, and my little 28-gauge Arizaga has a grip only 3¾ inches in circumference. This grip is in keeping with the elegant little gun and as nice to look at as the wrist of a lovely woman. Straight grips on many best-grade British and Continental guns are actually shaped like rounded diamonds on cross-section. I like the feel of them.

For the double with the single trigger, and any repeater, a pistol grip is more practical, more sensible, and gives better control of the gun than any other. The so-called semi-pistol grip, sometimes put on doubles in the old days, doesn't give much more gun control than the straight grip. I like a moderate curve, with the point of the grip about 4⅛ inches from the center of the trigger. Grips with excessive hook and lying close to the trigger seem clumsy and ungraceful to me and as cramping at the other extreme as the straight grip and far less handsome. However, some like them, and anyone is privileged to pay his money and take his choice.

THE BUTTPLATE

Cheap shotguns almost always have black composition buttplates which, though generally brittle, are satisfactory enough and easy to install. Guns of heavy recoil are generally fitted with a rubber recoil pad to alter length of pull and pitch. In some high-grade guns the end of the rubber pad is faced with leather so the rubber will not cling to the clothing. The fanciest doubles are generally made with no buttplate at all and have the bare wood checkered, but some, such as the late-lamented Parkers, had skeleton buttplates to protect the outside areas of the butt, leaving the center portion bare for some good-looking checkering.

THE FOREND

The short, "splinter" forend still is favored in Europe, but most American shooters want more forend to hang on to (with the left hand) for better control. All automatics and most pumps have plenty of forend, and most doubles made for the American trade

The slide handle of a pump shotgun should have ample wood for the shooter's hand and plenty of sharp checkering to keep it from slipping.

are fitted with beavertail forends. All Winchester 21s have beavertails and so do the majority of foreign doubles now being imported for the American market. Sporting goods dealers tell me that doubles with the old splinter forends are hard to sell. The beavertail gives the shooter more to hang onto, lets him get his left hand farther forward for better gun control and puts his hands more nearly in line for fast pointing. I believe that shooters began to realize the value of larger forends when pump and automatic shotguns became common, and they also learned from trap and skeet. Both games have had a great deal of influence on stock design. They are responsible not only for the beavertail forend but for the Monte Carlo comb and the straight stock.

WOOD FOR SHOTGUN STOCKS

Because shotguns use two-piece stocks, it is much easier to secure handsome wood in them than is the case with a rifle blank. Choice for most high-grade American arms is American walnut with good

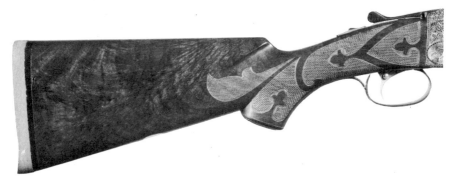

This Winchester Model 21 double has a burl walnut stock, checkered with a fancy pattern, and a rubber recoil pad.

burl and generally cut from the portion of the trunk where roots or limbs branch off. With the contrast in color and the swirly grain, some of this wood is very handsome but care should be exercised to see that the burl does not run into the grip itself or it is seriously weakened.

Europe's high-grade doubles are always stocked with one of the various varieties of European thin-shelled walnut, which is probably the world's handsomest stock material. The wood is very hard, close-grained and generally has more color and contrast than American walnut. Most of the wood comes from France, but Italy has a good supply, and some very handsome stuff is seen on shotguns made in Spain. The British and Belgians seem to prefer straight-grained wood with long, handsome, dark streaks. The Spanish go in for burl. This European walnut is hard, tough, light in weight and a joy to work. Light-colored woods such as maple and myrtle have gained some popularity in this country in the past 20 years or so, for shotgun stocks as well as rifle stocks. For those who like a light-colored stock, the best of these woods is very good indeed.

Good, sharp, well-executed checkering not only keeps the hands from slipping at grip and forend, but also enhances the beauty of the stock. In the good old days of made-to-order shotguns, the checkering went with the grade. The higher the price of the gun, the better the wood (Parker used European walnut on its best grades), the finer the diamonds and the fancier the design. For my taste some of the checkering designs got too intricate. I like plenty of fine, precise checkering, but simple fleur-de-lis or diamond designs. American wood is softer than French and most of it won't hold diamonds finer than 20-22 lines to the inch, and the worst won't hold diamonds that run over 18. But the harder American wood and good European walnut will take diamonds that go 24 and 26 lines to the inch, and these are the sizes I prefer. Some fine old British and Belgium guns have checkering that runs 28 and even 30 lines to the inch, but this is more ornamental than useful.

The dimensions and the fit of the stock are what count in the field and at trap and skeet. But if the stock combines fit and utility with good looks and fine workmanship, so much the better!

CHAPTER THIRTY ONE

How to Hit with the Shotgun

THERE IS NOTHING MAGICAL ABOUT THE PROPER FORM OF SHOOTING a shotgun, just as there is nothing magical about the best form in swimming, playing golf and tennis or in bowling. In any sport, good form is simply the easiest and most efficient way of doing what you want to do and is the result of a lot of thought and experiment.

It is a depressing fact that good form is not very common with most shotgun shooters. A lot of them are self-taught and acquire about five bad habits for every good one. They don't shoot enough to acquire skill or even to become used to handling guns. They stand wrong, mount their guns wrong, hold their heads wrong, and even close one eye when they sight—thus cutting down vision and handicapping themselves in their ability to judge distance.

I have a pal who is a real gun addict and a pretty good trap shot. Before we got acquainted I used to watch him shooting traps now and then and I thought he had suffered some terrible and crippling injury. When he was about to call for a bird his left leg was sharply bent and his right was thrust far out behind him. His body was inclined forward at an angle of about 45 degrees.

The poor guy had obviously been in an automobile wreck or had suffered some congenital deformity. Otherwise there was no accounting for his shocking condition. Then one day I happened to be watching when his squad got through. He strolled back to the club house upright and normal, as spry and pert as he could be.

"Look at that character!" I said to a bystander. "He's *walking!* I have been watching him shoot and I thought he was crippled!"

"No," said my friend. "There's nothing wrong with him. That mad crouch he uses is simply his idea of the best form for trapshooting."

In spite of his astounding form, this man isn't a bad trap shot.

420

He has good eyes, good coordination, and lots of enthusiasm. But every time he shoots he handicaps himself almost as badly as if he were trying to run a 100-yard dash wearing hobnailed logger boots and carrying a calf. His form keeps him off balance and cramps his swing.

THE PROPER STANCE

The right-handed shooter should shoot with his left foot advanced, his heels about 1 foot apart and the line of his shoulders at an angle of about 45 degrees to the left and away from the line of his gun. His knees should be slightly bent and he should lean slightly into the shot so the recoil will not put him off balance. With his feet fairly close together he can shift his weight from one leg to another as he swings and he can rotate his hips for smooth, even gun movement. Good stance helps him relax and swing, whereas he simply cannot maintain his balance and swing freely if his feet are wide apart, if he is in an exaggerated crouch, or if he stands feet together and bolt upright. In both trap and skeet shooting many men with bad form make very respectable scores but they do so in spite of their form and not because of it. All would shoot consistently higher scores if their form was better.

If the beginning scattergunner is skeptical of what I say, he should try swinging his shotgun through a wide arc from an exaggerated crouch with his feet far apart; from a bolt upright position, and from the position recommended here. He'll find that in either of the extreme positions his swing is cramped and that particularly in the crouch his hips are locked. The good shotgun shot swings by rotating his hips, and not by horsing his gun around with his arms.

It is an excellent idea for the beginning scattergunner (or for that matter for anyone) to form the habit of stepping into the shot with his left foot forward. Many a bird has flown on untouched by the shot charge because the man behind the gun has been flustered by a sudden flush and has tried to shoot off the wrong foot. Correct stance should be entirely automatic.

MOUNTING THE GUN

Another place where the beginning shotgun man (as well as many experienced shooters who have formed incorrect habits) goes wrong

Mounting a shotgun: Focus your eyes on the bird, then start to push gun out as head comes forward.

With your eyes still on the bird, thrust the gun out at arm's length so the stock will clear your body.

is in mounting the gun. I can attest to that because every season I miss several pheasants because a sudden flush startles me and I mount my gun poorly. The shotgun should be pushed out and back to the shoulder in line with the direction of the shot. If the gunner attempts to bring up his weapon from a point directly under his shoulder, he will often catch the butt under his armpit on his hunting jacket. Then he won't be able to get the butt in the proper position. His timing will be destroyed and he'll miss.

One fall I hunted birds on a gimpy leg and couldn't cover much territory and the misses I made broke my heart. I remember one of them. My dog was working a running pheasant that knew all the tricks of survival. It was sneaking low through the stubble, twisting, turning, doing everything possible to confuse the dog. I was watching my dog when the cock, which had doubled back, burst out at my feet. I jumped as if someone had given me the hot foot, jerked the butt of my gun up *under* my shoulder instead of bringing it out and back. The butt caught. I was so spooky that the bird seemed to be traveling 90 miles an hour. With the low position of the butt I couldn't get my head down enough. I saw too much barrel and both shots went right over that derisively cackling and wily old pheasant. If I had mounted that gun correctly, the shot would have been an easy one.

It is an old saying among shotgun aficionados that the good shot puts his gun to his face, the poor shot puts his face to his gun. Watch a good shot in the field sometime and you'll notice that he steps into the shot, and as he pushes his gun out so that he can bring it back to his shoulder unimpeded, he thrusts his head out into the position it will be in when he shoots. Then as the butt settles to his shoulder his eye is in line with the barrel and he is ready to shoot. *In effect he has already aimed with his head and with the position of his feet before the butt touches his shoulder.*

Keeping your head down, begin to bring the gun straight back to your shoulder and lean into the shot.

As the gun meets your shoulder, your eye should be right in line with both the barrel and bird.

The common and incorrect habit of putting the face to the gun—or to put it another way, of mounting the gun and then putting the head down—is one of the major reasons for misses. A bird bursts out. To the excited hunter it appears to be traveling as if jet-propelled. He hastily mounts his gun, sees the bird over the barrel. Then instead of getting his head down he blazes away—and overshoots. The man who puts his gun to his face seldom makes this error.

It is axiomatic among shotgun shooters that clay targets as well as game birds are either missed by shooting over or behind. As we have seen most of the overshooting comes from mounting the gun before the head is down. Likewise a lot of the shooting behind comes from poor stance that locks the shooter's hips and cramps his swing. The spraddle-legged, crouching shooter has his hips locked and has to swing with his arms instead of by rotating his hips. The feet-together shooter is likewise cramped and off balance.

HOW TO AIM

Precisely where the notion got started that the correct way to aim was by closing one eye, I'll never know, yet give a gun to a beginner, tell him to point it at something, and he will almost invariably close one eye. Many shoot all their lives with a squint. In doing so they narrow their field of view and they lose the advantage of the binocular vision that mankind has. The one-eyed shooter has a much more difficult time in judging range than does the shooter who uses his God-given binocular vision. Rifle, handgun, shotgun—all should be shot with both eyes open. The only exception to this rule is for that unfortunate who has a left master eye but who is right-handed. This gunner must either learn to shoot from the left shoulder with both eyes open or from the right

Keep both eyes open when mounting your shotgun. Focus them on the bird, not on the barrel.

shoulder with the left eye closed. Probably the last alternative is the easiest.

Aiming a shotgun as one would a rifle is also responsible for a lot of bad shooting. Because a shotgun is fired quickly at a moving mark and because the shooter has a large pattern to work with, the shotgun is *pointed* rather than aimed. Let us explain these terms by saying that the rifleman and the pistol shot concentrate on their sights, the shotgunner on his target. The eyes of the shotgun shooter should be focused on the bird and he should see the end of his barrel in relation to the bird. This concentration on target instead of barrel is shown by the fact that many shots declare they are never conscious of seeing the barrel at all. They *do* see the barrel, of course, because if they shoot correctly it is in their line of vision, but they see it a bit out of focus and are so target-conscious that they pay little attention to it. I knew one chap who had a pump gun with a large gold bead front sight. One day when we were hunting together he discovered that his front sight was gone. He also discovered that it had been off so long that the threads it was screwed into were rusted. He had been shooting for weeks and had not noticed the loss.

The shotgun shooter should *never* attempt to line up front sight and receiver as if they were front sight and rear sight. If he tries this he gives himself the tough job of trying to focus on three

things at once. He tends to get so interested in his aiming that he
loses sight of the bird, and he also tends to become a slow, dawdling
shot. He who tries to line up front sight and receiver while a
pheasant is flying straight away from him is lost. For one thing
the bird may be beyond the effective range of the gun before he
touches old Betsy off. For another he'll almost always undershoot.
The thing to do is to see the bird over the foreshortened barrel,
shoot *up* a bit at it, and never try to put the front bead in the middle
of the bird as if it were a heart shot on a whitetail buck. The man
who *aims* his shotgun as if it were a rifle is slow and generally
shoots behind.

Birds that aren't missed by overshooting are generally missed
by shooting behind, and those who shoot behind generally do so
because they want to be dead sure they'll hit and aim instead of
point. In order to get things just right they slow or stop their
swing—and then they miss. The beginning shooter should train
himself to shoot quickly even if he has all the time in the world,
because when he shoots quickly he doesn't give himself time to
aim, to slow or stop his swing. If he shoots fast and misses he
shouldn't worry; it is far better for the beginner to miss in good
form than to hit in poor.

My own besetting sin in shotgun shooting is taking too much
time on easy crossing shots. At skeet I often miss the No. 4 post
where a man has all day to get a shot off. Often I take all day—and
I shoot behind.

During the last dove season I noticed that when a bird sneaked
up on me from a blind angle and I shot instantly I almost never
missed. I missed when the birds were in sight a long time and I
could afford the luxury of a nice, slow precise swing. The reason?
I was slowing down or even stopping.

One season most pheasants were in stubble and were lying well
to my dog. I killed the majority of my birds with a 12-gauge bored
modified and improved modified at from 15 to 25 yards. A good
many of them were pretty badly shot up, and my wife's wails when
she inspected the mangled meat were terrible to hear. So I went
out resolved to wait the birds out and not to take any under 30-35
yards. At once my shooting fell off.

The answer, of course, was that in shooting fast at a jumping
pheasant I was shooting with the gun moving and the movement
was taking care of the lead. I'd shoot right at a climbing bird and

hit it because the muzzles of the gun were moving faster than the bird. When I waited my birds out, the gun had settled down, was slow or even stationary, and the birds climbed over the shot charge. I solved the problem by putting on an extra set of barrels bored Skeet No. 1 and No. 2, and from then on I must have averaged nine out of ten.

What a fast swing will do to correct a lead must be seen to be believed. This last fall I was down on a side hill in some brush and my dog was ahead of me acting birdy. I heard the dog's bell stop and knew he was on point, but as I headed toward him, I heard a pheasant flush and cackle and caught a glimpse of a beautiful cock shooting through an opening about 30 yards away. I swung fast and shot, but as the gun recoiled, I knew the muzzles hadn't caught up with the bird and I was behind by 6 inches. Much to my surprise I heard the bird hit the ground with a heavy thump. In the interval between the time I had told myself to shoot and when the shot had left the barrel that racing muzzle had caught up with and passed the bird—or else I never would have hit him.

The rules for the beginner with the scattergun, then, are relatively simple. Learn the correct stance, the correct mounting, put the gun to the face, not the face to the gun, point rather than aim, and shoot fast.

Anyone who follows these rules and practices them enough to make them become habits is going to be a good shot.

THIS BUSINESS OF LEAD

Just about once a month some happy inventor perfects a gadget that takes all the guesswork out of leading properly with a shotgun. From now on, these enthusiasts always say, shooting the scattergun will be simple. All the gunner must do is to buy the gadget, read the instructions, and then go out and knock them cold.

Now, I am a great hand for equipping my firearms with everything from radar to hot-and-cold running water and adorning them with portraits of Old Bones, my pet coon hound. Buying and trying out gun gadgets has kept me continually in the shadow of the poorhouse and has often caused me to go barefoot through the bitterest of winters. Alas, although I have tried out no end of these devices to ease the intellectual and physical burden on the poor shotgun user, I am still convinced that hitting something with the shotgun is more of an art than a science.

There have been many schemes for taking the headaches out of shotgun shooting. One I saw was an optical ring sight which is perched on the breech on the gun. With one of these, you have only to know how fast the bird is coming and how far away he is; then, theoretically anyway, you can slap the proper ring on him, touch her off, and down will come our little feathered friend. Another scheme is to use a bar rear sight with V's, white dots or notches. When the bird comes over, all you have to do is line up the front bead, with the proper dot or whatever it is, and the rest is history. Sometimes these bar-sights are put on the muzzle. Now and than a globe front sight is used, and the theory is that the gunner can tell how far his bird is away by the proportion of the globe it fills. Then, when the gunner knows how far he is from his prey, he can make some quick mental calculations and dope out how far ahead he must hold.

In the same category are the tables on how far to lead various birds at various ranges. If I have seen one of those tables I have seen dozens. Problem No. 1: Canvasback at 40 yards, flying at 60 miles per hour; correct lead 9 feet 3 inches. If you miss him, you didn't lead him right.

I realize that there is a great demand for something to take the guesswork out of swinging a scattergun. I wish that I had it myself, but I am fearful that I will never see it.

All of these "helps," these shortcuts, forget the variables that make shotgun shooting so complicated, so exasperating, and so wonderfully interesting. Even in skeet shooting, where the birds move at a uniform velocity and at known angles, one man's lead is another's headache.

Let's take some examples. One good skeet shot of my acquaintance tells me that in breaking the No. 4 high-house target, which is crossing at right angles, he fires the instant his gun barrel passes the bird. An equally good shot tells me that he leads that same target 5 or 6 feet. I am not in the class with either of those experts, but the birds break for me when I am apparently about 4 feet ahead of them at that station. If I shot like my pal, I would in one case be behind and in the other case I might be too far in front, in spite of the fact that the shot string makes shooting too far ahead difficult. Who's right? We're all right. We're different people!

Once a friend and I were shooting doves and both of us were doing very nicely. Most of the birds were coming in at a rate of what appeared to be about 30 or 35 miles an hour, flying right over low trees about 20 feet above the ground and from 25 to 30 yards away. I was swinging fast and touching off the shot when the muzzle was apparently about 1 foot in front of the birds. As a matter of curiosity, I asked my pal how far *he* was leading. He told me he was getting out about 3 feet ahead. If I had used his lead I would have missed and vice versa.

Let's take a look at the variables that make this business of wing shooting so complicated and uncertain. The birds themselves differ enormously in their flight—in speed, in angle, in distance from the gun, and in height from the ground. Lead which will get a bird at 30 yards will miss the same bird at 40 yards; lead which will get a bird flying at 30 miles an hour will miss him if he is sailing along at 40 or 50. Further, many a bird is missed because the shooter has misjudged the angle of the flight in relation to the ground. Let us say that our bird is rising or dropping. Even though the charge is thrown the correct distance ahead, it will go over or under the bird and either miss him entirely or merely catch him on the edge of the pattern. Who hasn't overshot a canvasback or a bluebill when he was busting in to the decoys because the angle of his flight was down?

The trouble with birds is that they are exceedingly uncooperative. If they would only come in at uniform speed and at known angles, the gunner could learn to do as well on them as he does at skeet, where a good shot will average 93-100 per cent. The darned birds, however, just won't play right.

Shotgun shooters themselves are pretty unpredictable fellows, and no two of them are just alike. Some men swing fast, some swing slowly. Some have quick reaction time, some do not. Some try to snap-shoot their birds, that is, throw the gun the proper distance ahead and touch her off so that the bird will run into the pattern. Others use the sustained lead, and try to shoot with the muzzle of the gun apparently traveling as fast as the bird. Still others use the fast swing and start behind the bird, overtake him and pull the trigger as the muzzle goes ahead.

Of course, some swing faster than others. Personal reaction times differ also enormously and further complicate the picture. All of us *think*, of course, that we have very speedy reaction times, and that we fire the moment our brain tells us to. Actually, there is a considerable time-lag. Our brains register the desire to shoot, the impulse goes to our fingertips, the muscles of the trigger finger act; the firing pin must fall, the primer must ignite, the powder begin to burn and then push the shot charge out of the barrel. All this occupies a perceptible interval of time and is by no means as instantaneous as most of us would like to believe.

This is the reason why the lead necessary to kill a bird with a stationary gun is so much greater than the lead needed with a swinging gun. I tried a little experiment during the past dove season. After killing birds regularly with about a two-foot lead and a fast swing as they came over a certain tree, I tried to hit them with a gun held still. I found I didn't do any good until I was out 10 or 12 feet ahead of them, five or six times as far as I apparently was when I swung!

Now, suppose we have a gunner who swings fast but whose reactions are slow. He would require less apparent lead because his gun would travel in the interval between the time his brain told his finger to press the trigger and the time that the gun actually went off. Such a shooter may actually *think* he doesn't lead but he is getting way out there ahead of them just the same. On the other hand, a second gunner may swing rather slowly but have a fast reaction time. He is the chap who requires a great deal of lead.

THE FAST SWING

There are two styles of swing, and the necessary amount of lead varies with each style. One is the fast swing. The gunner starts with the muzzle behind the bird, swings the gun apparently faster than the bird is moving, passes the bird and gets off his shot when his experience tells him he is out in front far enough. This style of swing is often used in skeet shooting—and in other types of fast shooting. The dove hunter who gets the birds as they come over openings in forests of low trees, such as the mesquite thickets of the Southwest, must swing it fast. So must the quail hunter in the jackoaks of Missouri or the grouse hunter of New England. The faster the swing, the less apparent lead is needed because of the velocity at which the gun barrels are moving ahead of the bird.

The crack quail and grouse shot is always a fast swinger. He is also usually a short swinger, who starts his swing only a little way behind the bird, overtakes it and fires. I have seen some crack shots of this school whose swings were so short and so fast that they appeared to be snap-shooting—throwing the gun up and shooting with stationary barrels at the place where the bird was going to be. I have seen men who use the fast short swing even on ducks and doves, who flash their guns to their shoulders, take a fast swing and shoot before you could say *scat*. These are top wing shots who are magnificently equipped with quick-focusing eyes and marvelous muscular coordination.

THE SUSTAINED LEAD

For the more deliberate pass shooting at ducks, doves and geese, most gunners like the sustained lead, which is slower than the fast swing but easier to master. In this style of shooting, the gunner starts his swing ahead of the bird and keeps the barrels pointing in front of the bird and moving apparently with the same speed as the bird. When he is sure of his lead he touches her off. This method of leading is also the one most often used with a rifle for shooting running game in the open. It is slower than the fast swing that has to be used on most upland game and, with a rifle, on running deer in the brush. It is slower—but more accurate and easier to check. I believe also that it is a method of leading and swinging that gives more consistent performance, one less apt to go sour and give the gunner a bad day.

As I write about hitting moving game with a moving gun and with the moving shot charge I am constantly reminded of tennis. The principles of tennis are much the same as those of wing shooting. Some tennis players take the ball on the rise. They play a fast game, and when they are good they are very, very good. Their timing, however, must be precise and when they are off and have a bad day they are often terrible. The more deliberate type of player, who takes the ball at the top of its bound, plays a more consistent game even though he is less speedy. The same thing is true of the gunner who uses the sustained lead in pass shooting. He is not so spectacular, but day in and day out he'll probably get more ducks and doves. I know that I am a more consistent dove and duck shot than I am a quail shot. For pass shooting I always use the sustained lead and shoot consistently. For quail I use the fast swing; on my good days, I do well, but let me get a bad one and the results would break your heart!

Either style of swing enormously simplifies the problem of leading, because the faster the bird is moving, the faster the gun must be swung to overtake and pass it or to stay ahead of it, and the faster the gun is moving the *farther* it will move in the interval that elapses between the time the brain says to shoot and the instant the shot leaves the muzzle.

Whatever the style of shooting, the gun must be kept moving because if it is slowed or stopped, the bird will be missed—not by inches but by feet. Particularly for clay bird shooting, where two or three shot will knock a piece off the target or even shatter it, it is almost impossible to overlead, as the shot string is stretched out for several feet, even at the short ranges at which skeet is shot. With a tough game bird like a pheasant, it is something else again. The pheasant has to be pretty well centered or he will shed a few feathers and fly away wounded. On the other hand a fragile bird like a dove will be brought down by relatively few shot.

No man can tell another the proper lead, not only because speeds of swing differ and reaction times differ, but because judgment of distance differs. Six inches to one man may look like a foot to another and four feet might be three feet to one, six to another. So, if someone tells you he leads a passing mallard 4 feet at 40 yards take it with a grain of salt. His "4 foot" lead may be 8 feet or 2½ feet and his 40 yards may be 30 or it may be 50.

Anyone who considers himself an accurate judge of range should make a practice of checking his guesses against actualities. Some years ago, I was hunting black bear on the Alaskan mainland with Ralph Young, the guide and outfitter. We were stalking a juicy black when we ran out of cover. Ralph asked me if I thought I could hit it from there. I reckoned as how I could, settled down, and knocked over the bear. As we walked over we discussed the range and agreed that it was less than 200 yards, probably about 175 or 180. When we got to the bear, though, we began to have misgivings, as the log from behind which I had shot looked a long way off. So as we went back we paced it. The distance was about 240-250 yards. The error of two old and experienced big-game hunters was over 30 per cent, and that is not exactly good.

Every man has to learn to lead all by himself and usually he does so slowly and painfully. Experience shows him that if a mallard looks about *so* big and is moving about *so* fast it will fall if he leads it about *so* far with his own particular speed of swing and reaction time. He'll tell you that he leads a fast-flying mallard 3 feet at 35 yards, let us say. Usually that doesn't mean much. The duck may not be 35 yards away and he may not lead it 3 feet. But he *thinks* he does and he kills his bird and he's happy.

TYPES OF LEADS

Here are some leads that work for me on various game birds. At least they *look* that way. When he is getting his flight underway old John Pheasant is a very easy bird to hit and doesn't require much lead. If he takes off directly away or slightly quartering, I swing up fast and shoot the instant I see him over the top of the barrel. If he takes off at right angles and is within 25 yards, I never lead him more than 1 foot. If I think he is 30-35 yards away I try to get 2 feet or so ahead of him. Now and then I get a right-angle shot at 40-45 yards and when I go I am about 3 feet ahead with a swinging gun.

Slowest of all birds and the easiest to hit once the gunner is used to them are the lumbering sage grouse. They get up so slowly that it is very easy to drop them with very little lead. Up to 30 yards I shoot right at their beaks—with a moving gun, of course.

When a dove is rolling by at his usual cruising speed of 35 miles per hour, and about 40 yards away, I try to get what looks like about 4 feet ahead. The faster flying duck at that distance would require more lead—6 or 8 feet, let us say.

Shot is round and ballistically inefficient. It loses its velocity with great rapidity. Therefore lead should be increased with distance. A good shot I know tells me that he doubles his lead with each 5 yards of range. If, for instance, he is leading 1 foot at 30 yards, he leads 3 feet at 35, 4 feet at 40, and 8 feet at 45. That may work for him, but it might not work for you or for me. The main thing is to get ahead of the bird with a swinging gun, as a good fast swing covers a multitude of bad guesses as to speed and range. The faster you swing, the less you have to lead and the less you have to guess. Anyone who follows the cardinal rules of wing shooting—keep the head down, keep the gun swinging, and get ahead—isn't going to do badly.

Proper leading, like all shotgun skill, is the result of a vast

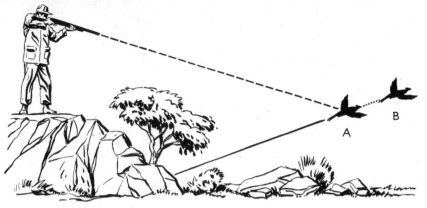

When a bird flushes from below, many hunters think it is a straightaway shot and aim at A. The bird will be at B when the shot arrives.

amount of experience that enables the shooter to size up a situation and react almost automatically and unconsciously. The veteran shot gives about as much actual thought to lead as he does to jumping when he sits down on a tack. He had to learn it slowly and painfully, and at first he had to *think* about it. Now he reacts instantly. He just shoots and because most of his processes have been subconscious, he'd have a tough time telling you how far he had lead and what. But the bird was centered and down it came!

HOW TO MAKE A DOUBLE KILL

One of the greatest joys that can befall a scattergunner is to make a pretty double, particularly if he can shoot fast enough to have both birds falling at once.

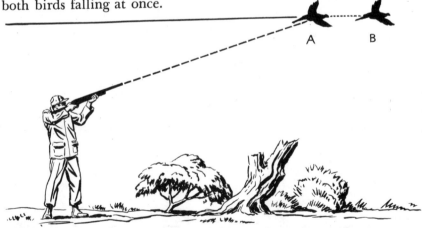

This shot would seem to call for a dead-on hold, but actually the bird is at an angle. The hunter should hold at B.

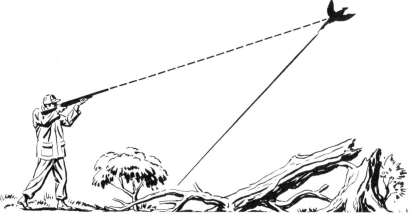

A pheasant usually rises sharply and if the hunter shoots fast with an open-bore, high-shooting upland gun, he'll probably connect.

But making doubles isn't easy because the proper technique is contrary to human nature. Most of us want to take the easiest and most conspicuous bird first, and we want to watch the bird until he hits the ground. The best way to make a double is to take the hardest and least conspicuous bird first, kill it and forget about it the instant you see it's hit, and then to take the easy shot. Many a time I have flubbed doubles because I took the easy one first and then, by the time I got around to it the hard one was out of range. I have also flubbed shots by worrying about the second while I was making the first—a fine way to miss both.

In shooting doubles, the skeet shot cracks the outgoer first, then the easier incomer. If he tried the incomer first the outgoer would be out of range. The game shot should follow the same technique on birds flying away. I remember one fall when my Brittany spaniel Mike took off at a dead run up a brushy fence, turned at right angles onto another, ran about 50 yards and slammed into a point. From the way he acted I was convinced he was on a cock so I galloped toward him like a 5-ton truck on a couple of flats. I heard birds flush and in the moment they cleared the fence row—two fine cocks, colors flashing, tails streaming. One was well ahead of the

This is a true, though seldom seen, straightaway shot that calls for a dead-on hold.

The natural instinct to want to see what you are shooting at may cause you to hold dead-on an overhead, incoming bird. Actually, you should lead as shown here.

other. The muzzles of the little 20 settled right on the one farthest away. The gun cracked and as I moved over to the other bird I saw the first falling. I fired the other barrel and saw the second bird hit the plowed ground. The two fine cocks lay within five feet of each other and 35 paces from the gun. If I had shot the close one first, the second might have been right on the edge of the 20's killing range and chances were I would have lost him.

If one bird takes off close to the ground and another towers, take the flat flying bird first because he isn't wasting any time gaining altitude. In addition he is harder to see, easier to shoot over and requires more careful holding. Shoot him and then take the one that is more conspicuous against the sky.

When ducks or doves are coming in, I like to make up my mind as to which will be No. 1 and which No. 2. Then I like to swing up quickly, take No. 1 as I would the high-house bird at the No. 8 station at skeet, then crack No. 2 in the same place.

Take the hardest and least conspicuous bird first, then forget about him and concentrate on killing the second. If you worry about the second while you're trying to hit the first you're licked and if you wonder if you made a clean kill on the first while you are getting on the second, you are likewise whipped.

The greatest help I have ever had in making doubles on running pheasants is a good dog. Before I got my Brittany I used to worry about the possibility of the first bird getting away because if you merely wound a cock pheasant, you may never find him. This worrying gave me a tendency to pick the easy bird first, make certain of it, and then turn to the hard one—only to miss or feather it. But since I have hunted with Mike I know that a wounded pheasant has about as much chance of getting away from him as a kidnapper has of throwing the FBI off his tracks. Now I very seldom miss what I'd call a fair shot—but I must admit that it is really my dog that makes me look good.

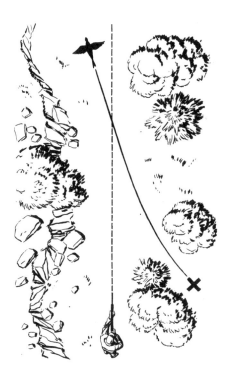

It is necessary to lead a bird flushed at X and flying off at a slight angle. Thinking he has a straightaway shot, the hunter shown here holds dead-on—and misses.

A flurry of feathers in the sky marks where the hunter connected with a low-flying bird. Note how he leans into the shot.

CHAPTER THIRTY TWO

Clay Target Shooting

THERE ARE TWO PRINCIPAL CLAY-TARGET GAMES IN THIS COUNTRY— traps and skeet. Each is shot all over the United States, and most fairly large communities have skeet or trap clubs, or clubs that feature both games. As anybody can see by glancing at sketches of the layouts, the two games are quite different.

Traps is shot from five positions 3 yards apart at single birds that come at varying angles out of a trap house at the call of the shooter. After each string of five shots, the shooter moves to another station, and so on until he has shot from all five. Thus he gets varying angles, since a bird that presents a straightaway from one station is in sharply angled flight at another.

In ordinary singles shooting, the targets come out of the trap house 16 yards from the gun, and the average trap shooter breaks them at about 33 yards. If he is a fast man with a gun, the good trap shot may break his birds as close in as 30 yards. If he is slow, he may hit them at 35 or 36. If he gets nervous and freezes up—something that happens at times to all but the experts—he may break (but more likely miss) some targets at 40 yards or even farther, since they fly 50 yards from the trap house and 66 yards from the shooter.

The mechanics of 16-yard singles are simple. The shooter takes his place at his station and mounts his gun with his cheek firm on the comb and his eye right down the rib. He trains the muzzle on the spot where the bird is to appear, then calls "Pull!" The bird, tripped by electricity, flashes out almost simultaneously with the call. The gunner swings up with the target and, without slowing his swing in the slightest, passes it and presses his trigger. If he has tracked in the right path, if he gets far enough ahead or above, if he doesn't slow or stop his swing, the target breaks as the shot charge strikes it. Flights vary from straightaways to fairly sharp right and left obliques. Shots are much like those the upland gunner gets when birds come up ahead of a dog, because the targets, like most upland game-birds, are always rising.

While trapshooting is good practice for the upland gunner, it isn't perfect practice. For one thing, the trap man has his gun mounted and his cheek on the comb before he calls for his bird. For another, he knows exactly when his target will appear and from what spot. True, he doesn't know the angle it will take, but if he is relaxed, doesn't try to outguess the trap, and busts them as they pop up, he'll find one angle no more difficult than another.

Traps will teach him swing and timing that will pay off in the field. One flaw of such shooting, from the standpoint of the bird hunter, is that the clay target isn't a pheasant or a quail. The clay starts off fast and then slows down, whereas the game bird gets off slowly and picks up speed. The pheasant, for example, gets off the ground like an icewagon with wings, but picks up speed as he goes. At 50 yards he is making speed; at that distance, the clay target is falling to the ground.

Another form of traps is single shooting at handicap distances. The individual shooters are put back according to their skill. One man may shoot at 16 yards, another at 25.

DOUBLES IN TRAPS

Perhaps the most difficult of all clay-target games is doubles. Two birds come out of the trap house simultaneously 16 yards from the gun, each on a fixed course, and it is up to the shooter to break both. He takes the straightaway first, then the angled bird. Knocking that second clay off before it hits the ground is no cinch. But it trains you for doubles in the field.

CHOOSING A GUN FOR TRAPS

The man who simply wants to acquire some skill in handling his gun can shoot some respectable scores at traps with practically any sort of scattergun that is bored modified or tighter. Most special trap guns are bored full choke (70 per cent or more), because they are used at handicap rises as well as at the 16-yard rise; but for 16-yard targets alone, a modified barrel (55-60 per cent) is all anyone needs.

On one occasion I shot a round with a Winchester Model 21 skeet gun with 26-inch barrels. I used the left (Skeet No. 2) barrel, approximately modified choke. I missed my first target because I tried to outguess the trap. I then broke the next 24—and most of them were powdered. Actually, the fast shot who uses a full-choke barrel for 16-yard targets alone is handicapping himself.

The special trap guns are usually long of barrel—30 inches if pumps, and 30 or 32 inches if singles like the famous Ithaca single-barreled trap guns. They are generally bored full choke or improved modified, and have raised or ventilated ribs and two sights. Only Ithaca now makes a single-barreled trap gun, but Winchester, Remington, and Ithaca make pumps stocked and equipped for trapshooting.

If the trapshooter has only one gun and plans to shoot doubles, this weapon, of course, must be either a repeater or a double. Automatics are seldom used at traps because the ejected shells bother the man at the shooter's right (shooting is in squads of five), and fixtures like the Weaver-Choke, Cutts Comp, and POWer-Pac are not in order since their muzzle blast would irritate the other men on the squad. (Both variable-choke devices and autoloaders are legal in skeet.) The Winchester Model 21 double-barreled trap gun is particularly popular for doubles shooting.

Since the targets are always rising, and since the gunner mounts his piece and gets his cheek down on the comb before he calls for a bird, the trap gun generally has a longer and straighter stock than a field gun. A gun so stocked shoots high—in effect, it has a built-in lead for the rising targets. I find, though, that in traps I can take my regular Winchester Model 21 (which I use for skeet, pheasants, quail, etc.), place my cheek so I see more barrel than I would for skeet, and do as well with it as I can with any gun. The casual trapshooter does not need a special gun, nor, in my opinion, is he greatly handicapped without one.

SKEET SHOOTING

Skeet is a relative newcomer among clay-target games, having been invented in the nineteen twenties by the late William Harnden Foster, who became skeet editor of *Outdoor Life*. Many will disagree with me, but I think it highly probable that skeet is better practice for the field shot than is trapshooting. It's a faster and more spectacular game, and presents a much greater variety of shots and angles.

The skeet layout has two houses which contain traps for throwing birds. They're called the "high house" and the "low house," since one starts its targets high, the other low. The targets from each house always follow the same path, but the shooter gets different angles by moving around a semicircle that starts at the high house, and shooting at seven stations, the last at the low house. There's another station, No. 8, in front of the semicircle and directly between the high house and the low house. He shoots a pair of singles at each station, one from the high house, one from the low. Angles vary from straightaways and slightly angling incomers at Stations 1 and 7, to shots that are approaching right angles or are true right angles at Stations 4 and 5. At the forward station, No. 8, the targets come almost directly toward the shooter —shots that are sometimes duplicated in the duck blind. The two shots at Station 8 are the bugaboo of the beginner, but actually are easy once the technique is learned.

The skeet gun can be mounted before the bird is called for, but for the sake of field practice I keep the butt of my gun below my right elbow. The sharp angles, large variety of shots, and great apparent speed make the game of skeet a natural for the man who wants to be sharp in the field. Unlike traps, skeet mixes singles and doubles in the same round. After the gunner has taken his Station 8 targets, he shoots pairs of doubles at Stations 1, 2, 6 and 7. He cannot dawdle. Curiously, the beginner usually scores better at doubles than at singles because he knows he has to shoot fast; most skeet targets are missed because they are ridden out until they drop below the shot pattern.

GUNS FOR SKEET

Any good upland gun is satisfactory for skeet if the shooter is not out to become a tournament ace. I have done most of my skeet shooting with a couple of Winchester Model 21 skeet guns, one a 12 and one a 16, and I have also shot a good deal with an Ithaca 20-gauge double, bored improved cylinder and modified. All three guns are stocked just alike—1½ x 2¼ x 14¼ inches.

Probably the most efficient of all skeet guns is the automatic. The Remington Model 58 and the Winchester Model 50 are favorites, as were the old Remington Model 11 and the Browning. An automatic is easier to use than a pump on double targets (although many fine shots use the Winchester, Ithaca and Remington pumps) and the new gas- and short-recoil operated automatics soften the kick. Most top skeet shots use either the Cutts Compensator with the spreader tube or the POWer-Pac with the short-range tube. Neither gives wider patterns than the special skeet borings of automatic and pump skeet guns, but many believe that the patterns are more regular. And these compensating devices have the virtue of further softening recoil.

There is skeet competition in a variety of gauges: all-bore (12 or 16 gauge); 20 gauge; small-bore (the .410 or 28 gauge with ¾ ounce of shot); and subsmall-bore (the .410 with ½ ounce). Many skeet enthusiasts own a whole battery of guns so they can take part in all events. The man who simply wants to be a good gun handler and has no yen to lug home cups and medals can do pretty well in all his shooting with one gun, and he may possibly be a better all-around field and duck shot if he sticks to one. My 12-gauge Winchester Model 21 has two sets of barrels—one set bored Skeet No. 1 and No. 2 (about improved cylinder and modified), the other set bored modified and improved-modified. By changing barrels I can make respectable scores at any kind of trapshooting, at skeet, on upland game and waterfowl. A pump gun with a 26- or 28-inch barrel bored modified is also an all-around gun, and if it has two interchangeable barrels, one bored improved cylinder, the other bored full or improved modified, its owner is all set.

OTHER CLAY-TARGET GAMES

Besides the standard competitive games of trap and skeet, there are other less formal types of clay-target busting. Some clubs have towers that throw targets 50 feet or more above the ground to provide practice in flight shooting. Another variation is the "quail walk"—the one at Abercrombie & Fitch's shooting school on Long Island, N.Y., is a tough one. The shooter moves along a walk near which small traps have been placed. An attendant behind him trips 25 of about 35 possible targets. They come at the shooter, go away from him, fly in singles and pairs, move in the open and through trees. On a visit there, my son and I each broke 16, which, I was told, is about par for the skeet shooter on his first exposure. No one has ever broken a "straight" on the quail walk. The highest score is 23, and that was shot by a chap who practiced for months. It's a tough course, but it's the nearest thing to upland shooting I know of.

WHY SHOOT TRAPS AND SKEET?

Once upon a time, when junior reached a certain age papa simply handed him a shotgun and a box of shells and turned him loose to harass the quail and cottontails that existed precariously on the edge of town, dodging hawks, cats and predatory small boys. Some degree of skill with a scattergun was deemed an essential masculine accomplishment in those days, akin to the ability to carry a part in a barbershop arrangement of "Sweet Adeline," or to block a roundhouse right.

Each weekend, the countryside surrounding the small town where I grew up was covered by youngsters armed with single-barrel shotguns, popping away at assorted birds and small mammals. Seasons were long then, wardens were scarce, there were fewer hunters and more small game. By dint of a lot of shooting and much thought, many of those lads became good shots and good sportsmen. But most lost interest and turned to other diversions.

Actually this system of learning to shoot is about as good as the sink-or-swim method of learning to keep afloat. Once when I was a second-grader at a church picnic, I was standing on the edge of a deep swimming hole admiring the reckless and remarkable deeds of the older boys when someone shoved me in. I discovered that by making certain motions I could keep from drowning. From then on I was a swimmer, though a poor one.

My two daughters are better swimmers than I ever was because they learned from a swimming instructor; and my youngest son is in many ways a better shotgun-shooter than I am because he did his first skeet shooting under proper instruction. Instead of getting a dozen bad habits he'd have to break later on, he learned to mount, lead and shoot correctly from the very beginning.

In these days of short seasons and limited bags, it is usually impossible for a tyro to get enough practice on game to develop any real skill. In many sections, for instance, the pheasant is the only game bird available to most gunners, and the pheasant season lasts only five days and the limit is two cocks a day. The lad who shoots only under such circumstances can expect to be a grandfather before he becomes a good shot.

The best and easiest way to acquire shotgun skill is to start with good instruction at a gun club where either traps or skeet is shot. Also beneficial is the shooting of clay targets thrown from a hand trap, especially if the young shooter has a good coach.

The young shooter is often reluctant about beginning at a gun club where he and his scores will be under the eyes of strangers. He is fumbling and inept, and he is both impressed and discouraged by the fancy trap and skeet guns and by the shooting jackets plastered with tabs announcing that their wearers have broken 25 straight, 50 straight, 100 straight. What he doesn't consider is that every veteran was once a beginner and that the old-timers welcome new blood to the shooting game and will make sympathetic coaches.

Another advantage to the tyro in shooting at a gun club is that even if he gets no coaching, he can learn a lot just by watching. The first time I ever shot a round of traps I simply picked up a gun, walked to my station and started shooting. I broke 16 clays out of a possible 25, which isn't good. I shot again, and broke 13. Figuring I must be doing everything wrong, I stopped shooting and just watched some good shots for a while. The next time I took a turn at the traps, I broke 22.

Sadly enough there is one great drawback to any clay-target shooting—the cost. A round of skeet or traps sets a man back anywhere from $2.50 to $3.50, including the price of a box of shells and 25 clay targets.

Breaking clays with a scattergun is by no means a 100 per cent satisfactory substitute for the real thing. But it presents the one big chance for any man to become a good shotgun performer.

CHAPTER THIRTY THREE

Taking Care of Your Gun

WELL-MADE MODERN FIREARMS SELDOM WEAR OUT—THEY ARE RUINED by mistreatment. The man who throws a fine rifle or shotgun in the back of his car with the chains, the jack and the tire irons will ruin it just as surely as the man who never cleans his gun. The man who yanks open a fine double gun as though he were breaking a stick of firewood over his knee has no right to moan when it begins to rattle after a time.

Most gun owners either ruin their firearms by neglect or kill them with kindness. There's the man who boasts that his old .30/30, bought 22 years ago come September, hasn't had a cleaning rod through it yet, and there's the oversolicitous fellow who keeps his guns swimming in oil and swaddled in flannel-lined gun cases.

The .30/30 belonging to the first citizen is coated with rust, the action works as if it were lubricated with sand and the stock has long since lost any vestige of finish. The barrel is rough and pitted, the rifling is almost non-existent. This gun not only looks neglected but it shoots poorly. When it was new it would keep its shots in a 3-inch circle at 100 yards. Now its shot group is about the size of a meat platter, and any hit beyond 100 yards is just an act of God.

The rifle owned by the well-meaning man who has tried to baby it along is in not much better shape. Years of over-oiling have made the whole action gummy with layer after layer of dried lubricant. Squirted into every nook and cranny, into anything that looked like a hole, the light gun oil has penetrated the wood and rotted it. In spite of all this oil, the rifle has collected some rust, because the flannel lining of the gun case has absorbed moisture, which has been trapped in the closed case.

It takes all kinds of gun owners to make a world. To some a gun is simply a tool like a hatchet or a garden rake, to be neglected and kicked around and discarded when it no longer operates. Others are interested in the shooting and functioning of their arms, but

445

have no interest whatsoever in their looks. Still others are far more interested in having beautiful, unmarred guns than in using them.

One chap I know has a 30-year-old .30/30 carbine which he claims has never been cleaned. What holds the stock on I wouldn't dare guess, there is no rifling in the barrel that I can detect, and all the wood looks as though seven generations of porcupines had been feeding on it. Another man has a whole case full of gleaming big-game rifles, not one of which has ever fired a shot.

THE CLEANING KIT

Actually it's not hard to keep guns new-looking for years in spite of hard use. All that's needed is a cleaning outfit containing the following:

One-piece steel cleaning rod for small-bore rifles, with proper tips, bristle and brass brushes in correct size for each caliber

One-piece steel cleaning rod for big-bore rifles (.27 caliber and up), with similar accessories

Jointed steel rod or pull-through for field use

Jointed wooden cleaning rod for shotguns, with brass brushes for various gauges, felt balls, etc.

Set of screw drivers to fit guard screws, scope-mount screws, etc.

Bottle of linseed oil

Can of lubricating oil

Tube of graphite in oil

Can of solvent

Tube or bottle of rust-preventive grease or oil

Cut patches of proper size

CARE OF THE RIFLE BARREL

Since the barrel is the heart of any firearm, let's find out first how to take care of it. The job is vastly more simple than it used to be back in the days of corrosive primers and cupronickel jackets on rifle bullets. Not much more than a score of years ago, all primers employed potassium chlorate, which in burning produced potassium chloride, a moisture-attracting, rust-causing salt.

The smaller the bore and the greater the proportion of priming compound to powder, the more vicious the action of those primers was. In a damp climate a .22 barrel would be ruined in a matter of months and so would small centerfire calibers like the old .22 W.C.F. and the .25/20. Big-bore rifles didn't go so quickly but even those usually were ruined by rust rather than by wear. Because the villain in the piece was a salt, earnest cleaning with oil did no good, and the barrels would start to rust as soon as the weather got damp.

The curious part of it all was that for years no one knew the answer, and gun writers wrote learnedly of the "acid fouling of smokeless powder" and how "high pressures drove the acids into the pores of the steel." When I was a lad doing big-bore target shooting with an old 1903 Springfield, we were taught to clean the bore with a solution of baking soda, which, because it was alkaline, presumably "neutralized" those harmful acids. We cleaned those barrels, dried them, and oiled them. They never went bad, because the water had dissolved the primer salts. The baking soda had nothing to do with it one way or another.

Today all commercial ammunition is loaded with non-corrosive (not rust-causing) primers, so there's no need to brood about primer salts. However, government military ammunition for the .30/06 is still being loaded with the Frankford Arsenal No. 70 primer containing potassium chlorate. Further, many handloaders are buying and using those primers because they are cheap.

If a rifle is fired with a cartridge containing a chlorate primer, there is only one way to clean it—with water. The easiest method is to fill a can with boiling water, drop a few soap flakes in it, and insert the muzzle of the rifle in the water. Next put a reasonably snug-fitting patch on a cleaning rod, push it through the breech, and pump the water back and forth through the barrel. Then push two or three dry patches through. This is enough. The water will make the barrel very hot, and in a few minutes the heat will have dried the barrel thoroughly. Next push through an oily patch— and that's that!

The best way to get patches, by the way, is to buy them already cut and of good cotton flannel. Using patches torn off the tails of somebody's shirt or cutting up someone else's pajamas leads only to trouble.

To clean a big-bore rifle that has been used with ordinary non-corrosive commercial primers, first push a clean dry patch through the bore. Follow with a patch or a bristle brush saturated by any one of a number of fine-powder solvents or all-purpose oils. If the rifle is to be used again in a week or two, that's enough. If it is to be stored and not used for some months the bore should be protected by a gun grease or by a rust-proofing oil.

The same procedure should be followed with a lever-action rifle except that it will have to be cleaned from the muzzle and care exercised not to damage the lands.

If any fairly fluid oil is used, set the rifle in the rack muzzle down. In this way, surplus oil can drain out the muzzle and not run back into the chamber and action, where it will cause oil to squirt into the eye, keep the case from clinging to the chamber walls and increase the back thrust on the bolt or breech-block.

Until about 25 years ago most bullet jackets were made of cupronickel, and metal fouling, which usually showed up first as lumps on the lands near the muzzle, was a terrific problem and necessitated regular cleaning with ammonia dope. Now that gilding metal and pure copper are used for jacket material, metal fouling rarely develops. Usually a thin copper-colored wash, hardly more than a stain, can be seen by looking diagonally into the muzzle in good light. This microscopically thin film has no effect on accuracy. I pay no attention to it except to run a brass brush through the bore occasionally and to use a solvent which tends to remove it. There is some slight possibility of its setting up an electrolytic action with the steel and causing pitting, although I think this is very slight. The film can be removed with an ammonia dope. If, with modern bullet jackets, a barrel still metal-fouls to the extent that lumps show, it is usually a sign that the bore should be lapped, or polished —a job which a good gunsmith will perform at little cost.

Wear in a well-kept barrel is first apparent in erosion at the throat. At first the rifling just forward of the bullet seat will appear dark when viewed at an angle from the breech. Next it will appear rough and the darkness will be apparent farther up the barrel. Sometimes accuracy will fall off before throat erosion has progressed very far. Occasionally a barrel will still shoot well with bad erosion six inches up the barrel. A worn-out barrel can be told by a general rounding of the lands.

CLEANING THE CHAMBER

Unless the chamber of a larger-caliber rifle is regularly wiped out, it will accumulate surplus oil (particularly if the rifle barrel is cleaned and immediately set butt down in a rack) not to mention dust and even leaves and twigs. The chamber should be clean to facilitate the easy seating and extraction of cases, and dry so the expanding case will cling to the chamber walls under pressure and not come whanging back against the face of the bolt or breech-block.

A good thing to use in cleaning the chamber is the bristle brush on a short wire handle that is made for cleaning large-caliber revolvers. Or you can wrap flannel around a short rod and do the job. Don't neglect the chamber. If rust pits it, extraction is difficult. If it is oily and the cases slide on firing, the pounding may cause the rifle to develop excessive headspace. A pitted or rusted chamber will slow up the functioning of the rifle.

When used with waxed or greased bullets, a .22 rimfire rifle does not need to be cleaned at all. The combination of non-corrosive priming and grease protects the bore nicely. However, if different brands of ammunition with different types of priming are used, it is wise to clean and oil the bore to preclude the possibility of chemical action resulting and causing pits.

THE SHOTGUN BARREL

To clean a shotgun barrel, I like to put a patch on the standard felt or yarn ball that comes with most cleaning rods, saturate it

The first step in cleaning a rifle bore is to push a clean dry patch through and follow up with a patch saturated with fine-powder solvent or oil.

with a good oil, and then shove it through. I usually follow with another oiled patch and let it go at that. Most new guns will accumulate a little lead just forward of the chamber for a time. A good brass brush, used in combination with a light solvent, will usually remove the lead. As the gun is used the friction of the shot tends to smooth up the bore and eventually most leading will stop.

If a barrel persists in leading, it can be polished by using a mild

Watch for lead that tends to accumulate in a new shotgun barrel just foward of the chamber. The lead can be removed with a brass brush used with light solvent.

abrasive on a tight patch over the felt ball of the cleaning rod. Or you can remove the leading by coating the inside of the barrel with common mercurial or blue ointment (obtainable at any drug store), leaving it in a couple of days, and then wiping it out. The mercury in the ointment will amalgamate with the lead. Occasionally a bore is so rough that it should be turned over to a gunsmith for lapping.

The greatest enemy of the metal on the outside of a gun is the sweaty hand. Many an irate gun owner has found the fingerprints of an admiring friend perfectly etched in rust on his favorite weapon. A gun should always be wiped lightly with an oily rag before it is put in the rack, particularly in hot, humid weather. The metal should also be wiped after the gun is handled. If a rifle is scope-sighted, wipe the scope tube, the mount and particularly the

bright slide of the receiver sight with an oily rag. Be careful, however, not to get oil on the lenses of the scope.

If the gun is to be left in storage for some months, all metal, inside and out, should be coated lightly with a good gun grease or
some special rust-preventing oil. If a scope is attached, the lens
covers should be kept on to protect the lenses from dust. The best
place for a gun is in a case or rack, either in the open or behind
doors. The family clothes closet is a very hazardous place for a
gun. It is liable to be knocked down and marred, and damp
clothing may cause it to rust. The gun should be where air can
circulate, the barrel should not be plugged and it should not be
smothered in a moisture-collecting sheepskin case.

Most gun owners put so much oil on their weapons that it is a
nuisance. They squirt it freely into every crevice, including the
gas-escape vents in the receiver ring and bolt. It is enough to put
an occasional drop of good lubricating oil on the working parts
where actual friction occurs.

If a gun is to be used in zero weather, all working parts should
be thoroughly cleaned in gasoline to remove the last trace of oil,
then lubricated with powdered graphite. Otherwise, with most oils
anyway, the gun will not function. Every year I get letters, particularly from Pennsylvania and upstate New York deer hunters,
who tell of pump and automatic rifles that have frozen tight, and
of firing pins so sluggish that they wouldn't dent a primer.

CARE OF THE STOCK

Almost all factory guns come with varnished or lacquered stocks
for the simple reason that such a finish is quick and easy to apply.
Even an increasing number of custom stocks are wearing varnish
in some form—and for exactly the same reason. To my notion
putting such a finish on a fine custom stock is something like clothing
a lovely girl in a thousand-dollar Hattie Carnegie dress and then
ornamenting her with dime-store jewelry.

If the gun is to be kept in the cabinet or used only on the skeet
field or target range, where it can be gently taken care of, the various forms of varnish finish look very nice. In the field, however,
where a gun must necessarily take some kicking around even in
careful hands, nothing stands up so well as a straight linseed-oil

finish—or a finish in which linseed has been mixed with spar varnish or shellac to fill the pores of the wood.

A good linseed-oil finish is tough, whereas a varnish finish is brittle. I have a friend with a fine super-grade Model 70 Winchester in .270. He has hunted a lot, and the surface of his rifle stock looks leprous. My old .270, on the other hand, has an oil finish over an oil and spar-varnish base. No one would take it for a brand-new gun, but considering the fact that it has been carried literally hundreds of miles in a saddle scabbard and toted other hundreds of miles over rough mountains, the stock is in remarkable shape.

About the only thing you can do with a varnish finish is to wipe it off with an oily rag to remove dust, dirt and fingerprints. A little linseed oil won't hurt, though. Put a few drops on the palm of your hand and rub into the stock. Then rub hard with a clean dry cloth and finally polish with the slightly oily hand. The thin layers of oil so built up will help, but basically the finish is brittle and will chip off.

The same procedure should be followed in caring for the oil-finished stock. Every now and then a few drops of linseed should be rubbed on with the hand so hard that hand and stock become hot. Then wipe off all surplus oil with a dry cloth and polish the stock with the cloth. In this way layer after layer of tough, microscopically thin coats of oil build up. If the finish is scratched, another light application of oil will take the scratches out.

Except for the first few rub-ins, when the pores of the wood are still absorbing oil, don't use anything but the very thinnest coats.

Both varnish- and oil-finished stocks can be preserved by rubbing a few drops of linseed oil in with the palm of the hand, rubbing hard with a dry cloth, then applying a little oil with the hand.

Unless all oil possible is wiped off it will become sticky and take a long time to dry. Great care, of course, should be used to keep the oil out of the checkering; otherwise it will gum and fill the lines to the surface. If that happens, the only thing to do is to protect the adjoining part of the stock with masking tape and then clean out the checkering with varnish remover and a brush with very fine bristles.

Sling straps, scabbards and leather cartridge boxes should be cleaned with saddle soap occasionally and oiled with neat's-foot oil. With this treatment the sling strap particularly will stay soft and pliable.

All screws in a gun will work loose under recoil and vibration. Many a rifle that has been performing poorly has been cured by the simple expedient of tightening up the guard screws or those in the scope mount. Every gun owner should own a set of screw drivers that fit the various screws on his guns. If the screw drivers do not fit, they chew up the screws and mar the looks of a gun in otherwise perfect condition.

Never take a gun out of the cold into a warm room, or a fine dew will form all over it and rust will quickly result. In the Arctic, trappers and prospectors hang their rifles on pegs outside the cabin. A gun will not rust in subzero temperatures for the simple reason that the moisture in the atmosphere is frozen.

Caring for a gun is relatively simple and takes but little time, effort or investment in material. The well-treated gun looks, shoots and lasts better. Gun care is economy of the highest order.

Glossary of Rifle and Shotgun Terms

ACTION. The breech mechanism of a rifle or shotgun which locks the cartridge in the chamber. The most common actions in use today are the single, double, bolt, lever, pump, semiautomatic and automatic.

ANVIL. That part of the cartridge primer which is a solid surface, against which the firing pin strikes to set off the priming powder.

AUTOLOADING. See SEMIAUTOMATIC.

AUTOMATIC. A firearm that will insert, fire and eject continuously all cartridges in its magazine with a single, continuous trigger pull. This is the true machine gun, not to be confused with the semiautomatic rifles and shotguns which are at times erroneously called "automatics."

BALL. The round lead missile propelled by smoothbores in the days of early firearms. The term is sometimes used today when referring to the cylindrical and conoidal bullets fired from rifled barrels.

BALLISTIC COEFFICIENT. A number given a bullet which tells how its shape, length, weight, diameter and nose design affect its stability, velocity and range against air resistance.

BALLISTICS. The study of what happens to moving projectiles, including their trajectory, force, impact and penetration. The term is divided into "internal" ballistics (what happens inside the barrel before the bullet or shot leaves the muzzle) and "external" ballistics (what happens after the bullet or shot emerges from the barrel).

BARREL. The metal tube, made of iron or steel, of a firearm through which the bullet or shot charge passes.

BASE WAD. The paper filler at the rear of the powder charge and inside the head of a shotgun shell.

BATTERY. The metal arm of a flintlock mechanism, against which flint strikes to create sparks in the flashpan. Also called the frizzen.

BEAVERTAIL. A wide, flat forend of a rifle or shotgun.

BEDDING. That part of the stock into which the barrel fits.

BELT. The narrow band around the rear portion of a cartridge case just forward of the extractor groove. The belt arrests the progress of the case into the chamber and hence controls headspace.

BERDAN PRIMER. See PRIMER.

BLACK POWDER. A finely ground mixture of three basic ingredients—saltpeter (potassium nitrate), charcoal (carbon), and sulphur which was made into cake-like form and broken up into uniform "grains" by passing the cake through fine screens. The burning rate of the black powder was controlled by the size of the grains—the smaller the grain, the faster the burning rate. Black powder was the most commonly used firearm propellant before development of smokeless powder.

BLOWN PATTERN. A shotgun pattern with erratic shot distribution, generally caused by gas escaping past the wads and getting into the shot.

BLUING. A process of boiling the metal gun parts in a bath of metallic salts and water, thereby coloring them in various shades of blue to prevent rust.

BOATTAIL. The tapered rear end of a bullet. Also called "taper heel," this design is used to increase ballistic efficiency at long range.

BOLT. A steel rod-like assembly which moves back and forth in a bolt action, sealing the cartridge in the chamber during firing.

BOLT FACE. The forward end of the bolt which supports the base of the cartridge and contains the firing pin.

BORE. The hole in the barrel of a firearm.

BORE DIAMETER. The measurement from one side of the bore to the other. In a rifled barrel this means measurement of the bore before the rifling grooves are cut or, to put it another way, from land to land. (See also LAND and RIFLING.)

BOXER PRIMER. See PRIMER.

BREECH. The rear end of the barrel. In modern arms, the portion of the barrel into which the cartridge is inserted.

BREECHBLOCK. The part in the breech mechanism that locks the action against the firing of the cartridge.

BREECHLOADER. A firearm loaded in the breech as opposed to one loaded through the muzzle.

BUCKSHOT. A large shot used in shotguns for hunting game at short ranges.

BULLET. The projectile fired from a rifle.

BUTT. The rear end of a rifle or shotgun stock; the portion that rests against the shoulder.

BUTTPLATE. That which covers the wood of the butt of a rifle or shotgun. Buttplates are made of plain or checkered steel, hard rubber, plastic, or Indian buffalo horn. Some steel buttplates have trap doors covering a recess for storage of cleaning equipment.

CALIBER. Generally the diameter of the bore of a rifle before the rifling grooves are cut. In the United States caliber is usually measured in hundredths of an inch. (.22, .30, etc.); in England caliber is usually measured in thousandths of an inch (.270, .455, etc.), and in Europe and Asia caliber is measured in millimeters (7 or 10 mm., etc.).

CANNELURE. A groove around the circumference of a bullet or case. Examples are the lubrication grooves of lead bullets, or the grooves into which the mouth of the cartridge case is crimped, or the extractor groove of the rimless or belted case.

CANT. To tip or lean gun to one side when in aiming position. Cant usually results in inaccurate shooting.

CAP. See PERCUSSION CAP.

CARBINE. Generally a shortened version of a military rifle.

CARTRIDGE. In the modern sense this means the metallic cartridge which consists of the brass or copper case, the powder charge, the primer and the bullet. Before development of the metallic cartridge the term was used, as its French derivation *(cartouche)* implies, for a roll or case of paper containing powder and shot. Modern cartridges are generally classified in three catagories—centerfire metallics, rimfires, and shotshells. Centerfire metallics include all metal cartridges that have primers in the center of the base. Rimfires include all cartridges in which the priming powder is sealed in the soft rim around the base. Shotshells include all cartridges that contain "shot," or small pellets instead of a single bullet.

CENTERFIRE. (Abbreviation C.F.) See CARTRIDGE.

CHAMBER. The enlarged portion of the barrel at the breech in which the cartridge is placed for firing.

CHECKERING. A diamond-like pattern on forends and grips of rifles and shotguns. The diamonds are made by cutting crossing lines into the wood with special gunshop tools.

CHOKE. The constriction in the end of a shotgun barrel by which the shot pattern is controlled.

CLIP. A metal case designed to hold a number of cartridges for loading into the magazine of a rifle.

COCK. To set the action into position for firing. On some weapons the action has an intermediate position; this is called half cock. On early weapons such as flintlock and percussion cap, the hammer was called a cock.

COMB. The upper edge of a rifle or shotgun stock upon which the cheek rests.

CONE. The sloping portion at the front end of a shotgun chamber in which the diameter is decreased to muzzle diameter. Also, the rear portion of the choke at the muzzle of a shotgun.

CONOIDAL BULLET. A cone-shaped bullet.

CORDITE. A double-base smokeless powder made of nitroglycerine and guncotton which is used in the form of long, stringy cords. Cordite is used extensively in Great Britain.

CORE. The part of a bullet that is covered by a jacket.

CORROSION. The eating away of the metal of a rifle or shotgun barrel, caused by rust.

CREEP. The movement of the trigger (also called drag or crawl) before it lets go.

CRIMP. The portion of a cartridge case that is bent inward to hold the bullet in place, or in the case of a shotshell, to hold the shot charge in place. The term "pie crimp" is sometimes used because some crimps look like a pie that has been cut for serving.

CROSS HAIRS. The sighting lines in a telescope sight.

CUPRONICKEL. A material of about 60 per cent copper and 40 per cent nickel, formerly widely used for bullet jackets. Often called "German silver" because it is white in appearance. Cupronickel was superseded in the nineteen twenties by gilding metal.

DAMASCUS BARRELS. Barrels made of strips of iron and steel welded around a mandrel. They have not been made for about fifty years.

DETERRENT. A material added to an explosive to reduce its burning rate.

DOUBLE-BASE POWDER. A rapidly burning powder made by absorbing nitroglycerine and nitrocellulose. Cordite is a double-base powder.

DOUGHNUT PATTERN. A shotgun pattern with a hole in the middle generally caused by the interference of the top wad.

DRIFT. The departure of a bullet or shot charge from the normal line of flight. This can be caused by wind or the spinning of the bullet. A bullet fired from a barrel with a right-hand twist drifts to the right; one from a left-hand twist drifts to the left.

DRILLING. A three-barrel gun generally of German manufacture with a rifle barrel beneath two shotgun barrels.

EJECTOR. The mechanism which throws the fired cartridge case free from the gun.

ELEVATION. The amount a rear sight or telescope sight reticule must be raised to cause the bullet to strike higher on the target.

ENERGY. The amount of work that is done by a bullet, expressed in foot pounds. To determine the energy of a bullet, you square the velocity of the bullet in foot seconds and divide the result by 7,000 to reduce from grains to pounds. Divide this quotient by 64.32. This gives you the striking energy for each grain of bullet weight. Multiply this by the weight of the bullet and you have the amount of energy in foot pounds. An easier way to determine a bullet's energy is to look it up in a cartridge catalog.

EROSION. The wearing away of a barrel's metal surface by a bullet or shot charge or by the heat of powder gases.

EXTRACTOR. A hook device which pulls the fired case from a rifle chamber as the breech mechanism is opened. The extractor generally brings the case within reach of the ejector, which then flips it out of the gun.

FEED. The action of pressing live cartridges from the magazine of a rifle or shotgun into the chamber.

FIRING PIN. The part of the breech mechanism which strikes the primer of the cartridge. The term is called "striker" in British parlance.

FLINCH. To move or jerk a weapon at the instant of firing.

FLINT. A piece of quartz held in the cock of an early weapon, which when striking the steel battery causes a shower of sparks to fall into the flashpan and ignite the powder.

FLINTLOCK. The system of ignition for early firearms in which flint was thrown against steel to ignite the powder charge. The flintlock action was the universal means of ignition from the late Seventeenth Century until the invention of the percussion cap in the early Nineteenth Century.

FLOOR PLATE. The detachable metal plate at the bottom of the cartridge magazine of a bolt action rifle. The floor plate is usually hinged at the front and held by a release spring located just ahead of the trigger guard.

FOREND. The forward portion of a shoulder-arm stock. Located under the barrel, the forend serves as a hand-hold for the left hand in the case of a right-handed shooter.

F.P.S. (also sometimes F.S.) Abbreviation for "feet per second," a term used in giving the velocity of the travel of a bullet.

FRIZZEN. See BATTERY.

FULMINATE OF MERCURY. A highly sensitive explosive used for many years after its initial use in 1807 by the Scottish clergyman, Reverend Alexander Forsythe, as a means of igniting gunpowder with detonation by a blow.

GAIN TWIST. Barrel rifling which increases in pitch from the breech to the muzzle to accelerate the spin of a bullet.

GAS CHECK. A metal cup placed on the end of a lead bullet to protect the lead against the hot gases of the burning powder charge.

GAS PORT. A small hole in the barrel of a gas-operated weapon through which expanding powder gases escape to power the autoloading system.

GAUGE. Measurement of shotgun bores derived from the number of bore-sized balls of lead to the pound. For example, 12 balls which fit the bore of a 12-gauge shotgun weigh one pound.

GRIP. The small portion of the stock gripped by the trigger hand. The name varies depending on its shape—pistol grip, straight grip, etc.

GRIP CAP. A cap made of metal, plastic, rubber or horn material fastened over the end of a pistol grip.

GROOVES. See RIFLING.

GROUP. A series of shots fired with the same sight setting and the same aim. The group center is generally found by measuring from center to center of the widest shots.

HALF COCK. See COCK.

HAMMER. The part of the action that drives the firing pin forward.

HAMMERLESS. In the nontechnical sense, referring to a firearm whose hammer and striker is concealed within the metal frame. Technically, referring to a firearm which employs a striker rather than a hammer. In the latter sense, a weapon with a concealed hammer is not considered hammerless.

HAND CANNON. One of a variety of small, crude cannons used in the early fourteen hundreds, attached for individual use by adding wooden stocks to rest against the shooter's chest, shoulder or leg.

HANGFIRE. Delay in firing a cartridge after hammer or striker has been released. See also MISFIRE, with which it should not be confused.

HARQUEBUS, ARQUEBUS. A term meaning "gun with a hook" originally used to designate the early smoothbore matchlocks used in Europe in the mid-Fifteenth Century. As the wheellock and flintlock shoulder arms were developed, the term Harquebus came to denote a gun of fine workmanship as distinguished from the musket, or common military arm.

HEADSPACE. The distance between the base of the cartridge and the face of the bolt or breechblock. This is determined by the rim of rimmed cartridges, the belt of belted cartridges and the shoulder of rimless cartridges. Some cartridges (the .45 Auto for example) headspace on the mouth of the case.

HEEL. The rear end of the upper edge of the gunstock or, to put it another way, the top of the buttplate. Also the base of a bullet.

HIGH INTENSITY. A term which has never caught on very well but which refers to cartridges giving velocities of around 2,700 feet per second and above.

HIGH POWER. An obsolescent term applied to the first smokeless powder cartridges with velocities of around 2,000 feet per second.

HOLDING. Term used in aiming, keeping the sights on target while applying pressure to the trigger.

HOLLOW POINT. A bullet with a nose cavity designed to increase expansion on impact.

IGNITING CHARGE. In early firearms, the charge used to ignite the propelling charge. In modern cartridges the igniting charge is in the primer.

INERTIA FIRING PIN. A firing pin which moves freely forward and backward in the breechblock so that a blow of the hammer or striker impels it forward while the explosion of the primer impels it backward.

INTERNAL BALLISTICS. See BALLISTICS.

IRON PYRITES. See PYRITES.

JACKET. The outer covering over the lead core of a bullet. Jackets in the United States are generally made of gilding metal, an alloy of copper and zinc, or a similar alloy. The jacket is called "envelope" in Great Britain.

JAWS. The vise-like device on a flintlock hammer used to hold the flint in place.

JUMP. The amount of change in the bore axis, computed both vertically and horizontally, while the projectile, upon being fired, moves from the chamber to the muzzle.

KENTUCKY RIFLE. A flintlock rifle with a long barrel and short, crooked stock with a rather small bore, developed in the Eighteenth Century by Americans of German descent. It was developed in Pennsylvania but was called the "Kentucky" because in those days Kentucky was the frontier. Sometimes called the "Pennsylvania rifle."

KEYHOLING. The failure of a bullet to remain gyroscopically balanced in flight so that it enters the target sideways, leaving an elongated opening.

KICK. The force of a firearm against the shooter's shoulder brought about by recoil as the projectile leaves the weapon.

KNURLED SURFACE. A metal surface which contains a series of ridges or beads to help grasp it without slipping.

LAND. In the rifling of a bore one of the uncut portions of the surface left after the rifling grooves have been cut into the metal. See also RIFLING.

LEADING. A type of fouling in a firearm bore consisting of particles from bullet jackets adherring to the metal surface through heat or friction.

LEDE. The beveled portion of the rifling at the rear end of the barrel and the forward portion of the chamber where the bullet first engages the lands.

LENGTH OF STOCK. The distance from the front trigger of a shotgun to the center of the butt.

LEVEL POINT. In the trajectory of a bullet, the point on the descending curve at the same altitude as the muzzle of the weapon firing the projectile.

LEVER ACTION. An action operated by a lever located on the underside of the frame. Generally, a secondary purpose of the lever is to serve as a trigger guard.

LINE OF BORE. A straight line which is a projection of the center of the bore of a firearm.

LINE OF SIGHT. The straight line from the eye through the sights of a weapon to the target.

LOAD. As a noun, one charge of powder and one projectile or, used loosely in the modern sense, a cartridge. As a verb, to prepare a gun for firing by inserting ammunition into it.

LOADING GAGE. A cover opening on a hinge which allows cartridges to be inserted into the magazine.

LOCK. The firing mechanism of a muzzle-loading weapon. In breech-loading weapons, it is generally the firing mechanism and breech-sealing assembly.

LOCKING LUGS. A series of projections on the bolt of a firearm designed to fit into corresponding slots in the receiver to lock the action in closed position for firing.

LOCKPLATE. A metal plate on which the firing mechanism is mounted on percussion and earlier firearms.

LOCK SPEED. Also called Lock Time. The interval of time between the release of the firing pin and the firing of the cartridge.

L.R. Abbreviation for Long Rifle.

MACHINE GUN. A weapon which fires small-arms ammunition at a high rate of fire on the automatic principle. See AUTOMATIC.

MAGAZINE. The part of a repeating firearm which holds the cartridges or shells in position ready to be impelled one at a time into the chamber. The magazine may be an integral part of a weapon or a separate device attached to the action.

MAGNUM. A term derived from a Latin word meaning large or great and applied to cartridges of considerable power, such as the .300 Magnum rifle cartridge and 12-gauge, 3-inch Magnum shotshell.

MAINSPRING. A strong spring which actuates the striker or hammer of a firearm.

MATCH. A long cord of hemp, flax or cotton which has been saturated in saltpeter or the lees of wine in order to burn slowly without a flame, used to ignite the powder in early firearms.

MATCHLOCK. The first "action" used with shoulder arms employing a serpentine or S-shaped piece of metal that held the smoldering match by pressing the lower end of the serpentine, while the upper end brought the burning match into contact with the priming powder in the pan.

METAL CASED. A bullet with the forward portion enclosed in metal as in bullets used for military purposes and for taking heavy game such as elephants. The British call such bullets "solids."

METALLIC CARTRIDGE. A term used to designate the modern cartridge as opposed to early cartridges made of linen, paper, etc.

METALLIC SIGHT. See SIGHT.

MID RANGE. In trajectory, the point halfway between the muzzle and the target.

MILLIMETER. A metric measurement equaling .03907 inches. MM is its abbreviation.

MINIE BULLET. An elongated lead bullet with a pointed head and a cup-shaped hollow in its base which spread as it was fired, forcing the metal into the rifle grooves. The most widely used rifled projectile by both North and South forces in the Civil War. It was invented by the French Captain of Infantry, C. E. Minie.

MIQUELET. An early flintlock developed in Spain. Its name is derived from the robber bands of Catalonia, famous users of the weapon.

MISFIRE. Failure of a cartridge to discharge after the weapon's firing pin has struck the primer.

MOUTH. The open end of a cartridge case into which the bullet is inserted.

MUSHROOM. The shape many bullets assume when the forward position has expanded upon striking game. Expanding bullets are sometimes called "mushroom bullets."

MUSKET. A military smoothbore shoulder arm.

MUSKETOON. A musket shortened for cavalry use.

MUZZLE. The forward end of a barrel.

MUZZLE BLAST. The violent disturbance in the atmosphere after discharge of a weapon, caused by expansion of powder gases into the air.

MUZZLE BRAKE. A device in the form of a slotted tube which is attached to the muzzle of a rifle to trap the escaping gases and utilize them as a counter-recoil force thus lessening the kick of the weapon.

MUZZLE ENERGY. A measurement expressed in foot pounds of the blow struck by a bullet as it emerges from the muzzle of a rifle.

MUZZLE FLASH. The bright flash at the muzzle of a firearm as a result of expansion of powder gases, burning powder grains and ignition of oxygen.

MUZZLE LOADER. A firearm that is loaded through the muzzle instead of in the breech.

MUZZLE VELOCITY. See VELOCITY.

NAKED BULLET. A bullet not covered by a metal jacket or patch.

NECK. The small, forward portion of a bottlenecked cartridge case. Also the small portion of a rifle chamber in which the neck of the cartridge case rests before the cartridge is fired.

NEEDLE GUN. The first rifle known to use a bolt action. It was invented by Nicholas Dreyse and used by the Prussian Army as early as 1841.

NIPPLE. A small metal tube extending through the breech of a percussion weapon through which the flame passed from the percussion cap to fire the main powder charge.

NOMENCLATURE. Systematic classification of the different parts of a weapon.

NOSE. The point of a projectile.

OBTURATION. Sealing the breech against escape of gas by expansion of the cartridge case.

OPEN SIGHT. See SIGHT.

OPTICAL SIGHT. See SIGHT.

OVER-AND-UNDER GUN. A firearm with two or more barrels placed one over the other.

PAN. The small cup-shaped container on the side or top of a matchlock, wheellock or flintlock weapon used to hold the priming powder charge.

PARALLAX. The seeming displacement of an object viewed from two different positions. As applied to telescope sights, for example, the apparent movement of the reticule in relation to the target when the eye is shifted.

PARKERIZING. A non-reflecting gray rust-preventive finish used on the metal of firearms.

PATCH. A piece of leather or cloth about the size of a quarter which was greased and placed around a bullet before it was rammed down the barrel of a muzzle-loading rifle. The patch improved the spin of the bullet, lessened the escape of gas past the bullet and helped to keep the barrel clean.

PATCH BOX. An indentation with a cover in the buttstock of a muzzle-loading rifle used to carry patches or other small items.

PATTERN. Distribution of the shot in a shotgun charge. This is measured at a standard distance of 40 yards and in a 30-inch circle. For example, a full choke charge is supposed to throw a pattern of at least 70 per cent of the shot into a 30-inch circle at a distance of 40 yards.

PENETRATION. The distance traveled by a projectile into wood, ground, armor, or other substance before coming to a stop.

PENNSYLVANIA RIFLE. See KENTUCKY RIFLE.

PERCUSSION CAP. A small metal explosive-filled cup which is placed over the nipple of a percussion shoulder arm. As the cap is struck by the hammer, it explodes and sends a flame through the nipple to the main powder charge. The percussion cap was in use from the time it began to supersede the flintlock in the mid-Nineteenth Century until the early development of self-contained cartridges at about the end of the Civil War.

PINE BOARDS. Often used for testing bullet penetration.

PISTOL GRIP. See GRIP.

PITCH. The angle at which the rifling of a bore has been cut in relation to the bore axis. Pitch is generally computed by a number of turns in an inch, such as one turn in 24 inches, or 1–24. This measurement is often called TWIST.

POWDER. The general term for any firearm propellant. The two major types are black powder, which is a mechanical mixture of charcoal, sulphur and saltpeter, and smokeless powder, which is not actually powder but a cast form of nitrated organic compounds.

PRESSURE. The thrust of burning gases in all directions against the cartridge case and base of a bullet, and the chamber and bolt face of a rifle. This is measured with metal "crushers" one inch ahead of the breech and is recorded in pounds per square inch.

PRIME. To prepare, or load an early weapon for firing.

PRIMER. The small cap fitted in the pocket in the head of a centerfire cartridge case or enclosed in the folded rim of a rimfire case. The primer contains a sensitive explosive compound which, when struck by the firing pin, ignites the powder charge. There are two basic types of centerfire primers: the Boxer, which is most generally used in the United States, and the Berdan, which is used in Europe.

PRIMER CUP. The housing in a cartridge base which holds a centerfire primer.

PRIMER POCKET. The depression in the base of a centerfire cartridge which contains the primer cup.

PRIMING PAN. See PAN.

PROJECTILE. Often loosely called a bullet. In ballistics, a bullet is a projectile only when it is in flight.

PROPELLANT. The explosive which, when ignited, sends the projectile on its way.

PUMPKIN BALL. A round ball of lead used in shotguns in the past for deer hunting but now largely replaced by the rifled slug.

PYRITES. A mineral used to produce sparks in wheellock firearms and in some early flintlocks. It was superseded by flint which has more suitable igniting qualities.

RAMROD. Also called a rammer, a wood or metal rod used to impel the wad and bullet down the barrel of a muzzle-loading firearm. In the modern sense a cleaning rod is sometimes called a ramrod.

RANGE. The distance traveled by a projectile from the weapon to the target. Pointblank range is the distance a projectile will travel before it drops to the extent that sight adjustment is required. Effective range is the greatest distance a projectile will travel with accuracy.

Extreme range is the maximum distance a projectile will travel without regard to accuracy.

RECEIVER. The metal frame which contains the breech, locking and reloading mechanism of a rifle or shotgun.

RECEIVER RING. The forward end of a rifle receiver which is threaded so the barrel can be attached to it.

RECEIVER SIGHT. A sight attached to the receiver of a rifle. Because of its location, it is always of the "aperture" or "peep" variety.

RECOIL. The rearward motion of a firearm caused by expansion of powder gases which impels the bullet out of the barrel. Recoil is measured in foot pounds along the line of the weapon's barrel. Since the line of the barrel is generally above the point of resistance (where the butt rests against the shoulder) the muzzle tends to swing upward with the force of recoil.

R.F. Abbreviation for RIMFIRE.

RIFLE. A firearm with a rifled barrel, designed to fire one projectile at a time and to be operated by one man from the shoulder with the use of both hands.

RIFLED SLUG. A projectile that is used in shotguns for big-game hunting. Those made in the United States are of pure, soft lead and have hollow bases which swage down when they hit the construction of the shotgun's choke. They are rifled on the outside, but do not actually spin. They fly fairly accurately because they are weighted in front and therefore fly point on.

RIFLING. A given number of spiral grooves cut into the bore of a barrel to impart a rotary motion to the bullet, giving it gyroscopic stabilization. The cut-away portions of the rifling are called GROOVES while the uncut or raised portions are called LANDS.

RIM. The projecting edge or flange of a cartridge case. On rimmed cartridges, the rim stops the progress of the case into the chamber. It's also the part of the case of which the extractor takes hold.

RIMBASE. The shoulder of a rifle stock on which the breech rests.

RIMFIRE. A cartridge in which the primer is sealed in the soft metal around the rim of its base.

ROLLED CRIMP. See CRIMP.

ROLLING BLOCK ACTION. A breech-loading action developed in the eighteen sixties with a short circular breechblock that was thumbed back to open the chamber and thumbed forward to close and seal the chamber for firing.

SAFETY. A device that blocks the firing mechanism of a firearm so it can't go off accidentally.

SALTPETER. One of the three basic ingredients of black powder.

SCATTER GUN. A shotgun whose barrel has been shortened in order to obtain a wide shot pattern.

SEAR. The mechanism which is the link between the trigger and the firing pin, designed to hold the latter at full or half cock and release it when the trigger is pulled.

SECTIONAL DENSITY. The relationship between the weight of the bullet and the cross-sectional area. This is termed by the formula (W/d^2) .7854. One divides the bullet's weight expressed in pounds by the square of the diameter of the bullet and then multiplies the result by .7854. To get the weight of the bullet in pounds, divide the weight in grains by 7,000.

SEMIAUTOMATIC. The modern mechanism in which the loaded and cocked firearm fires the cartridge, ejects the fired case, inserts a live cartridge and recocks the action, all with one pull of the trigger. This mechanism is powered by the gases of the exploding propellant. Also called self-loading and autoloading. Not to be confused with AUTOMATIC.

SERPENTINE. See MATCHLOCK.

SETSCREW. A screw that regulates the amount of pressure in the trigger mechanism.

SHOTGUN. A shoulder arm with a smoothbore designed to fire small pellets called shot, or rifled slugs.

SHOULDER. The sharply sloping portion of a bottleneck cartridge joining the body and neck.

SIGHT. The device on top of a firearm barrel designed to help the shooter aim the weapon accurately. Sights generally have two parts, front and rear. A front sight (sometimes called foresight) is located above the muzzle of the barrel and generally protrudes like a post (post sight) or in triangular shape like a pyramid (pyramidal sight). Some front sights have a circular hood over them (hooded sight) and others have a notch in the post (notch sight). The rear sight is located at the rear end of the barrel, near and sometimes on the receiver (receiver sight). An open rear sight is a small plate with a V-notch mounted vertically on the barrel. An aperture sight is a tube-shaped rear sight pierced by a circular hole through which aim is taken. An optical sight is a tube-like unit that contains a series of lenses aligned for aiming. Small-arms sights of this type are generally telescopic, but not always.

SLACK. The amount of movement in a trigger mechanism before it engages the sear or other release mechanism.

SLING. A leather or web strap used as an aid to carrying and shooting a rifle.

SLING SWIVEL. A metal loop, which may or may not be detachable, by which the sling is attached to a rifle.

SLUG. Any of a number of metal pieces propelled from a firearm. See also RIFLED SLUG.

SMALL BORE. In American parlance, generally a rifle of .22 caliber. From the British point of view, any rifle under .30 caliber.

SMALL OF THE STOCK. The narrow portion of the stock between the comb and the receiver of a shoulder arm.

SMOKELESS POWDER. See POWDER.

SMOOTHBORE. A firearm with a bore that is not rifled.

SNAPHANCE, also SNAPHAUNCE. An early flintlock dating from the Sixteenth Century, generally considered to be of Dutch origin. The snaphance action was similar to that of later flintlocks except that the flashpan cover was operated manually.

SNAP SHOT. A quick shot taken without considered aim.

SPANNER. A small metal wrench used to wind the mechanism of a WHEEL-LOCK.

SPENT BULLET. A projectile which has lost nearly all its velocity and hasn't the force needed to penetrate, or in some cases wound, the object being fired at.

SPITZER. A bullet which has a sharp point for better ballistic efficiency.

STOCK. The part of a shoulder arm by which the weapon is held for firing, and into which the metal parts are fitted. The stock is usually made of wood but sometimes of plastic, metal or other rigid material.

STRAIGHT-PULL ACTION. A bolt action in which the bolt is pulled and pushed straight backward and forward instead of up, back, forward and down as in the classic Mauser turn-bolt system. Examples of rifles employing the straight-pull action are the Winchester Lee and the Ross.

STRIKER. The forward part of a firing pin which strikes the cartridge's primer.

SWIVEL. An oval-shaped metal ring used to attach a sling to a rifle.

TANG. A metal strip which extends rearward from a rifle or shotgun receiver through which screws are driven to attach the barrel to the stock.

THROAT. The forward portion of the chamber, where it is tapered to meet the bore.

TOE. The bottom part of the butt of a rifle or shotgun.

TOUCHHOLE. A small hole in the top rear of a barrel of an early hand cannon through which a burning stick or "match" was thrust to ignite the propelling powder.

TOUCHPAN. The flashpan of an early firearm.

TRAJECTORY. The path a bullet takes from muzzle to target.

TRIGGER. The part of a rifle mechanism by which the firing pin is released to ignite the cartridge.

TRIGGER GUARD. A metal loop around the trigger designed to protect it and prevent accidental firing. On lever-action rifles, the lever doubles as the trigger guard.

TRIGGER PLATE. The metal part under the receiver of a rifle or shotgun through which the trigger projects.

TROMBONE ACTION. Pump, or slide, action.

TURN-BOLT ACTION. A bolt action which is locked by pressing the bolt handle in and down, thereby turning its locking lugs into recesses in the receiver.

TWIST. The inclination of rifling grooves in relation to the axis of the bore, generally measured in the number of inches to a complete turn, as one to ten (1—10) or one to twenty-two (1—22).

VELOCITY. The speed at which a bullet travels, usually measured in feet per second or meters per second.

WAD. See BASE WAD.

W.C.F. Abbreviation for Winchester Centerfire.

WHEELLOCK. An early firearm mechanism in which a wheel with serrated edges is wound against the tension of a strong spring and spins against a piece of iron pyrites, sending a shower of sparks into the pan to ignite the charge. The wheellock followed development of the early matchlocks, but because it was expensive to make and slow in firing, it was superseded by the simpler flintlock actions.

WILDCAT CARTRIDGE. A non-standard cartridge not loaded by the large cartridge manufacturers, and assembled by individuals who use hand dies to change shapes of standard cartridges.

WINDAGE. The lateral drift of a bullet in flight, caused by wind. Also a term used in the lateral, or horizontal, adjustment of a rear sight moving to right or left to compensate for wind currents.

W.R.F. Abbreviation for Winchester Rimfire.

ZERO. Sight adjustment so that the bullet will strike center at a range from which other adjustments can be made. A rifle, let us say, is "zeroed" at 100 yards.

Index

Index